ECONOMICS, INDUSTRY, AND DISABILITY

ECONOMICS, INDUSTRY, AND DISABILITY
A Look Ahead

edited by

William E. Kiernan, Ph.D.
Director of Rehabilitation
Developmental Evaluation Clinic
UAF-Children's Hospital
Boston

and

Robert L. Schalock, Ph.D.
Chairman
Department of Psychology
Hastings College
and
Mid-Nebraska Mental Retardation Services
Hastings

·P·A·U·L·H·
BROOKES
PUBLISHING Co

Baltimore · London · Toronto · Sydney

HD
7256
U5
E36
1989

Paul H. Brookes Publishing Co.
Post Office Box 10624
Baltimore, MD 21285-0624

Typeset by The Composing Room of Michigan, Grand Rapids, Michigan.
Manufactured in the United States of America by
The Maple Press Company, York, Pennsylvania.

Library of Congress Cataloging-in-Publication Data
Economics, industry, and disability.

  Bibliography: p.
  Includes index.
  1. Handicapped—Employment—United States.   2. Vocational
rehabilitation—United States.   3. Work design—United States.   4.
Social integration—United States.   I. Kiernan, William E., 1945–
II. Schalock, Robert L.
HD7256.U5E36   1989   331.5'9'0973   88-14493
  ISBN 1-55766-008-5

CONTENTS

CONTRIBUTORS

Ansley Bacon, Ph.D.
Director
Mental Retardation Institute
Westchester County Medical Center
Valhalla, NY 10595

J. Michael Barcus, M.Ed.
Assistant Director
Training
Rehabilitation Research and Training
  Center
Virginia Commonwealth University
1314 West Main Street
Richmond, VA 23284

Barry Bluestone, Ph.D.
Frank L. Boyden Professor of Political
  Economy
Department of Political Science
05/70 Wheatley Hall
University of Massachusetts-Boston
Boston, MA 02125

Shawn M. Boles, Ph.D.
Microcomputer Decision Support Center
College of Education
University of Oregon
Eugene, OR 97403

Sharon A. Borthwick-Duffy, Ph.D.
UC Riverside Research Group at
  Lanterman Developmental Center
Box 100-R
Pomona, CA 91769

Marcia Bredar, Esq.
Law Division
Mutual of Omaha Insurance
Mutual of Omaha Plaza
Omaha, NE 68175

Eugene Bronstein, M.B.A.
Director
School of Management Honors Program
Marketing Division
Boston College
Fulton 301-D
Chestnut Hill, MA 02167

Jay Buckley, Ed.D.
Research Associate
Specialized Training Program
135 Education
University of Oregon
Eugene, OR 97403

Carl F. Calkins, Ph.D.
Director
Institute for Human Development
University of Missouri at Kansas City
2220 Holmes Street
Kansas City, MO 64108

Joseph F. Campbell, Ed.D.
Executive Director
Incentive Community Enterprises
Box 598
Northampton, MA 01061

Ann Carter, M.B.A.
Assistant Vice President
First Winthrop Corporation
1 International Place
Boston, MA 02110

Ronald W. Conley, Ph.D.
Special Assistant to the Commissioner
Administration on Developmental
  Disabilities
Hubert H. Humphrey Building
200 Independence Avenue, S.W.
Washington, DC 20201

Daniel B. Crimmins, Ph.D.
Director of Psychology
Mental Retardation Institute
Westchester County Medical Center
Cedarwood Hall, Room 324
Valhalla, NY 10595

Lizanne DeStefano, Ph.D.
Associate Director
Secondary Transition Intervention
  Effectiveness Institute
University of Illinois at
  Urbana/Champaign
110 Education Building
1310 South Sixth Street
Champaign, IL 61820

Shari Miller Dunstan, M.A.
Research Analyst
Mathematica Policy Research
P.O. Box 2393
Princeton, NJ 08543

Tammi L. Goldsbury, M.A.
Assistant Rehabilitation Psychologist
Department of Psychiatry
Creighton–Nebraska Universities Health
  Foundation
42nd and Dewey Avenue
Omaha, NE 68105

David A. Goode, Ph.D.
Assistant Professor of Community and
  Preventive Medicine
New York Medical College
Valhalla, NY 10595

Bradley Googins, Ph.D.
Associate Professor of Community
  Organization, Management and
  Planning
School of Social Work
Boston University
264 Bay State Road
Boston, MA 02215

Mark L. Hill, M.S., Ed.
Director of Supported Employment
Virginia Department of Mental
  Retardation
Madison Building
Richmond, VA 23284

Deborah A. Johnsen, M.A.
Marketing Director
Mid-Nebraska Mental Retardation
  Services
2727 West 2nd Street
Landmark Center
Hastings, NE 68901

John Johnson, M.A.
Illinois Supported Employment Project
College of Education
University of Illinois
Champaign, IL 61820

Barbara T. Judy, R.N., M.S.
Manager
Job Accommodation Network
West Virginia University
809 Allen Hall/Box 6122
Morgantown, WV 26506

Orv C. Karan, Ph.D.
Director
Connecticut University Affiliated
  Program on Developmental
  Disabilities
University of Connecticut
991 Main Street, Suite 3A
East Hartford, CT 06108
and
Associate Professor of Educational
  Psychology
University of Connecticut
Storrs, CT 06268

William E. Kiernan, Ph.D.
Director of Rehabilitation
Developmental Evaluation Clinic
The Children's Hospital
300 Longwood Avenue
Boston, MA 02115

Kari Knutson, M.Ed.
Employment Training Specialist
Developmental Evaluation Clinic
The Children's Hospital
300 Longwood Avenue
Boston, MA 02115

Frank Lattuca, Jr., Ed.D.
Associate Professor
University of Massachusetts-Amherst
HRTA
Flint Lab
Amherst, MA 01003

David M. Mank, Ph.D.
Assistant Professor
Division of Special Education and
Rehabilitation
135 Education
University of Oregon
Eugene, OR 97403

Janine Matton, M.A.
Research Analyst
Mathematica Policy Research
P.O. Box 2393
Princeton, NJ 08543

Lori Mettel, ABD
Instructor
Madison Area Technical College
Madison, WI 53705
and
Program Assistant
Waisman Center on Mental Retardation
and Human Development
University of Wisconsin
1500 Highland Avenue
Madison, WI 53750

M. Sherril Moon, Ed.D.
Assistant Professor of Special Education
and Director of Training
Rehabilitation Research and Training
Center
Virginia Commonwealth University
1314 West Main Street
Richmond, VA 23284-0001

John H. Noble, Jr., Ph.D.
Professor of Social Work and
Rehabilitative Medicine
191 Alumni Arena
State University of New York at
Buffalo
Buffalo, NY 14260

Gary Roberts, M.S.
Senior Vocational Rehabilitation
Counselor
Massachusetts Rehabilitation
Commission
10 Green Street
Jamaica Plain, MA 02130

Sean Rowland, M.Ed.
Research Associate
The Children's Hospital
Developmental Evaluation Clinic
300 Longwood Avenue
Boston, MA 02155

Frank R. Rusch, Ph.D.
Director
Secondary Transition Intervention
Effectiveness Institute
College of Education
University of Illinois
Champaign, IL 61820

James S. Russell, Ph.D.
Lewis and Clark College
Business and Administrative Studies
Portland, OR 97219

Paul Sale, Ed.D.
Project Coordinator
Supported Employment
Master's Program
Rehabilitation Research and Training
Center
Virginia Commonwealth University
1314 West Main Street
Richmond, VA 23284

Raymond Sanchez, M.S.W.
The Administration of Developmental
Disabilities
Employment Initiative Director
200 Independence Avenue, S.W.
Room 350E
Washington, DC 20201

Robert L. Schalock, Ph.D.
Chairman
Department of Psychology
Hastings College
522 East Side Boulevard
Hasting, NE 68901

Howard Shane, Ph.D.
Director
Communicational Enhancement Clinic
Department of Otolaryngology and
 Communication Disorders
The Children's Hospital
300 Longwood Avenue
Boston, MA 02115

Jack A. Stark, Ph.D.
Associate Professor of Medical
 Psychology
Department of Psychiatry
Creighton–Nebraska Universities Health
 Foundation
42nd and Dewey Avenue
Omaha, NE 68105

Craig V.D. Thornton, Ph.D.
Senior Economist
Mathematics Policy Research
P.O. Box 2393
Princeton, NJ 08543

Jeffrey Tines, Ph.D.
Illinois Supported Employment Project
College of Education
University of Illinois
Champaign, IL 61820

John Trach, M.A.
Illinois Supported Employment Project
College of Education
University of Illinois
Champaign, IL 61820

Richard W. Venne, M.Ed.
Vice President
Community Incentive Enterprises
Box 598
Northampton, MA 01061

Bruce A. Wald, M.A.
Project Consultant
Oregon Technical Assistance
 Corporation
3857 Wolvereen Street, N.E.
Building C, Suite 20
Salem, OR 97305

Hill M. Walker, Ph.D.
Director
Center on Human Development
Clinical Services Building
College of Education
University of Oregon
Eugene, OR 97403

Paul Wehman, Ph.D.
Director
Rehabilitation Research and Training
Virginia Commonwealth University
1314 West Main Street
Richmond, VA 23284

Claude Whitehead, M.A.
Mary E. Switzer Research Fellow
and
Consultant
Employment Related Services
46-A G Street, S.W.
Washington, DC 20024

Debbie Winking, M.A.
Illinois Supported Employment Project
College of Education
University of Illinois
Champaign, IL 61820

Wendy Wood, M.Ed.
Project Coordinator
Traumatic Brain Injury Demonstration
 Project
Rehabilitation Research and Training
 Center
Virginia Commonwealth University
1314 West Main Street
Richmond, VA 23284

Yan Xiaoyan, Ph.D.
College of Education
University of Oregon
Eugene, OR 97403

FOREWORD

Expanding employment opportunities for persons with disabilities is one of the most important challenges facing the disability field. The work that has been done to ensure the integration of persons with disabilities into our communities will remain unfinished so long as large numbers of them are unemployed. It is not enough for persons with disabilities to be part of the social mainstream. They should be part of the economic mainstream because work enhances self-worth and contributes to the overall quality of life.

However, increasing employment opportunities for persons with disabilities is not an easy task. Despite decades of effort by persons with disabilities, their families, and public and private agencies, a great deal remains to be done. The results of a recent survey by Louis Harris and Associates demonstrate the magnitude of the challenge we face. According to the survey findings, two-thirds of all persons with disabilities in this country between the ages of 16 and 64 are not working. This situation exists despite the fact that a reported 66% of unemployed working-age persons with disabilities would like to have a job.

We in the Office of Special Education and Rehabilitative Services (OSERS) have sought to improve the prospects of employment for these individuals. One part of this effort has been an increased emphasis on preparing special education students for the transition to employment. Young people with disabilities continue to experience high levels of unemployment despite the increased educational opportunities available to them under Public Law 94-142. We are encouraging school systems and adult service providers to work with young people, parents, and employers to make appropriate plans for each student's transition and to develop services that will support their entry into the world of work.

Efforts are also underway to expand employment opportunities for persons with severe disabilities. A model for training and support of workers with severe disabilities at the worksite, known as supported employment, is being used to train persons with severe disabilities for jobs in communities throughout the country. Companies in the service sector of the economy that rely upon a diminishing pool of younger workers for their work force have expressed interest in this model as a means of utilizing the talents of persons with severe disabilities. Although initially used to train persons with mental retardation, the application of the supported employment model extends to other categories of persons with severe disabilities including persons with long-term mental illness, traumatic brain injury, and severe physical disabilities. As a result of the Rehabilitation Act Amendments of 1986, supported employment services will be available in every state in the nation in the years ahead.

No official support or endorsement of this book by the U.S. Department of Education is intended or should be inferred.

Through our work we have learned that the employment prospects of persons with disabilities cannot be viewed in isolation. Trends developing both within the disability field and in the larger society affect the employment outlook for persons with disabilities. The interest of service industries in workers with severe disabilities as a result of fewer young workers entering the force is an example of such a development.

Our initiatives in transition and supported employment are part of a changing response to the challenge of putting the productive capacity of persons with disabilities to work in the American economy. The outlook for ultimate success is promising, but we still have a long way to go. One of the most important steps we can take is to inform ourselves about the obstacles we face and the tools available to us in overcoming them. *Economics, Industry, and Disability: A Look Ahead* does just this by providing a broad overview of developments that affect the way we approach the task of expanding employment opportunities. This book is written by professionals in economics, vocational rehabilitation, rehabilitation engineering, and other disability-related fields. The chapters focus on the economic, demographic, and legislative influences on employment; the application of marketing concepts to creating jobs for persons with disabilities; the use of technology, training, and support techniques to ensure job success; and the importance of quality of life and quality assurance issues. The authors make specific recommendations regarding marketing, placement, documentation of changes in service delivery, and approaches to policy planning. In doing so, they respond to the need for a synthesis of information on current methods of integrating persons with disabilities into real jobs for real pay.

The ideas put forth by the authors can help provide a basis for action. The expansion of employment opportunities should be promoted with the same zeal that has characterized our efforts in education, independent living, and deinstitutionalization. To do less would be to leave unfinished the great work begun by so many committed individuals. The task is not only to ensure persons with disabilities vocational opportunities, but also to awaken society to a productive resource that has been too long ignored. Persons with disabilities have claimed their rights as citizens; now they eagerly look forward to bearing their share of the responsibility for the work that must be done in this society.

Madeleine C. Will
Assistant Secretary
Office of Special Education and Rehabilitative Services

PREFACE

Evolutions in the demands of the marketplace, the dwindling labor supply, and changing employment patterns all contribute to the need to develop concepts and techniques to guide the expansion of employment for citizens with disabilities. Since the late 1960s, with the move from a manufacturing to a service economy in the United States there has been a significant shift in the types of job opportunities. The shift in the economic focus has been accompanied by changes in the population distribution as well. The continued decrease in the number of younger workers (ages 15–24) available for employment, the increase in the number of individuals over the age of 65 years, and the expanded needs of the information and service industries have placed considerable demand upon the dwindling labor resource. Furthermore, the movement of populations toward the South and West and away from the Northeast implies that shifting population patterns will create additional regional-specific pressures on the labor market.

Individual worker behaviors have likewise changed. Job seekers have become more mobile, and job permanence less significant for the new entrants into the employment world. Fewer than 1% of the population remain on their first job for more than 10 years. In addition, during the average employment history, an individual will work for 10 or more employers. Thus the focus is upon job change and job mobility rather than on job permanence.

Even with recognition of the job climate, unemployment for adults with severe disabilities continues to be considerably greater than among the nondisabled work force. In the past this situation resulted as much from a lack of available jobs as from lack of opportunity. Today the continued high level of unemployment for persons with disabilities points out the need for change on a number of fronts if the potential of this generally untapped labor resource is to be maximized. By focusing on economics, industry, and persons with disabilities, this book addresses key issues in the employment picture for adults with severe disabilities.

If the current federal, state, and local efforts to expand employment opportunities for adults with disabilities are to be sustained, there must be adequate documentation of changes in both levels of economic self-sufficiency achieved through employment and of the improvement in the quality of life of the individual. In an effort to highlight the issues, a number of specific recommendations are made here in the areas of marketing, placement, documentation, and forward policy planning relating to the employment of persons with disabilities.

MARKETING/ADVOCACY

Increase awareness among parents, human services providers, educators, industry, and persons with disabilities regarding their own abilities and the employment opportunities available.

Reinforce the idea of job change and establish the view of job mobility as a positive step in the development of employment skills for persons with disabilities.

Assure an active role for adults with disabilities in all employment-related decisions.

Design educational curricula and experiences that develop vocational skills among students in special education.

Increase integration opportunities for employees with a disability within the social and work environments.

Develop an integrated approach to the provision of vocational, social, and residential services for adults with severe disabilities.

PLACEMENT

Increase the variety of jobs available to persons with disabilities.

Design support models that will ensure that adequate on-site supports are available for persons in supported employment programs.

Design industry-based support strategies to assist employees with disabilities who are in need of assistance at various times (i.e., Employee Assistance Programs).

Develop placement opportunities that provide fringe benefits to persons in supported or competitive employment.

Expand vocational educational and work study options for students in special education programs.

Design support services such that persons with disabilities will be able to retire and have adequate resources to live and recreate as independently as possible.

DOCUMENTATION

Develop and implement a national data collection procedure for day and employment programs. Such a data system may provide mechanisms for identifying best practices in the delivery of day or employment-related services, may identify new or more effective or efficient strategies for service delivery, and/or may provide a mechanism for measuring the impact of current and future practices in employment.

Design measurement procedures for documenting changes in quality of life for persons with disabilities as a result of employment, including the levels of integration achieved by such persons.

Document changes in economic impacts for the individual, the family, the industry, and society through all types of integrated employment options.

Develop longitudinal research activities that will examine placement, training, and support strategies for persons with disabilities.

POLICY PLANNING

Analyze changes in economic factors and their impact upon obtaining and maintaining employment for persons with disabilities.

Examine the changing role of the workplace and its impact upon the quality of life of the worker.

Analyze the economic and health effects upon persons with disabilities who enter or return to work.

Design strategies to look at trends of the whole person and the role of work in ensuring the adjustment of the worker.

Design incentives that encourage industry to open up employment and career opportunities for persons with developmental disabilities.

The preceding recommendations reflect some of the issues that will need to be examined if employment opportunities and increased levels of economic, social, and emotional independence are to be realized for persons with disabilities. This book addresses many of these concerns and describes current, state-of-the-art work in integrating persons with disabilities into real jobs for real pay. Sections of the book relate, respectively, to understanding economic, demographic, and legislative influences on employment; applying marketing concepts in creating opportunities; using technology, training, and support mechanisms to ensure job success; and stressing the importance and implementation of accountability and quality of life issues.

Our major motivation in editing this book has been to facilitate the successful employment of persons with disabilities. We and the other contributing authors have attempted to capture the excitement and challenges surrounding the movement toward generic employment with support services, and to present techniques and strategies that will improve readers' efforts in the field. The legislative, economic, and service delivery changes currently being experienced in the human services area have created significant information and technical needs for (re)habilitation personnel. We trust this book will fulfill those needs and thereby increase employment opportunities and outcomes for persons with disabilities.

ECONOMICS, INDUSTRY, AND DISABILITY

I

OVERVIEW
Economic, Demographic, and Legislative Influences on Employment

The improvement in recent years in employment opportunities for people with disabilities is a reflection of many factors, including the economy, population distributions by age and geographic region, and legislative initiatives. The four chapters comprising this book's first section discuss these changes and their impact upon employment opportunities for persons with disabilities. Chapter 1, by W. E. Kiernan, R. L. Schalock, and K. Knutson, stresses the philosophy and rationale for shifting our (re)habilitation focus to the person's natural residential, recreational, and vocational settings. In addition, the authors summarize population and economic trends that should enhance the employment outlook for persons with disabilities. The chapter concludes with a summary of data from a 2-year employment study supporting the need for continued placement into generic employment with support services and documenting recent progress in that regard.

Chapter 2, by B. Bluestone, summarizes the employment prospects for persons with disabilities and suggests that based on the 1987 Harris poll data, a large percentage of persons with disabilities want jobs. Bluestone then stresses the need to understand the American labor market and the barriers that such people will face in the late 1980s and 1990s.

There is no doubt that the service delivery system is changing. Those changes and the major legislative basis for them are detailed in Chapters 3 and 4. In Chapter 3, C. Whitehead reviews a number of important factors to keep in mind relating to state and federal policy development, including federal policy principles, special populations and special needs, and policy interpretation as a threat to program implementation. In addition, one needs to be aware of recent legislative changes, well-summarized in the chapter, in order that momentum generated by these changes can be maintained. Chapter 4, by R. W. Conley and J. H. Noble, Jr., summarizes the changes that have occurred in the service system for persons with disabilities and the implications stemming from those changes. Finally, the authors review in more depth the regulations pertaining to supported employment and federal guidelines used in establishing supported employment as a service of the Rehabilitation Services Administration.

Individually and in combination, these factors all contribute to the employment picture for adults with disabilities. It is essential that readers be knowledgable about and understand the implications of changes in the economy, population, and policy so that development of positive and constructive employment opportunities for people with disabilities can continue to progress.

Economic and Demographic Trends Influencing Employment Opportunities for Adults with Disabilities

William E. Kiernan, Robert L. Schalock, and Kari Knutson

The focus of rehabilitation has moved toward the provision of services for people with disabilities in the individuals' natural residential, recreational, and vocational settings. In the early 1900s, with the establishment of large institutional care facilities, it was felt that the clustering of persons with disabilities in specialized care programs would be the most efficient and humane way to meet the needs of people with severe disabilities (Baker, Seltzer, & Seltzer, 1974). However, the difficulties in delivering quality service in large, congregate living arrangements have been documented by the numerous class action suits that have resulted from the belief that people with disabilities are more appropriately served in integrated, community settings (Conway & Bradley, 1985; Gilhool, 1976; Seltzer & Seltzer, 1978; Wolfensberger, 1967).

The development of employment training programs is following a course similar to that of residential services. Initially, with the expansion of sheltered employment programs in the 1940s and 1950s, it was felt that persons with disabilities would perform best and be served most appropriately in segregated employment environments (Goldman & Soloff, 1967; Massie, 1967). However, changes in training technologies and in population distributions, and the movement from a manufacturing to a service-based economy, have pointed out the need for and appropriateness of providing employment services for adults with severe disabilities in integrated work settings (Kiernan & Stark, 1986).

The philosophical principles of deinstitutionalization, mainstreaming, and the least restrictive environment have brought to the forefront the utilization of integrated residential, social, and vocational settings in the provision of services to people with disabilities. In addition, the movement has stressed the development of specific, individualized service plans. The emphasis on the establishment of the individualized written rehabilitation plan (IWRP), individualized education program (IEP), individualized service plan (ISP), individualized habilitation plan (IHP), and individualized transition plan (ITP) has underscored a commitment to develop services according to the specific needs of the person rather than according to his or her diagnostic classification. These plans look not only at short-term interventions but at longer-term service needs to increase clients' productivity, independence, and integration into society (McCarthy, Everson, Barcus, & Moon, 1985; Schalock, 1983).

This chapter examines the interaction of economic factors, the needs of industry, and the nature of the person with disabilities in the movement to develop increased independence for people with disabilities in the mainstream of society.

PHILOSOPHY AND RATIONALE FOR CHANGE

The role of work in our society is significant. Work not only provides the individual with a means for economic independence but is central in the development of self-concept, peer relations, and one's basic identity in society (Holland, 1983; Super, Starishevsky, Matlin, & Jordaan, 1963). Society values employment and assigns status to various occupations. This status, combined with economic gains realized through employment, often serves to define the social, interpersonal, and residential environments within which the individual operates (Warr, 1984).

A look at some of the current opinions and beliefs of employed U.S. citizens provides enlightenment on the role of work and of the worker in our society. In surveys conducted by Harris (1987), persons employed in a wide variety of jobs reported their levels of satisfaction, job mobility, and general feelings about job security. On the issue of job satisfaction, Harris noted that 88% of persons surveyed expressed satisfaction with their jobs, with 50% very satisfied and 38% somewhat satisfied. This confirmation that individuals are satisfied with their employment was viewed by Harris as an affirmation that the vast majority of employed persons were deriving a sense of accomplishment, contribution, and self-esteem through the tasks they performed.

Harris (1987) noted, however, that in today's society there is a great deal of mobility among the work force. The concept of movement and of not being wedded to the job were exemplified in Harris's findings by the fact that 39%

of workers surveyed indicated that in 5 years they did not intend to hold the same job. Thirty-one percent said they intended to leave their current job, while another 25% of the sample indicated they did not know what they would be doing in 5 years (Harris, 1987). A study of job mobility showed that fewer than 1% of those in the work force remain on their first job for more than 10 years. The average worker will have 10 different jobs, although not necessarily different employers, over a work career. These findings clearly indicate that the work force in the United States is extremely mobile.

A contributing factor to the level of job satisfaction and the amount of mobility in the workplace is that the vast majority of workers surveyed by Harris (1987) felt that with a minimum of effort they would be able to find another job that would meet or exceed their current levels of reimbursement and satisfaction. Only one-quarter of workers surveyed felt it would be difficult to find a new job. Thus, the sense of high job satisfaction, of a commitment to job mobility, and of being able to find a comparable or better job support the observation that the work force is mobile.

In a similar series of investigations, Harris (1987) attempted to examine worker expectations from employment. In the early 1930s the major expectations of employees were good pay and job security (Harris, 1987). These expectations and the struggles of workers to achieve these goals lead to the development of unions and of lobbying for job tenure. However, employee needs and expectations have been changing since this time, with a marked shift apparent over the past 5 years. About one-half of the workers responding to recent Harris polls have reported that they want their job to be important and to give them a sense of accomplishment. One out of five feels that a chance for advancement is central to his or her job, while a slightly smaller percentage feels that pay is an important motivator. Less than 1 in 10 want security from being fired. Thus, the average worker's expectations have shifted from economic independence and security to a sense of satisfaction and contribution (Harris, 1987).

A study conducted by the International Center for the Disabled (ICD, 1986) in conjunction with Harris (1987) surveyed 1,000 persons with disabilities. The findings showed striking parallels to the previously noted observations, in addition to the finding that the overwhelming majority of disabled people believed that life had improved over the last decade. This improvement, however, was related to the social and integration opportunities that persons received rather than to their vocational opportunities. In the survey, two-thirds of the respondents indicated that they were currently unemployed. Of those employed, 24% held full-time jobs and 10% held part-time jobs. Many of the persons surveyed were viewed as not in the job market, owing to being discouraged about obtaining employment. However, it was notable that of the two-thirds who were unemployed, when asked if a job became available would they be interested, two out of three indicated that they would engage in employment. This extremely high level of unemployment among persons with disabilities would thus appear not to be an issue of motivation but rather of a lack of opportunity. Clearly, this problem must be addressed if employment opportunities for adults with disabilities are to expand. The consequences of not increasing employment options is significant, as alluded to by Harris in noting that "those who do not work feel left out, alone, and largely useless" (1987, p. 196).

Persons with disabilities have a great desire to be accepted by their fellow human beings. The primary way that society can accord them the respect and acceptance they are owed is to expect them to be gainfully employed and to create job opportunities for them. In recent years, people with disabilities have viewed themselves as a cohesive and disadvantaged minority much like the black and Hispanic populations. In a manner similar to the way in which other minority groups have demanded their fundamental rights, a grass-roots disability civil rights movement has emerged to compel the integration of persons with disabilities in all aspects of society (Haveman, Halberstadt, & Burkhauser, 1984). Harris's just-mentioned conclusion (1987) reflects his contention that a common identity is emerging among youth with disabilities, spurred by a conviction that the types of adversities and inequities experienced in the past can be overcome. This sense of personal and group conviction may provide the essential impetus to heighten society's awareness of inequitable patterns of living and of employment discrimination against citizens with disabilities.

The movement toward self-advocacy and an expanded awareness of the abilities, interests, and motivations of people with disabilities is demonstrating that this group will have considerably more to say in the future about the services and employment opportunities provided them. They will increasingly attract attention as an overlooked minority whose members should be hired essentially because it makes good sense (Stevens, 1986).

POPULATION TRENDS AND DEMOGRAPHICS

The expanded advocacy among persons with disabilities is not the only factor that will have an impact upon enhanced employment opportunities. Changes in population trends are likewise exerting a major influence on employment opportunities.

The population growth in the United States, that is, the birth rate minus the death rate plus net immigration, is expected to stabilize over the next several years, showing a decline from the 9.3% growth rate in 1983 to a 5.9% growth rate in the year 2000. The changes in population trends are significant not just from the perspective of changes in birth and death rates but also because of changes in the distribution of the age categories. Since 1880 the proportion of youth and children has declined by about 60%, while the old age component is now more than three times what it was in 1880 (Bogue, 1985). This is largely due again to a declining birth rate. As shown in Table 1.1, the changes in age distribution from 1940 to 1980 are considerable. The percentage of persons between the ages of 18 and 64 has held somewhat constant, while the percentage of those over 65 has increased considerably. More notably, there has been a decrease in the numbers of people in the childhood and youth categories. This change in population age distribution will have a major impact upon the available labor pool in the years to come.

The shift in the age distribution to an older population is a product of two chief factors: 1) the increased life expectancy, and 2) the lower birth rate. For example, the median age in 1970 was 28; in 1983, 30.8 (Bogue, 1985). Advances in health and medical services have allowed elderly persons to maintain a much more active and longer life. These factors are important for family life, housing, labor force participation, Social Security, and politics.

The share of the labor force held by the 20- to 24-year-old group is expected to decrease substantially, from 24% in 1975 to 14% in 1995 (Baxter, 1986). With this substantial decline in younger workers, industries such as fast food and hospitality that have depended on youth as an employment resource are becoming more pressed to find viable labor resources. The estimated 20% reduction in the number of 20- to 24-year-old workers available to enter employment in the year 2000 has raised significant questions in certain industries about expansion (Silvestri, Lukasiewicz, & Einstein, 1984). Moreover, the shortage of a labor pool has led many industries to begin to look toward populations that in the past have not commonly been viewed as viable, such as the disadvantaged, elderly, and disabled populations (ICD, 1986). Thus, although people with disabilities will be competing with individuals from other minority groups, the plentiful openings for full- and part-time work in many service-oriented fields is certainly an advantageous situation. Given the needed training and support, adults with severe disabilities can enjoy the opportunity to increase their share of the labor force.

Table 1.1.   U.S. population distribution by major stages of the life cycle

Age range	Life stage	Percentage of total population in		
		1940	1960	1980
0–8	Childhood	14.4	19.8	12.9
9–17	Youth	16.2	16.1	15.2
18–64	Adulthood	62.5	55.1	60.6
65+	Elderly	6.8	9.0	11.3

Adapted from Bogue (1985).

ECONOMIC TRENDS

General Labor Force

In examining the changes in employment opportunities for adults with disabilities, it is essential to review what has occurred in the general labor force over the past several years. It is also imperative to look at future projections to see what opportunities may arise owing to changes in labor force participation rates and population distributions as well as overall changes in the economy resulting primarily from the movement to service-based industries.

The labor force has grown rapidly since 1965, due primarily to the entry of the baby boom generation. Significant numbers of persons sought employment between 1960 and 1980, with a reduction after 1980. In addition, the number of women entering the labor force has grown rapidly; in 1940, 25% of the new entrants into the labor market were female, as opposed to 54% in 1984. Regarding all males in the labor force, there has been a decline from 87% participation in the labor force for this group in 1948 to 78% in 1984. Many changes are due to longer school attendance, and, therefore, later entry into the workforce for younger workers, and to earlier retirement for individuals over the age of 55 (Bogue, 1985). There is a continuing trend toward retirement from the labor force at earlier ages. In 1970, 89% of the males age 55–59 were in the labor force. This percentage dropped to 79 in 1983. However, the per capita income of this age group (55–59) is greater than that of any other age group (Slater, 1987).

Given these observations, slower growth can be anticipated in the labor force in the years to come, specifically among younger workers. The number of female participants probably will not exceed that of males, and therefore will most likely plateau during the next two generations. The baby bust that began in 1957 and reached major proportions in 1960, along with the reduced birthrate, is leading to fewer entrants into the labor force in upcoming years. Changes in the retirement age and opportunities for early retirement show that in 1940, 42% of males over 65 were employed, whereas in 1983, only 17% of males over 65 were employed. Thus, more older workers will be withdrawing from the labor force in the years ahead if this trend continues as expected. It is also projected that by the year 2000, 45.6% of those in the labor force will be female. It is anticipated that most of the females who choose to work will have the opportunity to do so, and that there will be no untapped surplus of workers among this group (Bogue, 1985).

The preceding trends will have a significant future impact upon the growth of the economy, upon employment prospects for coming generations, upon retirement options for those generations, and upon formulation of immigration policy. Changes in the entry of females into the labor force and the redistribution of the labor force geographically provide many opportunities for employment for individuals who in the past were considered nondesirable candidates or participants, including persons with disabilities.

Employment Opportunities

In studying the changing employment opportunities, a trend is occurring in the general labor force that has similar implications for increased employment opportunities for people with disabilities. In 1969, 29% of all nonfarm employment was in manufacturing, whereas in 1987, this figure dropped to 19%, adding almost 32 million jobs. However, over 1 million fewer persons were employed in manufacturing in 1986 than in 1969 (Slater, 1987).

The service industry has shown explosive growth in the past 15 years. In addition, services appear to be less affected by recessions and by international competition (U.S. Department of Labor, 1986). Service employment trends are showing less regional variation; specific services will likely be offered in all regions, whereas in manufacturing, it is more probable that regions will specialize, such as the Detroit area's automotive industries. However, one must be cautious when looking at the service industry from a macro perspective since not all sectors of the industry will grow at the same pace. Certain clusters within the broad category of services have shown considerable growth, including health care, hospitality, and business/professional services (U.S. Department of Labor, 1986).

Although manufacturing has not duplicated the dramatic gains of the service industries, the manufacturing side will continue to grow. It is estimated that from 1982 to 1995, one in six new jobs will be in manufacturing. Although this represents absolute growth, the proportion of manufacturing to service jobs will decline. In 1959, manufacturing represented 25% of all jobs, whereas in 1982, this percentage dropped to 19%. However, this rate will probably stay steady through 1995 (U.S. Department of Labor, 1986).

A continued decline in unemployment rates can also be expected. In 1982, the unemployment rate rose to 9.7%. In 1987, it had dropped to 7.6% and is anticipated to be around 6% in 1995. This drop in unemployment is a reflection of the restructuring of the available labor resource pool, due, in part, to the declining birth rate and to earlier retirement as well as to expansions in the demand for workers, particularly in the service industries.

These changes provide those involved in enhancing employment opportunities for adults with disabilities with reasons to feel optimistic, yet cautious, about the future. The high-growth industries, particularly many of the service industries, will require a different training approach. The placement of persons with disabilities will have to be on-site, with adequate training and support provided, if in fact the human services field is to respond to the needs of the marketplace. Many service jobs require social and interactive skills that will need to be taught to people with disabilities. Thus, the focus on increasing rates of productivity will have to be balanced with increases in interpersonal and social skill development. Clearly, the challenge in expanding employment opportunities for adults with disabilities will be one of creative utilization of integrated work environments, design of structured support systems, and the integration of individuals in the work setting.

NATIONAL EMPLOYMENT DATA

Given the preceding trends, one can predict that employment opportunities for adults with disabilities could increase significantly in the years to come. A look at the history of the integrated employment movement will help to clarify the opportunities and options for the future.

The movement toward accessing integrated employment opportunities as opposed to sheltered employment has been underway for several years (Kiernan & Stark, 1986; Rusch, 1986; Schalock, 1983; Wehman, 1981). Activities sponsored by the federal government through the U.S. Office of Special Education and Rehabilitative Services (OSERS), the U.S. Department of Education, as well as the U.S. Administration on Developmental Disabilities (ADD) in the Department of Health and Human Services have encouraged the expansion of employment training programs, particularly in the development of supported employment (see Chapters 3 and 4 in this volume; and Bellamy, Rhodes, Mank, & Albin, 1988). One can assume that the successes realized through supported employment are a reflection of changes in placement and support strategies, advances in technology and its application in the work setting, changes in the availability of labor as a resource, changes in the economic environments, and increased awareness of the ability of persons with disabilities in the workplace.

Many states have modified their approach to meeting the employment needs of adults with disabilities by utilizing various supported, transitional, and competitive employment options (Rusch, 1986). Consequently, the focus of many state efforts has shifted from the use of sheltered workshops, day habilitation programs, and work activity centers as the first-choice option to the consideration of integrated work settings as viable alternatives.

A parallel movement has been the increasing focus upon the transition from school to work (McCarthy et al., 1985; Schalock, 1986; Wilcox & Bellamy, 1983; also Chapter 15 in this volume). With the passage of the Education for All Handicapped Children Act (PL 94-142), it was hoped that special needs students would be more effectively prepared to exit the educational system and assume roles as productive adults in society. However, data show that many of the graduates of special education programs do not go into employment but more than likely are referred to sheltered employment, work activity centers, or day habilitation programs (Hasazi, Gordon, & Roe, 1985; Mithaug, Horiuchi, & Fanning, 1985; Schalock, 1986). This realization has led to the development of several efforts to assist special needs graduates to move into supported employment, transitional training, and/or competitive employment (McCarthy et al., 1985).

The shift in philosophy from a structured and separate work or day program to an integrated work environment for special needs graduates has lead to a concerted effort on the part of the federal government to encourage more integrated employment opportunities with necessary supports for:

Those exiting special education and transitioning from school to work
Those in sheltered employment who have not had the opportunity to engage in integrated employment
Those in work activity or day habilitation programs who were perceived in the past as being too severely disabled to have any type of employment as a realistic goal

These changes have lead to the reconceptualization of service delivery systems. Earlier efforts in providing training and employment services are now being viewed by many as limiting the opportunities for adults with disabilities (Wehman et al., 1985). For example, in 1981, the average earnings of a person with mental retardation in sheltered employment were about 35% of the then-prevailing minimum wage and amounted to only $417 per worker per year (Schalock, 1983). Other reports (Karan, 1978; Rusch & Mithaug, 1980) have indicated that individual productivity and movement into competitive employment for the worker with a disability are not sufficiently enhanced in a sheltered employment setting. Advocates of supported and transitional employment designs suggest that the natural work setting is a more desirable work training environment even for workers with severe disabilities (Bailis, Jones, Schreiber, & Bernstein, 1984; Horner & Bellamy, 1979; Riccio & Price, 1984).

In an effort to document actual employment opportunities, a national study of the placement activities of more than 3,652 facilities, organizations, and/or agencies providing vocational services to developmentally disabled adults was conducted by the Developmental Evaluation Clinic, a university affiliated facility at Boston's Children's Hospital (Kiernan, McGaughey, & Schalock, 1986). The survey was conducted over a 12-month period (October 1, 1984–September 30, 1985) and documented the placement of individuals with developmental disabilities into transitional training/employment, supported employment, and competitive employment. The data in Table 1.2 present the findings of the general survey, including the numbers of persons employed full- and part-time (a total of 20,050 individuals), the average age, the wages per hour, the hours worked per week, and the yearly placement comparisons. The table makes clear that placement in transitional and supported employment generally tends to be on a part-time, as opposed to a full-time, basis, while the inverse is true for those placed in competitive em-

Table 1.2. National employment data for adults with developmental disabilities placed into transitional, supported, or competitive employment (general survey, 10/1/84–9/30/85)

| | Employment environments | | |
Variable	Transitional training/ employment	Supported employment	Competitive employment
1. Number placed:			
Full-time	2,797	1,440	7,521
Part-time	3,201	2,464	2,627
2. Average age at placement (weighted means)	29.0	30.8	28.6
3. Wages per hour (weighted means)			
Full-time	$2.67	$3.16	$3.96
Part-time	$2.11	$2.26	$3.56
4. Hours worked per week (weighted means)			
Full-time	35.8	35.7	38.3
Part-time	19.9	19.2	20.8
5. Yearly placement comparisons			
Full-time			
'83–'84	1,737	1,020	4,993
'84–'85	2,797	1,440	7,521
Part-time			
'83–'84	1,462	1,222	1,448
'84–'85	3,201	2,464	2,627

Source: Kiernan, W. E., McGaughey, M., & Schalock, R. L. (1986). National employment survey for adults with developmental disabilities. Boston: Children's Hospital, Developmental Evaluation Clinic.

ployment. Also, it should be noted that there was a continual increase in earnings and hours worked for those placed in transitional, supported, and competitive employment.

In addition, data were collected on the numbers of persons in sheltered employment (not shown in Table 1.2). The information collected looked at earnings in relationship to hours of employment. The employment status indicated that 32% of those persons in sheltered employment worked on a full-time basis, while 68% were employed on a part-time basis. Full-time persons averaged 30.5 hours of work per week at $1.47 per hour, and part-time persons averaged 23.3 hours per week at $1.24 per hour. In looking at the average earnings of those in sheltered employment, more than 50% of the individuals received $1.09 per hour or less. (Kiernan, McGaughey, & Schalock, 1986). This information confirms 1981 data showing that persons in sheltered employment continue to receive approximately one-third of the prevailing minimum wage. Although the absolute dollars may have increased, the percentage of earnings in relationship to the prevailing minimum wage has not increased for more than 6 years.

As important as is placement, measures of employment retention over time are equally important. For those in competitive employment, a measure of retention was calculated. Seventy-seven percent of the sample remained in employment for 60 days or more. A subanalysis of the data showed the retention rate over a 22-week period to be 73%. This would indicate that three out of four individuals placed in employment are able to maintain their positions for more than a 5-month period (Kiernan, McGaughey, & Schalock, 1986).

This survey examined employment from the perspective of numbers of persons placed as well as earnings. It clearly does not demonstrate the complete picture of employment for persons with disabilities. In the future, analysis and documentation of the actual change in quality of life of the employed individuals will be essential.

It is undeniable that many economic and social benefits are realized by individuals and society when employment opportunities are provided for adults with disabilities. Adults with developmental disabilities specifically realize gains through increased disposable income, improved quality of life, and increased sense of self-worth. An increased opportunity for integration with nondisabled persons can provide additional social opportunities as well as the chance to learn more appropriate and effective social interaction skills. The gains made by placing persons in employment, particularly in light of this chapter's discussions regarding population and economic trends, are attributable also to industry. The reduction in job turnover, more effective matching of individual abilities to the job requirements, and the integration of disabled workers into the work setting will certainly reduce costs from an industry perspective. Furthermore, society realizes economic and humanitarian gains by having a contributing member rather than a dependent member.

From all perspectives, then, the increased emphasis on employment placement makes good sense—economically, socially, and emotionally. The movement to create employment opportunities for adults with disabilities has broad-based support and should receive continued investment from government, industry, professionals, parents, and adults with disabilities.

CONCLUSIONS

Changes in the demographic and economic trends as documented in this chapter clearly provide opportunities for human services to respond to industry's employment needs by creating a better match of individuals to jobs. The editors' primary purpose in developing this book is to present readers with strategies and techniques for providing opportunities for regular employment and ensuring the success of that employment. The text also anticipates further changes in the economic environment, it discusses methods for approaching industry from a marketing rather than a selling perspective, it describes new developments in technology that may enhance the person-job match, and examines alternative support strategies to further the integration of the individual into the employment setting. Moreover, the book addresses how to measure the impact that this employment will have on industry, the individual, and society. Finally, the book examines the issue of quality of life, the less well-defined but critically important measure of gain that persons with disabilities will realize through employment in integrated work settings.

REFERENCES

Bailis, L.N., Jones, R.T., Schreiber, J., & Bernstein, P.L. (1984). *Evaluation of the BSSC supported work program for mentally retarded persons*. Watertown, MA.: Cadmus Group.

Baker, B.L., Seltzer, G.B., & Seltzer M.M. (1974). *As close as possible: Community residences for retarded adults*. Boston: Little, Brown.

Baxter, N. (1986, Spring). New projections to 1995. *Occupational Outlook Quarterly, 30*(1), 31–34.

Bellamy, G.T., Rhodes, L.E., Mank, D.M., & Albin, J.M. (1988). *Supported employment: A community implementation guide*. Baltimore: Paul H. Brookes Publishing Co.

Bogue, D.J. (1985). *The population of the United States: Historical trends and future projections*. New York: Free Press.

Conway, J.W., & Bradley, V. (1985). *The Penhurst longitudinal study: Combined report of five years of research and analysis*. Philadelphia: Temple University, Developmental Disabilities Center; and Boston: Human Services Research Institute.

Gilhool, T.K. (1976). The use of courts and of lawyers. In R. Kugel (Ed.), *Changing patterns in residential services for the mentally retarded* (pp. 155–184). Washington, DC: President's Committee on Mental Retardation.

Gliedman, J., & Roth, W. (1980). *The unexpected minority*. New York: Harcourt Brace Jovanovich.

Goldman, E., & Soloff, A. (1967). Issues in rehabilitation workshops. In L. Stahlecker (Ed.), *Occupational information for the mentally retarded: Selected readings* (pp. 528–536). Springfield, IL: Charles C Thomas.

Harris, L. (1987). *Inside America*. New York: Vintage Books.

Hasazi, S., Gordon, L., & Roe, C. (1985). Factors associated with the employment status of handicapped youth exiting high school from 1979 to 1983. *Exceptional Parent, 51*, 455–469.

Haveman, R.H., Halberstadt, V., & Burkhauser, R.V. (1984). *Public policy toward disabled workers*. Ithaca, NY: Cornell University Press.

Holland, J.L. (1983). Vocational preference. In M. Dunnette (Ed.), *Handbook of industrial and organizational psychology* (pp. 521–571). New York: John Wiley & Sons.

Horner, R., & Bellamy, G.T. (1979). Structured employment: Productivity and productive capacity. In G. T. Bellamy, G. O'Connor, & O. Karan (Eds.), *Vocational rehabilitation of severely handicapped adults: Contemporary service strategies* (pp. 85–102). Baltimore: University Park Press.

International Center for the Disabled. (1986). *The ICD survey of disabled Americans: Bringing disabled Americans into the mainstream.* New York: Author.

Karan, O.C. (1978). *Habilitation practices for the severely developmentally disabled* (Vol. 2). Madison: University of Wisconsin, Research and Training Center in Mental Retardation.

Kiernan, W.E., McGaughey, M., & Schalock, R.L. (1986). *National employment survey for adults with developmental disabilities.* Boston: Children's Hospital, Developmental Evaluation Clinic.

Kiernan, W.E., & Stark J.A. (1986). Current and future directions in employment of adults with developmental disabilities. In W.E. Kiernan & J.A. Stark (Eds.), *Pathways to employment for adults with developmental disabilities* (pp. 305–316). Baltimore: Paul H. Brookes Publishing Co.

Massie, W. (1967). Sheltered workshops: A 1962 portrait. In L. Stahlecker (Ed.), *Occupational information for the mentally retarded: Selected readings* (pp. 537–541). Springfield, IL: Charles C Thomas.

McCarthy, P., Everson, J., Barcus, J.M., & Moon, M.S. (1985). Issues in school to work transition and persons with severe disabilities. In P. McCarthy, J. Everson, M.S. Moon, & J.M. Barcus (Eds), *School to work transition for youth with severe disabilities* (pp. 3–17). Richmond: Virginia Commonwealth University, Rehabilitation Research and Training Center.

Mithaug, D., Horiuchi, C., & Fanning, P. (1985). A report on the Colorado statewide follow-up survey of special education students. *Exceptional Children. 51,* 397–404.

Riccio, J.A., & Price, M.L. (1984). *A transitional employment strategy for the mentally retarded: The final STETS implementation report.* New York: Manpower Demonstration Research Co.

Rusch, F.R. (1986). *Competitive employment issues and strategies.* Baltimore: Paul H. Brookes Publishing Co.

Rusch, F., & Mithaug, D. (1980). *Vocational training for mentally retarded adults.* Chicago: Research Press.

Schalock, R. (1983). *Services for developmentally disabled adults: Development, implementation and evaluation.* Austin, TX: PRO-ED.

Schalock, R.L. (1986). *Transitions from school to work.* Washington, DC: National Association of Rehabilitation Facilities.

Seltzer, M.M., & Seltzer G. (1978). *Context for competence.* Cambridge, MA: Educational Projects.

Silvestri, G.T., Lukasiewicz, J.M., & Einstein, M.E. (1984). Occupational employment projections through 1995. In U.S. Department of Labor, *Employment projections for 1995* (Bulletin 2197, pp. 35–47). Washington, DC: Bureau of Labor Statistics, U.S. Department of Labor.

Slater, C. (1987). Who's hiring? *American Demographics, 9*(11), 70–84.

Stevens, G. E. (1986). Exploding the myths about hiring the handicapped. *Personnel 63,* 57–60.

Super, D.E., Starishevsky, R., Matlin, V., & Jordaan, J.P. (1963). *Career development: Self-concept theory.* New York: College Examination Board.

U.S. Department of Labor. (1986). *Occupational outlook handbook* (Bulletin 2250). Washington, DC: Bureau of Labor Statistics, Author.

Warr, P. (1984). Work and unemployment. In P.J.D. Drenth, H. Thierry, P.J. Willems, & C.J. deWolff (Eds.), *Handbook of work and organizational psychology* (Vol. 1, pp. 413–443). New York: John Wiley & Sons.

Wehman, P. (1981). *Competitive employment: New horizons for severely disabled individuals.* Baltimore: Paul H. Brookes Publishing Co.

Wehman, P., Hill, M., Hill, J., Brooke, V., Pendleton, P., & Britt, C. (1985). Competitive employment for persons witn mental retardation: A follow-up six years later. *Mental Retardation 23*(6), 274–281.

Wilcox, B., & Bellamy G.T. (1983). *Design of high school programs for severely handicapped students.* Baltimore: Paul H. Brookes Publishing Co.

Wolfensberger, W. (1967). *Normalization.* Toronto: National Institute on Mental Retardation.

Employment Prospects for Persons with Disabilities

Barry Bluestone

In the middle of the 19th century, a young and still largely unknown Karl Marx observed, in what became known as his *Economic and Philosophical Manuscripts of 1844* (1971), that nothing so determines the status and well-being of an individual as does his or her relationship to the means of production. How individuals are valued by society and how individuals intrinsically value themselves are circumscribed by their relationships to the world of work and to the ownership of property. While family ties and friendships also contribute to a sense of self-worth and to social status, there is unquestionable wisdom in the young Marx's claim. The realm of production confers upon individuals much of their identity, not to mention standard of living. To be outside the world of work is therefore to be largely outside society. Those who are disabled, or better put, "physically challenged," have learned this lesson well. In the words of Louis Harris, the national pollster:

> The decisive decision between hope and no hope among the disabled is between working and not working. Those who work by and large feel they are part of the human race. Those who do not work feel left out, alone, and largely useless. (1987, pp. 195–196)

Given the centrality of work, it is appropriate to ask: What are the job prospects for physically challenged people in postindustrial America? This chapter endeavors to provide some answers to this question.

DISABLED PEOPLE AND THE WORLD OF WORK

According to a Harris poll (1987), there were 27 million Americans in 1985 with a disability or health problem that prevented them from participating fully in work or in school. This is equivalent to one out of seven people in the United States age 16 and over. In 1982, the federal government counted 13 million Americans with some form of work disability—a number more than 50% greater than the total number of people who were counted by the U.S. Department of Labor as unemployed (U.S. Bureau of the Census, 1985, Table 640, p. 378). Of those who have disabilities that affect work or the potential for work, 6.7 million were men, while 6.4 million were women. Only about one-third of this group was in the official labor force, compared with more than three-fourths of those without disabilities. No more than one in five of the persons with disabilities who was working was employed full-time, while the unemployment rate among persons with disabilities was almost double that of the rest of the population. Forty percent of persons with disabilities have never finished high school (compared to 15% for nondisabled people), a factor that contributes to low wages when jobs are found. As a consequence of poor labor market prospects, more than half of those with disabilities live in families with incomes below $15,000, and they are twice as likely as nondisabled persons to live in poverty (Harris, 1987, p. 195).

It is not for lack of ambition that persons with disabilities have been unable to locate adequate work in the job market. Among the two-thirds in the Harris poll (1987) who were reported not working, two-thirds said they would like to have a job. If they had their way, 78% would be working, not the 33% as is now the case. Unfortunately, half believe that employers are convinced that they are not fit to work. Four out of 10 who are not working have little idea where to find a suitable job, and of those working, one-third report that the only reason they were able to find employment is that they found employers who went far out of their way to recognize their capacity to work at a full-time job. For mentally or physically challenged people, getting work—like so many other things in their lives—is no easy matter.

UNDERSTANDING THE AMERICAN LABOR MARKET

To understand the economic barriers facing this population, it is necessary to probe the inner workings of the labor market. Essentially, two key factors influence employment opportunity for any group of workers. One is the nature of the labor market "queue"; the other is the "tightness" of the market itself (Thurow, 1975). To see how these factors interact to provide or deny access to a job for a given individual, one can imagine the labor market as a movie theater with variable seating capacity and a long queue of potential theatergoers standing in line hoping to obtain tickets for the next performance. As opposed to a movie queue, however, tickets in the labor market queue are not distributed on a first-come, first-served basis. Instead, within broad occupations, potential workers are arrayed from the head of the queue to the end, based on employer perceptions of the characteristics of these prospective employees. In the ideal world, the queue would be arranged simply on the basis of the skills each individual possessed. Employers would have sufficient information to judge the productive capacity of each worker, and on the basis of this knowledge, would always choose the most appropriate worker without prejudice. In the real world, of course, this optimal arrangement does not prevail. Employers seldom have comprehensive information about the potential value of job candidates, and they often harbor biases with regard to race, gender, age, beauty, or impairment. Given the peculiar set of prejudices in our society, white men have traditionally been the first in the labor market queue, with women, blacks, elderly, and disabled workers almost automatically consigned to places farther back in the line. Persons with disabilities have usually been at the very end, so that when the movie theater was small, they were left outside, unemployed in large numbers.

The "tightness" of the labor market effectively determines how many seats are in the theater. During periods of high unemployment, the theater shrinks in size, leaving no available tickets for many disadvantaged persons. Only during periods of close to full employment do people at the end of the queue get past the ticket window. Moreover, it is only during such times that wages are bid up as a direct result of labor scarcity. Having exhausted their traditional sources of labor supply, employers are forced to hire workers they would normally have passed over—and they often are compelled to offer higher wages to coax workers into their theater. Hence, full employment is most crucial to those at the end of the queue, including persons with disabilities, because: 1) it provides greater job opportunity, and 2) it tends to drive wages up as a consequence of employers competing among themselves for the few workers still standing outside the theater waiting for seats.

The Labor Market in the 1980s and 1990s

Trends in the nature of the U.S. labor market are therefore critical to the job prospects of people with disabilities. What is known about these trends? For one, we know that America has built a "great jobs machine" (Bluestone & Harrison, 1986). Between 1973 and 1986, this country created 26 million new jobs. This was an extraordinary performance, especially compared to all of western Europe, which, with a population exceeding that of the United States, failed to create a single net new job during the same period. The growth in employment in the United States since 1982 has been sufficient to reduce the national unemployment rate from nearly 11% to under 6%. This is still well below full employment, but is a significant improvement nonetheless.

Not all of the job news, however, has been so positive. While the quantity of job growth has been satisfactory, the quality of the jobs created has been disappointing. In inflation-adjusted dollars, average weekly earnings in America peaked in 1973. Today, the average real wage is lower. Along with the decline in average wages, it has been found that low-wage em-

Table 2.1. Low-wage employment[a] in the United States, 1963–1985 (in percent)

	1963	1973	1979	1985
All workers	35.2	31.8	30.4	31.5
Year-round/full-time	21.2	13.0	13.8	16.1

Source: Bluestone and Harrison (1987, p. 6).

[a]Low-wage employment for all workers is defined as $7,400 or less in 1986 dollars. Low-wage employment for year-round/full-time workers is defined as $11,103 or less in 1986 dollars. The $7,400 low-wage cutoff for all workers and the $11,100 limit for year-round, full-time workers is a standard based on taking half the computed median wage in 1973 for each group, respectively, and then adjusting these two medians for inflation for every year between 1963 and 1985, using the consumer price index (CPI) for all items.

ployment has proliferated in recent years (Bluestone & Harrison, 1986; 1987a,b). If one defines a "low-wage job" as one that paid $7,400 or less in 1986, one finds that the proportion of low-wage jobs in the economy declined steeply between 1963 and 1979. After 1979, however, the percentage reversed and is now higher than in earlier periods. This pattern, which resembles a U-turn, is even more pronounced for the 60% of the labor force who work full time year-round. For them, the percentage falling below $11,100 a year declined from more than one in five in 1963 to little more than one in eight in 1973. By 1985, however, the proportion of low-wage employment was back to nearly one in six. A summary of these data is presented in Table 2.1.

This increase in low-wage employment can be seen even more clearly in terms of employment growth (see Table 2.2). Between 1963 and 1973, about one in five of the net new jobs created paid less than $7,400 per year. Roughly the same proportion held between 1973 and 1979. Yet, between 1979 and 1985, the proportion of new jobs paying low wages more than doubled, to 44%. Once again, the pattern is even sharper among year-round, full-time workers. The proportion of low-wage jobs actually fell by almost 10% in the earliest period, grew by only 12% in the middle period, but accounted for more than one-third of all new year-round, full-time job growth between 1979 and 1985.

Why has the great American jobs machine led to a proliferation of low-wage employment? There appear to be two dominant reasons. The first, and

Table 2.2. Low-wage percentage[a] of net new employment, 1963–1985

	1963–1973	1973–1979	1979–1985
All workers	19.1	19.9	43.9
Year-round/full-time	−9.8	12.4	33.5

Source: Bluestone and Harrison (1987, p. 6)

[a]See Table 2.1 for annual earnings cutoffs.

clearly the most important, has been the nation's poor productivity performance during the past decade. Labor productivity—the amount of real output produced per hour of work—has grown by an average of less than 1% per year since the early 1970s (in contrast to close to 3% per year in earlier years). Since real wages over the long term cannot grow any faster than the rate of productivity growth, wages have generally stagnated. This shows up in the form of more and more low-wage jobs as well as in a falling average wage.

The second reason is the loss of relatively high-wage manufacturing jobs juxtaposed to the extraordinary growth in the postindustrial service sector. In 1986, hourly earnings of production workers in the manufacturing sector averaged $9.73 an hour, while the average for all jobs in the private nonfarm sector was nearly a dollar less, at $8.75 (Council of Economic Advisers, 1987, p. 15). Hence, as manufacturing employment shrank and workers were displaced from jobs in auto, steel, and other production industries, high-wage jobs disappeared.

In their place, the expansion of retail trade and services created a disproportionate number of low-wage jobs. The average wage in retail trade in 1986 was $6.05 an hour, only 62% of the average wage in manufacturing. Even the average wage in professional service industries such as finance, insurance, and real estate trailed the manufacturing sector by almost 13%. The jobs machine created jobs galore, but at a lower wage level than before. Nearly 40% of all service workers earned $7,400 or less in 1985, compared to only 17% of those in manufacturing.

Near-Term Future of the Labor Market

The labor market trends of the most recent past are expected to continue into the future. According to the U.S. Bureau of Labor Statistics, the 1995 labor force will continue to shift away from old patterns (Fullerton, 1985). For one thing, more than two-thirds of the expected 15 million to 16 million new labor force entrants will be women, thus continuing the trend toward a "feminization of the labor force." Second, a smaller proportion of the labor force will be young, and the share of jobs held by those age 55 and over will also shrink (see Chapter 1 in this volume). In 1995, there will be 21 million more prime-age workers, while the ranks of those age 16–24 will decline by 3.8 million and the cohort over age 54 will shrink by 1.6 million.

Following existing trends, nearly four out of five of the new jobs will be in the service sector, with the most optimistic forecast suggesting that while the hemorrhaging of manufacturing industries may cease, this sector as a whole will do little better than hold its own. Moreover, contrary to popular perception, the high-tech industries will add only 1.7 million jobs out of the projected 16 million. The booming sectors will be those shown in Table 2.3.

Table 2.3. Projected high-growth industries, 1984–1995

		Employment growth (in millions)
1.	Business services	2.633
2.	Retail trade	1.691
3.	Eating and drinking establishments	1.203
4.	Wholesale trade	1.088
5.	Medical services	1.065
6.	Professional services	1.040
7.	New construction	0.558
8.	Doctors'/dentists' services	0.540
9.	Hotels and lodging places	0.385
10.	Credit agencies	0.382
	Total	10.590

Source: Personick, V. A. (1985). A second look at industry output and employment trends through 1995. *Monthly Labor Review, 108*(11), 31, Table 3.

IMPLICATIONS OF LABOR MARKET TRENDS FOR DISABLED PEOPLE

The trends just outlined—in particular, the slowdown in the growth rate of new labor force participation and the continued expansion of the service economy—provide some good news, but also some discomforting news for people with disabilities.

On the positive side, reduced numbers of younger workers just entering the labor market will force employers to explore additional sources of labor to fill their personnel needs. In some areas of the nation, particularly in the Northeast, employers are already scrambling for workers. Unemployment rates hovering around 3% in New England indicate that the pool of traditional workers there is all but exhausted. Employers are therefore compelled to turn to workers near the end of the labor market queue to meet their production goals. In so doing, firms are having to develop and adopt new training programs in order to provide skills for these workers. Even then, employers are finding that they are required to offer higher compensation to lure workers away from "the competition." In New England, wage trends are moving in the opposite direction from the national trends just reported. The proportion of low-wage jobs in that region of the country is actually declining, while the number of middle- and high-wage jobs is expanding (Bluestone & Harrison, 1987a). To the extent that slower labor force growth combined with continued job creation leads to intensified competition for labor and additional employer-provided training and higher wages, persons with disabilities will benefit from expanding employment opportunities over the next decade. While the laws of supply and demand are imperfect laws, they do affect the labor market, and these should be to the benefit of persons with disabilities. Of course, however, the laws work both ways. A major recession would dash many of these projections.

New technologies are also providing more job opportunities for persons with physical and mental disabilities. Lighter weight and more easily maneuverable personal transport devices facilitate job opportunities for paraplegics and quadraplegics. As noted in Chapters 11 and 12, the introduction of the computer and the microprocessor-controlled robot as standard machines in the workplace opens up new types of jobs for those with limited cognitive capacity or physical mobility. Modern telecommunications also provide opportunities in telemarketing that did not exist until recently. Extraordinary devices for blind and deaf people are also leading to job openings for many who would have languished at the end of the labor market queue a decade ago.

But not all of the news is so encouraging. The reports of labor market shortages are far from universal. The extremely tight labor markets of parts of the Northeast have still not permeated the deindustrialized "dust bowl" of the Midwest and the South. Even after the longest peacetime economic recovery on record, hundreds of cities and towns continue to sustain jobless rates in excess of 7% and 8%. Thus, while McDonald's Restaurants are forced to pay $5.50 an hour in Boston's suburbs to find enough workers to fry hamburgers and operate cash registers, Detroit's and Birmingham's unemployment rates are such that the same company can offer the minimum wage of $3.35 and attract all the workers it needs.

The shift to a postindustrial service economy is also a mixed blessing in a manner unique to persons with disabilities. Many, if not most, service jobs involve face-to-face contact not only with the employer but the consumer as well (e.g., waiters, waitresses, hotel clerks, accountants, lawyers, doctors, nurses, dental hygienists, hairdressers, department store clerks, financial advisers, and photocopier repairpersons). The service economy no longer provides a "sheltered workshop"—in this case, sheltered away from the consumer. Unlike the manufacturing facility where the worker's identity is hidden from the sight of the consumer, in service jobs the two are in close proximity. What this means is that the worker with physical and mental disabilities faces not one, but two forms of potential discrimination: employer and consumer. The prejudices of the consumer can coerce even the most unbiased employer to be concerned about the outward appearance, speech patterns, or manner of the person he or she hires. In a society so imbued with a sense of what is "normal," consumer sovereignty can be devastating to the job prospects of those with highly visible handicaps.

IMPROVING EMPLOYMENT PROSPECTS FOR DISABLED PEOPLE

The preceding review of labor market dynamics provides at least three important lessons concerning the employment prospects for persons with disabilities. The first is that there is no substitute for a full-employment economy in ensuring job opportunities for disadvantaged people. A full-employment labor market is the ultimate weapon against employer discrimination and the most powerful incentive toward innovation in training and hiring.

The second lesson is that to move persons with disabilities closer to the front of the labor market queue, it is necessary to constantly educate and inform employers about the employability of those who are physically and mentally challenged. In this effort, trained professionals are needed to work both with disabled people and with employers to improve the skills and competencies of the potential worker and to deal with the biases of employers who have traditionally hired from the front of the queue.

Finally, given the service-based nature of the new postindustrial society, it is ultimately the customer—essentially everyone—who must be sensitized to the needs and potential of persons with disabilities. Just as barriers are being broken down with regard to race and sex, albeit still too slowly, the process of dismantling the barriers between persons with disabilities and those without disabilities must begin in elementary school and be carried on through the rest of life.

That an increasing number of persons with disabilities understand these lessons and are ready to organize around them augurs well for the basic social changes that will be necessary. Again, Louis Harris (1987) aptly sums up the situation. People with disabilities, he writes,

> . . . do not want pity. They want a chance to achieve self-respect. And that will come only when they can feel independent and self-reliant. Significantly, by 45% to 42%, a plurality of the disabled now view themselves as a cohesive and disadvantaged minority, much like blacks and Hispanics. The young who are disabled feel particularly deeply about this. And fully 74% of the disabled report they have a common identity with all others who are disabled. With this common bond and a powerful determination born of their desperate and lonely plight, the disabled are beginning to feel they can overcome. (p. 199)

REFERENCES

Bluestone, B., & Harrison, B. (1986, December). *The great American jobs machine.* Report prepared for the Joint Economic Committee of the U.S. Congress.

Bluestone, B., & Harrison, B. (1987a). *The dark side of labor market flexibility. Falling wages and growing income inequality in America.* [Occasional paper.] Geneva: International Labor Office.

Bluestone, B., & Harrison, B. (1987b). *The increasing incidence of low-wage employment in the U.S.* Unpublished manuscript, University of Massachusetts, Boston.

Council of Economic Advisers. (1987, April). *Economic indicators.* Washington, DC: U.S. Government Printing Office.

Fullerton, H.N., Jr. (1985). The 1995 Labor Force: BLS' latest projections. *Monthly Labor Review 108*(11), 80, 92d.

Harris, L. (1987). *Inside America.* New York: Vintage Books.

Marx, K. (1971). *Economic and philosophical manuscripts of 1844.* (D.J. Struick, Ed., and M. Milligan, Trans.). New York: International Publishing. (Original work published 1932)

McLellan, D. (Ed.). (1977). *Karl Marx: Selected writings.* Oxford, England: Oxford University Press.

Personick, V.A. (1985). A second look at industry output and employment trends through 1995. *Monthly Labor Review, 108*(11), 31.

Thurow, L. (1975). *Generating inequality.* New York: Basic Books.

U.S. Bureau of the Census. (1985). *Statistical abstract of the United States: 1986.* Washington, DC: U.S. Government Printing Office.

3

Influencing Employment through Federal and State Policy

Claude Whitehead

People with disabilities have experienced significant and substantial improvement in their efforts to penetrate the regular labor market in recent years. A variety of individuals and organizations have been credited with this success. Unfortunately, one frequently finds less than optimal success in legislative initiatives in this area, either because of failure to act, or the development of complex regulations for major programs, or failure to appropriate funds for these programs. Human services professionals have frequently worked collectively in the private and public sectors to get new federal and state legislation passed, but have failed to realize that the legislative action is only a first step. Thus, this chapter focuses on the importance of understanding state and federal policy and implementation strategies. In particular, it is essential to remember that there is wide variation in federal resource allocation; therefore, persons or organizations seeking to influence a federal program need to be familiar with the power vested in the respective state or local agency.

STATE AUTHORITY IN POLICY MAKING AND ALLOCATION

An important development in establishing service programs is the trend to give the states wide discretion in establishing policies and allocating funds. Examples of this trend include the block grant approach of allocating funds without imposing controls, as seen in the Social Services Block Grant, Maternal and Child Health Block Grants, and the Community Development Block Grants. Other major programs affecting services to persons with disabilities (e.g., the Job Training Partnership Act [JTPA] of 1982 and the Rehabilitation Act of 1973) include an element of state discretion and choice and are considered to be a modified or limited form of block grant. In both of these latter

27

programs, states are given considerable latitude in allocating funds and supporting state and local service delivery systems. In recent efforts to persuade the U.S. Department of Labor (DOL) to establish special earmarking of training and employment (JTPA) funds for persons with disabilities, human services professionals were unsuccessful, mostly because of the DOL policy of giving states and local communities the right to establish individual community priorities, with the primary power resting with the local private industry councils operating under the guidance of the state jobs training coordinating council.

The Rehabilitation Act traditionally has provided for a strong statefederal program, with the states exercising considerable power in determining specific policies and practices. In this relationship, the state vocational rehabilitation (VR) agency is more in control than the federal Rehabilitation Services Administration. The state VR agency influence in the design and development of the Title VI, Part C, Supported Employment Services Program in the 1986 reauthorization of the Rehabilitation Act (PL 99-506) was much in evidence. Efforts of advocacy groups to impose requirements for total funding of the supported employment program under the Title I Basic State Grant were thwarted; Congress opted for an extension of the traditional time-limited funding approach.

Entitlement programs, however, most often are subject to stronger federal control, especially in the establishment of performance standards and controls. Disability-related programs funded under the Social Security Act, Title II Disability Insurance (DI), Title XVI Supplemental Security Income, (SSI), and Title XIX Medicaid operate under various levels of federal influence.

POLICY DEVELOPMENT FACTORS

The development of policy is a complex undertaking. The process often begins with presenting the rationale for establishing such policy: Why is specific attention needed? What results are likely? What happens in the absence of policy? In the development of policy changes, one is always concerned with such considerations as:

Target population to be served; eligibility criteria to be used; who will be included; who will be excluded and why
Equity in service availability to the target group and other special needs groups
Legal and ethical implications
Cost implications of the proposed change
Quality assurance provisions, performance requirements
Impact on service providers

Burden likely to be imposed on the states in terms of additional administrative and resource requirements, including fiscal (accounting and reporting)

FEDERAL GOVERNMENT POLICY PRINCIPLES

The U.S. government is the responsible party for ensuring that its citizens enjoy their freedom, express themselves without fear, and have other protections. In the current environment, there is also increasing concern for the independence of the individual. The government through Congress is charged with ensuring an individual's independence through such activities as:

Ensuring that people who want to work will have that opportunity

Providing income support for persons who, because of their physical or mental disability, are unable to work

Providing training and other assistance to people with disabilities who want to work and providing ongoing support for persons with severe limitations who need support in order to keep their jobs

Providing health coverage for people with severe disabilities who are unable to get health and hospitalization insurance through their jobs and are otherwise unable to afford or secure health isurance

Providing for wage adjustments but retaining the right to commensurate wages if the worker or job candidate with a disability is unable to meet the production requirements

Setting aside or reserving certain jobs in government that people with disabilities are able to do

Targeting government contracts for affirmative action and requiring contractors doing business with the federal government to employ qualified persons with disabilities under certain conditions

Guaranteeing persons with disabilities a free and appropriate education, thereby improving their chances for a job in the community rather than adult nonwork activities after school completion

Providing assistance to help the individual to live independently, if the person is unable to work

SPECIAL POPULATIONS AND SPECIAL NEEDS

Competition and conflict sometimes develop among special populations, especially when there is a shortage of resources to meet special needs. The most common competition in recent years has been between categories of disabled people, such as between those with developmental disabilities and those with physical disabilities. Although there are certain common needs, each subgroup also has unique needs in terms of access to housing, transportation, and jobs.

A second competing relationship involves persons who are aged and persons with developmental disabilities. Both have needs for extended services, especially in the case of medically limited elderly persons, but the needs may require dramatically different services systems. However, the need for employment takes on similarities because of the limitations imposed by age or disability.

In addition, conflict sometimes occurs when there is resistance by older persons or by those with mental illness to being associated in a program with persons who are labeled as mentally retarded—the labeling conflict. The irony of this conflict is that grouping persons with physical limitations with persons with mental limitations would permit combining the mental skills of one person with the physical capabilities of the other to achieve a productive outcome. A recent innovative project involved training persons disabled by mental retardation to be personal care workers or domestic assistants for older persons unable to live independently without such help. Another project under consideration would employ displaced older workers as job coaches for persons with disabilities in supported employment programs.

POLICY INTERPRETATION
AS A THREAT TO PROGRAM IMPLEMENTATION

The recent experience of states in developing and implementing federal programs has not always been positive. In some states, new programs have been implemented only to have related expenditures disallowed when federal auditors reviewed the records. In some instances, states have been found to have stretched the new authority beyond intended limits; in other situations, there was simply a lack of understanding of the regulations or other requirements.

This problem has been especially acute in the funding of community-based vocational services for persons with developmental disabilities and the redirection and reallocation of Title XIX (Medicaid) funds originally designed for institutional services. Efforts to reconcile the conflicts continue, but the impact likely will be increased reluctance by states to authorize program expenditures in areas where the threat of audit and subsequent disallowance exists.

The basic problem centers around the concern of federal or state government that the funds should go for appropriate, intended services. This problem appears to be increasing as federal and state governments delay the publication of rules and regulations in an effort to ensure that requirements and provisions are legally and technically correct, and as recipients continue to protest regulations that are technically complex and difficult to interpret. In order to protect the intent and goals of the program, unreasonable delays are becoming common.

LEGISLATIVE REFORM:
REMOVING BARRIERS AND INCREASING INCENTIVES

In the final days of its 99th session, Congress conducted a "legislative sweep" that removed barriers and improved incentives to employment for persons with severe disabilities. The remainder of this chapter reviews the status of these new opportunities.

1. Rehabilitation Act Changes included: providing special recognition and status to supported employment through changes in the Title I program to authorize supported employment as a specific vocational rehabilitation service and through adding Title VI, Part C, Supported Employment Services, as a specific formula grant program; and revising the definition of *severe handicap* to make it compatible with the Developmental Disabilities Act as amended by PL 98-527. Final regulations implementing the new Title VI, Part C, Supported Employment Services Program, were published in September 1987, following an extended comment period, and funds were subsequently distributed to the state VR agencies.

2. Education for the Handicapped Act Rules for implementing early intervention, the major provision of PL 99-457, have been finalized after extensive delays, and the funds for the Part B program have been distributed following state plan amendments. Although the major amendments focus on early (preschool) intervention, other important changes involve the tightening of transition planning requirements and specific listing of supported employment as a goal. While results of the early intervention program implementation are likely to be evident in later years for the transitioning student, states and local communities will be required to improve employment-related planning in the immediate future.

3. Work Incentive Improvements Act Authorized under PL 99-643, the amendments gave prominence to the Social Security Act, Section 1619, provisions of the Supplemental Security Income (SSI) program involving continuing support of cash assistance and medical (Medicaid) services for persons who work in spite of their disability. The changes, effective July 1, 1987, also addressed problems of eligibility and program reentry, SSA staff training, and informing persons of eligibility.

The key new terms *break-even point* and *threshold of earnings* replace *trial work period* and *extended period of eligibility,* thereby making the entry to the world of work a safer venture. These changes are likely to have a major impact on employment for people with severe handicaps. The gradual phaseout of the cash assistance benefits under Section 1619(a) permits the recipient to use cash earnings to replace SSI payments. The Medicaid eligibility continuation under Section 1619(b) is especially important for persons who go to work and are not provided health and hospitalization insurance coverage by their employers.

Most persons with severe disabilities are eligible for Medicaid under the Title XVI (SSI) program, while others are eligible for Medicare under the Title II Disability Insurance (DI) program. The PL 99-643 amendments affect persons receiving SSI and a portion of those receiving Disability Insurance benefits as an adult disabled child, but problems continue for persons with disabilities who have need for medical coverage but have earnings that take them out of the eligibility range. For that group of individuals, the issue of medical coverage becomes one of availability and affordability. A Disability Advisory Council, established by the U.S. Department of Health and Human Services in 1987, was created to address the need for comparable provisions under the Disability Insurance program, along with other problems in the SSA disability program.

4. The Fair Labor Standards Act (FLSA) The changes in PL 99-486 removed severe restrictions on earnings and mobility limitations in sheltered workshops and work activity centers. The revised program replaces a complicated multiple-certificate program with a single certificate available to all employers in which subminimum wages are involved. A "right to fair wages" provision ensures workers with disabilities of improved consideration of their productive work through establishing a special procedure. On the employer's side, the process of securing a certificate and paying commensurate wages was improved, but the requirements to justify wage rates were tightened. It is important to note that the commensurate wage payment requirement relates to "prevailing wage rates in the vicinity," rather than to the statutory minimum hourly rate; the prevailing rate is most often more reflective of the community wage levels and is higher than the statutory rate set by FLSA legislation.

Proposed regulations implementing the FLSA Section 14(c) changes have experienced extensive delays, reportedly because of the Department of Labor's concern that the procedures would be legally and technically unworkable, especially the wage payment appeal process. In the interim period, employers have been advised by DOL that the single-certificate provisions and the work activities center segregation elimination changes are considered to be in effect.

5. The Consolidation Omnibus Budget Reconciliation Act (COBRA) The changes included in PL 99-272 pertaining to provisions for funding employment-related services under the Home and Community Based Care Program of Title XIX have produced disappointing results to date, mostly because of a strict interpretation of the amendment by the Health Care Financing Administration (HCFA). The targeted case management authorization has likewise seen limited implementation through state plan amendments approval by HCFA.

The 1987 Omnibus Budget Reconciliation Act (PL 100-203) included additional refinements in the Title XIX Home and Community Care Waiver program, which clarified intent regarding habilitation services, including pre-vocational services and supported employment. In addition, clarification was provided for the Title XIX basic Medicaid authorization regarding targeted case management being available to address special problems in service coordination, including extended support for employment-related services. Congressional staff have privately assured this author that future legislative changes will provide special attention to removing the current prohibition regarding reimbursement of specialized employment services, including supported employment, as a day program under the Title XIX program for intermediate care facilities for the mentally retarded (ICFs/MR). All of these changes are directly related to the needs of individuals with mental retardation and other developmental disabilities for continued support in securing and maintaining employment in an integrated setting in the community.

6. *Tax Reform* The changes contained in PL 99-514 involve restoring two important employment incentives for persons with disabilities: Targeted Jobs Tax Credit and tax credits for renovations and alterations to improve physical access to buildings and transportation. Job placement people report good response to the restoration of these programs.

To summarize, the benefits of these six recent legislative reforms have not been fully realized to date; but hope remains. As mentioned previously, the process of implementing change in federal policy has become much more difficult in recent years. The change is attributed to a number of factors, including legal considerations and realization of the potentially vast implications of any government action, the drive for cost containment, the competition among special need groups, and the constant campaign for expanding services. The best approach for human services advocates seems to be to seek alternative strategies for working with the system and its barriers, to seek incremental changes rather than major reform, and to actively collaborate with groups who have similar needs to strengthen lobbying power.

A remaining challenge relates to long-range funding. More and more states report that they face a cap in state funds for community-based services for persons with severe disabilities; yet they are being asked to expand residential and community-based services to meet the needs of persons on waiting lists and to continue the process of expanding opportunities for integrated community living. Some states report the possibility that future growth in congregate community living may require that residential facilities now operated mostly with state and local funds be reorganized administratively and operationally so that they can be certified as ICFs/MR in order to have federal participation in the operating costs. But this requires meeting stricter, and often less appropriate, standards of care and treatment. In other words, there is concern that the change will represent both reduced flexibility and a regression in the move toward independence, productivity, and community integration.

The significance of the problem is best illustrated in Braddock's study (Braddock, Hemp, & Howes, 1985) of state use of Title XIX funds. The federal share of expenditures for an ICF/MR ranges from 55% to 78% of the cost of these institutional services. By contrast, federal funds cover only about 25% of the cost of community services. It seems difficult to expect continued growth of community services (that is, movement from an ICF/MR to a noncertified residence and entry to non–federally supported employment services) when the money does not follow the individual and when state costs continue to grow. The Title XIX Home and Community-Based Services Waiver program was designed to address this problem and to have the money follow the individual. To date, efforts to enact the waiver have been disappointing, but plans for further refinement to this significant program are currently under consideration in Congress.

MAINTAINING THE MOMENTUM

Many of the states have made outstanding progress in expanding employment opportunities and options over the past few years, with much credit owed to the collaboration between state VR and state mental retardation/developmental disability (MR/DD) agencies. The opportunities ahead will depend upon continuing this momentum through actions at the state and local levels such as the following:

1. *Take full advantage of the SSI and SSDI benefits available to persons with continuing disabilities.* One needs to make certain that all qualified/eligible persons are enrolled and receive full benefits. Equally important, persons with developmental disabilities most often do not receive hospitalization insurance as part of their employment benefits and, consequently, eligibility for Medicaid (or Medicare) is especially important.
2. *Expand the Home and Community-Based Services Waiver (HCBSW) through "active pursuit" by state MR/DD agencies and others to secure additional amendments.* The complexity of federal regulations for the HCBSW is unprecedented and unsurpassed.
3. *Address services coordination needs in planning for long-range services.* Such services include employment support in retaining and reobtaining employment. The COBRA (PL 99-272) changes authorized "targeting" of service coordination in the revision of case management under the Title XIX programs, but this provision requires concentrated effort to identify the target group, to specify the services to be provided, and then

to coordinate the services. A modification in the states' Medicaid Plan is necessary, but the support implicit in the COBRA changes should justify this effort for which other funding is not generally available.

4. *Monitoring of the publication of proposed federal regulations is very important.* States should not assume that national organizations will cover their concerns. In reality, federal regulators often pay more attention to comments of provider agencies at the local level.

5. *Secure additional changes in medical insurance provisions for persons with developmental disabilities who are not covered by the Section 1619(b) changes.* Some of that population group may be receiving assistance under the Title II Disability Insurance provision (as disabled workers or childhood disability beneficiaries); others will not be eligible for extended coverage because their earnings level is above the allowable limit. One segment of the needs of the SSDI group is addressed in provisions for continuation of Medicare coverage for 24 months after the person achieves substantial gainful activity (SGA) and is no longer receiving benefits under the DI program. Unfortunately, the time limit may not be adequate for people with severe and continuing disabilities. Additional revision is under consideration by SSA and Congress as an amendment to the Title II Disability Insurance program, similar to the SSI Section 1619 revisions. In the availability and affordability area, there will be greater need for assigned risk insurance pools and for similar programs as persons with severe disabilities increase earnings but find health coverage unavailable or not affordable.

6. *Continued attention must be given to transitioning programs.* The federal legislation has only laid out an agenda or program format in terms of transitioning youth with disabilities into the world of work. Public school programs will need to be revised and staff trained to implement a new employment-directed transition planning program. They will need encouragement in recognizing that this group needs preparation for work rather than daily nonwork activities, as is too often the case.

In conclusion, a number of significant federal legislative reforms have recently been enacted whose intent is to provide additional living and employment opportunities for persons with developmental disabilities. Despite these legislative changes, one should be sensitive to the important role that regulatory bodies and state agencies play in the actual implementation of (re)habilitation programs. As might be expected, efforts to ensure continuation of the current gains are coupled with concern regarding cost containment. However, any program that shows evidence of reducing public costs through improving productivity and self-sufficiency will likely continue to receive the attention of Congress and federal and state government.

REFERENCES

Braddock, D., Hemp, R., & Howes, R. (1985). *Public expenditures for mental retardation and developmental disabilities in the United States.* Chicago: University of Illinois at Chicago, Institute for the Study of Developmental Disabilities.

4

Changes in the Service System for Persons with Disabilities

*Ronald W. Conley
and John H. Noble, Jr.*

Most Americans with severe disabilities will receive services from many different public and private agencies during their lifetime. All children with disabilities will receive educational services. As adults, they may receive income support, medical care, vocational rehabilitation, counseling, attendant care, case management, and a wide variety of other services.

Collectively, the programs that provide these services constitute a system of services. One important fact must be emphasized in this connection: The level and type of social adjustment that people with disabilities achieve is dependent upon the combined and interacting effects of this system of services and not upon any one component by itself. Whether or not a severely disabled person is able to work, for example, may depend upon the type of educational program he or she received, the availability of vocational rehabilitation services, the incentives or disincentives inherent in the income support and health care financing programs, as well as the effects of other programs. Of course, the optimum combination of services will differ among individuals.

Forty years ago, the service system for people with disabilities was relatively small and simple. Many necessary services were not available and, as a consequence, numerous persons with severe disabilities went unserved. For example, many Americans grew to adulthood without any educational services. At that time, little was expected of persons who had severe disabilities. Employment was generally considered not feasible, as was any

This chapter was written by the authors in their private capacity. No support or official endorsement by the U.S. Department of Health and Human Services is intended or should be inferred.

degree of community integration. Many persons with severe and not so severe disabilities were placed in institutions that provided few services and maintained a subsistence standard of living. During the past 40 years, however, enormous changes have occurred in the service system. This chapter briefly reviews a number of these changes, including the new supported employment programs, and discusses the implications of these changes in terms of the economic and human services environments within which adults with disabilities live and work.

CHANGES IN THE SERVICE SYSTEM

There have been five dramatic changes in the service system for adults with disabilities. These are discussed briefly next.

Change #1. The service system has become very large. No precise measure of the cost of the service system is possible. The National Council on the Handicapped (1986) estimated that federal expenditures alone on disability programs exceeded $60 billion in 1986. Berkowitz and Hill (1986) reported that total government (federal, state, and local) and private expenditures on disability programs were $121.5 billion in 1982.

Another way to emphasize the enormous size of the system of programs serving persons with disabilities is to observe that during 1986 (National Council on the Handicapped, 1986) approximately:

3.9 million persons with disabilities were receiving Social Security Disability Insurance benefits.

1.9 million persons with disabilities were receiving Supplemental Security Income.

2.8 million persons with disabilities were receiving Medicare.

3.2 million persons were receiving Medicaid because of disability.

2.2 million persons were receiving veteran's compensation for service-connected disabilities and 676,000 persons were receiving a pension for nonservice-connected disabilities.

4.2 million children were being served with partial federal funding under the Education of Handicapped Children program.

An unduplicated count of the total number of persons with disabilities being served by the service system cannot be developed. Data are lacking on a number of the programs that provide services to persons with disabilities, and there is little information on the number of persons receiving concurrent services. However, the number of persons with disabilities receiving services would certainly exceed 5 million and is probably closer to 10 million.

Change #2. The service system has become increasingly comprehensive. A wide range of services is available, including: income support through the Social Security Disability Insurance program/Childhood Disability Benefits program (SSDI/CDB) and through the Supplemental Security Income (SSI) program; health care financing through the Medicare and Medicaid programs; employment services through state vocational rehabilitation agencies and employment services; social services through the Social Services Block Grants; housing services through the intermediate care facilities for the mentally retarded (ICFs/MR) program (which also provides social services and limited vocational services) and U.S. Department of Housing and Urban Development (HUD) programs; and medical and other services through the Maternal and Child Health Block Grants. Although these programs are among the largest in the service system, many other programs also provide or fund services and other support. For example, public and private retirement programs often offer income support to adult children of beneficiaries whose disability began in childhood.

Change #3. The service system has become complex and is poorly understood by most people. An individual program may appear straightforward and simple to the individuals who administer it, but to persons with disabilities and their families who seek access to services, the experience is often bewildering. This is partly because each program was established independently and is separately administered, and program administrators are not required to take account of the impact of their actions on other programs. Moreover, the goals of individual programs tend to be narrowly defined. For example, the primary purpose of the Social Security program is to provide income support, not to encourage employment. In addition, eligibility conditions vary widely among programs.

Another factor contributing to the complexity of the system is the sheer number of programs. The National Council on the Handicapped (1986) identified 46 separate federal programs providing support and services to persons with disabilities, while acknowledging that the actual number of programs was understated. For example, the list did not include the Food Stamp program; the Social Services Block Grants; the Maternal and Child Health Block Grants; the Alcohol, Drug Abuse, and Mental Health Block Grants; or the childhood disability components of the federal Civil Service Retirement and Railroad Retirement programs. To these federal programs must also be added those programs that are funded solely by state and local governments (such as some housing programs) and the many private (profit and nonprofit) programs that provide services and support to persons with disabilities.

Finally, the system's complexity is exacerbated because the programs are operated both publicly and privately, and the public programs are operated at different levels. For example, the SSDI/CDB, SSI, and Medicare programs are administered by the federal government, the vocational rehabilitation and Medicaid programs by state governments, and some housing and social service programs by local governments.

Change #4. There has been a major shift to a reliance on federal funding, particularly for adult services. As examples, the federal government funds 100% of the costs of SSDI/CDB, SSI (other than the state supplements), Medicare, and veteran's programs. The federal government funds about half of the Medicaid program and about 80% of the state-federal vocational rehabilitation program.

In 1984, federal expenditures for persons (adults and children) with mental retardation or other developmental disabilities were about 55% of total federal and state expenditures for these programs (Braddock, Hemp, & Howes, 1985). Federal expenditures undoubtedly constituted an even larger percentage of expenditures made for adults with mental retardation or other developmental disabilities. Adults with mental retardation are more likely to receive federally funded income support payments and health care financing, while children with mental retardation are universally enrolled in education programs funded by state and local government.

Change #5. During the past 40 years, there have been rapid and dramatic changes in the goals set for people with mental retardation or other developmental disabilities. Initially, it was largely believed that most persons with mental retardation, even those with mild mental retardation, had limited capacity to learn or to work. Consequently, emphasis was placed on developing programs for institutional reform (the ICF/MR program), income support (SSDI, SSI), and day activities. However, these goals are rapidly changing. It is now generally accepted that most (some people say *all*) persons with mental retardation or other developmental disabilities can learn and develop in a classroom setting, can live in community-based housing and participate in community activities, and can work in substantial jobs in integrated worksites.

IMPLICATIONS OF SERVICE SYSTEM CHANGES

Several important observations, based in part on the five trends just described, should be noted.

Observation #1. The large size and comprehensiveness of the service system means that policy analyses should be primarily oriented toward "how-to" issues. The broad question that should be asked is: How can existing resources be used more effectively to achieve social goals, or more efficiently to achieve these goals at less cost? The authors are not arguing that sufficient resources already exist in the service system to meet all of the service needs of clients. Unfortunately, information to determine whether resources allocated to the service system should be increased or decreased is not available and probably will continue to be unavailable for some time. However, given the substantial resources currently being used, the authors believe that the payoff for more efficient and effective use of resources will often be greater than the payoff from adding additional resources. Thus, the authors believe that the overall cost of the service system can be reduced while increasing the well-being and independence of its clients.

Examples of "how-to" issues related to this overall concern include:

Should funds be reallocated from work activity centers and day care to supported work?

What are the most effective techniques for providing supported work to persons with different types of disabilities?

To what extent can home services avoid the need for placing persons in out-of-home care?

Observation #2. States often organize their service systems in ways that assure them of the receipt of federal funds rather than in ways that are most suitable for clients. This is the result of two factors. First, the substantial contribution of federal dollars to the service system is usually accompanied by restrictions on who may receive the funds and on what types of services may be provided. Second, states place a high priority on minimizing their own fiscal burden by qualifying for as many federal dollars as possible.

In urging change in federal programs, state officials sometimes acknowledge that they behave in this fashion. As examples, the wish to capture Medicaid dollars has inhibited the changeover from institutional to community-based care for persons with mental retardation, and has impeded the changeover from day care services to employment services. As another example, the desire to maintain SSDI and Medicare coverage for clients, which, as mentioned, are 100% federally funded, may cause some state administrators to hesitate to place dual SSDI/SSI beneficiaries in jobs that would jeopardize continuing SSDI and Medicare eligibility, despite the positive work incentives now available under the SSI and Medicaid programs. Even though Medicaid coverage may continue, it would increase the financial burden on the state since Medicaid is partially state financed.

Observation #3. In evaluating the effectiveness of services, one must consider the combined and interacting effects of all programs, not of any one program alone. If one tries to evaluate the effects of any single program on an individual, one inevitably begins to ascribe to that program part of the contributory effects of other programs on that individual. Thus, the failure of a rehabilitation program to place a client in a job may not be due to inadequacies in the rehabilitation program, but to work disincentives contained in income support and health care programs.

Observation #4. When initiating a new program, or altering an existing program, one should consider not only the immediate effects on the program being changed but also the effects on other programs. For example, cutting back on employment programs may eventually lead to an increase in the costs of the income support and health care financing programs.

Observation #5. Evaluation of the service system must be based upon the goals set for individuals. The authors (Conley, Noble, & Elder, 1986; Noble & Conley, 1981) have been critical of various programs for creating barriers to the attainment of employment or community-based living arrangements for people with disabilities. A frequent rejoinder has been that the authors were criticizing programs for failing to do what they were never designed to do. For example, the ICF/MR program was not designed to promote community-based care in the least restrictive mode possible, nor were the SSDI or SSI programs designed to promote the employment of disabled persons. Although true, this defense of program activities is not relevant. The issue is whether or not the programs are providing the types of services that people with disabilities need in order to achieve social goals. If not, then the programs clearly need to be changed, regardless of their original intent.

Observation #6. In spite of the magnitude and comprehensiveness of the service system, and the dramatic changes that have been occurring, much remains to be accomplished for persons with severe disabilities. Despite the optimistic beliefs about what persons with mental retardation or other developmental disabilities can accomplish, numerous such individuals still live in large institutions, and few persons with severe limitations have actually been placed in substantial jobs. Bruininks et al. (1983) reported that about 80% of the persons with mental retardation in out-of-home care still lived in institutions with 16 or more residents. Unfortunately, little information is available on the extent to which the residents take part in community activities, and very limited national information is available on the employment status of persons with severe limitations (Kiernan, McGaughey, & Schalock, 1986). However, a recent survey (Buckley & Bellamy, 1985) indicated that large numbers of people with mental retardation are still in day care or work activity centers.

Observation #7. The programs in the service system have not kept up with changing goals and treatment philosophies for persons with mental retardation and developmental disabilities. In fact, many programs were designed to meet goals that were set in past years and have not changed substantially since then. Consequently, the service system is riddled with contradictions and inconsistencies and with program requirements that are inconsistent with the goals now established for persons with severe disabilities. (See Chapter 25, in this volume, for a review of some of the more important of these inconsistencies and contradictions.)

THE NEW SUPPORTED EMPLOYMENT PROGRAM

The 1986 Amendments to the Rehabilitation Act of 1973 created a revolutionary new state formula grant program for supported employment of people with severe disabilities. This program is designed to assist persons with severe disabilities to achieve substantial employment. The target population comprises persons for whom competitive employment has not traditionally occurred or has been interrupted or intermittent as a result of severe disabilities and who have been evaluated as having the capability to engage in supported employment. In other words, eligibility for the new program is based on the inability to function independently in employment without ongoing support services for the duration of employment (*Federal Register*, May 27, 1987). Any person with a sufficiently severe disability can qualify for the supported employment program, including persons with mental retardation, spinal cord injury, blindness, or mental illness, if deemed capable of working an average of 20 hours per week with ongoing service supports. The supported employment program can be viewed as providing legislative authority for the federal-state vocational rehabilitation program to provide extended services to persons whose disabilities are so severe that they would not be considered eligible for traditional time-limited services. Not all persons with severe disabilities will be eligible for the new program, since they must be evaluated as capable of working an average of 20 hours per week with ongoing service supports.

There are several noteworthy characteristics of the new program, including:

1. Although the supported employment program has separate legislative authority and funding, it is an integral part of the basic vocational rehabilitation program. Of particular importance is that many of the services received by persons who enter into supported employment will be funded by the basic program. For example, the proposed regulations explicitly state that any evaluation of prospective clients for supported employment must be supplementary to the evaluation of rehabilitation potential conducted under the basic program. Certain other rehabilitation services, such as the provision of prostheses, are to be paid for by the basic program. Services provided with supported employment funds are to supplement basic vocational rehabilitation services and are to be provided *after* clients are placed on jobs. Such postemployment services include the funding of a job coach, long-term follow-up, supervision at the worksite, or other services needed to assist the client to maintain employment.

2. Funding of postemployment services by the federal-state vocational rehabilitation program is limited to a period not to exceed 18 months, at which point the funding responsibility must be shifted to another agency. The new legislation refers to postemployment services paid for by another agency as "extended services."

3. Coordination and joint agreements with other agencies are mandated under this new program. An individualized written rehabilitation plan (IWRP) must be developed that complements the individualized plans prescribed by

other federal or state legislation such as the individualized education program (IEP) under PL 94-142, the individualized habilitation plan (IHP) under the Medicaid ICF/MR program, and the IHP required by the Developmental Disabilities Act. More important, provisions must be made for the assumption of funding for postemployment services by other state or private, nonprofit agencies following termination of vocational rehabilitation support after 18 months.

4. Placement of workers with severe disabilities into competitive work in an integrated work setting is the only vocational goal sanctioned by the new supported employment program. The proposed regulations define the following key terms. *Competitive work* refers to work that averages at least 20 hours per week and for which an individual is compensated in accordance with the Fair Labor Standards Act. *Integrated work setting* refers to job sites where most of the co-workers are without disabilities. Although it is preferable for the client to be placed in a work group where most other workers do not have disabilities, the proposed regulations permit clients to be placed in small work groups of disabled workers of no more than eight individuals, provided the group has regular contact with nonhandicapped persons who are not providers of support services in the immediate work setting. This apparent exception to the full integration of clients is deemed necessary to enable persons with severe disabilities to work as members of mobile crews or in sheltered enclaves in regular work settings. The supported employment program cannot be used to fund clients in sheltered workshops or work activity centers.

5. The regulations permit services to be offered to persons with chronic mental illness who are in "transitional employment." However, *transitional employment* is defined in the same way as *competitive employment* (i.e., it must be provided in integrated work settings), with the additional proviso that the job need not be considered permanent. This exception is made to accommodate the special needs of persons with chronic mental illness to allow them to work in shared jobs when their fluctuating psychiatric symptoms permit work activities.

The development of a federal supported employment program represents a major advance in a movement that only a few short years ago existed as a visionary technology practiced in a few academic centers with the temporary support of discretionary funds from public agencies. The new federal legislation gives impetus and support to the continued development of supported employment programs that have been initiated by an increasing number of states with federal discretionary funds.

SUMMARY

This chapter has highlighted a number of recent changes, including the new supported employment program, that have occurred in the service system for persons with disabilities. The implications of these changes have also been discussed as they affect the economic and service environments within which disabled adults live and work. The chapter provides a transition from the first section of the book, which has focused on economics and human services, to the second section's emphasis on applying marketing concepts to create employment opportunities. The changes in the service system cited here are affording increasing numbers of people with disabilities the opportunity to work in integrated employment settings. As the second section emphasizes, however, that opportunity must be "marketed" to industry and the private sector. Without effective marketing, many potential opportunities may well be lost.

REFERENCES

Berkowitz, M., & Hill, A.M. (1986). Disability and the labor market. In M. Berkowitz & A.M. Hill (Eds.), *Disability and the labor market: An overview* (pp. 1–28). Ithaca: Cornell University, New York State School of Industrial and Labor Relations; ILR Press.

Braddock, D., Hemp, R., & Howes, R. (1985). *Public expenditures for mental retardation and developmental disabilities in the United States*. Chicago: University of Illinois at Chicago, Institute for the Study of Developmental Disabilities.

Bruininks, R.H., Hauber, F.A., Hill, B.K., Lakin, K.C., McGuire, S.P., Rotegard, L.L., Scheerenberger, R.C., & White, C.C. (1983). *Brief #21: 1982 national census of residential facilities: Summary Report*. Minneapolis: University of Minnesota, Center for Residential and Community Services.

Buckley, J., & Bellamy, G. (1985). *National survey of day and vocational programs for adults with severe disabilities: 1984 profile*. Eugene: University of Oregon Specialized Training Program, College of Education.

Conley, R., Noble, J., & Elder, J. (1986). Problems with the service system. In W. Kiernan & J. Stark (Eds.), *Pathways to employment for adults with developmental disabilities* (pp. 67–83). Baltimore: Paul H. Brookes Publishing Co.

Federal Register. (1987, May 27). 52 (101): 19817–19920.

Kiernan, W.E., McGaughey, M., & Schalock, R. (1986). *National employment survey for adults with developmental disabilities*. Boston: Children's Hospital, Developmental Evaluation Clinic.

National Council on the Handicapped. (1986). *Toward independence*. Washington, DC: U.S. Government Printing Office.

Noble, J., & Conley, R. (1981). Fact and conjecture about the policy of deinstitutionalization. *Health Policy Quarterly, 1*, 99–124.

OVERVIEW
Application of Marketing Concepts in Creating Opportunities

As noted in Section I, a number of economic, demographic, and policy factors must be taken into account when examining employment opportunities for people with disabilities. The following section examines some approaches that can be used by agencies, facilities, and organizations to enhance employment opportunities for adults with disabilities.

Chapters 5 and 6 (by W. E. Kiernan, A. Carter, and E. Bronstein; and D. A. Johnson and R. L. Schalock, respectively) present an overview of the principles of marketing and some specific applications of marketing within the rehabilitation network. The overall theme of these chapters is the need to continue to encourage the development of skills within the individual, based on an analysis of existing needs in the community. This theme again highlights the move away from pretraining and toward identifying community needs and then training within the integrated work setting. In addition, the authors of both chapters demonstrate how the concepts of marketing have been utilized and integrated into the service delivery system of rehabilitation programs.

The focus on marketing and its application in rehabilitation is a continuous theme throughout the book.

Chapter 7, by F. Lattuca, Jr., R. W. Venne, and J. F. Campbell, stresses the importance and application of marketing concepts to the building and maintaining of supported work and training alliances. The authors give examples of such partnerships throughout the country and emphasize the principle of ''marketing for quality partnerships'' by determining the organization's capabilities and the needs of the target market.

In Chapter 8, J. S. Russell provides an overview of the applications of assessment in regard to placement of adults with developmental disabilities. The chapter presents a number of challenges to those who view assessment as either noncontributory or totally predictive for employment of persons with disabilities. Russell highlights some of the advantages of generalized assessment practices, but also advises against applying assessment too rigidly in matching persons with disabilities to employment.

The overall focus of this section is to familiarize readers with strategies for developing marketing approaches; for utilizing information available in industry to identify needs; and finally, to present methods for responding to those needs by placing people with disabilities in integrated work settings.

5

Marketing and Marketing Management in Rehabilitation

William E. Kiernan,
Ann Carter, and Eugene Bronstein

There are several ways to define *market-ing*. Many of us think of marketing as a business concept. However, since this country's explosive entrance into the service industry arena and the introduction of the Great Society, marketing has become a matter-of-course activity for numerous health care and other nonprofit organizations and agencies.

Marketing as a discipline is focused on the wide array of potential and actual buyers. Its major purpose is to bring buyers and sellers together. When Calvin Klein, for instance, wants to sell a men's fragrance called Obsession, the company must make several decisions both before and during the production of the product: Who is the potential buyer? Where should the product be placed? What should be the price? With these answers in hand, the company is ready to go to the public, or the marketplace. To accomplish this, a distribution channel to reach the ultimate customer must be established. In other words, the company uses marketing strategies to bring customers and product together. Marketing techniques are used to pinpoint customer groups (through market research), to select channels of distribution and promotion techniques, and finally to sell these channels.

Perhaps the most important marketing concept to remember is that product development activities take place in response to the public's changing needs and wants. The marketing process begins with customer analysis before the product or service is ever developed. An example of a product developed in response to consumer needs is the microwave oven. Among other needs, the oven answered the demand for speed of food preparation on the part of the dual-career couple. In the employment field, the changing demands in the marketplace and the increased focus upon service will place many new demands upon both the employer and the employee, leading to increased interest in utilizing the limited labor force as effectively and efficiently as possible. These changing needs in the marketplace are creating enhanced employment opportunities for persons with disabilities.

This chapter provides a broad overview of the principles of marketing and of how these principles relate to the employment of persons with disabilities. Elements such as customer identification, strategies for the completion of needs assessments, approaches to market segmentation, and designs for dissemination of information regarding the availability of a good and service are discussed here in global terms. Subsequent chapters in this section outline specific steps in implementing marketing plans in rehabilitation and human services.

WHAT IS MARKETING?

One often hears that *marketing* is just another term for selling. In fact, many dictionaries define *marketing* as a selling process. Actually, selling is one arm of the marketing plan. Market research establishes what buyers will want to purchase, what form the product should take, what price the market will pay, in what location the product should be made available, and when it should be made available. Without answers to these questions, the introduction of a new product or service will be extremely risky. It is this type of risk that most industries prefer to avoid; thus, they engage in varying degrees of market research.

Kotler (1986) in his book, *Principles of Marketing,* defined *marketing* as "human activity directed at satisfying needs and wants through exchange processes" (p. 4). This definition notes that there must be a need, a want, a product, and a willingness to engage in an exchange process. These are the simple elements of business. On the one hand, needs reflect what is perceived as lacking by an individual or group of individuals. Wants, on the other hand, reflect a personal preference or desire. Market research analyzes whether the marketplace reflects an absence of a good or service or whether it prefers something in a different shape, form, time, or location.

Once the need or want is established, the potential buyer must view the good or service being offered as satisfying a need or want better than any other available good or service. It is the packaging and support of a good or service that assure an ongoing relationship with the customer both for purposes of repurchase and for influencing initial purchases by other potential buyers.

Marketing can thus be viewed as the successful analysis of a need, the design of a good or a service to meet that need, the linking of that good or service to a potential user, and the utilization of a good or service by the buyer. This, however, is not to say that an exchange is a one-time event. It can also be a recurring purchase of a good or service. In all cases, the marketing process should be viewed as a dynamic activity often reflecting the evolving relationship of the deliverer of a service to the needs of a buyer.

MARKETING IN HUMAN SERVICES

In the past, human services agencies—particularly those focusing on employment opportunities for adults with disabilities—have approached business from a selling perspective. This approach, as can be seen from Table 5.1, generally looks to the development of a product, in this case, the training of a person with a disability, who has specific skills or abilities that are then matched to a job in industry. Often the training is done based on the assumption that once the individual has mastered the required skills, a placement will be sought. Such an orientation, however, does not consider the evolving needs of the customer, that is, industry, but instead looks at the deficits or limitations of the product, that is, the person with a disability (Johnsen, Schik, Koehler, & Schalock, 1987). The agency thus risks developing or producing a product for which there is no need at that time, in that place, and/or at that cost.

From a marketing perspective, the customer's needs are paramount; thus, the specific training of the individual will be directed to meeting an already-identified need within the industry environment. Similarly, the value of the end product, the work performed, is reflected in the customer's satisfaction. In this case, a marketing focus identifies a need and a response to a need, while the selling focus prepares an individual with skills and then attempts to match the individual to a need that may or, unfortunately, may not exist within the community. A common selling strategy of rehabilitation facilities has assumed that with sufficient skills an individual can be assimilated into the labor market. Although there have been some successes with this strategy, the movement from a manufacturing to a service economy (see Chapter 2 in this volume) has meant that required job skills are changing. A more effective approach to job training would be to analyze the existing needs within the labor market and then deliver a product, in this case a worker with disabilities, to meet those specific needs.

Table 5.1. A comparison of selling and marketing concepts

Focus	Means	Ends
A Selling Concept		
Products	Selling and promoting	Profits through sales volume
The Marketing Concept		
Customer needs	Integrated marketing	Profits through customer satisfaction

In viewing the ultimate goal of marketing as the satisfactory completion of an exchange process for both the buyer and the seller, it is appropriate to examine the steps that should be taken to achieve this goal. Critical to the design of a marketing plan is the identification of needs within a specific industry or group of people. The next section looks at some techniques for identifying needs.

IDENTIFYING THE MARKETPLACE

In analyzing the universe of needs and wants, clearly the seller of a good or service must narrow down the marketplace. The first stage in establishing a market plan is to identify the various elements in the marketplace. Each potential seller of a good or service must take a series of steps prior to establishing a viable product line. Those steps involve pinpointing various industries or organizations that are in the selected geographic territory that may be potential buyers, conducting an analysis of the needs or wants within those industries or organizations, identifying who within the industry or organization is most affected by those needs or wants, and developing a strategy for letting those individuals know that you have a product that may be attractive to them.

In human services, and more specifically in endeavoring to enhance employment opportunities for adults with disabilities, a similar series of steps must be taken. The first step in establishing a marketing plan is for an agency, organization, or facility to note clearly those companies within the geographic territory that have job openings. The second step is to survey those companies to ascertain their needs and wants, particularly in relationship to the availability of a qualified labor resource base. The third step is to determine which individuals in those companies are most affected by these needs and wants and thus most logically the targets for a marketing campaign. The final step is to establish a public relations or information dissemination strategy to inform these companies, and specifically those individuals most affected, that the human services agency is offering a good or service to meet their needs and wants. The following paragraphs briefly suggest ways in which a human services agency may put these steps into place.

1. *Identifying Potential Buyers* The first step is to compile a list of employers in the general area. A number of resources are available for accomplishing this, including telephone Yellow Pages and business community telephone directories. These sources list companies but provide no information regarding size, range of goods, services provided, or names of individuals to contact.

Manufacturing or service directories are also available through chambers of commerce or trade associations. Local divisions of employment security often contain company job listings. In addition, trade association membership lists provide information on groups such as hospitality industries, recreational organizations, and manufacturing associations. Local unions, too, often have company membership listings and other information about the companies; however, these lists may not always be available.

The preceding suggestions will yield information about where jobs are, but not much about what the need may be. For the latter information, a regular review of the help-wanted ads, and in some instances, of job postings outside of companies, are good places to start. State employment services may also, through their job bank listings or labor market analysis reports, give some indication of the type and/or magnitude of the labor needs in a specific area. It should be noted that many of the possible job openings and job opportunities (yet-to-be-available jobs) may not appear in the help-wanted ads, owing to the costs of advertising and the limited return on this investment for many companies. The listings of employers will provide a base from which more specific employment data may be collected.

2. *Grouping Potential Employers*   Once a list of potential employers is prepared, it may be advantageous to separate the market, that is, assemble distinct groups of buyers, in order to identify the needs and wants of specific employers. Markets can be segmented according to the types of products developed or services delivered, the size of the organization, and the geographic territory served, or according to many other strategies. The market segmentation procedure adopted will be determined by the available resources (i.e., staff, budget) of the individual agency, facility, or organization.

Once the segmentation process is complete, a more in-depth analysis of the needs and wants of organizations and companies within the designated grouping can be initiated. Sometimes the help-wanted ads will provide enlightenment on the specific needs of employers. However, since, as noted earlier, many industries use other sources to recruit employees, it is advisable to also ask for the assistance of the job bank of the local division of employment security, as well as of job-finding agencies to determine the needs and wants of certain industries.

Another strategy is to conduct a series of informational interviews with certain industries. These interviews are generally brief and can be conducted over the telephone or in person. The informational interviewing technique can be used both to identify a need that had not previously emerged as well as to confirm needs that have emerged through other sources. In addition, depending upon the nature of the data gathered, opportunities for the future can be ascertained and the agency has the chance to inform the company of the possible resources that the agency can offer. Often this can serve as the first contact leading to a follow-up meeting to discuss specific jobs.

3. *Identifying Areas for Concentration*   The next step is to evaluate the target segments and select one or more areas on which to concentrate. In this phase, efforts should be made to identify who in fact is most affected by the identified need or want. Not all needs have the same significance for all persons. In certain industries, for instance, a president or chief executive officer may sense a need without the need having a direct day-to-day impact on him or her.

If, for instance, the pressing issue is a lack of workers, the employee (e.g., personnel director responsible for recruitment) may be the key individual toward whome one's marketing efforts should be directed. The line manager, who is responsible for the production of a good or service and for meeting deadlines, may be another likely target. It may not be sufficient to identify a company and market as to its global needs; one may also need to expend additional effort to establish the most logical place on which to focus the marketing effort. One may therefore have to conduct one or more interviews before actually reaching the person most interested in the good or service one is offering.

4. *Getting the Word Out* The fourth major component in the marketing plan is to publicize to the buyer that the product that has been identified as needed or wanted is available through one's agency, facility, or organization. This step aims to send the right message to the right audience through direct action, that is, through a public relations effort. In organizations geared toward the employment of adults with disabilities, public relations can involve spreading the word about opportunities, thus multiplying the impact of success stories, so as to affect people's opinions. The public media are basic publicity tools to accomplish this—radio, television, print, cable, trade journals, and so forth.

Spreading the word does not have to begin after all of the previously described steps have been completed. The public relations techniques discussed in the paragraphs following encompass a broad information-sharing effort. While these activities are frequently directed at the general market, the messages conveyed have a common theme that is also meaningful to specific audiences. A message must capture the audience's interest in order to have an impact. Clearly, then, the public relations effort must respond to a need or it will be viewed as irrelevant. The following is a review of three public relations tools.

a. Press Kit A press kit is a primary vehicle for achieving community awareness of one's program. It is a folder of information geared toward members of the press and potentially containing a one-page history of the agency or organization, biographies of influential individuals associated with the organization, a description of two or three successful programs, articles that have appeared in other newspapers or journals, and other relevant information. The press kit should provide information concisely and efficiently, thus making the job of a reporter easier. Reporters rarely have time to digest reams of detailed information; therefore, materials in the kit should be straightforward and graphically appealing.

b. Press Release   The press release contains information written in the same concise and effective manner as that in the press kit, but dealing with a specific event or topic. Although of potentially general appeal, the release must be prepared with a specific audience in mind and directed at answering who, what, when, where, and why questions. As simple as the strategy seems, it is frequently not used to advantage by human services agencies. Answering these questions, again, makes it easier for a reporter to cover a story. A specific example may be the announcement of a new project or service directed at meeting labor market shortages. The press release should give the broad community some idea of what goods or services are available through the program while directing industry's attention to the fact that the program can respond to their needs. Although not targeted to a specific industry, if the appropriate audience exists, the press release can be a very specific instrument for directly communicating a message.

c. Photography   For purposes of streamlining information, photography is a good publicity tool. A well-placed action photograph can often substitute for the written word and serves as an additional way to add impact to a message. Photographs should reflect the theme of a story or the spirit of an organization, and should not be staged pictures.

Armed with the basic tools of publicity, the program or agency must compile a mailing list and a target audience. As noted earlier, this effort parallels that of finding out who will most benefit from the good or service. To reiterate, the more clearly the target audience is identified, the more precise the message can be. Materials should be written in a language that is meaningful and appropriate for the selected audience. Jargon may turn off members of the media. With the target audience identified, a direct mail and telephone follow-up strategy can be initiated.

In some cases where the conduit to the key audiences has yet to be identified, general mailings or other strategies can be tried. For example, a strategy for collecting valuable media information is to call five different companies and speak with their personnel directors or vice presidents, asking them to name the five publications of most relevance for their industry. News releases can then be sent directly to those publications, in addition to the companies themselves. Since fiscal resources are frequently very limited, this strategy can save valuable advertising dollars in targeting the market segment.

The establishment of a public relations effort is an affirmative step in telling industry that one has a labor resource that can respond to unmet labor needs in their company. Systematic information sharing can be highly beneficial and can lead to many jobs within industry. The preceding strategies— identifying where the jobs are, finding out what the need is within those companies, finding out who is most affected within the corporation by those needs and wants, and developing a public relations campaign—are essential steps in developing an organization that can effectively and efficiently answer industry needs while successfully accomplishing the goal of enhancing employment opportunities for disabled adults.

OTHER MARKETING CONSIDERATIONS FOR REHABILITATION PROGRAMS

The foregoing material looks at a selected market segment, that is, the industry segment. For a rehabilitation facility to expand employment opportunities for adults with disabilities, the organization must be responsive to a wide variety of market segments. Such segments include the employee and the community, the parent and the family, and the person with a disability.

In developing a comprehensive market plan, the same questions apply—locating persons with disabilities and their families, determining their needs and wants, finding out who is most affected by those needs and wants, and publicizing the availability of a service that can efficiently and effectively respond to those needs.

CONCLUSIONS

Marketing is a process of identifying a need and responding appropriately to that need. The role of rehabilitation programs in the future will be to match the needs of industry with the needs of disabled individuals as well as with the other various market segments and also provide supports sufficient to assure that all parties are satisfied with the services rendered.

This chapter has focused primarily upon developing a marketing plan for enhancing integrated employment opportunities in industry for adults with disabilities. Other chapters in this section present strategies for assuring a good fit of the individual's abilities with the demands of the job and the social requirements of the workplace, as well as specific approaches to marketing, particularly relating to human services agencies and organizations. Marketing is a concept that must be adopted by human services agencies if they are to be viewed by industry as resources in meeting labor market needs.

REFERENCES

Johnsen, D.A., Schik, T.L., Koehler, R.S., & Schalock, R.L. (1987). *Developing a customer-oriented employment services program.* Hastings: Mid-Nebraska Mental Retardation Services.
Kotler, P. (1986). *Principles of marketing* (3rd ed.). Englewood Cliffs, NJ: Prentice-Hall.

6

Meeting Consumer Needs by Developing a Marketing Orientation

Deborah A. Johnsen
and Robert L. Schalock

The importance of focusing on employment of adults with disabilities, although noted in the Rehabilitation Act of 1973, was not fully recognized until the passage of the Comprehensive Rehabilitation Services Act of 1978. Since that time, numerous programs throughout the country have demonstrated the success of nonsheltered employment for adults with disabilities. In addition, the movement from sheltered employment to employment within real work settings, as documented by Kiernan, McGaughey, and Schalock (1986), has created both opportunities and challenges: opportunities for persons with disabilities to enter the mainstream of economic America, but challenges to those of us involved in ensuring services to provide meaningful employment opportunities for people with developmental disabilities. This chapter suggests that these opportunities and challenges can best be met when human services and rehabilitation training programs adopt a marketing orientation to create job opportunities and enhance employment success.

Implementing a marketing-based approach and procedures is not easy for most human services and rehabilitation training agencies, however, for they have a strong legacy in sheltered employment and dependency-producing policies and procedures. This legacy is reflected in the following characteristics:

Readiness training based upon traditional psychomotor or job sample assessment
Prevocational skill training
"Place and pray" mentality
Job placement into available jobs with only limited on-site training and follow-up

Job failure attributed to the client's poor behavior, low motivation, and/or poor work skills

This chapter is based on the authors' belief that in order to meet the challenges of working effectively with business in developing and retaining work opportunities, human services providers need to become market oriented. To do so, agencies will probably face a struggle in attempting to evolve from their current predominantly production-oriented status to adopting a marketing-oriented approach that considers customer needs as the foremost priority. This chapter suggests that this struggle can be eased and successfully overcome if agencies can accomplish the following three goals: 1) become marketing oriented, 2) implement a marketing plan, and 3) evaluate their customer-referenced outcomes.

BECOMING MARKETING ORIENTED

Marketing consists of much more than sales and advertising. As noted in Chapter 5, marketing begins with identifying customer needs—not with the production process. Marketing anticipates needs, translates these needs into production and accounting components, and directs and coordinates all the activities of the company. Some human services agencies, in an attempt to "market," have added placement or sales components to their programs. Unfortunately, these components are often compartmentalized in the same manner as their production or training counterparts. Marketing personnel are expected to "go out and get placements." This simplistic approach to marketing frequently overlooks the need to emphasize that marketing is not merely moving or selling the product but is the development of the product or service so that it will move itself. Peter Drucker (1973) described this process as follows:

> There will always be a need for selling, but the aim of marketing is to make selling superfluous. The aim of marketing is to know and understand the customer so well that the product or service fits him and sells itself. Ideally, marketing should result in a customer who is ready to buy. All that should be needed then is to make the product or service available. . . . (pp. 64–65)

Adoption of a marketing-oriented approach as opposed to a production-oriented process often requires unlearning current philosophies and discarding current practices. The marketing orientation manifests itself in a "customer first" commitment to providing services. The differences between a production and marketing orientation are summarized in Table 6.1. As can be seen, becoming marketing oriented means that a program's employment services component considers customer needs as the foremost priority. What must not be overlooked in that process is that there are at least two sets of customers: the employee (i.e., the person with disabilities) and the prospective employer.

Table 6.1. A marketing orientation versus a production orientation

Marketing orientation	Production orientation
Customer needs determine company plans.	Customers should be glad we exist and appreciate the services available.
Company makes what it can sell.	Company sells what it can make.
Marketing research determines customer needs and level of customer satisfaction.	Marketing research is used for determining reaction, if used at all.
Innovation focus is on creating new opportunities.	Innovation focus is on cutting costs and technology.
Placement rate projections are determined by customer need.	Placement rate projections are determined by available resources.
Customer needs determine availability and use of on-site training, transportation services, prosthetics, and job modifications.	Agency resources and policy determine the availability and use of on-site training transportation services, prosthetics, and modification. Emphasis is on convenience and minimizing cost.
Quality of services and customer outcomes are crucial concerns.	Adherence to regulation and correct process are primary concerns.
The roles of advertising are to describe need and convince the customer of the benefits of products and services.	The role of advertising is to describe product features and how products are made.
The role of the sales force is to help customers to buy, if the product fits their needs, while coordinating with the rest of the company, including the training component.	The role of the sales force is to sell the customer, not to worry about coordination with the rest of the company.
The customer's needs and wants are the stimulus and primary consideration for all decisions.	Policies, regulations, procedures, current staff resources, convenience of staff, and/or cost are primary stimuli and considerations in decision making.

Adapted from Vizza, Chambers, and Cook (1967).

The role of an employment service program is to bring together these two customers in a mutually beneficial relationship. How one human services agency (Mid-Nebraska Mental Retardation Services, with which the authors are associated) has done this through implementing marketing plans is discussed in the next section.

Implementing a Marketing Plan

Table 6.2 summarizes guidelines regarding the four components of a marketing plan, including research, plan development, implementation, and

Table 6.2. Marketing planning guidelines

1. Research
   A. Research the needs of prospective customers, including those of people with disabilities, their families, and employers.
   B. Find groups of customers with similar needs.
   C. Aggregate customers with similar needs into target markets or market segments.
   D. Identifying marketing mix considerations.
   E. Develop marketing mixes to meet target market needs.
2. Plan development
   A. Complete strategic plan.
   B. Complete tactical plan.
   C. Develop the marketing program.
3. Implementation
   A. Set sales objectives.
   B. Set timelines.
   C. Assign responsible persons.
4. Monitoring and evaluation
   A. Update plans.
   B. Use quality circle approach.
   C. Measure and reward adherence to strategic and tactical plans.
   D. Measure and reward outcomes.
   E. Measure customer satisfaction through active listening.

monitoring/evaluation. This section of the chapter discusses four of these guidelines, including researching customer needs, aggregating customers with similar needs into target markets, identifying marketing mix considerations, and completing strategic and tactical planning. Full details regarding each guideline are found in Johnsen, Schik, Koehler, and Schalock (1987).

1. *Researching Customer Needs* Customer needs are determined via research. This research may include observation, survey, or experimentation to test hypotheses. Companies who actively listen to their customers are among the most effective, according to Peters and Austin in *A Passion for Excellence* (1985), which identified the hallmark characteristics of the nation's most successful companies. Many of these organizations practice active listening in order to determine customer needs. They orchestrate opportunities for getting close to customers and require active listening on the part of all of their employees.

In reference to the employee, careful listening will indicate the following customer needs:

Doing a job that interests them
Making good money

Working enough hours to support themselves
Receiving benefits such as sick leave, life insurance, vacation, retirement
Working with people they like
Good working conditions
Career advancement opportunities

Similarly, if one listens carefully to potential employers, their primary need can also be clearly identified: a stable, productive work force within the context of a particular business or industry.

Once customer needs are researched, a second part of the marketing plan can then be developed. This involves aggregating, or clustering, customers with similar needs into target markets.

2. *Developing Target Markets* A target market is a group of customers with similar needs to whom the (company) wishes to appeal. A target market consists of persons (both employees and prospective employers) with homogeneous needs or interests. Segmentation, the process by which a target market is defined, involves studying customer needs and aggregating groups of customers with similar needs. For example, customers who share needs, and therefore represent target markets, include employers who are interested in financial incentives or reduction of employee turnover, and employees or their families who desire a meaningful job, paid work, or integrated employment. The role of a marketing-oriented employment specialist is to unite these targeted markets in a mutually beneficial relationship. This is best done by developing a "marketing mix" to meet the needs of this well-defined target market. This process is described next.

3. *Identifying Marketing Mix Considerations* Once a target market is defined, a marketing mix consisting of product, price, placement, and promotion is assembled to meet the needs of the target market. These "4 Ps" of marketing are defined as follows:

Product: Having what the target market customers need or want
Price: Making the product available to the target market at an acceptable cost
Place: Offering the product where, how, and when it is needed to meet the target market
Promotion: Making the target market aware of and interested in the product and selling it to them

Table 6.3 lists examples of some of the marketing mix considerations for an agency's employment services component. The customers' needs determine what mix of these considerations will satisfy the target market. For example, targeted tax credits as a price consideration may be the primary tool to reach an employer with a primary financial concern, whereas on-site training and job assistance may be the best approach to sell a prospective employer who is concerned with initial job training and maintenance.

Table 6.3.　Marketing mix considerations

Product
　Job match
　On-site training, assistance, support
　Work design
　Environmental modifications
　Prosthetics
　Job restructuring
　Customer service (follow-up and agency services)

Price
　Targeted tax credits
　Vocational rehabilitation funds, on-the-job evaluation, on-the-job training
　Job Training Partnership Act funds
　Green thumb funding
　Association for Retarded Citizens On-the-Job Training funds
　Credit terms

Placement/Distribution
　Employment services training-placement component(s)
　Individualized transition plan
　Intersector agreements
　Not-for-profit corporations
　Vendor/brokerage functions

Promotion
　Advertising—media type
　Publicity
　Promotional blend
　Personal selling
　Public relations

4. *Completing Strategic and Tactical Planning*　Strategic planning identifies the broad, long-range activities of the company in a particular market. A strategic plan describes: 1) the marketing mix the company plans to offer to a specific target market; 2) the resources that will be needed; and 3) sales projections. Continuous feedback and control procedures should be integrated into the strategic plan. These built-in indicators quickly identify areas of the plan that may require adjustment.

Tactics are developed to implement strategic plans. Tactics are short-run decisions or activities required to effectively carry out strategies. Tactical decisions must fall within the guidelines of strategic policies. These decisions are made on a regular basis, perhaps even daily or weekly. The following are examples of strategic and tactical planning:

Product strategy: Provide on-site training for as long as needed to ensure the success of the employee and the satisfaction of the employer.

Tactic: Check site progress weekly to determine staffing needs and to review training programs, level of staff assistance, and the follow-up from the customer contact notes. Adjust staffing level as indicated.

Tactic: Use weekly quality circle (discussion) approach to review the job site follow-up reports and to compare the perceptions of agency staff involved in the job site.

Price strategy: Promote the use of employer reinbursement programs by training sales representatives to use the reimbursement programs.

Tactic: Check with employer reimbursement programs on a regular basis to determine availability of funds and qualifying procedures.

Promotion strategy: Target companies for sales based on the job interests expressed by the prospective employee. Focus sales calls and follow up on only the best sales leads in targeted areas.

Tactic: Update the sales leads on a monthly basis for each individual, based on the individual's job-interest preference, qualifying information, and the rank order of sales leads.

The various strategic plans for different markets are integrated into one marketing program or plan. A company will have as many strategic plans as target markets it wishes to serve. The process of defining a target market, formulating a marketing mix for each market, developing strategic and tactical plans for various markets, and integrating these into a marketing plan is shown in Figure 6.1.

Implementing the marketing plan often results in a change in a program's employment services component. Processes are frequently adjusted to produce more customer-oriented outcomes. An example of a flow-chart is presented in Figure 6.2, which outlines the experiences of Mid-Nebraska Mental Retardation Services, based on a marketing orientation and the marketing planning guidelines summarized in Table 6.2.

Figure 6.1. The marketing planning process.

Research prospective employee and employer needs.

↓

Identify target market.

↓

Develop a marketing mix to meet target market needs.

↓

Procure targeted opportunity.

↓

Match person to job requirements.

↓

Use work design, prosthetics, environmental modifications, and on-site training assistance and support to reduce mismatches between person and job.

↓

Fade only when the customer is satisfied and bonds are strong.

↓

Measure and reward adherence to plans.

↓

Measure and reward outcomes.

↓

Update marketing plan.

Figure 6.2. The Mid-Nebraska Employment Services System: An employment services flow chart based on a marketing orientation and market planning.

EVALUATING CUSTOMER-REFERENCED OUTCOMES

Employment service programs must constantly evaluate their effectiveness. Part of this evaluation involves active listening, and part involves customer-referenced outcome measures. Active listening should involve both of the customers—the employee and the employer. Asking customers how they feel, what they like or dislike, what they want, or what they want changed can provide significant input. Many human services organizations make a mistake in not really listening to customers; rather, they use only objective data or written evaluations that frequently miss the important nonverbal and verbal messages that they would get if they simply talked with their customers.

However, evaluation also involves the development of customer-referenced outcome measures. The development of these measures ensures a constant focus on evaluation and revision based on whether customer needs are met. To provide readers with examples, the customer-referenced outcomes currently employed by Mid-Nebraska Mental Retardation Services are listed in Table 6.4.

SUMMARY

In summary, developing a marketing orientation requires listening to and understanding customers. It often demands a significant change in philosophy, policy, and practice for most human services agencies. The technology of marketing becomes a common sense approach when the agency adopts a customer-first orientation. Developing effective employment services is made easier when all the members of an organization accept the following basic customer-related premises:

1. The customer is the most important person.
2. The customer is the stimulus for every decision made.
3. The employment service functions as a brokerage, bringing together an employee and employer who need each other.
4. The employment service is a business, providing services to employee and employer customers. It is not a human service agency, government program, or charity.
5. The employment service is in business to provide opportunities to help customers get what they want.

When human services agencies listen to customers and market to them, significant change can result. The costs of such change are insignificant when compared to the costs of ineffective programs that do not meet customer needs. The authors believe that in order to successfully interface industry with disabled people, human services and (re)habilitation programs must become more customer referenced and marketing oriented. This chapter has endeavored to suggest ways by which this might be done.

Table 6.4. Customer-referenced outcome measures

Employee-referenced	Employer-referenced
Type of job	Rate of establishing accounts
Hours worked per week	Growth of accounts
Wages per hour	Retention of accounts
Level of integration	
Benefits received	

Adapted from Schalock (1988).

REFERENCES

Drucker, P.F. (1973). *Management: Tasks, responsibilities, practices.* New York: Harper & Row.

Johnsen, D.A., Schik, T.L., Koehler, R.S., & Schalock, R.L. (1987). *Developing a customer-oriented employment services program.* Hastings: Mid-Nebraska Mental Retardation Services.

Kiernan, W.E., McGaughey, M.J., & Schalock, R.L. (1986). *Employment survey for adults with developmental disabilities.* Boston: Children's Hospital, Developmental Evaluation Clinic.

Peters, T., & Austin, N. (1985). *A passion for excellence.* New York: Random House.

Schalock, R.L. (1988). Critical performance evaluation indicators in supported employment. In P. Wehman & M.S. Moon (Eds.), *Vocational rehabilitation and supported employment* (pp. 163–174). Baltimore: Paul H. Brookes Publishing Co.

Vizza, R.F., Chambers, T.E., & Cook, E.J. (1967). *Adoption of the marketing concept: Fact or fiction.* New York: Sales Executive Club, Inc.

7

Building and Maintaining Supported Work and Training Alliances for Persons with Severe Disabilities

Frank Lattuca, Jr., Richard W. Venne, and Joseph F. Campbell

People with severe disabilities have suffered, perhaps more than any other minority, from the hardships of unemployment. Officially, they are often not perceived as among the ranks of the unemployed and therefore are not included in most state and federal unemployment statistics. These individuals have not historically been identified as candidates for work, but rather as persons in need of welfare-type supports. Even leading vocational organizations for handicapped persons have focused more upon sheltered workshop services than on providing an opportunity for employment in a natural setting.

Throughout the 1980s, however, a new phenomenon has begun to emerge in the American workplace. Individuals once served in isolated work centers are now working amidst regular employees in nearly every type of industry across the United States. Many of these employees with disabilities continue to receive support on an ongoing basis. Their employment arrangements are usually described as "supported employment" (see Chapter 4). While individual supported workers may often hold regular positions and have a normal employee relationship with their employer, in other cases, due to particular individual needs, the employee may be part of a work group from a vocational agency that typically contracts with the "host industry" for labor services. In any event, two sets of needs are being addressed: The employer's need for suitable workers is fulfilled and the unemployment problem of the person with a disability is solved.

Labeling the problem of these individuals as one of unemployment has assisted human services organizations to conclude that the solution actually lies with industry—with employers generally, as opposed to the vocational agency itself (Campbell, 1985). Similarly, it has pushed these organizations toward reexamining their own performance and role in providing nonisolated employment opportunities for their clients. As a result, many vocational organizations have become successful brokers, or creative liaisons, matching people with disabilities with needs in industry. There has emerged a growing emphasis on marketing and the development of partnerships around employment and training arrangements. This partnership concept now embraces not only natural employment situations but, as this chapter explains, generic educational establishments as well.

ALLIANCES IN THE HOSPITALITY INDUSTRY

Perhaps most productive in the authors' experience have been the growing partnerships between nonprofit vocational agencies and employers in the hospitality industry. A major reason for this is that many positions in food service establishments and in hotel/motel businesses are entry level and generally provide an opportunity for learning on the job. In addition, the food service industry, the third largest industry in the United States, suffers from chronic labor shortages and high job turnover. The scarcity in labor supply for this industry is projected to grow at a rate greater than that of any other American industry. Between now and the turn of the century, employment opportunities for food service workers will grow at a rate close to 40%. The National Restaurant Association (1988) reports that eating and drinking places are expected to employ 2.5 million more people by the year 2000, generating the largest number of new jobs in any industry. This growth in the industry coupled with a decrease in available workers from traditional sources, such as the 16- to 18-year-old population, will continue to cause problems for food service employers. The scarcity in the traditional labor pool coupled with an estimated turnover rate of between 300% and 400% (a level greater than in the economy in general and larger than in the industries competing with food services for the same labor pool [Davis & Wasmuth, 1983]) has caused many employers to scramble for solutions to the mounting problem (Schapire & Berger, 1984).

It is estimated that 2 million employees will be needed in the food service industry by the year 2000 (Lattuca, 1987). This figure includes 126,000 cooks, 145,000 fast food workers, and 304,000 kitchen helpers. Given this growing labor crisis, the industry is well disposed toward developing partnerships leading to supported employment arrangements for persons with disabilities. A wide variety of partnership arrangements are possible and have the potential for including not only private service providers but also public sector funding sources and college or university food service training programs.

Numerous examples of hospitality industry partnerships have sprung up across the country. The authors are particularly familiar with the efforts of Incentive Community Enterprises (I.C.E.) in Massachusetts, a private human services organization that has brokered partnerships with approximately 150 employers (mostly in food service) who daily provide jobs for almost 400 of the agency's clients. I.C.E. marketing staff have been especially successful in building cooperative arrangements with food service employers. For example, the organization has a unique partnership with the University of Massachusetts School of Hotel, Restaurant, and Travel Administration. This arrangement provides university-based training to 10 students with mental handicaps annually and exposes a group of college juniors, who are destined to become tomorrow's employers, to the benefits of working with people with handicaps. This program is described in section #2 in the paragraphs following, along with other noteworthy I.C.E. partnerships.

1. *A Friendly Resource* Foremost among the food service partners with I.C.E. has been the Friendly Corporation, now a subsidiary of Hershey Foods Corporation. Friendly has facilitated the employment of more than 100 I.C.E. workers since the beginning of the relationship in the late 1970s.

In 1985, the Friendly Restaurant management approved and initiated a highly successful group training site at the company's Ingelside Mall restaurant in Holyoke, MA. I.C.E. hired a veteran Friendly's employee to act as coordinator and trainer at the restaurant-based site. Trainees are exposed to a cross-section of restaurant duties, including food preparation, waiting, and busing. During the training period, which lasts 3–6 months, individual clients are paid and managed by the I.C.E. organization. The program is funded by the Massachusetts Rehabilitation Commission, and trainee wages are paid to I.C.E. by Friendly's. Upon completion of training, all graduates are hired directly by the restaurant. In 1987, Friendly's extended the partnership to its Greenfield, MA, restaurant, which acts as a fieldwork base for I.C.E. students/clients participating in the University of Massachusetts Food Service Training Program.

2. *Food Service Training in a University* The University of Massachusetts Food Service Training partnership with I.C.E. commenced in 1986. The program is the result of special collaboration between the university, I.C.E., and the funding agency, the Massachusetts Department of Mental Retardation. The program focuses on food service training for persons with disabilities and at the same time offers a four-credit course to undergraduate hotel, restaurant, and travel administration (HRTA) majors on "Training the Disabled in the Food Service Industry." The course was designed by the university's special education faculty in the school of education. HRTA undergraduates train the handicapped workers in the department's commercial kitchen and dining room laboratory facilities for 5 hours, 3 days a week. On the remaining days, clients receive on-the-job training in area food services, including Friendly's and McDonald's restaurants and in the dining facilities of nearby Amherst College.

In addition, there are other examples of public educational and private organization partnerships providing training and employment to handicapped workers in the food industry. For instance, a number of school districts throughout the nation have training programs for their students with special needs. Tri-County Consortium for Special Education in California is located in the foothills of the Sierras and includes Calaveras, Tuolumne, and Amador counties. It provides on-the-job training for its high school students (ages 18–22) in 25 area businesses after they have received vocational training in one of the district's high schools. The major supporters of this effort are the fast-food restaurants, which assist the schools in matching the students' interests with available positions (Schneider, 1986).

The students with special needs benefit by receiving state-of-the-art vocational training on a university campus and on-the-job training at area businesses. The HRTA undergraduates benefit by acquiring the knowledge and necessary practical experience to enable them to make decisions regarding the employability of persons with disabilities as they assume leadership roles in the hospitality industry. Local food service employers benefit by the availability of the program's graduates as new or continuing employees.

This particular style of partnership model has excellent potential for replication at educational institutions throughout the country. There are over 175 4-year and over 600 2-year hospitality-related programs throughout the nation. Most have commercial food service training facilities. An unprecedented opportunity lies ahead to combine the resources at these institutions with those of local and state vocational rehabilitation organizations and area businesses. The conceptualization and brokering of these partnerships is a highly suitable role for the community vocational rehabilitation organization.

3. *Hotel and Restaurant Training* Incentive Community Enterprises has also developed employment and training arrangements with a number of hotels and motels throughout western New England. These include such establishments as Days Inn, the Marriott Corporation, Sheraton, Holiday Inn, Hilton International, and Motel 6. Jobs include a variety of general hotel functions, but the greatest number of positions is in guest room preparation. In 1987, I.C.E. employment and training crews regularly maintained approximately 100 hotel rooms in partnership with these employers. In addition, these and other hospitality establishments employ many Food Service Training program graduates directly. In some of these cases, support services continue to be available to the new employees for an indefinite time period.

These ventures involving cooperative arrangements between typical vocational agencies, local businesses, and public institutions provide an excellent alternative to the more isolated sheltered employment options. The authors emphasize, however, that I.C.E.'s previous experience as a sheltered workshop provider helped in establishing many of the needed skills both in program development and in marketing to the local community.

In evolving from a center-based agency to an entirely industry-integrated employment system, I.C.E. staff acknowledge the key role of marketing in successfully forging productive partnerships with the organization's employer allies. During its 10 years of industry-based employment services, the agency has clarified its marketing posture and built a successful, ongoing marketing program to increase its partnership network. This topic is discussed in the next section.

MARKETING FOR PARTNERSHIPS

There are numerous approaches to successful marketing, which vary depending upon the product or service offered and the specific mission and values of the organization. Employment and training organizations recognize that they must present disabled workers to potential employers in a manner that not only addresses the needs of industry but, perhaps more important, addresses the needs of the individual. In this dual objective lies the primary difference between general marketing strategies and those of agencies seeking to enhance employment for disabled persons. This leads to the first important step in the marketing process.

1. *Determine the Individual's Capabilities* Before addressing employers, agency staff must first establish the capabilities and job interests of the person with a disability. While workers may eventually perform in groups, it is essential that a marketing focus recognize the importance of the individual. Presenting workers as capable of more than they can reasonably handle will obviously lead employers to become dubious and cynical of future efforts (Lumbrinos & Johnson, 1985). Although there is a tendency among marketing staff to give primary attention to the needs of a target market in industry, the human services agency's mission will generally require a primary concentration on individual client needs and reasonable capabilities. The second focus of the agency is the identification of the need in industry.

2. *Determine the Needs of a Target Market* Although the disabled client and the client's funding source are theoretically target markets for each supported employment organization, the authors refer here to a *target market* as the industry market—the potential employment environment. Recognizing the importance of becoming market focused is essential. A well-focused marketing effort will eliminate or reduce significantly the need for investment in the sales and procurement activity of typical traditional vocational re-

habilitation organizations (see Chapter 5). Peter Drucker (1973) suggests that "the aim of marketing is to make selling superfluous. The aim of marketing is to know and understand the customer so well that the product or service fits him and sells itself" (p. 64). Drucker's comment alerts us to the importance of learning the customer's needs so that individual and group placements are a suitable match. If placements are not based on customer needs, they will survive only until the customer recognizes their unsuitability. Then the placement process must begin all over again and will ultimately exhaust both the agency's reputation and customer base. Since it is virtually impossible to become totally familiar with the specific needs of every potential industry and customer, some organizations may choose to use a vertical marketing approach. This involves choosing a particular industry or, more specifically, an industry segment. For example, an organization might choose to target the hospitality industry and further focus on hotel/motel or restaurant employers. Maintaining excellent services for industry will usually involve continued efforts to keep informed about employers' requirements. Following are some techniques for doing this.

Market Survey   Many organizations find that a survey or questionnaire can be an effective starting place for a vertical marketing activity. A typical questionnaire introduces the employment agency and includes validating affiliation. For example, membership in the chamber of commerce is highlighted, or funding by the state to train potential employees for business is mentioned. The questionnaire is designed to glean maximum information concerning employment needs and conditions. Questionnaires should be simple and brief and should always promise some benefit to the respondent—for example: "Could you use the services of a state-funded training program in preparing potential employees?" The survey results can be used in a variety of ways.

Market Test   The market survey can produce excellent information, essentially establishing the beginnings of a market data base. Moreover, each market survey respondent is a candidate for further follow-up. Follow-up to the questionnaire must always be formal and highly professional. For instance, a particular respondent may be "chosen" as the "most typical" or perhaps the "most impressive," and become the base of a publicly funded "market test." Such an offer will often draw positive responses and agreement to participate.

A market test is in essence a sample product or service to determine its viability and demonstrate its performance capacity. The market test is in itself a way of selling service by the provider. In the case of a supported employment provider, the market test site has the potential to become a training site from which trained employees can be placed directly into jobs with other employers. Ideally, the market test will become an outstanding example to the industry of how disabled workers can be successfully integrated into their work force. If an agency operates in different geographic regions, it might be wise to "sell" from a market test site in each region. Should an employment and training organization develop the capacity to extend its vertical marketing into a number of market areas (e.g., hospitality industry and printing industry), test sites in each industry obviously would be important.

The most important selling tool is the reputation of the good or service. Quality is the concern not just of the persons delivering and supervising the good or service but also of the marketing staff. For this reason a somewhat experimental market test or training site should be subjected to rigid quality standards and checks. Building a reputation will enhance opportunities and reduce the selling effort and expense.

3. *Employment Advisory Committee* Among the most popular strategies in the authors' experience for developing employment opportunities continues to be the employment advisory committee. This committee is composed of industry representatives who are knowledgeable about employment opportunities in the area and selected human services agency staff. From its inception, the committee must understand that its reason for existence is to promote and accomplish employment and training placements for agency clients. The committee should start small and gradually expand as members understand and feel comfortable with their roles. Initially, members may be recruited by agency staff; however, new members will normally result from employer-member networking.

The typical committee meets monthly. Early morning meetings with coffee and doughnuts work best. Meetings should have an agenda, start on schedule, and last approximately 1 hour. This allows businesspeople to reach their offices by 9:00 A.M. Each meeting should feature a report from agency staff on current achievements in developing employer partnerships and should identify current prevailing needs. This approach allows the chairperson to assign related follow-up tasks to members. Each meeting should also include reports on these assignments. The employment advisory committee, while prompting employment opportunities, also ensures that agency staff stay alert to the needs and realities of employers. The committee should investigate trends and prepare reports on future employment needs in its respective industries. For these reasons, it is important that committee members be competent spokespersons for their respective industries. College business schools, U.S. Small Business Administration offices, chambers of commerce, banks, and investment firms are often good recruiting grounds for committee members.

4. *Marketing Presentation Kit* It is very difficult to make a good presentation to a potential employer without some visual aids or evidence of the organization's successful track record. This is why even the most simple marketing presentation kit or manual is extremely valuable. An excellent kit can be developed at practically no cost beyond the price of an attractive photograph album or similar folder. Ideally, the kit or manual should have removable plastic pages that can be easily updated. It should be large enough so that a marketing representative can place it on a desk and comfortably share the contents with a potential customer. A typical manual might include:

An attractively presented logo with organization name
A condensed (four- or five-line) mission statement
A map of the area served, highlighting service bases
A brief description of employment services
Attractive photographs of consumers at work in local industrial settings
Letters of reference from leading industrial participants

An organization may wish to include additional items, but, remember, presentation time will be limited. The manual serves as an agenda for less experienced marketing staff and usually provides for a more relaxed yet effective presentation. It is important to note that merely reviewing such a manual with a potential employer cannot be considered a complete marketing presentation. Ultimately, the discussion must focus on the host industry, its specific needs, and how the vocational agency can help solve these.

THE FINAL WORD—QUALITY

Numerous marketing approaches have proven effective in building working relationships with industry. It merits reiterating, however, that nothing surpasses the value of reputation. When partnerships have been established and workers are placed, then the service relationship has just begun. Maintaining a high quality of service will normally keep the partnership healthy. Poor quality will ultimately lead to the loss of the site and thus to the need to develop a new one. A good service reputation is a marketing activity in itself.

Since the quality of services is so crucial, it is important for supported work providers to have an active quality assurance program specifically related to their industrial relationships. Naturally, those agency staff who directly supervise the cooperative venture with the industry are primarily responsible for ensuring the quality of their service or product as well as a positive working relationship. It is necessary, however, to go further in assuring quality. The authors have found it advisable for the final stages of a quality assurance process to be directed by staff other than those whose quality of performance is perhaps being checked. An example of a final review of quality is the "satisfaction survey." This is a brief, one-page form that asks employers directly if they are satisfied with such areas as quality of work done, relationship with agency staff, communication levels with the supported employment organization, and so forth. These areas are normally rated as excellent, good, fair, or poor. A couple of lines should also be available for employers to respond to: "How can we improve our services to you?" This form should be mailed to employers with a stamped, self-addressed return envelope.

The satisfaction survey is in itself an excellent marketing tool, in that it suggests that the vocational organization is conscientious and available to solve problems. Therefore, it is useful to have this component of quality control handled by the marketing staff. How regularly the survey is distributed will vary, depending on the length of the relationship and the results obtained, but, ideally, the instrument should be used at intervals sufficient to provide early warning signals. The regularity of testing should change based on findings. If, for example, time after time no problems are found, then the frequency of testing can be reduced. If, however, problems begin to develop, then the frequency of testing should be increased until quality is back under control (Grove, 1983). Employers will not terminate the arrangement simply because problems emerge; they will drop out, however, when the supported work provider fails to recognize and address problems in a professional and timely fashion.

Thomas Peters and Robert Waterman in their much-acclaimed book *In Search of Excellence* (1982) noted that the excellent companies identified were not only committed to service but were also obsessed by quality. This obsession pays off in reputation. Among the excellent performers enumerated, Peters and Waterman included Caterpillar Tractor and shared the story of a Vietnam veteran who had the responsibility for ordering construction equipment for the Navy during the war: "We would go to almost any ends, stretching the procurement regulations to the limit, to specify the always more expensive CAT equipment" (Peters & Waterman, 1982, pp. 171–172). Quality service cements relationships and secures stability in human services agencies' employment partnerships.

Developing and maintaining quality relationships with industry is the foundation for stable employment arrangements for people with severe disabilities. Building such arrangements requires program creativity and well-planned marketing efforts. Most important, however, is that service providers, while being committed to quality services for their disabled clients, also be dedicated to building strong and stable alliances with host industries.

REFERENCES

Campbell, J.F. (1985). *Supported work approaches for the traditional rehabilitation facility.* Washington, DC: National Association of Rehabilitation Facilities.

Davis, S.W., & Wasmuth, W.J. (1983). *Cornell Hotel-Restaurant Administration Quarterly, 23*(4), 16–18.

Drucker, P.F. (1973). *Management: Tasks, responsibilities, and practices.* New York: Harper & Row.

Food service and the labor shortage. (1986, January). Washington, DC: National Restaurant Association Current Issue Report.

Grove, A.S. (1983). *High output management.* New York: Random House.

Lattuca, F. (1987). Training the mentally disabled for the Ford service industry. In *Proceedings, 1987 Annual Council of Hotel, Restaurant, and Institutional Educa-*

tion Conference. Atlanta: C.H.R.I.E. (Council of Hotel, Restaurant, and Institutional Educators).

Lumbrinos, J., & Johnson, W. (1985, Spring). Discrimination against the handicapped. *Journal of Human Resources,* p. 265.

National Restaurant Association. (1988).*NRA pocket factbook: Food service industry 1987–88.* Washington, DC: Author.

Peters, T.J., & Waterman, R.H., Jr. (1982). *In search of excellence.* New York: Harper & Row.

Schapire, J.A., & Berger, F. (1984). Responsibility and benefits in hiring the handicapped, *Cornell Hotel-Restaurant Administration Quarterly, 26*(2), 59–67.

Schneider, I.A. (1986, February). Dollars for education, *School Product News* (2), 6.

8

Identifying Opportunities through the Creative Use of Aptitude Tests

James S. Russell

The recent emphasis on placing more people with disabilities into private employment has resulted in a dilemma for employers and placement personnel. While there is a severe need to secure competitive employment for persons with disabilities, at the same time employers are beginning to increase the use of aptitude testing, which screens out persons with disabilities. Although this chapter focuses on research related to employment for individuals with developmental disabilities, the research techniques are general and apply to persons with all types of handicaps. The chapter is divided into four sections, including: 1) a brief introduction to the need for placing developmentally disabled people into employment; 2) a description of the reasons employers are increasingly using cognitive and psychomotor aptitude testing; 3) a description of a research effort designed to analyze the ability of aptitude testing to predict job performance for developmentally disabled people; and 4) a discussion of important factors related to aptitude testing that will increase the potential for placing people with developmental disabilities.

THE NEED TO PLACE DEVELOPMENTALLY DISABLED PEOPLE

Public sector placement services need assistance from private employers to place persons with developmental disabilities. Such help would add resources from the private sector and reduce the employer resistance faced by placement personnel attempting to "push" people into competitive employment. Ideally, information could be given to employers that would create a demand for the labor market of persons with disabilities, essentially "pulling" clients from the social services system. Unfortunately, as indicated, the opportunity to create such a demand is colliding with an increasingly effective employment practice that is gaining new advocates: employment testing.

Employment testing is increasing in popularity after a 20-year hiatus that was caused by a combination of inconsistent research results, inappropriate research methods, and civil rights legislation. Research in the 1960s and 1970s found that validities of aptitude tests varied widely, even for aptitudes tested in similar jobs (Ghiselli, 1973). This led to the conclusion that validity was job specific; that is, each job had to be studied to determine factors that predicted job performance, and then tests that measured those factors had to be developed. Employers also deemphasized testing because civil rights guidelines made tests difficult to develop, and sample sizes were frequently not large enough to obtain accurate results.

The renewed popularity of employment testing is due to recent research demonstrating that standardized tests of cognitive ability are valid predictors of job performance across a wide variety of jobs (Hunter & Hunter, 1984). The conclusion about widespread validity is based on a technique called meta-analysis, which calculates weighted averages of validities and makes corrections for statistical artifacts (Hunter, Schmidt, & Jackson, 1982). Research demonstrated that earlier studies were based on small sample sizes and contained procedures that provided questionable results. Such findings now allow researchers to conclude that tests were valid predictors for broad categories of jobs (Madigan, Scott, Deadrick, & Stoddard, 1986). The implication is that job-specific studies are not necessary. This broad applicability of aptitude tests has been labeled *validity generalization*.

Based on early work in validity generalization, the U.S. Employment Service (USES) sponsored research (U.S. Department of Labor, 1970) on 515 validity studies that had used the General Aptitude Test Battery (GATB). The results indicated that the GATB was a valid predictor of job performance across a wide range of jobs (Hunter, 1983). Specifically, weighted combinations of cognitive, spatial, and psychomotor aptitudes were found to be valid predictors for five job families that represent 12,000 jobs coded in the *Dictionary of Occupational Titles* (*DOT;* U.S. Department of Labor, 1977).

The five job families were identified by using the "things" and "data" worker function codes of the *DOT* (U.S. Department of Labor, 1977). The first job family consists of all jobs with a things code of "0"; and the fifth job family consists of all jobs with a things code of "6." The remaining job families are jobs that are not coded "0" or "6" for things and do have data codes of "0–2" (job family two), "3–5" (job family three), or "6–8" (job family four). The five job families are identified, with typical jobs in each family, in Table 8.1. The weightings for the combination of aptitudes within each job family are also summarized in Table 8.1. The job family numbers are arranged in order of complexity: Job family 1 is viewed as the most complex

Table 8.1. *DOT* job families and weightings for the combination of aptitudes within each job family

	Percentage of aptitude composite		
	Cognitive	Perceptual	P-Motor
Job family	GVN	SPQ	KFM
1. Prepare/adjust machines.	59	30	11

Get a machine to do a particular kind of job. Machine changes and settings require considerable judgment.

Examples: drill-press set-up operator, tool machine set-up operator.

2. Originate/interpret—Manage/ problem-solve.	100	–	–

Bring information together and discover new ideas.

Examples: experimental psychologist, tax economist, historian.

Examine information and determine what should be done and how it should be done.

Examples: financial analyst, applied statistician, astronomer.

3. Examine/collect/calculate.	73	–	27

Study and determine the value of information. Then, suggest actions to take.

Examples: law clerk, patent examiner.

Collect or classify information. Then, report results and/or carry out an agreed-upon action.

Examples: file clerk, fingerprint classifier.

Do arithmetic operations. Then, report the results and/or carry out an agreed-upon action.

Examples: accounting clerk, cost clerk, payroll clerk.

(continued)

Table 8.1. *(continued)*

	Percentage of aptitude composite		
	Cognitive	Perceptual	P-Motor
Job family	GVN	SPQ	KFM
4. Copy/compare.	44	–	56

Rewrite or copy information. Examples: addresser, typist, telephone agent.

Determine how data, people, or things are the same or different. Examples: proofreader, film viewer, packager, sorter.

5. Feed/remove materials from machines.	13	–	87

Place or remove materials from machines or equipment that are automatic or are tended by others.

Examples: print shop helper, washing machine loader.

GVN = Composite cognitive scores of general, verbal, and numeric aptitudes.

SPQ = Composite perceptual scores of spatial aptitude, form perception, and clerical perception.

KFM = Composite psychomotor scores of motor coordination, finger dexterity, and manual dexterity.

and job family 5 the least complex. The multiple correlations for the validities ranged from 0.59 to 0.49, with an average of 0.53 (Hunter & Hunter, 1984).

An understanding of how the process works leads to the conclusion that mentally retarded people will be at a significant disadvantage in competing for jobs. First, cognitive ability is a factor in every weighting scheme (see Table 8.1), although the weighting in the least complex job family is only 13%. Second, total scores are calculated on the basis of the percentages described in Table 8.1. Using job family 3 as an example, and cognitive scores of 200 and psychomotor scores of 400, the total score would be 254 (0.73 × 200) + (0.27 × 400). Consequently, low cognitive scores cannot be fully overcome by high scores in psychomotor or spatial abilities. Third, employers receive lists of clients ranked by their percentile score within their ethnic group. The USES (U.S. Department of Labor, 1970) recommends that clients be hired from the top down. This means that instead of the employer selecting any client who scored above a cutoff score, the USES recommends employers select the person with the highest percentile first, and then work down the list until the cutoff point is reached. This again puts people with developmental disabilities at a disadvantage, because they will have difficulty attaining the best scores.

REASONS FOR INCREASED USE OF APTITUDE TESTING

Based on the results of these studies (U.S. Department of Labor, 1970), the USES is promoting the use of the GATB in employment placement. Over 30 state employment services have begun implementing a testing system using weighting schemes derived from the research, and preliminary reports have been positive (Hawk, 1986). At least 25% of the states use a procedure that replaces interviewing with the GATB test for applicant screening and placement (Madigan et al., 1986). Michigan has implemented the program with automotive companies and has referred 26,000 applicants out of 73,600 persons tested (Madigan et al., 1986).

One of the reasons that testing is becoming more acceptable relates to the concept of utility. Utility analysis calculates the economic return to an employer of using a valid selection test (Boudreau & Berger, 1985). The essential assumption is that employees selected by more valid employment tests will have an average performance that is superior to employees hired with less valid tests. The increased performance is linked to dollar returns for employers in the form of increased productivity and reduced turnover.

The use of a test that has a validity of 0.53 generates considerable return for employers in comparison to hiring practices, such as the interview, that have less validity. This text does not warrant a full explanation of the formulas, which are complex, but, briefly, using a selection device that gains 0.20 in validity when hiring 100 people at the minimum wage for 5 years could yield over $300,000 in savings, excluding turnover savings (Miller & Russell, 1985). The actual dollar value of the utility is not as important as the fact that the procedures used to estimate the utility are generally viewed as conservative, which means employers will find it worthwhile to invest in new testing procedures.

A RESEARCH EFFORT TO ASSIST
DEVELOPMENTALLY DISABLED PEOPLE

The remainder of this chapter discusses a research project underway to overcome employment testing hurdles for persons with disabilities. The study's specific tasks are to: 1) apply meta-analytic techniques on studies that have assessed and measured aptitudes and work performance for persons with low cognitive abilities; 2) apply meta-analytic techniques to analyze existing data on competitive employment to identify tasks and jobs that can be performed effectively by people with low cognitive skills; 3) prepare an employer's guide for identifying such tasks and jobs and the associated economics for employing people with developmental disabilities; and 4) disseminate the information to employers and job placement personnel.

Predictions of Employment

Predicting job performance for persons with developmental disabilities is sometimes confused with assessing clients for rehabilitative purposes. As Cobb (1972) has explained, the philosophy of personnel selection is aimed at selecting those people who have the highest probability of job success. This is in contrast to assessing people for vocational guidance, which is aimed at maximizing the potential of an individual client. These conflicting goals have caused resistance to using global aptitude tests for rehabilitation work (Bolton, 1981; Cobb, 1972). However, this reason alone should not preclude testing for selection purposes.

Reviews of the predictability of aptitude tests for predicting job performance are universally pessimistic (Bolton, 1981; Browning & Irvin, 1981; Cobb, 1972). Essentially, the arguments against the use of employment testing include administrative problems connected with such testing, its impracticality for rehabilitative purposes, and nonvalidity.

Although administrative problems and the impracticality of testing affect validity, they appear to be solvable issues. For example, the arguments concerning administration are that the tests rely heavily on verbal directions (Browning & Irvin, 1981), and that only test personnel who are familiar with the particular disability should be allowed to administer the tests (Bolton, 1981). It is important to note that these two arguments do not preclude the use of tests, but only require that administration be done effectively.

The need to effectively administer tests to persons with disabilities is echoed by employment law that requires employers to use standardized testing procedures. The research literature indicates that the GATB can be administered to persons who have developmental disabilities if standardized procedures are used. The GATB was administered to 656 developmentally disabled people in three separate tests (U.S. Department of Labor, 1970) utilizing such standards. Furthermore a nonreading version of the GATB (NATB) is available, which uses six tests that are identical to GATB tests and two that are parallel to ones in the GATB. One study found the NATB could be administered to people with mild and moderate mental retardation but not to those with severe and profound retardation (Carbuhn & Wells, 1973).

The second objection to testing, that the results are impractical for rehabilitative purposes, is not an issue for employers. Employers want to know how functional the person is at the time of placement, so tests should be administered when the person is ready for placement.

The major argument addressed in this chapter and in this author's research is that aptitude tests have not been found to be consistently valid. Reviews have concluded that few studies use psychometric data that can be cumulated, that sample sizes are small, that data reporting is incomplete, that statistical and research procedures may be less than satisfactory, and that the independent variables are too heterogeneous to be compared (Browning & Irvin, 1981; Cobb, 1972). Note that these criticisms are the same ones that were leveled at employment testing and can be overcome by meta-analytic techniques (Hunter et al., 1982). In addition to early prediction research, recent work has added a number of variables that have been used to predict a variety of criteria. Research in the past 10 years has focused on which client characteristics can predict successful deinstitutionalization. Schalock and his colleagues (Schalock & Harper, 1978; Schalock, Harper, & Genung, 1981) have administered a comprehensive battery of tests and found that several psychomotor and intelligence measures predict movement along a community-integration continuum. A number of client characteristics have also been identified in other studies (cf. Bell, 1976; Crawford, Aiello, & Thompson, 1979; Heal, Sigelman, & Switzky, 1978; McCarver & Craig, 1974). While these studies provide more comprehensive data, the results are still inconsistent and limited to small sample sizes. Categorizing the tests into global abilities such as cognitive, spatial and psychomotor abilities, and combining other variables into general categories may reduce the number of independent variables to an interpretable level.

Another criticism of tests of global aptitudes is that their prediction powers are not as great as tests of specific job performance (Browning & Irvin, 1981). Browning and Irvin labeled the latter type of testing *applied performance testing*. This term refers to testing for the purpose of matching specific aptitudes with specific work samples, and has resulted in correlations that exceed 0.70. Browning and Irvin conclude that "validity coefficients in the 0.40 to 0.50 range are simply inadequate as the foundation for client selection and placement decisions" (p. 376).

While correlations of 0.70 are better than correlations of 0.40 to 0.50, it is a serious error to conclude that global tests should not be used for prediction purposes. In fact, the lower correlations are to be expected, and discarding them leads to detailed job analyses that may not be necessary for all clients. This problem can be best understood by recognizing the relationship between aptitude tests, work sample tests, job knowledge, and job performance. For example, one research project reviewed validity results for a series of studies on predictors of supervisory ratings of job performance (Hunter, 1986). Supervisory ratings were significantly correlated with general cognitive ability ($r = 0.47$), job performance on a work sample ($r = 0.52$), and job knowledge ($r = 0.56$). A path analysis of the four variables established the path diagram

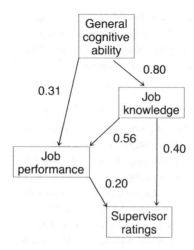

Figure 8.1. Path analysis of cognitive ability, job knowledge, job performance, and supervisor ratings. (From Hunter, J.E. [1986]. Cognitive ability, cognitive aptitude, job knowledge, and job performance. *Journal of Vocational Behavior, 29,* 340–362.)

shown in Figure 8.1 (Hunter, 1986). It shows that cognitive aptitude tests are excellent predictors of job knowledge. While job knowledge is an excellent predictor of work sample performance, cognitive aptitudes also play an important part. That is, even with comprehensive training to provide job knowledge, global aptitudes will contribute to work sample performance. Both work sample performance and job knowledge predict job performance.

Applied performance testing uses an aptitude test composed of a specific sample of the actual work that should be performed. Typically, the aptitude is a specific item such as a multiplication problem, which would be found on a global aptitude test. The results on the specific aptitude test are compared with the results of either a work sample, such as calculating prices on an invoice, or job knowledge, such as relating prices to quantity. The correlations between the test and the dependent variable are high.

This testing process is directly analogous to employment testing of global ability, job knowledge, work sample tests, and supervisory ratings. Correlations between general cognitive aptitudes and global supervisory ratings are understandably smaller than correlations between applied performance tests of specific aptitudes and of specific job performance measures (see Figure 8.1). While applied performance testing is effective at verifying the tasks that are important for development, extensive and time-consuming procedures are required before evidence can be presented to employers demonstrating that the clients are capable of acceptable levels of job performance. Where the purpose of assessment is to predict employment success, and therefore entice the private sector to assume some of the effort in completing the detailed work analysis, it would be more efficient for placement services to provide employers with the validities of global aptitudes and their respective utilities. Utility analysis would still indicate that the lower correlations of 0.40 to 0.50 are rewarding to employers, and thus would get the employers more involved.

Validity for Developmentally Disabled People

In addition to the meta-analyses described previously, the author's second research thrust has been to analyze existing validity studies of people in the working population to determine which job characteristics would moderate the predictive validity of cognitive aptitudes. The term *moderated* here means that the validities of the cognitive and psychomotor aptitudes in jobs with particular work characteristics are significantly different from those in jobs without such characteristics (Peters & Champoux, 1979). In the author's initial work (Russell, Brawner-Jones, Lucke, Dodson, & Ferguson, 1986; Russell & Lucke, 1987), two job characteristics were identified that appear to moderate job validities. Much of the description that follows is taken from those studies.

The search for moderators of the predictive validity of cognitive psychomotor aptitudes has established that increases in job complexity correspond with increases in the validity of cognitive aptitudes and decreases in the validity of psychomotor aptitudes (Gutenberg, Arvey, Osborn, & Jeanneret, 1983; Hunter, 1983). The major work in this area was the USES study (Hunter, 1983) reported earlier, where five job families were established from an analysis of 515 validity studies of the GATB for jobs coded in the *DOT* (U.S. Department of Labor, 1977). One of this author's research efforts (Russell & Lucke, 1987) has been to identify potential moderators that reduce the validities of cognitive aptitudes within those five job families.

Hunter (1983) cited a study in which the cognitive validity was low for jobs that were restricted to following a set of instructions. The work by Townsend, Prien, and Johnson (1974) established that jobs in a sheltered workshop were characterized by manual control, structured work, little information coming from people, little decision making, and little technical activities. Of course, research has demonstrated that developmentally disabled people could perform work where jobs were structured so that workers were able to repeat a set of procedures and attain clear standards of performance (Bellamy, Peterson, & Close, 1987).

This author's first analysis used job characteristics already coded within the *DOT* job classification system. The job characteristics are called "temperaments" and refer to the type of adjustments workers must make in job situations. In light of the research on potential moderators, two temperaments of jobs were identified where developmentally disabled people might be able to perform effectively.

The first temperament was "situations involving repetitive or short cycle operations carried out according to set procedures or sequences," and the second temperament was "situations involving the precise attainment of set limits, tolerances, or standards" (U.S. Department of Labor, 1965, p. 654). Jobs with the former temperament, labeled "repetitive operations," are referred to here as "RO jobs," and jobs with the latter temperament, labeled "precise limits," are referred to here as "PL jobs."

The study ran three analyses within each job family. Each analysis had the same hypothesis: Within each job family, jobs with either one or both of the temperaments would have significantly higher psychomotor validities than jobs without the characteristics. There were no jobs in job family 1 that had either repetitive operations or precise limits, so the analysis was restricted to job families 2 through 5.

The data analysis began with 722 validity studies accumulated by the USES. The studies included the 515 studies used to define the five job families for the USES (Hunter, 1983) and 227 additional studies subsequently compiled by the USES. Ultimately, 566 studies provided information on temperaments, aptitudes, validities, and job proficiencies that could be used in the study. The criterion was job proficiency, which was primarily measured by supervisory ratings.

The reporting in this chapter is restricted to the beta weights for regression equations to predict job proficiency from cognitive and psychomotor aptitudes for each of the different job families and temperaments. For a full report of the data, see Russell and Lucke (1987).The results are listed in Table 8.2, along with the original beta weights and multiple Rs from the Hunter (1983) study. The higher beta weights for cognitive scores found by Hunter most likely reflect undetected miscoding of the data provided to Hunter.

Overall, the results indicate that jobs with repetitive operations and precise limits have lower betas for cognitive aptitudes and higher betas for psychomotor aptitudes than jobs without those temperaments. For job family 2, the cognitive beta is less for PL jobs than for non-PL jobs. For job family 3, all jobs with those temperaments have lower betas for cognitive aptitudes and higher betas for pyschomotor aptitudes than jobs without those temperaments. In fact, the cognitive aptitude beta is *less* than the psychomotor aptitude beta for RO and PL jobs, which is a reversal of the pattern found by Hunter (1983) in job family 3.

In job family 4, another reversal pattern exists for RO jobs. For RO jobs, the cognitive beta is less than the psychomotor beta. The betas in the rest of job family 4 follow the same pattern found by Hunter. The betas in job family 5 are more dramatic than the other job families, although the data are not as comprehensive as preferred. The 21 jobs all have repetitive operations, and 10 studies had both repetitive operations and precise limits. The beta for cognitive aptitudes for RO and PL jobs is -0.10, while the beta for psychomotor

Table 8.2. Beta weights and multiple Rs for cognitive and psychomotor aptitudes

Job family	Repetitive operations			Precise limits			Combined temperaments		
	Betas		Mult. R	Betas		Mult. R	Betas		Mult. R
	GVN	KFM		GVN	KFM		GVN	KFM	
2 With	.—	.—	.—	.45	.04	.47	.—	.—	.—
Without	.49	.05	.51	.51	.04	.53	.49	.05	.51
Hunter,	.58	.—	.58	.58	.—	.58	.58	.—	.58
83	.25	.22	.38	.34	.15	.42	.15	.31	.39
3 With	.37	.13	.43	.38	.12	.44	.37	.13	.43
Without	.45	.16	.53	.45	.16	.53	.45	.16	.53
Hunter,	.19	.34	.44	.22	.31	.44	.21	.33	.44
83	.28	.22	.41	.17	.32	.43	.20	.31	.42
4 With	.28	.33	.50	.28	.33	.50	.28	.33	.50
Without	.07	.42	.45	−.10	.56	.53	−.10	.56	.53
Hunter,	.—	.—	.—	.22	.30	.43	.22	.30	.43
83	.07	.46	.49	.07	.46	.49	.07	.46	.49
5 With									
Without									
Hunter,									
83									

GVN = Composite cognitive scores of general, verbal, and numeric aptitudes.
KFM = Composite psychomotor scores of motor coordination, finger dexterity, and manual dexterity.

aptitudes is 0.56, in comparison to betas that are 0.22 and 0.30, respectively, for the non-RO and PL jobs. The negative beta in the RO and PL job data suggests that cognitive aptitude is acting as a suppressor variable. This interpretation is based on the fact that cognitive aptitudes are correlated with psychomotor aptitudes ($r = .34$; Hunter, 1983), and thus psychomotor aptitudes are already accounting for the variance in performance.

Considering that all of the results are within job families, it appears that the repetitive operations temperament moderates validities of cognitive and psychomotor aptitudes, and that the precise limits temperament is a significant moderator in combination with repetitive operations.

THE POTENTIAL FOR PLACING
PEOPLE WITH DEVELOPMENTAL DISABILITIES

The results of the preceding study have implications for employment practices in job families 3, 4, and 5. Together, these jobs represent 82.8% of the jobs surveyed by the USES (Hunter & Hunter, 1984). For developmentally disabled people, the beta weights in job families 2 through 4 still indicate that cognitive aptitudes make a significant contribution to job performance. One avenue for future research is to identify tasks of jobs in these three job families that would moderate cognitive validities.

In job family 5, the study suggests that cognitive scores be given no weight for those jobs with both temperaments. These results must be treated with caution because a review of the jobs included in the studies indicates that all the studies with repetitive operations and precise limits were cannery worker jobs, a very limited data base. The limitations are a reflection of the job family itself, which only represents 2.4% of the jobs surveyed by the USES (Hunter & Hunter, 1984). Additional research that would add to the variety of jobs in job family 5 may identify more opportunities to employ developmentally disabled people.

The present studies suggest that information commonly available within the *DOT* coding scheme could serve as a guide to identifying moderators. These results complement the work by Gutenberg et al. (1983), who found that information processing moderated the validities of cognitive aptitudes using the information available in the Position Analysis Questionnaire, a widely used job analysis system. Placement personnel and employers who want to identify jobs that can be effectively performed by persons with developmental disabilities will find the two readily available job analysis systems provide better information than procedures currently recommended by the USES.

REFERENCES

Bell, N.J. (1976). IQ is a factor in community lifestyle of previously institutionalized retardates. *Mental Retardation, 14*(3), 29–33.

Bellamy, G.T., Peterson, L., & Close, D. (1978). Habilitation of the severely and profoundly retarded: Illustration of competence. *Education and Training of the Mentally Retarded, 14*, 131–137.

Bolton, B. (1981, Spring). Assessing employability of handicapped persons: The vocational rehabilitation perspective. *Journal of Applied Rehabilitation Counseling, 12*, 40–44.

Boudreau, J.W., & Berger, C.J. (1985). Decision-theoretic utility analysis applied to employee separation and acquisition. *Journal of Applied Psychology, 70*, 581–612.

Browning, P., & Irvin, L.K. (1981). Vocational evaluation, training, and placement of mentally retarded persons. *Rehabilitation Counseling Bulletin, 25*, 374–408.

Carbuhn, W.M., & Wells, I.C. (1973). Use of the Non-reading Aptitude Test Battery (NATB) for selecting mental retardates for competitive employment. *Measurement and Evaluation in Guidance, 5*, 460–467.

Cobb, J.V. (1972). *The forecast of fulfillment: A review of research on predictive assessment of the adult retarded.* New York: Teacher's College Press.

Crawford, J.L., Aiello, J.R., & Thompson, D.E. (1979). Deinstitutionalization and community placement: Clinical and environmental factors. *Mental Retardation*, *17*(2), 59–63.

Ghiselli, E.E. (1973). The validity of aptitude tests in personnel selection. *Personnel Psychology*, *26*, 461–477.

Gutenberg, R.L., Arvey, R.D., Osborn, H.G., & Jeanneret, P.R. (1983). Moderating effects of decision-making/information-processing job dimensions on test validities. *Journal of Applied Psychology*, *68*, 602–608.

Hawk, J. (1986). Real world implications of g. *Journal of Vocational Behavior*, *29*, 411–414.

Heal, L.W., Sigelman, C.K., & Switzky, H.N. (1978). Research on community residential alternatives for the mentally retarded. In N.R. Ellis (Ed.), *International review of research in mental retardation* (Vol. 9, pp. 210–249). New York: Academic Press.

Hunter, J.E. (1983). *Test validation for 17,000 jobs: An application of job classification and validity generalization analysis to the General Aptitude Test Battery* (USES Test Research Report No. 45). Washington, DC: U.S. Department of Labor.

Hunter, J.E. (1986). Cognitive ability, cognitive aptitudes, job knowledge, and job performance. *Journal of Vocational Behavior*, *29*(3), 340–362.

Hunter, J.E., & Hunter, R.F. (1984). Validity and utility of selected predictors of job performance. *Psychological Bulletin*, *96*, 72–98.

Hunter, J.E., Schmidt, F.L., & Jackson, T.S. (1982). *Meta-analysis*. San Francisco: Sage Publications.

Madigan, R.M., Scott, K.D., Deadrick, D.L., & Stoddard, J.A. (1986). Employment testing: The U.S. Job service is spearheading a revolution. *Personnel Administrator*, *31*(9), 102–112.

McCarver, R.B., & Craig, E.M. (1974). Placement of the retarded in the community: Prognosis and outcome. In N.R. Ellis (Ed.), *International review of research in mental retardation* (Vol. 7, pp. 146–207). New York: Academic Press.

Miller, M., & Russell, J.S. (1985). The utility of predicting job performance for persons with disabilities. In M.S. Gould & G.T. Bellamy (Eds.), *Transitions from school to work and adult life* (pp. 149–187). Eugene: University of Oregon, Specialized Training Program.

Peters, W.S., & Champoux, J.E. (1979). The role and analysis of moderator variables in organizational research. In R.T. Mowday & R.M. Steers (Eds.), *Research in organizations: Issues and controversies* (pp. 239–253). Santa Monica, CA.: Goodyear Publishing.

Russell, J.S., Brawner-Jones, N., Lucke, J.R., Dodson, J., & Ferguson, P. (1986). An empirical analysis of repetitive validities. In P. Ferguson (Ed.), *Issues in transition research: Economic and social outcomes* (pp. 78–92). Eugene: University of Oregon, Specialized Training Program.

Russell, J.S., & Lucke, J.R. (1987, April). *Examining work temperaments that moderate DOT job family validities*. Paper presented at the Annual Meeting of the Society of Industrial and Organizational Psychologists, Atlanta.

Schalock, R.L., & Harper, R.S. (1978). Placement from community based mental retardation programs: How well do clients do? *American Journal of Mental Deficiency*, *83*(3), 240–247.

Schalock, R.L., Harper, R.S., & Genung, T. (1981). Community integration of mentally retarded adults: Community placement and program success. *American Journal of Mental Deficiency*, *85*(3), 478–488.

Townsend, J.W., Prien, E.P., & Johnson, J.T. (1974). The use of the Position

Analysis Questionnaire in selecting correlates of job performance among mentally retarded workers. *Journal of Vocational Behavior, 4,* 181–192.

U.S. Department of Labor. (1970). *Manual for the USES General Aptitude Test Battery.* Washington, DC: U.S. Government Printing Office.

U.S. Department of Labor. (1965). Occupational classification and industry index. *Dictionary of occupational titles* (3rd ed., Vol. II). Washington, DC: U.S. Government Printing Office.

U.S. Department of Labor. (1977). *Dictionary of occupational titles* (4th ed). Washington, DC: U.S. Government Printing Office.

III

OVERVIEW
Using
Technology and Training
to Ensure Job Success

$$T$$he "place and pray" concept of previous years is rapidly being replaced by the application of sophisticated technological and training strategies that ensure the successful employment of people with disabilities. Recent advances in person-environment analysis, behavioral analytic techniques, prosthetic procurement and use, and job and environmental modification have provided vocational and employment specialists with an array of techniques for enhancing employment opportunities for adults with disabilities. A review of these topics provides the focus for Section III of this book.

The techniques discussed in the following six chapters are attractive not only to habilitation personnel but to industry personnel as well, many of whom frequently need help in areas in which habilitation specialists are becoming proficient. Chapter 9, by A. Bacon and D. B. Crimmins, concentrates on the new developments in instructional technology that enhance a person's social capabilities. The authors examine the relationship between values and technology, the current research on habilitation practices, and the relevance of social competence and employment.

In Chapter 10, R. L. Schalock discusses the need to go beyond the short-term focus of evaluating and matching persons to appropriate jobs, to a long-term job tenure and maintenance perspective. The chapter summarizes current work on short- and long-term person-environment matching strategies and service delivery strategies that are necessary to transition employees from short-term to long-term employment status.

One such strategy is central to B. T. Judy's chapter (Chapter 11) on job accommodation and the JAN (Job Accommodation Network) program, which provides consultative services to programs and industry to facilitate job accommodation for persons with various disabilities. Among the physical accommodations discussed in the chapter include those involving the worksite, work station and work environment.

H. Shane and G. Roberts, in Chapter 12, describe how computers can be used or modified to enhance writing and keyboard accessing opportunities. This use of applied technology to improve work opportunity for persons with severe physical disabilities rests on a good assessment of a person's sensory status, attention to seating and positioning, and analysis of other possible ways to facilitate the link between the operator and the computer. The authors conclude the chapter with a discussion of technology in the workplace and home-based employment via the computer.

The importance of not overlooking the training needs of various persons is emphasized in Chapter 13, by O. C. Karan and L. Mettel, who summarize training needs in integrated settings. The authors stress not just the training needs of paraprofessionals, professionals, parents, and consumers but also the performance issues involved in this training.

The section concludes with a chapter by C. F. Calkins and H. M. Walker on the need for a habilitation planning guide focusing on social competence. In the chapter, the authors summarize their work to date on a planning guide to enhance employment outcomes and materials based on a person- and program-environment analysis and fit. Calkins and Hill anticipate that this approach to expanding employment outcomes will increase the knowledge base for decision makers, improve the system variables that affect the habilitation process, and better the quality of work life for persons with disabilities.

Throughout this section, the reader will be impressed with the degree of sophistication and applicability of the techniques presented. However, these techniques constitute only part of what is necessary to ensure a person's job success. Various support mechanisms are also necessary, as is seen in Section IV.

9

Enhancing Functional Social Capabilities

New Developments in Instructional Technology

Ansley Bacon
and Daniel B. Crimmins

Social and interpersonal skills are essential tools for adults with disabilities in their quest for successful employment. When a person's behavior is judged to be socially competent, more opportunities are available to that person. However, the lack of appropriate social behavior can result in either the loss of a job or the loss of an employment opportunity in an integrated setting. As the opportunities for integrated employment increase, human services professionals are challenged to develop a more sophisticated instructional technology for social competence that reflects society's changing values regarding people with disabilities. This chapter discusses how social competencies can be enhanced through recent developments in instructional technology. The major sections of the chapter include the relationship between values and technology, current research on habilitation practices, and a discussion of social competence and employment.

VALUES AND TECHNOLOGY

Values guide the development of new instructional technology. Over the past few years new values in the field of disability have evolved, as expressed in the professional literature, state and federal legislation, and organizational mission statements. The section following describes some of these new values.

Community integration refers to the presence and participation of people with disabilities in their communities. *Integration* means physical proximity *and* opportunity for social interaction between people with disabilities and typical peers and community members. The value of integration has led to a general recognition of the importance of the environments with which one interacts, and of the influence of those environments over a person's behavior. An emphasis on the relationship between the person and the social and physical environments has moved the focus of interventions from "fixing" the person to fit the environment, to one of either assisting individuals to develop their abilities or modifying the environment itself. One aspect of this new focus is the recognition of the importance of *social networks and supports* that will sustain continuous interdependent relationships with a variety of people.

The critical and dignifying *role of work* in adult life has been described extensively in the professional literature (Hill, Hill, Wehman, & Banks, 1985; Will, 1984), as has *productivity,* which is defined as contributing to one's community or household (*Developmental Disabilities Assistance and Bill of Rights Act,* 1984). Being productive at real work contributes to a valued social role for adults.

The concept of *social role valorization,* the successor to the principle of normalization as described by Wolfensberger (1983), is another important value. It is defined as "the creation, support, and defense of valued social roles for people" (p. 234), and is based on the assumption that the primary goal of services is to enhance and protect positively valued social roles for persons who are devalued. A related value that has been articulated frequently is the importance of chronologically *age-appropriate activities* and life-styles. For adults with disabilities, this refers to the value of living, working, and recreating in ways similar to those of typical peers. Another view that has emerged is that people with disabilities should participate in the process of planning their lives and have the right to exercise *choice* in the selection of their residential, employment, and recreational options.

The values just described refer to both goals and outcomes, as well as to the means to achieve them. They are all assumed to be related to the overall quality of life for individuals with disabilities, and have resulted in changes in service approaches. Innovative program models are providing opportunities and support for adults to engage in real work and to live and participate in integrated community settings. However, as programs and services attempt to effect changes consistent with these values, issues of social competence frequently arise. Again, it is widely recognized that a person's social competence is related to the opportunities available for leading a productive, fulfilling life.

The lack of adaptive, functional social skills and the presence of excess, problematic behaviors are frequently reported to be major barriers to successful integrated employment and community living. Some of the problems experienced by the new program models have led to a questioning of whether the current instructional technology has provided the necessary means to address the new values discussed previously. Traditional approaches may not be effective or appropriate for dealing with social competence issues in integrated employment or community settings, and, furthermore, may not be consistent with the new values. An instructional technology is now developing that facilitates social competence in a manner that is effective and consistent with the values expressed in the disability field and does so in the context of normalized, integrated environments.

HABILITATION PRACTICES: CURRENT RESEARCH AND TECHNOLOGY

The values noted in the previous section have led to the development of new approaches to habilitation planning. Employment-related social competencies must be addressed that facilitate the goals of positive interactions with others, the development of long-term relationships and systems of social support, and continued opportunities for learning. The challenge is to apply the available technology in innovative ways to assist people with disabilities to achieve these goals. One framework for this application is based on the following steps: 1) assessment of the social and physical environment, 2) assessment of the person's capabilities and characteristics, 3) assessment of the person/environment fit, 4) determining a focus of intervention, 5) implementing intervention strategies, 6) promoting generalization of skills, and 7) setting socially/ecologically valid goals.

1. *Assessment of the Social and Physical Environment* Rehabilitation counselors and job trainers have a well-developed technology for assessing the performance requirements of a particular job. Consideration of these requirements is an essential component in assessing the employment options for an individual. Clearly, a person is unlikely to be successful in a position for which he or she has no related job skills or aptitude. The social environment may be secondary in importance, but is often not considered at all in the placement decision. This is unfortunate, since problems in social/personal areas appear to be a major factor in job failure (Greenspan & Shoultz, 1981). An environmental inventory should be conducted that assesses the worksite in terms of the type of social demands and requirements (implicit or explicit) for social interaction. It is also important to identify the social skills that are critical or desirable and those excess behaviors that are unacceptable for a working setting. Further assessment would identify critical outcomes that need to be achieved for a person to fully participate in the environment, the flexibility of the physical environment in terms of its potential for modification or adaptation, and the availability of social support from co-workers and supervisors (for more detail see Chapter 10).

2. *Assessment of the Individual* The behavioral capabilities, including employment-related social competencies and challenging behaviors, should then be assessed with regard to the work environment. Capabilities and excesses can be further defined by functional analyses to examine what factors relate to the presence or absence of a behavior. In terms of capabilities, the assessment addresses the strengths and skills the person possesses that relate to the requirements of the employment setting. What skills does the person demonstrate that will facilitate the development and maintenance of social relationships? Can the person carry on a conversation? Does he or she talk too much? Does he or she cooperate with co-workers and the supervisor? Can he or she initiate social contact, such as inviting a person to sit down on coffee break? How does the person respond to frustration or to negative feedback? Does he or she solicit feedback from the supervisor? How will the person ask for help when faced with problems? All of these questions may not be relevant for every job, but they indicate the areas usually related to job success.

A functional analysis of a problem behavior asks a different set of questions. What are the typical consequences for this behavior? What factors affect the onset, duration, persistence, and occurrence of the behavior? In what situations does it typically occur? When is it typically absent? Why does it make sense for this person to do this? A new development in terms of the assessment of excess behavior is to determine the function or critical effect of that behavior. This approach has proven useful in demonstrating that behavioral excesses may persevere despite attempts at remediation, because they accomplish certain social-communicative functions (Donellan, Mirenda, Mesaros, & Fassbender, 1984; Durand, 1986). This is often true for persons who lack the verbal communication repertoires to meet their social needs, but can also be seen in persons who want to obtain an outcome at an inconvenient time. Common functions of problem behaviors are to gain the attention of others, to escape or avoid unpleasant situations, to obtain items or desired outcomes, and to provide sensory stimulation (Durand & Crimmins, 1988).

3. *Assessment of the Person/Environment Fit* The two sets of information collected in the previous two steps can be examined initially to determine discrepancies or mismatches between what is required in the work environment and what the person does independently, and then to select priorities for intervention. Schalock and Jensen (1986) provide one way to conceptualize this comparison of a person's behavioral capabilities and the performance requirements of a given environment using the "goodness-of-fit index," which identifies important mismatches and employs a decision matrix that facilitates selecting areas in which functional capabilities need to be enhanced.

Another approach currently under development (Calkins et al., 1987) utilizes a screening tool to assess the person and the environment on a set of critical/desirable and unacceptable/undesirable social behaviors. Each behavior is checked as present or absent for an individual, and as required to be present or absent or not needed in a specific environment. The scoring gives a match or mismatch for each behavior, resulting in an overall match quotient. The higher the number of matches, and therefore the higher the match quotient, the fewer interventions are required to match the person and that environment. This tool may be helpful in terms of comparing various environments for a person or for comparing several people for one environment in terms of the degree of person/environment fit.

4. *Focus of Intervention* Identifying areas of important mismatch through comparing the requirements of the environment and the capabilities of the person helps to pinpoint areas requiring intervention to achieve critical outcomes. Goals are selected with regard to the critical skills or functions necessary to participate successfully in specific environments. In addition, the goals are stated in terms of the outcome or desired effect on the environment.

Once goals are articulated, one must determine the best way(s) to achieve each critical outcome. New approaches are based on the assumption that many goals can be accomplished in more than one way. Habilitation planning procedures have traditionally emphasized the identification of skills and activities necessary to accomplish a critical function in a typical way, and the implementation of a teaching program to develop the skills. This approach has been based on the assumption that there is *one* best way to accomplish an outcome. It assumes that there are correct *forms* of a behavior and that specific behaviors can be described as correct or appropriate for a given situation. Similarly, it has been assumed that there are forms of behavior that are always incorrect for a situation. While it is true that there are forms of behavior that are likely to be generally acceptable to a majority of the population, the overall assumption has left us with insufficient means to assist people who because of physical or cognitive disabilities, or lack of instruction, are unlikely to attain those predetermined forms.

The increased emphasis on the *function* of behaviors has been particularly helpful in developing interventions with individuals who have difficulties learning new skills. If it is unlikely that a person will achieve a critical function using a typical form of behavior, a different form that accomplishes the desired purpose can be taught. For example, if writing the date is a requirement of a particular job but a person cannot perform this function without extensive instruction, the focus of the intervention could be modified to teach the person to use a date stamp.

The focus on behavioral functions is also important with regard to challenging behaviors. If an inappropriate behavior brings undue attention to an individual, the implications for intervention are clear. A socially acceptable means of gaining attention that is equally effective in accomplishing the purpose should be determined. A form of behavior can be selected to which significant others will respond (e.g., eye contact, a greeting, or approaching a person in a friendly way). In addition, one can teach the environmental cues for the appropriate time to use the behavior, and continue to monitor the skill to ensure that it is further developed. For example, a greeting is appropriate only when one has not seen the other person for a period of time; repeated greetings are inappropriate. An individual might also be assisted to develop a set of conversational skills in order to enter into and maintain reciprocal and interesting interactions with others.

Another new feature of intervention planning is a natural outgrowth of the consideration of the person/environment fit. Until recently, interventions focused primarily on changing the person's behavior to "fit" the environment. New developments have broadened the intervention focus to consider the use of environmental or ecological strategies to assist the person in accomplishing the critical function. For example, when an individual has problems adjusting to one situation, the situation can be changed, the person can be instructed in some means of coping with the situation, or a compromise between the environmental demands and the individual's capabilities can be worked out.

5. *Intervention Strategies* Environmental modification can focus on changing either the social or physical ecology. The strategies might include increasing the probability of some events (e.g., a co-worker taking responsibility for introducing a person to others during breaks; supervisor regularly scheduling performance checks to give feedback) and/or decreasing the probability of other events (e.g., changing a job assignment to reduce failure or negative feedback), with the overall goal of improving general adjustment to the work setting. Interventions of this nature are sometimes easier to accomplish because the focus of change is under the control of the worksite. Alternatively, the environment can be rearranged to prevent a behavior from occurring, such as allowing a person to work sitting down rather than standing up to reduce fatigue, or removing certain distractions from the worker's environment.

Schalock (1987) describes a second type of intervention that focuses on the development of prosthetic devices that reduce the person/environment mismatch. These allow an individual, who otherwise would be dependent on external assistance, to perform a function independently. Examples of common prosthetic devices are calculators, communication boards, and Velcro straps instead of shoelaces. In the employment setting, devices might include timers to assist in pacing one's work, audiotaped instructions, or sequenced pictorial instructions. Note that the individual may still require instruction (e.g., on how to use the calculator), but the goal of instruction is independence in achieving the desired outcome, rather than an academic skill.

Instructional procedures that facilitate the development of new skills are a third type of intervention. A well-developed technology of instruction is briefly described here. Task analysis procedures are used to break down certain complex skills into small steps that guide instruction. Various types of prompting, modeling, and consequating procedures are used. While a wide range of techniques are available to teach new behaviors, new developments have focused primarily on ways to facilitate the *use* of adaptive behavior in a variety of situations and contexts. For example, while task analysis has been used as a major teaching strategy, recent concerns have been expressed regarding the limited scope of the steps included in the task analysis and whether they incorporate all of the elements needed for the skill to be performed in a natural setting (Brown, Evans, Weed, & Owen, 1987). Brown et al. proposed a "component model of functional life routines" (p. 118), in which skill sequences are designed to facilitate the independent use of the skills within natural contexts. For example, components such as the initiation of the skill or the solving of problems that may arise during the performance of the skill are taught in order to make the skill sequence more functional. In addition, opportunities for social interaction during skill performance are specifically addressed.

The development of strategies to deal with excess behavior, based on the function of the behavior, has been a fourth major development in intervention strategies. Creativity in the use of these and the other strategies described here has resulted in more acceptable forms of intervention that can be used in typical environments with excellent results. Regardless of whether the most efficient and effective intervention focuses on changing the behavior of the individual, changing aspects of the environment, or a combination of the two, the most important point to stress is that there is often more than one way to achieve an outcome.

6. Generalization Issues Another issue that has received attention is that of developing strategies to enhance generalized changes in adaptive behavior. The traditional approach to employment has stressed client readiness to participate in integrated settings. That is, a person has been restricted from participating in an integrated environment until prerequisite skills for that environment were learned. It has been assumed that these skills could be taught in a segregated environment, and that the approach was justified because of a lack of technology or resources to deal with excess behaviors or to promote skill development effectively in natural environments. The approach has been criticized recently, however, because skills taught in one setting often do not generalize to other settings. The remediation of behavioral deficits or excesses that occur in a training environment is problematic because it is difficult to predict whether the behavior will be displayed in the integrated environment. The two settings are likely to differ in a number of ways. For instance, the availability of appropriate role models, the training and philosophy of the staff members, the contingencies that support excess behaviors, and the program models and standards may be very different in the natural as opposed to the training environment. Also, some behavior may be tolerated in workshops but not tolerated in integrated employment settings, and vice versa.

An intervention that takes place within the integrated environment enhances a person's functional capabilities in that environment. The approaches previously described here have been used successfully within integrated environments and can be implemented in the course of the daily routine. They may initially be more difficult to establish and conduct, but, in the long run, they avoid the need for developing elaborate transfer strategies from the training setting to the typical environment in which the behavior is expected to occur.

There is one case in which caution must be exercised, however. Overdependence on prosthetic devices and on environmental adaptations to the exclusion of skill development should be avoided, since the use of such devices may limit the person's opportunities. It should be determined whether the same function could be accomplished without artificial prompts, cues, and supports. If such devices are necessary, the training specialist should consider how dependence on them might be faded. For example, an environmental modification might enhance one's functional capability within a given setting, but if the capability is dependent on that modification, it will not occur unless that modification is always in place. In selecting any strategy, the extent to which the interventions used will support generalized responding in the greatest number of new environments should be evaluated.

While the focus of this chapter is on training in the natural setting, there are some circumstances in which simulation may be the most effective strategy to teach generalized responding (Horner, McDonnell, & Bellamy, 1986). For example, if the natural setting provides limited opportunities and a limited number of situations to practice a skill, acquisition of the behavior may be facilitated by simulation training. In addition, if failure to perform a skill correctly results in danger to the person or to others, practice in a simulated setting may increase safety. If simulation is used as a training technique, its use should be guided by the new values in the disability field. Horner et al. note that simulation must not unnecessarily restrict the person from participating in integrated settings. If instruction in the natural setting would result in skill acquisition just as quickly, it should occur there. But, if the behavior could be learned more quickly in a simulated setting, and would therefore lead to increased integration in a shorter period of time, simulation should be considered. In addition, materials and techniques used in simulation must be age appropriate and must respect the dignity of the individual. In all cases, if simulation is used, it should be used in combination with community training.

7. *Social/Ecological Validity Issues* *Social/ecological validity* refers to the subjective evaluation of the outcomes of an intervention by those persons most affected by a client's behavior change, such as employment supervisors and co-workers (Wolf, 1978). It is based on a number of questions that assess the importance of the behavior selected for intervention, whether the change was perceived as meaningful, and whether the change enhanced the social competence of the individual. For example, requesting assistance when needed is an important skill; improving the rate of this skill, however, from 1 time in 20 opportunities to 1 in 10 may not be viewed as a discernible difference by others and may not have an impact on the life of the individual. Social validity also refers to the acceptability of various instructional practices or interventions within community settings. Time-out procedures, for example, are frequently used in therapeutic settings, but are not likely to be accepted in integrated environments. The following guidelines are proposed for selecting interventions that are socially valid in integrated environments:

1. The intervention must be consistent with the new values described in this chapter.
2. The intervention should not call undue attention to the individual.
3. Prosthetic devices and other supportive materials should be age and setting appropriate.
4. The intervention must be integrated into the typical daily routine.

A LOOK AHEAD: SOCIAL COMPETENCE AND EMPLOYMENT

This chapter has been based on the premise that social competence is a critical factor in developing and maintaining integrated employment opportunities for adults with disabilities. Some of the changing social values and their relationship to a developing technology for improving social competence have been described, as have new approaches to assessment and intervention strategies to enhance functional capabilities and modify excess behavior, and the important issues related to social validity and generalization.

The future presents many challenges in the employment outlook for people with disabilities. As was indicated in Chapters 1 and 2, employment opportunities are increasing for this population. However, effective and ecologically valid habilitation strategies to facilitate access to those opportunities should continue to be developed and implemented. This will necessitate expanded emphasis both on social competence issues and on specific job skills.

Many problems in social competence are linked to personal and environmental variables. The personal histories of many adults with disabilities reflect negative social conditions and inadequate social supports. Extended involvement in segregated settings has isolated people from interaction with their peers. In addition, these settings provide models of inappropriate behavior, and the behavior standards and expectations differ from those in the community at large. It is not surprising, then, that research findings document that excess behavior is more prevalent in persons who live and work in more restrictive settings. Yet, even with increased community-based opportunities (Willer & Intagliata, 1984), problems related to social competence remain. These present major obstacles to implementation of community integrated options for employment. A means of providing the appropriate support and intervention approaches described in this chapter is needed.

The types of intervention strategies required may well begin to change with the young adults now leaving public schools and entering the job market. These adults often have very different histories because of Public Law 94-142 (The Education for All Handicapped Children Act of 1975) and the least restrictive environment requirements. Some will have job histories, while many will have had extensive opportunities to interact with typical peers and the community. They will have learned various functional skills in the context of the community. These different histories will present a new and different set of challenges and priorities.

To fully address the changing social values, it will be necessary to examine carefully the design of the service system. The most common design is a "continuum of services" model, in which people move through the continuum from one service to the next, with resources decreasing as people gain more independence. The disadvantages of this approach are, first, that, in reality, people rarely move through the system. In addition, the person must be transferred to where the necessary resources are located, rather than bringing the resources to the person. An alternative model, referred to as the "array of services" model (Warren & Juhrs, 1984), provides the resources and services needed in the context of community-integrated environments. That is, services necessary to support the person in integrated community settings are provided in those settings. As the person's needs change, services can be added, reduced, or eliminated.

Finally, there is a clear need to reduce the gap between new research and technology and its implementation. Only the continued development, dissemination, and replication of adaptive and functional habilitation practices and service models will assure that people with disabilities have access to the same opportunities as other members of the community.

REFERENCES

Brown, F., Evans, I.M., Weed, K.A., & Owen, V. (1987). Delineating functional competencies: A component model. *Journal of the Association for Persons with Severe Handicaps, 12,* 117–124.

Calkins, C.F., Walker, H.M., Kiernan, W., Schalock, R.L., Bacon-Prue, A., Boles, S., Crimmins, D., & Griggs P. (1987). *Enhancing employment outcomes: A practical guide to the habilitation planning process.* Unpublished project report, University of Missouri at Kansas City.

Developmental Disabilities Assistance and Bill of Rights Act. (1984). 42 U.S.C. Sec. 6000.

Donellan, A.M., Mirenda, P.L., Mesaros, R.A., & Fassbender, L.L. (1984). Analyzing the communicative functions of aberrant behavior. *Journal of the Association for Persons with Severe Handicaps, 9,* 201–212.

Durand, V.M. (1986). Self-injurious behavior as intentional communication. In K. Gadow (Ed.), *Advances in learning and behavioral disabilities* (Vol. 5, pp. 143–157). Greenwich, CT: JAI Press.

Durand, V.M., & Crimmins, D.B. (1988). Identifying the variables maintaining self-injurious behavior. *Journal of Autism and Developmental Disorders, 18,* 99–117.

Greenspan, S., & Shoultz, B. (1981). Why mentally retarded adults lose their jobs: Social competence as a factor in work adjustment. *Applied Research in Mental Retardation, 2,* 23–28.

Hill, M., Hill, J.W., Wehman, P., & Banks, P.D. (1985). An analysis of monetary and nonmonetary outcomes associated with competitive employment of mentally retarded persons. In P. Wehman & J. W. Hill (Eds.), *Competitive employment for persons with mental retardation: From research to practice* (Vol. 1). Richmond: Rehabilitation Research and Training Center, School of Education, Virginia Commonwealth University.

Horner, R.H., McDonnell, J.J., & Bellamy, G.T. (1986). Teaching general skills: General case instruction in simulation and community settings. In R.H. Horner, L.H. Meyer, & H.D.B. Fredericks (Eds.), *Education of learners with severe handicaps: Exemplary service strategies* (pp. 289–314). Baltimore: Paul H. Brookes Publishing Co.

Schalock, R.L. (1987, January 16). *Augmentative habilitation techniques.* Paper presented at the National Conference on the Challenge to Serve, Omaha, NE.

Schalock, R.L., & Jensen, M.C. (1986). Assessing the goodness of fit between persons and their environments. *Journal of The Association for Persons with Severe Handicaps, 11,* 103–109.

Warren, F., & Juhrs, P. (1984). Community philosophy: Continuum of services. *Community News, 1,* 1–2.

Will, M., (1984). *OSERS programming for the transition of youth with disabilities: Bridges from school to work life.* Washington, DC: Office of Special Education and Rehabilitative Services.

Willer, B., & Intagliata, J. (1984). *Promises and realities for mentally retarded citizens.* Baltimore: University Park Press.

Wolf, M.M. (1978). Social validity: The case for subjective measurement or how applied behavior analysis is finding its heart. *Journal of Applied Behavior Analysis, 11,* 203–214.

Wolfensberger, W. (1983). Social role valorization: A proposed new term for the principle of normalization. *Mental Retardation, 21,* 234–239.

10

Person-Environment Analysis
Short- and Long-Term Perspectives

Robert L. Schalock

The human services field can point to significant recent advances in understanding the importance of person-environment matching, in assessing person-environment congruence, and in determining the goodness-of-fit between persons and their environments. As professionals in the disability area plan for the future, it is important to go beyond the short-term focus on obtaining and matching persons to appropriate jobs, to a long-term, job-tenure and maintenance perspective. To help readers gain insight into this necessary transition, this chapter is developed around the following four issues: 1) the relevance and importance of distinguishing between short-term and long-term perspectives, 2) the need to understand current approaches to environmental classification and assessment, 3) a proposed approach to person-environment analysis for disabled employees in tomorrow's world of work, and 4) the transitioning of employees from short-term to long-term employment status.

SHORT- VERSUS LONG-TERM PERSPECTIVE

Considerable evidence indicates that the initial successful adjustment of people with disabilities to their environments is related to both person-specific behavioral capabilities and setting-specific performance requirements. These results are consistent with a social ecological model that proposes that a person's successful adjustment depends on both the measurement and programming of person- and setting-specific factors and on the facilitation of the congruence between persons and their environments.

Recently, however, data from longitudinal placement studies suggest that long-term correlates of successful placement may be different for living environments (Schalock, Harper, & Carver, 1981; Schalock & Lilley, 1986) and work environments (Conley, 1986; Hill, Wehman, Hill, & Goodall, 1987). These results become increasingly important in light of recent federal and state employment initiatives whose major goal is long-term employment. These initiatives, plus recent data indicating that most persons with disabilities can work in regular employment for extended periods of time (Hill et al., 1985; Schalock & Lilley, 1986), suggest that human services professionals need to expand their focus and efforts from a short-term person-environment analysis to a long-term program-environment perspective. Before considering how this might be done, it is instructive to look briefly at current approaches to environmental classification and assessment.

ENVIRONMENTAL CLASSIFICATION/ASSESSMENT

Environmental Classification

The last 15 years have seen an upsurge in attempts to understand how environments affect behavior. This work can be found in disciplines such as social ecology, ecological psychology, social engineering, systems analysis, and human ecology (Conyne & Clack, 1981). Moos (1973), for example, presented six categories of human environments that affect human functioning. These environments included ecological, behavioral setting, organizational structure, inhabitant's behavior and characteristics, psychosocial climate, and functional reinforcement analysis. Table 10.1 contains a brief description of each of these environments.

The materials in this chapter focus primarily on an individual's behavior and characteristics (category 4 in Table 10.1). In that regard, a person's behavior is a function of the interaction between personality needs and environmental factors; thus, this approach stresses the congruence between persons and their environments.

Environmental Assessment

Environmental assessment can also be approached from a number of perspectives, as summarized in Table 10.1 (right side). To this author, environmental assessment is undertaken to maximize the person-environment fit (category 4 in the table) by determining the performance requirements of specific living or work environments. Once the person-specific behavioral capabilities vis-à-vis environment-specific performance requirements are assessed, these data can be used for a number of purposes, including providing an index of important matched and mismatched skills; quantifying the congruence for planning, monitoring, and evaluation purposes; permitting discrepancy analysis to establish habilitation strategies including skill training, prosthetic utilization, and/or environmental modification; and relating a person's goodness-of-fit

Table 10.1. Summary of environmental classifications and assessment approaches

	Environmental classification		Environmental assessment	
Category	Brief description		Approach	Reference
1. Ecological	Classifiers include geographical (terrain), meterological (weather), and physical design (buildings).		Functions of physical settings	Conyne & Clack (1981)
2. Behavioral setting	Physical location (such as office or church) require particular behaviors.		Space coding	Steele (1973)
3. Organizational structure	Includes descriptive analysis of the organization, plus demographic data such as size, organizational chart, and procedures.		Organizational/climate evaluations	Conyne & Clack (1981)
4. Inhabitant's behavior and characteristics	Environment reflects the personal characteristics and perceived behavior of its inhabitants. Behavior is a function of the interaction between personality needs and environmental factors (demands).		Person-environment analysis	French, Rogers, & Cobb (1974); Schalock & Jensen (1986)
			Template matching	Bem & Lord (1979); Cone, Bourland, & Wood-Sherman (1986)
5. Psychosocial climate	Includes three climate dimensions: relationship, personal development, and systems maintenance/change.		Social ecology	Lemke, Moos, Mehren, & Gauvain (1979); Moos (1979)
6. Functional reinforcement analysis	Stresses the environmental conditions that influence, support, and maintain particular behaviors.		Behavior and person-reference functional analyses	Meyer & Evans (1986)

Adapted from Conyne and Clack (1981).

107

index to that person's assessed quality of life (Schalock & Jensen, 1986; Schalock & Lilley, 1986).

Work to date of this author and others (Bem & Lord, 1979; Moos, 1979; Moos & Insel, 1974; Schalock & Jensen, 1986) regarding person-environment classification and analysis suggests a number of principles to keep in mind as one considers the next section, which contains a proposed approach to person-environment analysis of disabled employees in the working world of the future. These principles are summarized in Table 10.2. The top of the table lists a number of assumptions that underlie matching persons and environments; the bottom lists general criteria that one should use in constructing environmental assessment procedures.

PERSON-ENVIRONMENT
ANALYSIS AND THE DISABLED WORKER

Reference was made previously to the fact that the correlates of successful short-term job placement are different from those associated with long-term job tenure. This section outlines a proposed approach to person-environment

Table 10.2.   Principles concerning person-environment analysis

Assumptions underlying the matching of persons and environments[a]

1. Persons can be accurately described in terms of specific, measurable characteristics.
2. Environments are best described in terms of specific demand characteristics rather than by a general name or function.
3. The behavioral capabilities of persons can be objectively and reliably assessed.
4. The demand requirements of environments can be objectively and reliably assessed.
5. Persons and environments can be assessed in common terms (i.e., environments can be assessed according to which behavioral capabilities they require).
6. The characteristics of persons and environments can be compared and discrepancies identified.

General criteria for environmental assessment procedures[b]

1. Consistent with a conceptual approach.
2. Able to discriminate empirically among environments.
3. Demonstrated reliability and validity.
4. Tapping environmental dimensions that are meaningful to respondents and thus relevant to people in the setting.

[a]Adapted from Bem and Lord (1979) and Schalock and Jensen (1986).
[b]Adapted from Moos (1979) and Moos and Insel (1974).

analysis based on this distinction and the perceived needs of future disabled employees.

Short-Term Job Tenure Factors

The author has recently been involved in the development of two person-environment assessment instruments whose purpose is to assess the behavioral capabilities and social competencies of persons in reference to the performance demands of a particular job or work environment. The factors assessed by these instruments are listed in Table 10.3 (left and center). These factors are evaluated using the procedure outlined in detail in Schalock and Jensen (1986) and Schalock and Koehler (1984). The assessment results in a measure of the congruence (or goodness-of-fit) between the person's behavioral capabilities and the job's performance demands, as well as in an indication of significant matches and mismatches between capabilities and demands. Once the mismatches are identified, they can be reduced through behavioral skill training, prosthetic utilization, and environmental modification. Initial work (Schalock & Jensen, 1986) suggests that successful job placement and performance are related to a reasonable congruence between a person's behavioral capabilities and environmental demands.

Long-Term Job Tenure Factors

Table 10.3 (right column) also lists a number of factors cited in recent literature as associated with long-term job tenure. These are not person-environment factors so much as program-environment or social-ecological factors reflective of the three psychosocial climate dimensions of relationship, personal development, and systems maintenance (see Table 10.1, category 5). Assessment of these factors can be conducted using the following two-step process:

1. The requirements of an environment to sustain long-term successful employment would be determined. Critical factors to assess include those listed in Table 10.3 (right column), which either enhance or impair long-term employment. A simple yes/no scoring system can be used.
2. The program then assesses its (or the employer's) capacity to provide or procure certain factors (on the *Enhances* side of Table 10.3) or accommodate or overcome others (on the *Impairs* side of the table). Again, a yes/no scoring system is sufficient.

Once the analysis is completed, one determines the matches and mismatches between the environmental requirement and the agency's/employer's ability to meet those requirements. Significant mismatches need to be "remediated" along the lines suggested in Figure 10.1 and discussed in detail in the next section.

Table 10.3. Short-term and long-term factors assessed by two person- or program-environment assessment instruments

	Short-term			Long-term[c]	
Employment Screening Test[a]		Social competency[b]			
Physical demands	Temperament requirements	Enhances	Impairs	Enhances	Impairs
1. Standing	1. Directing, controlling, and/or planning activities of others	1. Asks questions	1. Steals	1. Leader/co-worker support	1. Seasonal work
2. Walking		2. Follows directions	2. Physically aggressive	2. Job satisfaction	2. Appearance inappropriate to setting
3. Sitting		3. Accepts criticism	3. Argues/refuses	3. Task variety	3. Family resistance
4. Reclining	2. Performing repetitive and/or short-cycle work	4. Follows rules	4. Late/absent	4. Job coach availability	4. Long-term tolerance
5. Lifting		5. Is neatly groomed	5. Lacks social awareness	5. Quantity of work	5. Economic disincentives
6. Carrying	3. Influencing people	6. Adapts to change	6. Whines/complains	6. Quality of work	6. Transportation
7. Pushing		7. Interacts appropriately	7. Easily distracted	7. Ability to learn job	7. Job burnout
8. Pulling	4. Performing a variety of duties	8. Courteous to co-workers	8. Displays bizarre behavior	8. Family support	
9. Climbing				9. Long-term job satisfaction	
10. Bending	5. Creative expression				
11. Crouching					
12. Crawling	6. Working alone				
13. Reaching	7. Performing effectively under stress				
14. Handling					
15. Fingering	8. Attaining precise measurement				
16. Touching					
17. Talking	9. Working under specific instruction				
18. Hearing					
19. Tasting/smelling	10. Dealing with people				
20. Visual acuity					
21. Depth perception	11. Making judgments and decisions				
22. Field of vision					
23. Numbering					
24. Reading					
25. Writing					
26. Driving					

[a]Employment Screening Test (Schalock, Johnson, & Schik, 1985).
[b]From EEO Match Scale (Boles, Walker, Schalock, Zouck, & Griggs, 1987).
[c]From Program Capacity Checklist (Boles et al., 1987).

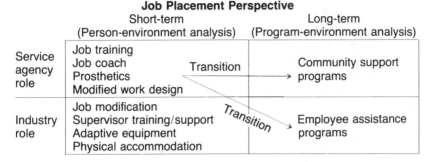

Figure 10.1. Service agency and industry roles in short-term and long-term job placement.

TRANSITIONING EMPLOYEES TO
LONG-TERM EMPLOYMENT STATUS

The concept of the individualized transition plan (ITP) is well established (see Chapter 16). The basic notion of the ITP is that one needs to plan for and provide assistance to people as they move from one life stage or living-work environment to another. The time has come, however, to conceptualize and implement a "second generation ITP process" that focuses on transitioning disabled employees from short-term to long-term employment status. This transitioning involves the two components shown in Figure 10.1, including evolving from a short-term agency responsibility to:

A long-term agency responsibility involving the use of community support programs (CSPs)

A long-term industry responsibility involving the use of employee assistance programs (EAPs)

The remainder of this chapter is devoted to discussing CSPs and EAPs, both currently available mechanisms that should provide the techniques and incentives for these two transitioning components.

Community Support Programs

The concept of community support programs is emerging from the long-term needs of persons with mental retardation, along with the demonstrated effectiveness of preventing institutionalization of elderly persons through the procurement of community supports (Carcagno et al., 1986; Stroul, 1984, 1986). The author feels that even though CSPs are not currently being used by persons with developmental disabilities, there are three critical aspects to this emerging CSP concept that are applicable to such persons living and working in the community. These aspects include instrumental activities of daily living (IADL), services necessary to maintain these activities, and a systems-level case manager to match needs and services.

1. Instrumental Activities of Daily Living (IADL) The IADLs include meal preparation, housekeeping, shopping, transportation, taking medication, money management, and telephone use. These are the activities that need to be procured as part of the service agency's long-term role (see Figure 10.1) to overcome many of the factors that can impair job tenure (see Table 10.3).

2. Services to Maintain IADLs Service needs are very specific to the person, but a list of probable services includes home aide, companion, transportation, medical assistance, mental health, adaptive and assistive equipment, and emergency assistance. These, too, are procured as part of the service agency's long-term role.

3. Systems-Level Case Manager A number of years ago, the author (Schalock, 1983) suggested the need for a systems-level case manager that would coordinate service delivery to persons in integrated living and work environments. Conceptually, this person would link person-specific needs to available generic services, with the ITP being the proposed mechanism. Funding for this function is increasingly becoming available through the Title XIX of the Social Security Act Case Management Waiver program.

Employee Assistance Programs

An EAP is a structural approach for problem solving to help employees return to productive and efficient levels of job performance. The first programs were started to help employees with alcohol problems that were affecting their job performance; currently, EAPs are concerned with drugs as well as other health and social problems. EAPs are voluntarily created and are run either internally by the company or externally by a private contractor. The term *broad brush EAP* has recently been coined to emphasize that the program works with all types of problems and needs (Hacker, 1986). (See Chapter 19, in this volume, for a detailed discussion of EAPs and their potential for developmentally disabled workers.)

The challenge to human services workers over the next few years is to develop incentives and intersector arrangements whereby industry and/or EAPs can either contract with or procure the long-term job-related needs of employees with disabilities. These long-term needs relate to the factors listed in Table 10.3 that either enhance or impair long-term job tenure. A number of incentives and intersector arrangements are briefly discussed below.

1. Incentives Other chapters in this book stress the importance of providing incentives to both hire and maintain employment for persons with disabilities. These incentives can be "marketed" to provide the *initial job opportunity,* but are insufficient to provide the *long-term incentives* that should ideally come from the employer's desire to maintain a valued employee. But that desire may be insufficient to cover the EAP costs of providing or procuring the appropriate counseling, treatment, and support services, for which the company may pay in whole or in part. Thus, one needs to ensure, if necessary, partial payment through third-party insurance, entitlement programs or employer-based insurance coverage.

2. *Intersector Arrangements* The 1986 Amendments to the Rehabilitation Act (PL 99-506) authorized grants to assist states in developing collaborative programs with appropriate public agencies and private nonprofit organizations for training and for traditionally time-limited postemployment services leading to supported employment for individuals with severe handicaps. According to the act, services that might be provided include, but are not limited to:

An evaluation of rehabilitation potential

Provision of skilled trainers who accompany the worker for intensive on-the-job training, systematic training, job development, and follow-up services

Regular observation or supervision of the individual with severe handicaps at the training site

Other services needed to support the individual in employment

As an example of how one might use intersector arrangements, the author has recently been involved in an intersector group, including public schools, community-based mental retardation programs, and vocational rehabilitation that were recently incorporated to provide and train job coaches for recently placed supported employment workers. The corporation is also planning to contract with a number of local EAPs to provide the more long-term job-related services needed by these workers.

Thus, transitioning employees from short-term to long-term employment status requires the development of community support programs and the active involvement of employee assistance programs. A possible relationship between these programs and the long-term employee is diagrammed in Figure 10.2.

SUMMARY

In summary, this chapter has focused on the need to extend person-environment analysis from its current short-term perspective to a long-term perspective that enhances a person's job tenure. To that end, the chapter has stressed the importance of this short-term/long-term distinction, has reviewed the current approaches to person-environment analysis, has suggested that one needs to analyze both the person-environment and the program-environment congruence, and has outlined a model that will permit the long-term employee with disabilities to interface with both community support and employee assistance programs.

Our society is entering a new era in its consideration of economics, industry, and disability. It is a challenging era and one that will require creative technology related to marketing and servicing the customer. At the

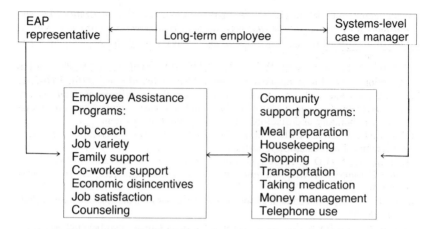

Figure 10.2. Relationship between community support and employee assistance programs and the long-term employee with disabilities.

heart of that technology is the product, the employee with disabilities whose long-term needs, capabilities, and environmental requirements cannot be overlooked.

REFERENCES

Bem, D.J., & Lord, C.G. (1979). Template matching: A proposal for probing the ecological validity of experimental settings in social psychology. *Journal of Personality and Social Psychology, 37,* 833–846.

Boles, S., Walker, H., Schalock, R., Zouck, E., & Griggs, P. (1987). *EEO match scale and program capacity checklist: Field test versions.* Eugene: University of Oregon, Center on Human Development–College of Education.

Carcagno, G.J., Brown, R.S., Kemper, P., Thornton, C., Will, J., & Davies, M. (1986). *The evaluation of the national long-term care demonstration.* Princeton, NJ: Mathematica Policy Research.

Cone, J.D., Bourland, G., & Wood-Sherman, S. (1986). Template matching: An objective approach to placing clients in appropriate residential services. *Journal of the Association for Persons with Severe Handicaps, 11*(2), 110–117.

Conley, R.W. (1986). Employment of developmentally disabled persons: Obstacles inherent in the service system. *Remedial and Special Education, 7*(6), 31–36.

Conyne, R.K., & Clack, R.J. (1981). *Environmental assessment and design: A new tool for the applied behavioral scientist.* New York: Praeger.

French, H., Rogers, W., & Cobb, S. (1974). Adjustment as person-environment fit. In G. Coelho, D. Hamburg, & J. Adams (Eds.), *Coping and adaptation* (pp. 150–186). New York: Basic Books.

Hacker, C. (1986). *EAP: Employee assistance programs in the public schools.* Washington, DC: National Education Association.

Hill, J., Hill, M., Wehman, R., Banks, P.D., Britt, C., & Pendleton, P. (1985). Demographic analysis related to job retention of competitively employed persons with mental retardation. In P. Wehman & J.W. Hill (Eds.), *Competitive employment for persons with mental retardation: From research to practice* (Vol. 1, pp. 74–87). Richmond: Virginia Commonwealth University, Rehabilitation Research and Training Center.

Hill, J.W., Wehman, P., Hill, M., & Goodall, P. (1987). Differential reasons for job separation of previously employed persons. *Mental Retardation, 24*(6), 347–351.

Lemke, S., Moos, R., Mehren, B., & Gauvain, M. (1979). *Multi-phasic Environmental Assessment Procedure (MEAP): Handbook for users.* Palo Alto, Ca: Social Ecology Laboratory and Stanford University School of Medicine.

Meyer, L.H., & Evans, I.M. (1986). Modification of excess behavior: An adaptive and functional approach for educational and community contexts. In R.H. Horner, L.H. Meyer, & H.D.B. Fredericks (Eds.), *Education of learners with severe handicaps: Exemplary service strategies* (pp. 315–350). Baltimore: Paul H. Brookes Publishing Co.

Moos, R. (1973). Conceptualizations of human environments. *American Psychologist, 28,* 652–655.

Moos, R. (1979). Improving social settings by social climate involvement and feedback. In R. Munoz, L. Snowden, J. Kelly, & Associates (Eds.), *Social and psychological research in community settings* (pp. 145–182). Palo Alto, CA: National Press Books.

Moos, R., & Insel, P. (1974). *Issues in social ecology.* Palo Alto, CA: National Press Books.

Schalock, R.L. (1983). *Services for the developmentally disabled adult: Development, implementation, and evaluation.* Austin, TX: PRO-ED.

Schalock, R.L., Harper, R.S., & Carver, G. (1981). Independent living placement: Five years later. *American Journal of Mental Deficiency, 86*(2), 170–177.

Schalock, R.L., & Jensen, C.M. (1986). Assessing the goodness-of-fit between persons and their environments. *Journal of the Association for Persons with Severe Handicaps, 11*(2), 103–109.

Schalock, R.L., Johnson, D.L., & Schik, T. (1985). *Employment screening test and standardization manual.* Hastings: Mid-Nebraska Mental Retardation Services.

Schalock, R.L., & Koehler, R.S. (1984). *Ecobehavioral analysis and augmentative habilitation techniques.* Hastings: Mid-Nebraska Mental Retardation Services.

Schalock, R.L., & Lilley, M.A. (1986). Placement from community based mental retardation programs: How well do clients do after 8–10 years? *American Journal of Mental Deficiency, 90*(6), 669–676.

Steele, F. (1973). *Physical settings and organization development.* Reading, MA: Addison-Wesley.

Stroul, B.A. (1984). *Toward community support systems for the mentally disabled: The NIMH community support programs.* Boston: Boston University Center for Rehabilitation Research and Training in Mental Health.

Stroul, B.A. (1986). *Models of community support services: Approaches to helping persons with long-term mental illness.* Boston: Boston University Center for Psychiatric Rehabilitation, Sargent College of Allied Health Professions.

11

Job Accommodation
in the Workplace

Barbara T. Judy

Any look ahead into the world of work for persons with disabilities must include an overview of job accommodation. Based on a thorough job analysis, jobs and work environments can be molded to fit the capabilities of workers and thereby benefit both employees and employers. This chapter presents an overview of job accommodations and of one service, the Job Accommodation Network (JAN), that provides free advice and technical assistance to counselors and employers when hiring or retaining disabled employees.

Labor market studies reviewed previously (see Chapter 1) demonstrate that the work force by the year 2000 will comprise workers who are older and probably more disabled. These data indicate clearly that there will be an increasing need to make adjustments in current practices regarding work environments in order to adapt to the changing population of available workers. An equally important outcome of this anticipated trend is the fact that opportunities have never been greater for meaningful employment for persons who experience some degree of physical or mental functional limitations.

If these opportunities are to become a reality, vocational and other rehabilitation personnel, plus employers, need to be aware of what job accommodation is and what it entails; they need to be apprised of the legislative basis for job accommodation; they need to know the incentives that can accrue to the employer for accommodating the workplace; and they need to be familiar with the help that is available to counselors and employers when hiring or retaining disabled employees. Each of these areas is addressed, respectively, in the four sections of this chapter. Although not discussed in detail here, the reader should recognize the importance of a good job analysis that provides a basis for understanding and implementing necessary accommodations. For more details regarding functional job analyses, see Judy (1987) or Mcloughlin, Garner, and Callahan (1987, chap. 12).

OVERVIEW OF JOB ACCOMMODATION

The practice of job accommodation is not new, for indeed "mankind has always reached for new ways to lighten the burden of work and make himself more productive" (McCray, 1987, p. 5). However, it is important to realize that, historically, most accommodations have been made with the needs of the average, everyday worker in mind. Thus, until recently it was rare to see job accommodations being made at the job site to enable "unemployable workers" to function successfully. In most cases,

> the handicapped individual was expected to find a less demanding, often menial job which better suited his supposed limitations. Little wonder then that stereotypes of blind men selling pencils on street corners, lame beggars, hunchbacks ringing church bells and other similar images evolved. What is perhaps even more unfortunate, however, is that many of these stereotypes and assumptions about the kinds of work people with handicaps can and cannot do persist in our culture even today. (McCray, 1987, p. 6)

However, attitudes are beginning to change regarding the work potential of persons with disabilities. Part of this change is due to advanced technology and, as discussed in the next section, part is due to legislative and fiscal incentives. One of the technological changes that has contributed to both attitudinal changes and job accommodation is the use of functional job analyses, which involve a detailed description of all of the tasks or operations required in a specific job, a listing of the duties and responsibilities of the position, and a summary of the environmental conditions in which the work takes place (Fera, 1984). Components of a functional job analysis (Judy, 1987) include:

Specific tasks to be performed
Processes and procedures required
Time factors
Environmental factors
Human relationships

Job accommodation has many different definitions. For example, while the Rehabilitation Act of 1973 (PL 93-112) requires that certain employers provide "reasonable accommodations" to qualified handicapped individuals, the regulations do not clearly define what a reasonable accommodation is. Instead, a list of examples of activities that may represent accommodation practice is presented, such as the following, which were issued by the Department of Health, Education, and Welfare, Title 45 of the Code of Federal Regulations, Subpart B, Section 84:12b:

Making facilities used by employees readily accessible to and usable by
    handicapped persons
Job restructuring

Part-time or modified work schedules
Acquisition or modification of equipment or devices
The provision of readers or interpreters
Other similar actions

A useful definition, which will be used throughout this chapter, was provided by Berkeley Planning Associates (1982), who stated that accommodations

> include the full range of adaptations or adjustments that make a worksite or job more suited to the needs and abilities of a handicapped worker. Accommodations include all modifications of work environment, job content, or work procedures that enable handicapped workers to compete equally for jobs with nonhandicapped workers. In some cases, accommodations are necessary for an individual to perform essential functions of his or her job. In other cases they enable handicapped workers to work more easily or more productively, or they expand the range of jobs an individual can perform. (pp. 2–3)

Table 11.1 summarizes some of the more common types of accommodations. Five types of accommodations are listed, including those involving the worksite, work station, work environment, job restructuring, and work ac-

Table 11.1. Common types of job accommodations

Worksite

Ramps	Flooring
Elevators	Restrooms
Doors	Enlarged working areas

Work Station

Adjustable desks and tables
Lighting
Equipment that includes speech, alternate input for motor impairment, moving work areas to benefit workers in wheelchairs

Work Environment

Heat/cold/noise/pollution controls
Reduced distractions
Safety from chemicals and radiation
Safety from productivity rate stress
Rest areas

Job Restructuring

Task reassignment
Reevaluation of tasks to update methods
Combining jobs to redesign total method of accomplishing goal
Job sharing

Work Activities Modification

Flex time (days), hours, or shifts
Alteration of break/rest periods

tivities modification. A different job accommodation classification system (McCray, 1987) might include:

Environmental accommodations, such as improved lighting, improved ventilation, and reduction of temperature changes

Physical accommodations, such as the use of adjustable tables, relocation of switches, and use of interchangeable light or sound signals

Minor worksite modifications, such as process flow modifications, rearrangement of equipment or machines, and organizational restructuring

Job restructuring, including task modifications, task eliminations (entirely or in part), task reassignments or recombinations of tasks to provide additional employment opportunities at lower skill levels, creation of additional needed promotional lines, provision of job enrichment, and the meeting of specific needs of disabled employees or qualified disabled job applicants

Other, such as use of flexible hours, compressed work weeks, and part-time helpers or aids

Regardless of how one classifies job accommodations, the key point is that each accommodation should address the unique needs of the worker and the demands of the job. Furthermore, accommodations are generally made for a number of different reasons, including those listed in Table 11.2.

LEGISLATIVE BASIS

The major legislative basis for job accommodation comes from Sections 503 and 504 of the Rehabilitation Act of 1973 (PL 93-112). Section 504, for example, states that

Table 11.2. Reasons for making job accommodations

1. For incumbent employees who are newly handicapped and seeking to return to work

2. For incumbent handicapped employees who, because of promotion, transfer, deterioration in their handicap, or other factors, require new accommodations

3. To comply with Sections 501, 503, and 504 of the Rehabilitation Act of 1973 or with Section 402 of the Vietnam Era Veterans Readjustment Assistance Act of 1974, which require the provision of accommodations to qualified handicapped persons

4. To increase access to employment opportunities for qualified handicapped job applicants

5. To provide benefit to business on a formal basis when accommodations are carefully documented and costs are analyzed

6. To provide benefit to business when relatively minor accommodations are needed and can be installed fairly quickly and easily

Adapted from McCray (1987).

no otherwise qualified handicapped individual—shall solely by reason of his handicap be excluded from the participation in, be denied the benefits of, or be subject to discrimination under any program or activity securing financial assistance.

Section 503 requires affirmative action of all public and private contractors of the federal government when the contract is in excess of $2,500. Contractors and subcontractors having contracts of $50,000 or more and 50 or more employees are required to specify and follow an affirmative action program. As employers, the recipients of federal funds must make reasonable accommodation to the handicaps of applicants and employees, unless the accommodation would cause the employer undue hardship.

Regulations issued May 4, 1977, give the mandate on reasonable accommodation as follows:

A recipient shall make reasonable accommodation to the known physical or mental limitations of an otherwise qualified handicapped applicant or employee unless the recipient can demonstrate that the accommodation would impose an undue hardship on the operation of the program.

Reasonable accommodation may include making facilities readily accessible to and usable by handicapped persons, and job restructuring, part-time or modified schedules, acquisition or modification of equipment or devices, the provision of readers or interpreters, and other similar actions. (Title 45 of the Code of Federal Regulations, Subpart B, Section 84.12)

Undue hardships are defined to give guidance to the employers in their consideration of what is a reasonable accommodation: 1) the overall size of the recipient's program with respect to the number of employees, number and type of facilities, and size of budget; 2) the type of the recipient's operation with respect to number and type of facilities and size of budget; and 3) the nature and cost of the accommodation needed.

The 1977 regulations further mandate program accessibility through the statement that "no qualified handicapped persons shall, because a recipient's facilities are inaccessible to or unusable by handicapped persons, be denied the benefits of, be excluded from participation in or otherwise be subject to discrimination under any program or activity to which this part applies" (Schwab & Buskey, 1987).

Thus *accessibility* to a program, activity, or building becomes the crux of reasonable accommodation. It includes one or more of the following (Wright, 1980):

Redesigning equipment
Reassigning meetings to accessible places
Providing transportation
Making aids available
Being able to circulate easily within the person's microenvironment of work
Caring for personal hygienic needs
Maintaining privacy

EMPLOYER INCENTIVES

Many employers are uninformed about job accommodation and its potential benefits to them. The general benefits include an increase in productivity, a safer and more efficient job site, and increased independence and productivity by the disabled worker (Schwab & Buskey, 1987). There are undoubtedly many reasons for being uninformed, but the most important ones include (McCray, 1987):

Employers with small staffs who often lack sufficient human relations resources to pay adequate attention to the issue
Vocational rehabilitation professionals who lack formal training in the area
Lack of enforcement by the office of Federal Contract Compliance programs within the U.S. Department of Labor because of personnel shortages and difficulties in interpreting the law

The major incentives for employers to do job accommodation involve increased worker productivity and potential tax deductions. Indeed, an increasing body of evidence from employers seems to suggest that they are strongly supporting the practice of job accommodation (McCray, 1987).

Berkeley Planning Associates (1982) found, for example, that employers viewed increased efforts on the part of rehabilitation counselors to promote job accommodation procedures as an important incentive to them to expand their accommodation efforts, because of the anticipated increase in productivity following the accommodations. In addition, the tax deduction for businesses that make their facilities or public transportation vehicles more accessible to and usable by handicapped or elderly persons has been made permanent and retroactive to December 31, 1985. The maximum that can be deducted is $35,000 for the tax year in which the expense was incurred. The deduction is claimed by identifying it as a separate item when reporting other standard business expenses to the IRS. Any amount in excess of the $35,000 may be added to the basis of the property that is subject to depreciation. However, in order for the expenses to be deductible, standards reflective of those summarized in Table 11.3 must be met.

THE JOB ACCOMMODATION NETWORK

A service that has been developed in an effort to assist employers in making accommodations or modifications for their employees is the Job Accommodation Network (JAN). For years, members of the Employers' Committee of the President's Committee on Employment of the Handicapped had discussed ways of offering assistance to other employers who were interested in hiring persons with disabilities. They believed that many employers were making accommodations, but that very little of this information was shared with

Table 11.3. Exemplary standards that must be met for accommodation expenses to be deductible[a]

Grading

The grading of ground must reach the level of a normal entrance to make a facility accessible to people with physical disabilities.

Walks

A public walk must be at least 48 inches wide and must not slope more than 5%. A walk of maximum or near maximum steepness that is fairly long must have level areas at regular intervals. A walk or driveway must have a nonslip surface.

Parking Lots

At least one parking space that is near a facility must be set aside and marked for use by handicapped people.

Ramps

A ramp, which must have a nonslip surface, must not slope more than 1 inch for each foot of length. The ramp must have at least one handrail that is 32 inches high, measured from the surface of the ramp. The handrail must be smooth and must extend at least 1 foot past the top and bottom of the ramp. However, this does not require a handrail extension, which is itself a hazard.

Entrances

A building must have at least one main entrance that is usable by people in wheelchairs. The entrance must be on a level accessible to an elevator.

Doors and Doorways

A door must have a clear opening at least 32 inches wide and must be operable by a single effort. The floor on the inside and outside of a doorway must be level for at least 5 feet from the door in the direction the door swings and must extend at least 1 foot past the opening side of the doorway.

Stairs

Stairsteps must have round nosing of between a 1 and $1\frac{1}{2}$ inch radius. Each step must not be more than 7 inches high.

Floors

Floors must have a nonslip surface. Floors on each story of a building must be on the same level or must be connected by a ramp, as discussed previously.

Toilet Rooms

A toilet room must have enough space for people in wheelchairs.

Water Fountains

A water fountain or cooler must have up-front spouts and controls and must be hand operated or hand and foot operated.

Public Telephones

A public telephone must be placed so that the dial and headset can be reached by people in wheelchairs. The public telephone must be equipped for those with hearing disabilities and be so identified with instructions for use.

(continued)

Table 11.3. *(continued)*

Elevators

An elevator must be accessible to, and usable by, handicapped people and the elderly on the levels they use to enter the building and all levels and areas normally used.

Controls

Switches and controls for light, heat, ventilation, windows, draperies, fire alarms, and all similar controls that are needed or used often must be placed within the reach of people in wheelchairs. These switches and controls must not be higher than 48 inches from the floor.

Markings

Raised letters or numbers must be used to mark rooms and offices. These markings must be placed on the wall to the right or left of the door at a height of 54 inches from the floor.

Warning Signals

An audible warning signal must be accompanied by a simultaneous visual signal for the benefit of those with hearing disabilities. A visual warning signal must be accompanied by a simultaneous audible signal for the benefit of blind persons.

Hazards

Hanging signs, ceiling lights, and similar objects and fixtures must be at least 7 feet from the floor.

International Accessibility Symbol

The international accessibility symbol must be displayed on routes to and at wheelchair-accessible entrances to facilities and public transportation vehicles.

[a]This is not a complete listing of all the standards and their associated criteria. A complete listing is available from the United States Commission on Civil Rights (1983).

others. They devised a plan to establish a location where such knowledge could be collected, classified, and later disseminated to employers who had similar needs. The concept included the use of consultants who would respond to telephone requests from employers who were seeking information about practical ways to accommodate an individual in a work environment.

With funding by the National Institute of Handicapped Research and later by the Rehabilitation Services Administration, the West Virginia Research and Training Center in Morgantown became the site at which JAN's services were established. The system, which began receiving calls in July, 1984, has become an information network and consulting service for employers, for rehabilitation professionals, and for other similar resource agencies providing field-tested solutions of ways to accommodate individuals with functional limitations. In 1987, 1,923 companies took advantage of JAN's informational services. As of early 1988, calls to JAN numbered well over 8,800. An unpublished Job Accommodation Network Evaluation Study conducted in March, 1987, found that of those who have called, 95% felt that the service provided was extremely helpful.

JAN looks at the manner in which an individual's functional limitation relates to a specific job task. This permits network users to concentrate not on job accommodation. In addition, society as a whole can reap enormous economic and social benefits through the application of job accommodation the disability but on the specific limitation with which they must be concerned in an employment situation.

The information available from JAN consists of descriptions of solutions acquired from employers across the nation who have made accommodations in their businesses, from materials provided by various manufacturers and distributors of products that are used in the workplace, from organizations or special interest groups who provide data and information for a specific population, and from a network of consultants throughout the nation who have or can provide individualized attention to a need.

JAN is available nationwide by means of a toll-free number (1-800-JAN-PCEH or, in West Virginia, 1-800-JAN-INWV) by both voice or TDD from 8:00 A.M. to 8:00 P.M. ET or on evenings or weekends by a telephone message service. While there is no fee for the use of JAN, users are asked to provide information about accommodations they have made to the network in order that it can be shared with other callers. Information requested will be provided by telephone or by mail. If the consultants do not have the desired information, the caller will be given suggestions of other resources that might be of assistance. The JAN service, then, is based on the concept of functional job analysis and has, even in its short existence, been helpful to many employers nationwide in their accommodation efforts.

In addition to JAN, other services are increasingly becoming available and are being implemented regarding job accommodation. One is the Clearinghouse on Computer Accommodation (COCA), which has been instituted within the U.S. General Services Administration. This service provides ongoing technical assistance to agencies in the area of hardware and software that can solve accommodation problems; short-term staff training; and a variety of other services. In addition, the Rehabilitation Services Administration has begun to provide more training in job accommodation techniques, including training in basic engineering and technology. Examples include augmentative or assistive devices, redesign of work stations, and job restructuring. The more important principles (Schwab & Buskey, 1987) involved in this training include:

The adjustment must meet an identified need in assisting the worker to do the job, which may include conserving energy.
The adjustment must be socially acceptable; that is, it cannot differ too radically from the way normal persons perform the task.

The adjustment must have both employee and employer acceptance.
There must be a favorable cost-profit ratio between the cost of the adjustment and the increase in worker efficiency and benefit of having a stable employee.

In conclusion, both the employee and the employer stand to gain from principles and practices. This benefit is well summarized by McCray (1987), who states:

> disabled individuals who become productive workers return millions of dollars in benefits, through the form of taxes, in economy each year. If these benefits are not in and of themselves substantial enough to warrant the expansion of proven return-to-work practices such as job accommodation, the "human factor" certainly is. For like anyone, disabled people, no matter how severe their disability, desire independence and opportunity. Job accommodation strategies offer each of them, as well as prospective employers and helping professionals one more weapon for achieving these important societal values. (p. 16)

REFERENCES

Berkeley Planning Associates. (1982). *Study of accommodations provided by federal contractors: Final report (Vol. 1); Study findings (Vol. 2); Ten case studies.* Prepared for the U.S. Department of Labor, Employment Standards Administration. Washington, DC: U.S. Department of Labor, Employment Standards Administration.

Fera, D.M. (Ed.). (1984). *Handicapped requirements handbook.* Washington, DC: Federal Programs Advisory Service.

Judy, B.T. (1987). Functional job analysis. In F.T. Waterman (Ed.), *Job match: Together for good business* (Module 111, pp. 13–29). Omaha, NE: Center for Applied Urban Research.

McCray, P.M. (1987). *The job accommodation handbook.* Verndale, MN: RPM Press.

Mcloughlin, C.S., Garner, J.B., & Callahan, M. (1987). *Getting employed, staying employed: Job development and training for persons with severe handicaps.* Baltimore: Paul H. Brookes Publishing Co.

Schwab, L., & Buskey, J. (1987). Adapting the workplace. In F.T. Waterman (Ed.), *Job match: Together for good business* (Module 111, pp. 51–80). Omaha, NE: Center for Applied Urban Research.

Title 45 of the Code of Federal Regulations, Subpart B, Section 84.12, U.S. Department of Health, Education, and Welfare.

United States Commission on Civil Rights. (1983). *Accommodating the spectrum of individual abilities.* Washington, DC: U.S. Government Printing Office.

Wright, G.N. (1980). *Total rehabilitation.* Boston: Little, Brown.

12

Using Applied Technology to Enhance Work Opportunities for Persons with Severe Physical Disabilities

Howard Shane and Gary Roberts

Before the advent of computers and other technical writing or data entry devices, few persons with severe physical disabilities were able to create text. Generally, writing was restricted to those individuals who, despite physical disabilities, had sufficient head or extremity control to manipulate a pen or pencil in order to write. The physical parameters of a keyboard—including its overall size, keypad dimensions, the pressure needed to operate it, and so forth—or the coordination needed to control a writing implement prevented many persons with severe physical disabilities from striking keys (typing) or moving a pen or pencil (writing). For the majority of such persons, therefore, creating text was an unattainable skill. It was also the case that for individuals who could access a keyboard or hold a writing implement (and who were also literate), the rate at which they generally were able to do so was so slow that the application of that skill for competitive work was highly improbable.

Prior to the introduction of computers and computer-based work stations, few techniques and strategies existed for giving persons with severe physical disabilities sufficient manual control even to consider a vocational future. The computer and related peripherals (which enhance the opportunity for accessing technology), however, provided an innovative and potentially productive tool for such persons. The emergence of the "Information Age" in Western society, which allowed the control and manipulation of information and data, greatly improved the chances of finding employment for persons who in the past would have been considered ineligible. This chapter discusses work opportunities for severely disabled persons, through computer literacy and keyboard control (whether by normal operation or alternative methods). Included is a description and classification of the severely disabled population, evaluation and rate enhancement techniques, writing and keyboard accessing methods, and vocational implications.

POPULATION OVERVIEW

Limitations in manual control occur in a variety of disabling conditions. Table 12.1 contains a classification of diseases that can lead to writing or keyboard accessing disorders specified as a function of a neurological disorder, a central or peripheral nervous system disorder, or as a musculoskeletal problem. Also included in the table are notations of nature of onset for each disorder (congenital or acquired) and the status of the disorder (progressive or nonprogressive). A considerable number of disorders classified as writing impaired have an acquired basis. However, the large number of persons with writing impairment within the congenital cerebral palsy grouping suggests that in terms of total number of cases there may be as many persons with a congenital writing impairment as an acquired one.

Progressive conditions require that a flexible intervention approach be taken. Flexibility here is in terms of the methods used to accommodate the changes that occur as the condition progresses. Furthermore, acquired writing disorders that are progressive in nature and have a neurological basis are often accompanied by declining speech and regression in upper extremity control and function. Whatever the origin of the limitation, the results are the same: The person cannot manipulate the environment with ease, resulting in disturbances to activities of daily living and vocational opportunity. In summary, the persons considered here experience difficulty with the mechanics of writing, relating to a central or peripheral neurological impairment or structural abnormality, all of which adversely affect the ability to generate written text or access a keyboard.

ENHANCED WRITING AND
KEYBOARD ACCESSING OPPORTUNITIES

It has become increasingly clear that techniques used to augment conversation and oral message transmission for the person who is nonspeaking pose analogous intervention dilemmas for individuals who are nonmanual, rendering them unable to write, access computers, or both. For the purposes of this chapter, these individuals are referred to as "nonmanual." The nonmanual person experiences a reduced capacity to control hands, arms, or shoulder movements owing to a congenital disorder, acquired disease, or accident.

Table 12.1. Common etiologies underlying severe writing, typing, and computer access disorders

Classification	Diagnosis	Nature of onset	Degree of progression
Neurological	Cerebral palsy	Congenital	Nonprogressive
Central nervous system	Amyotrophic lateral sclerosis	Acquired	Progressive
	Multiple sclerosis	Acquired	Progressive
	Cerebral vascular accident	Acquired	Nonprogressive
Peripheral nervous system	Myasthenia gravis	Acquired	Progressive
	Guillain Barré syndrome	Acquired	Progressive to resolution
	Spinal cord injury	Acquired	Nonprogressive
	Werdnig Hoffman disease	Acquired	Progressive
	Cerebral vascular accident	Acquired	Nonprogressive
Musculoskeletal system	Juvenile rheumatoid arthritis	Congenital	Progressive
	Arthrogryposis	Congenital	Nonprogressive
	Muscular dystrophy	Congenital	Progressive
	Fibrositis	Acquired	Progressive
	Congenital limb anomalies	Congenital	Nonprogressive
	Amputation (traumatic or surgical)	Acquired	Nonprogressive

Consequently, assistance is needed in carrying out activities of daily living (ADLs), independent living (IL activities), and/or work activities. This individual is forced into the position of relying on personal care assistants, health aides, and friends in order to fulfill ADL and IL functions.

In the vocational areas, manual function is of critical importance. A survey of the Sunday newspaper help-wanted pages yields few, if any, jobs that do not require some manual control. A telephone operator, for example, must be able to access a switchboard or a computer terminal in order to perform the job duties. Similarly, a clerk must be able to handle files and operate office machinery. And a vocational counselor is responsible for writing contact notes and correspondence.

Impaired written communication is typically associated with nonmanual individuals. This includes persons with mild writing impairments, often characterized by poor legibility, or a reduced rate of expression, as well as more severe written output disorders in which little or no writing is possible. This chapter emphasizes persons who experience a mechanical impairment of writing and not a developmental or literacy problem or specific language-based writing disorder. The typical person under consideration, therefore, is one for whom the mechanical aspects of writing are tedious, result in illegibility, or are impossible to execute. This individual may, or may not, be able to speak functionally; thus, written output is, in some cases, the principle output medium for conversation. For others with normal or near-normal speech but impaired ability to write, the ability to generate text can and will offer extensive opportunities for personal, educational, and vocational growth.

Alphanumeric text often becomes, out of necessity, a principle output medium for conducting a conversation. This becomes an especially powerful option when a brain injury or degenerative neurological disease abolishes previously normal speech. It is often the case, however, that a previously normal oral communicator, when faced with the choice of selecting output to substitute for a severe expressive speech impairment, will avoid an artificial voice alternative in favor of written text—albeit text that appears on a monitor screen, computer printout, typewritten letter, or handwritten record.

The inability to produce written material, whether through the use of handwritten notation or an advanced assistive device, is a major obstacle to personal independence. For the person who has severe physical disabilities and whose manual capacities are limited, the ability to write (and access keyboards or other data input instruments) greatly enhances his or her vocational potential. Furthermore, when a person with a disability is able to control an assistive device, job opportunities are greatly expanded. With the current availability of assistive devices that enable keyboard accessibility, and in the presence of a high demand for skilled personnel to operate computers, any job that requires computer operation might be thought of as a possible vocational option for a person who is nonmanual.

EVALUATION: A DETERMINATION OF ABILITIES AND NEEDS

Because of the diversity of abilities and needs of the severely disabled population, no one computer, computer accessing technique, or combination of techniques is suitable for all potential users. Thus, a systematic manner for determining the most appropriate systems and techniques must be identified. The selected method should result from a thorough evaluation, including an assessment of the individual's physical and psycholinguistic abilities as well as vocational history, aptitude, and needs. The assessment process is aimed at identifying those techniques that will allow an individual to generate text or input data in the fastest manner, for the longest amount of time, and with the least amount of effort. The individual's vocational interest (as discussed later in this chapter) and needs must also be considered as a key component of the evaluation process. Following are a number of aspects to consider in the evaluation process.

1. *Sensory Status* The evaluation process should begin with a screening of the individual's sensory status, since hearing and vision can significantly influence performance and, thus, the outcome of the entire evaluation process. Declining vision, for example, often a concomitant problem of multiple sclerosis, can affect the text size that can be read; thus, the software and hardware need to accommodate the sensory deficit that accompanies the disease.

2. *Seating and Positioning* Like sensory status, seating and positioning can profoundly influence job performance, albeit indirectly. Proper seating and positioning of the individual and the manner in which materials are positioned or placed before him or her are critical in gaining a realistic understanding of overall motor capability. The concept of seating and positioning goes beyond what is needed for evaluation or personal comfort purposes and looks at work capacity. Whether it is a home-based or a traditional worksite, the manner in which the work space is arranged and the individual seated within it will ultimately affect job performance. A well-conceived work space should improve job performance, as well as minimize fatigue, thus maximizing output.

3. *Control Site Evaluation* As a rule of thumb, no person should be considered too physically disabled to access a computer and use it as a tool for writing or other work-related tasks. This is not to say, however, that the rate of text creation or data input would necessarily be sufficient to allow the individual to perform satisfactorily in a work setting in which rate is tied to job success. The aim of the control site evaluation is to identify methods of input or means to facilitate writing that an individual can perform reliably, with consistency, and with minimal fatigue. Generally, several control and accessing routines are identified as potentially viable. Those sites will vary according to the unique abilities and needs of the user. Control can range from typical keyboard operation, with minimal or no modification, to control of the computer by elaborate and highly sophisticated equipment.

A great deal of clinical activity and research effort is directed at determining effective and practical methods by which to interface computers with persons who experience severe physical disabilities (Burkhead, Sampson, & McMahon, 1986). An ideal person-to-machine match is one in which the user can operate the computer as a vocational, educational, recreational, or personal tool. As such, the computer can enhance personal independence.

Typically, the effort to match persons with computers attempts to identify efficient and reliable techniques and strategies to enable persons who evidence a variety of disabling conditions that originate at birth or are acquired later in life to operate a computer. Preferably, the method or methods selected to interface an individual with the computer should offer the greatest amount of alphanumeric input given the least amount of physical effort.

4. Overview of Accessing Methods   Many ingenious high-technology solutions are now available to facilitate the link between the operator and the computer. In some cases control of the keyboard by a disabled operator is accomplished through the use of a substitute keyboard that is expanded or reduced in size or one in which repeat function is dismantled. The performance of a keyboard may also be emulated (simulated) through a number of peripheral hardware options (e.g., Computer Entry Terminal—a Prentke Romich Company product; or a Tetra Scan, made by Zygo Industries) or through firmware such as the Adaptive Firmware card (an Adaptive Peripherals product). Some applications are fully "transparent," allowing the operator to emulate all functions normally performed by the computer's standard keyboard, while other applications are only partially transparent, resulting in more limited operational capability. Appliances as simple as a keyguard (i.e., a shield containing holes corresponding to the keypad), hand splint, or pointer (generally attached to an appendage or to the forehead or chin, or inserted in the mouth) also enable effective access to and efficient operation of the computer. These low-technology solutions can be as powerful for certain operators as some of the high-technology solutions.

Methods currently exist to control the computer using a variety of physical movements, electrical impulses, or pneumatics. Switches located on or off the body, for example, can be activated by slight or gross movement of appendages, the trunk, or the head. Also controlled eye movement, muscle action potential, and respiratory activity can be calibrated to allow access and control of the computer. The essential ingredient in effective control is that the individual must be able to activate a targeted movement or impulse consistently, reliably, and without undue fatigue.

5. Computer Literacy   Computer use for writing, data entry, or other work-related applications requires a level of computer literacy that will vary according to the requirements of the job under consideration. As a rule, the greater the computer literacy required, the greater the extent to which the computer will be utilized on the job. A review of ''The Computer Access and Literacy Curriculum'' developed at Children's Hospital, Boston, for preparing persons with physical disabilities to use the computer as a work tool reveals that word processing and data-base management are important requirements to the majority of entry-level trainees, and knowledge of a computer disc operating system sets the stage for the trainee to perform other computer-related work applications.

The faster the rate at which an individual can enter or manipulate data into a computer or general text by hand, typewriter, or word processor, the greater the vocational opportunity and/or potential for academic success. Greater rate also increases the likelihood that the person will be willing or able to write in order to achieve personal independence.

6. *Rate Enhancement Techniques* The enhancement of writing, typing, and/or keyboard entry rate is usually accelerated in two ways:

1. Improved accessing routines (IAR)
2. Linguistic acceleration techniques (LAT)

In addition, normal factors such as rehearsal, instruction, and maturation also contribute to faster writing, typing, and data entry rates.

Improved accessing routines or the rate of input can be greatly accelerated by the manner in which a person accesses a writing or data entry device. Furthermore, rate of access can be enhanced using low- and/or high-technology techniques and solutions. Table 12.2 lists low-technology solutions meant to accelerate the rate at which an individual can generate text or input data. These methods and techniques improve rate indirectly because they improve accuracy of key selection, which in turn allows the user either to

Table 12.2. Low-technology solutions that enhance writing or keyboard access

Technique	Way in which technique enhances access
Seating/positioning	Decreases tone Improves visualization of material
Positioning of materials	Improves visualization of material Improves accuracy of selection
Splinting	Improves accuracy of selection Enables single key activation
Keyguard	Improves accuracy of selection Prevents inadvertent key selections Potentially decreases extremity fatigue
Pointers	Enables single key activation Enables use of alternate control areas

move faster or to move with greater accuracy. In either case, the result is overall improvement in rate. High-technology solutions also used to accelerate rate are listed in Table 12.3.

It is important to note that the solutions listed in Tables 12.2 and 12.3 are frequently utilized in combination to achieve maximum rate of writing or data entry. Most often, it is the use of one or more of the low-technology solutions in combination with a high-technology technique that brings about the highest rate of access.

The term *linguistic acceleration techniques* refers to the use of artificial intelligence (e.g., prediction schemas), linguistic principles (e.g., abbreviated expansions), or logical order (e.g., arrangement by frequency of occurrence) to reduce the overall number of required keystrokes needed to generate written materials or enter data. Table 12.4 contains a composite of linguistic acceleration techniques.

VOCATIONAL IMPLICATIONS

The ability to write—be it with an advanced assistive device such as a word processor or through handwritten notation—improves the opportunity for personal independence. Furthermore, reliable and efficient writing capability and computer access offer persons with severe physical disabilities greatly enhanced vocational potential. When an individual can effectively operate a computer, job opportunities afforded by this control are expanded. For example, any job that requires computer operation can be considered potentially

Table 12.3. High-technology solutions that enhance writing or keyboard access

Technique	Way in which technique enhances access
Variable size keypad	Accommodates unique movement
One-handed keyboard input	Accommodates movement to optimize one-sided access
Variable input acceptance time	Accommodates movement disturbances (e.g., tremor)
Audible review	Eliminates need to view monitor to verify entry
Infrared technology	Eliminates need to press keypad; allows multiple control site operation
Light pen technology	Allows multiple control site operation
Sonar detection technology	Allows keyboard control by head movement; eliminates need to press keypad
Voice recognition technology	Allows keyboard control by voice

suitable to the individual, disabled or not, who is both familiar with the computer requirements inherent to the job and can operate the computer reliably and efficiently. The positions of programmer, data input specialist, and writer represent some obvious job options suitable to such individuals. Other computer-assisted jobs do not require full-time computer operation or full computer literacy, but are nevertheless suitable for individuals with severe disabilities. Here job success usually demands not only some computer competency but also other essential qualifications such as the physical skills needed to complete the noncomputer tasks.

Within the past 10 years the presence of computers and terminals in the workplace has become an accepted and sometimes expected norm (Growick, 1983; Szeto, Allen, & Rummelhart, 1987; U.S. Department of Labor, 1986). Computer literacy is encouraged in educational settings and may be a requirement for many jobs. This emergence of technology in the workplace has significant bearing upon the employment future of many people with disabilities.

Recently, the Bureau of Labor Statistics in the U.S. Department of Labor noted that the number of jobs involving the use of computers has been steadily increasing in both volume and geographic distribution. Similarly, the semi-skilled labor market is shrinking in comparison to the need for task-specific skilled workers (U.S. Department of Labor, 1986).

Table 12.4. Overview of linguistic acceleration technique options

Technique	Way in which rate is accelerated
Linguistic prediction	Reduces keystrokes by anticipating future letter or word units
Abbreviated expansion	Reduces keystrokes by abbreviation of words or phrases
Semantic compaction	Uses meaning-based symbols to represent words or sentences
Arrangement of material by frequency of occurrence:	
1. Keyboard	Reduces excursion of impaired extremity
2. Materials in scanning array	Reduces time for cursor or pointer to reach most probable location
Retrieval of whole (stored) units:	
1. Glossaries	Minimal keystrokes retrieve whole units of information
2. Dedicated software	Minimal keystrokes retrieve whole units of information
3. Macro solutions	Minimal keystrokes retrieve whole units of information

The employment alternatives for the nonmanual person might be divided into groups: jobs that require the use of the computer as a central element and jobs that may use the computer as an assistive writing device. In the former group, some possible job titles include: data input technician, civil engineer, marketing manager, financial analyst, clerk, personnel benefits specialist, computer programmer, and writer. In the latter category, some job titles are: peer counselor, art therapist, educational administrator, real estate broker, social worker, receptionist, and program director. Whether the worker uses the computer as a primary tool or as an assistive writing device, the essential question remains the same: Can the user control the computer in such a way as to produce material that is both accurate and timely in concurrence with a job's requirements?

Viewing the computer as a tool to effect an action to complete a task can be a reasonable approach. The "tool" concept is the key that allows the nonmanual person to operate within the same work parameters as a non-disabled person. For the rehabilitation professional as well as for the user, this concept serves to demystify the computer as a complex and indecipherable entity and suggests its role as more of an effective device to facilitate job functioning.

Keeping the tool concept in mind, the rehabilitation practitioner can begin to determine the job match by developing a profile of the person's interests, acquired skills, and personality characteristics. The individual's ability to physically perform the functions of the job is not an immediate concern, since the initial step is to investigate jobs that match the person's profile. This task is easier to perform when physical limitations are disregarded temporarily. Once a profile is complete and the job requirements are understood, one then determines whether applied technology can bridge the gap left by the physical limitations. At this point in the job placement process, it may be advisable to refer the individual to a center that is routinely engaged in the selection and application of assistive technology. Following are some technology-related considerations in the job placement process.

1. *Technology in the Workplace*   At times, the introduction of new or different technology into the workplace has a negative effect and this possibility should be considered by the practitioner making the recommendation. Szeto, Allen, & Rummelhart (1987) maintain that successful employment by the worker with a disability is related to the flexibility and willingness of co-workers to accommodate new and different approaches. This assertion places considerable pressure on an employer to alter what may have been a homogeneous workplace in order to accommodate the disabled worker. It is important to emphasize to the employer at the outset the concept of how the new employee will "add to the quality of the workplace" and to deemphasize the notion that this new employee might detract from the work environment.

Fellow employees can become concerned when assistive technology is introduced into a worksite. Efforts should be made to ensure that the equipment does not have the reverse effect of alienating the new employee because normal work routines have been altered. Furthermore, the introduction of a computer into a work area may cause co-workers to become disgruntled or even jealous of the "perks" given to the new (disabled) worker. An effective approach to facilitating acceptance, in this case, might be to present the computer as a tool that enables the new employee to work at a competitive level with (and not necessarily above the level of) able-bodied employees.

It is also crucial to consider carefully the assistive devices that are selected for a person to function within a particular worksite. In addition to being cost conscious and thoughtful about technology's role for an individual worker, it is best to try to select the least obtrusive equipment. In this way the work environment will require the least modification, thus allowing the disabled employee to appear as normal as possible. While job modifications may be possible, it will not always be viable to make extensive modifications in order to effect successful job placement. In all circumstances, the need for and the presence of the adaptive technology should be minimized while the attributes and qualities of the prospective employee should be maximized.

Recently, the authors informally discussed the introduction of computers with six disabled workers who used assistive technology in the workplace. They indicated that their reception by their employers and co-workers had been positive. It was revealed that employer questions generally centered around the funding of the assistive technology. (In the case of these disabled employees, the technology was funded by the state's rehabilitation agency.) Once it was understood that the employers would not have to finance the extra technology, they were more willing to consider employing a disabled person. It is not unusual for a rehabilitation agency to take the position that the assistive device portion of technology (which enables the individual to adequately and successfully conduct the job) is the responsibility of the state agency, while the central processor (the usual or typical technical equipment for the job) remains the responsibility of the employer. The computer, in this case, was viewed as a device capable of improving an employee's rate and quality of work, and not as an intrusive element in the work environment.

2. *Home-Based Employment* Home-based computer-oriented employment through the utilization of a modem to a host computer is a work alternative for disabled persons. Many of the issues raised previously here regarding worker resentment or work space are of course avoided when this alternative is selected. And certainly for the person for whom health issues significantly interfere with job attendance, home-based employment through telecommunication is an attractive alternative. Home-based employment, however, has its own set of problems. First, social isolation is a prime concern. The individual's interpersonal expectations and needs should be taken into account and clearly analyzed in light of the social separation that can occur. This social disadvantage must be weighed in relation to the advantage of the individual's gaining meaningful and productive employment. Second, the difficulty of supervising the "telecommuter" should be weighed carefully by the prospective employer. Vagnoni (1986) considers contact between new and experienced workers to be a major factor in employee success. He states that employers, without exception, believe that computer programmers and analysts require 2–3 years of on-the-job experience before being capable of productive home-based employment. Furthermore, the team approach to problem solving would not be available to the home-based telecommuter. Finally, the decision to start a telecommunication home program is often fraught with technical problems. Compatibility with a host computer is the most frequent difficulty associated with such home-based employment.

3. *Funding Assistive Technology*   The cost of assistive technology is an important consideration for both the prospective employer and the potential employee. The price of technical equipment itself is often thought to be the exclusive factor in determining the cost associated with providing assistive technology. However, cost must also include associated fees for installation, maintainence as well as software and hardware customizations, modifications, and updates. Finally, the cost of training an individual to operate an assistive device and achieve computer literacy must be taken into account when calculating overall cost of applied assistive technology. Cost, therefore, may range from a few hundred dollars to many thousands of dollars, depending on the nature of the device, its purpose, and the amount of training required to achieve competency.

Attaining financial assistance to purchase assistive technology varies as a function of several factors. In general, several funding sources can be explored depending on the nature of the disability, the residence of the intended user, the overall purpose of the assistive technology, the type of employment the individual is seeking (e.g., competitive, sheltered), and the personal financial position of the potential employee.

Public funding sources may vary from state to state and between departments within the same state. These might include the departments of vocational rehabilitation, public health, developmental disabilities, or state-supported health insurance programs (Hoffman, 1982). An assistive device for an individual who will be employed in a sheltered workshop or in a volunteer job may be fundable by a public health insurance program. If competitive employment is the goal, then application to the state department of vocational rehabilitation or to a private insurer (e.g., workers' compensation) would be an advisable first step. For others, the Program to Achieve Self Support (PASS), administered through the U.S. Social Security Administration, may be a viable alternative.

In many cases, employer participation is possible. The potential benefits to the employer are numerous, including control over the type of computer purchased and the ability to update equipment as the workload warrants. When full employer participation is not possible, then a joint purchase venture might be explored. The possibility of shared costs may prove attractive to the employer. As noted previously, the employer may find it acceptable to purchase or provide the central processing unit (CPU), while those components necessary to enable a disabled operator to access the CPU are provided by the state agency. A further option might be for the employer to purchase the equipment and for the public or private service provider to fund installation and training.

Because the role of technology in enhancing job opportunity is still in its infancy, a complex justification process may be required to secure funding for assistive technology. Such justification often requires several layers of review before approval is secured. Perhaps the strongest justification for funding assistance is a genuine belief by the vocational practitioner that assistive technology can lead to meaningful employment.

CONCLUSION

It is the contention of these authors that sufficient technology is currently available to afford meaningful employment for persons formerly considered unemployable. Furthermore, it is believed that the greatest obstacle to full utilization of these technological tools is not limited financial resources or a lack of commitment to the achievement of human potential but rather, inadequate understanding of the power of this technology, including its ability to accommodate the most serious disabilities. These conclusions complement those of Burkhead et al. (1986), who suggested that the practitioner's lack of knowledge and a resistance to change underlie the slow acceptance of technological innovation in the rehabilitation profession.

REFERENCES

Bolton, B. (1979). *Rehabilitation counseling research*. Baltimore: University Park Press.

Burkhead, J.E., Sampson, J.P., & McMahon, B.T. (1986). The liberation of disabled persons in a technological society: Access to computer technology. *Rehabilitation Literature, 42*, 7–8.

Growick, B. (1983). Computers in rehabilitation: Current trends and future applications. *Rehabilitation Research Review Booklet # 17*. Washington, DC: National Rehabilitation Information Center.

Herr, E.L. (1985). Advanced technology. Theory and rehabilitation counseling. *Rehabilitation Counseling Bulletin, 29*(1), 6–16.

Hoffman, A. (1982). *The many faces of funding*. Mill Valley, CA: Phonic Ear.

Szeto, A.Y.J., Allen, E.J., & Rummelhart. M.A. (1987). Employability enhancement through technical communication devices. *American Rehabilitation, 13*(2), 8–29.

Thirteenth Institute on Rehabilitation Issues. (1986). *Rehabilitation technologies.* Menomonie: University of Wisconsin, Material Development Center, Stout Vocational Rehabilitation Institute.

U.S. Department of Labor, Bureau of Labor Statistics. (1986, Spring). The job outlook in brief. *Occupational Outlook Quarterly, 30*(1).

Vagnoni, J. (1986). Telecommuting: Homebased computer related employment for severely disabled persons. *American Rehabilitation,12*(3), 6–9 and 21–31.

13

Training Needs in Integrated Settings

Orv C. Karan and Lori Mettel

For most of us, work consumes only part of the day. What happens in other settings can and does influence what happens at work. This chapter considers the training needs not only of those who support the consumer with disabilities in integrated *work* settings but the training needs of those involved in other aspects of a person's life as well. Thus, the needs of paraprofessionals, professionals, parents, and consumers themselves are addressed.

PARAPROFESSIONAL TRAINING

While a variety of well-trained personnel are critical to the community integration movement, those who work directly with consumers are particularly important. Commonly referred to as paraprofessionals (Gartner, 1979), these direct care staff represent 80% of the people with whom developmentally disabled adults have daily contact (Schalock, 1983). Interest in paraprofessional training is growing. Among the reasons for this is the recognition that those who have daily contact with consumers can have the most influence. Many professionals have found that they can be most effective and efficient by working with and through paraprofessionals.

One might imagine that these paraprofessionals would be well trained and highly regarded. On the contrary, those who devote their time entirely to direct services are often the least well paid, the least respected, and the least trained (Schalock, 1983). It is also apparent from national staff turnover rates, which exceed 70%, that direct care staff do not find their work sufficiently satisfying or rewarding. And, as more integrated community options are created, the problem could increase, particularly if staff feel more isolated (Lakin & Bruininks, 1980).

Turnover does little to purge the system of dissatisfied employees. Instead, it prevents the development of meaningful relationships while seriously interfering with the implementation of well-intentioned community integration programs. Moreover, those who stay but would really rather be doing something else if they could find another job are not the best performing employees (Lakin & Bruininks, 1980).

In addition to the human costs related to turnover, there is an economic toll as well. It has been estimated, for example, that it costs in excess of $2,000 to replace each staff member (Lakin & Bruininks, 1980). Given these factors, it is clear that concern about service options for those with developmental disabilities must include attention to ways to encourage competent direct care employees to remain in their critically important jobs.

Training Needs

It has been estimated that from 70% to 90% of those providing direct services in community-based programs never received any formal training for their job (Bilvosky & Matson, 1977). Instead, the majority of such employees are entry-level personnel with no prior experience (Pfriem, 1979). These results suggest the need to consider two kinds of training. The first is inservice training to better equip the current work force; the second, and one that may be more fiscally sound in the long run, is to develop preservice training programs.

Inservice Training Frequently mentioned obstacles to inservice training include insufficient funds and logistics (Bruininks, Kudla, Wieck, & Hauber, 1980; Knowles & Landesman, 1986; Ziarnik & Bernstein, 1982). Budget restrictions have resulted in chronic staff shortages in many settings, and the release of direct care staff from their daily responsibilities to attend training may alter the remaining staff-to-client ratio to unacceptable levels. In addition, just because training opportunities are available does not assure the quality of the training. Training programs vary tremendously, and good quality training personnel and materials are not widely available (Knowles & Landesman, 1986).

At an absolute minimum, trainers must be qualified. However, they must also be well informed of their clients' training needs ahead of time, because unless staff development efforts are based upon competencies needed to work in a given setting with a specific population, they may be of minimal value (Richardson, West, & Fifield, 1985). Training must meet the demands of the job (Karan & Berger, 1986). In this respect, the desired outcomes should be identified before any training is actually undertaken, and the curriculum should be based on specific performance expectations rather than on general, nonspecific content areas (Ziarnik, Rudrud, & Bernstein, 1981).

A variety of outcome measures have been used to evaluate the effectiveness of staff inservice training programs, but no national data base exists for examining their relative impact (Knowles & Landesman, 1986). Thus, although there is some evidence suggesting that staff training results in small changes in staff behavior immediately after training (for certain skills only), overall it appears that the effectiveness of staff inservice training has yet to be conclusively confirmed (Ziarnik & Bernstein, 1982).

Preservice Training Preservice training programs for paraprofessionals have existed in one form or another for over a decade. The most durable have taken place within community and technical colleges, which offer several advantages. In general, these institutions attempt to be responsive to the needs of the community, and once a program has been initiated, its continuation depends on the availability of jobs for its graduates and sufficient enrollment. So unlike many grant-supported training programs, which rapidly end when the funding ends, these programs continue so long as there is a need. Finally, program graduates often stay within the immediate geographic area, providing an existing source of trained personnel to their local communities.

Many community and technical colleges throughout the country offer associate degrees in human services and related fields. However, most of these programs offer little content specifically relevant to developmental disabilities. However, a small, but growing, number of community and technical colleges are including specific courses along with clinical experiences in the field of developmental disabilities. Several of these, particularly those that have been in operation for 5 years or longer, have modified their existing human services or related training programs to incorporate coursework and practice in the specialty area of developmental disabilities. Institutions offering associate degree training programs are located, for example, in Iowa, Kansas, Nebraska, New Jersey, Texas, and Ohio. Newer programs, which are less than 5 years old, such as those in North Dakota and Wisconsin, however, have structured their associate degree programs exclusively to train paraprofessionals within the developmental disabilities area.

A review of many of these preservice training programs leads to the following general conclusions (Karan, 1987):

1. Most of the graduates go into jobs within school systems, institutions, and local community agencies. A relatively new job market has recently opened, however, and graduates are now being hired as job coaches, transition aides, and so forth.
2. The existing programs are not usually statewide but are found in one or two locations in the state.
3. Graduates are more likely to receive respectable wages and benefits within school systems. Those who enter community-based services, as represented by private nonprofit agencies, usually receive starting wages not unlike what they could have received without the training.
4. All preservice associate degree programs include clinical experiences as a significant part of their training.

5. There are not enough data to determine if these programs are making a significant difference in the quality of life of people with developmental disabilities or if the programs are altering the turnover rates of those who receive this training.

Performance Issues and Employment Needs

Regardless of the extent or quality of their training, staff performance, as determined by the quality of care, training, and supervision the staff provides to people with developmental disabilities, is related importantly to employment practices and to the ability of management to create environments that encourage and maintain these skills. While there is little doubt that new skills must be taught to direct care staff, recent research (Whitman, Sabak, & Reid, 1983) has indicated that staff training endeavors are frequently not sufficient to improve performance in day-to-day work situations.

It is often mistakenly assumed that staff lack necessary skills when, in fact, the problem may be more accurately described as the failure of the working environment to support the use of these skills. Certainly, the need for well-trained personnel is a serious concern. However, of equal if not greater importance is the need to find ways to support these individuals, financially and in other ways, to sustain them in the continuing provision of their services.

Direct care workers have two important and sometimes conflicting needs. On the one hand, they have employment needs like any person in any industry (i.e., they need decent pay, good working conditions, the opportunity to participate in decisions). On the other hand, they are heavily responsible for contributing to improving the quality of life of consumers. A balance between these two sets of needs is not always easily achieved (Karan & Berger, 1986). Unless supportive managerial practices with well-defined expectations and the right incentives are available to support direct care workers, there may be insufficient reason for them to sustain these skills or provide these services (Lattimore, Stephens, Favell, & Risley, 1984).

Systematic attempts to alter environmental conditions in an effort to improve human performance have recently emerged as a distinct discipline under the title of organizational behavior management (OBM; Frederikson & Johnson, 1981). To date, the application of OBM to direct care staff has consisted primarily of altering conditions related to: 1) goals and feedback, 2) consequences, and 3) cues. For example, several programs have been able to alter significantly staff performance, without a heavy financial investment, by simply informing staff of exactly what was expected and then providing feedback on how well expectations were met (Ziarnik & Bernstein, 1982). A fourth OBM approach that has come into recent practice is known as organizational level intervention and is represented by changes in policy.

With the growing use of computers, one can expect to see more applications of OBM in such areas as improving staff feedback or in identifying functional staff responsibilities. Such information may prove to be very useful not only in making direct care jobs more desirable but also in improving job performance. It is known, for example, that staff perceptions influence their actions (Slater & Bunyard, 1983), and that therefore any management approaches that can help the staff's perceptions, values, and attitudes to become more congruent with those who administer programs will ultimately benefit consumers (Karan & Berger, 1986).

PROFESSIONAL TRAINING

As the developmental disabilities field has begun to shift from its segregated and institutional models of service delivery to more integrated community-based options, a severe problem has emerged in the delivery of professional services, namely, that of shortages of qualified providers. Finding doctors, dentists, lawyers, psychologists, and so forth, who are *willing* and *able* to provide necessary services in the community to developmentally disabled people is often a challenge. The band of professionals from which to choose becomes even narrower if the person's level of handicap and/or behavior impairment is severe.

Some of the difficulty can be attributed to professional training, in that many practitioners have had little if any exposure to developmental disabilities. Even more of a deterrence, however, are the multiplicity of obstacles that serve as disincentives, mitigating any professional motivation to upgrade one's skills in this area and sometimes even penalizing those who do offer their services. The following sections examine these topics in greater detail.

Obstacles to Professional Training

In general, there has been a lack of synchronization among universities, community colleges, and service agencies in the development of joint planning to meet training needs (Gartner, 1979). One notable exception, however, is found among the national network of university affiliated programs (UAPs), whose members have taken a leadership role in preparing well-trained professionals knowledgeable in state-of-the-art interdisciplinary approaches. Yet, most systems of higher education that are not associated with a UAP lack the programs necessary to respond to future training needs.

In some cases, rigid university policies and/or the professional standards of specific disciplines make it very difficult to start new courses within an accredited program's course sequence. Although new courses, such as those on developmental disabilities, may sometimes appear as electives, the heavy demands made on the student's time as a result of required courses may limit the number of available students; students simply may have little time to take anything else. Or if they do have the time, any offerings in developmental disabilities may be competing with other more highly desired options.

The knowledge and interest of the faculty are also critical in promoting an environment in which training in developmental disabilities can be accomplished (Guralnick, Richardson, & Heiser, 1982). Yet, few academic departments and professional schools have faculty with extensive background, training, or interest in this area. Further, given the "publish or perish" climate of many universities, faculty may have little incentive to stray too far from their particular areas of expertise unless there is a compelling reason.

A professional license or advanced degree is an insufficient indicator of competence in working with individuals who have developmental disabilities. And, even if a provider is willing to offer services, he or she may be unable to acquire needed training and ultimately may be faced with an ethical professional dilemma about practicing with individuals whose special needs often dictate specialized knowledge. Without such knowledge, risks can range from simply bad advice to matters of life and death.

Obstacles to Professional Performance

To work effectively with developmentally disabled consumers means that professionals must have the necessary knowledge, must be able to transcend their traditional discipline boundaries, and must understand both the contexts within which consumers function as well as the values of the significant others in that consumer's life (Karan & Berger, 1986; Richardson et al., 1985). Unfortunately, many professionals may not perform well simply because they do not have these necessary skills. Others may be unaware of what other providers do, which may result in poor implementation or coordination of services. Still others may have difficulty effectively communicating with families, direct care personnel, and other professionals.

In some cases, the failure to provide services may be because professionals devalue the importance of families and direct care personnel and do not view them as equal partners (Donnellan & Mirenda, 1984). Much of it may also reflect on the professional's difficulty in translating his or her approaches and recommendations into methods clearly understood by those implementing the suggestions. Furthermore, "turf" issues, self-preservation, professional rivalries, and philosophical differences may also impede adequate services.

Finally, financial disincentives continue to play a major role as an obstacle to service delivery. Stated simply, many private health care practitioners can make considerably more money with far less paperwork by serving clients without developmental disabilities. Not only are they penalized by the loss of time and income, but there is no incentive for them to improve their skills in this area. As such, private mental health specialists in the developmental disabilities area, whose skills are so critical because of the greater likelihood for psychopathology among this population (Matson, 1984), are relatively rare.

PARENT TRAINING

Both by necessity and as a result of legal mandates, parents may play a variety of roles as decision makers, advocates, service providers, case managers, and evaluators. Few can argue against the view that parents bring a unique perspective to all of these roles. Not only are parents the child's first teachers, but they are in the best position to know what social support networks will be available over time (McDonnell, Wilcox, Boles, & Bellamy, 1985). Because of the variety of changing roles parents can play, they need adequate information and support (Allen & Hudd, 1987) to enable them to perform these roles as effectively as possible.

Just because parents have an unprecedented voice in decision making, however, does not necessarily mean they are taking an active role. Thus, although parents have the right to be treated as equal members of the professional team (Arnold, 1985) or in some cases even to be viewed as experts in areas pertaining to their child's abilities and needs (Donnellan & Mirenda, 1984), their roles are influenced by shortcomings in their own knowledge, continuing professional biases that work to undermine their influence, and often their own decision not to participate actively. In actuality, most parents assume a passive role in decision making (Allen & Hudd, 1987). Indeed, those who question professional advice or persist in seeking services that are not typically available are often negatively labeled by the professional community and lay society (Donnellan & Mirenda, 1984).

Recently, McDonnell et al. (1985) surveyed parents regarding their projections of service needs for their children and found that a significant number received no information about postschool services available in their communities. Without such information, parents are unable to plan effectively for their child. In addition, even when parents actively seek information, they may find that obtaining it can be time-consuming and frustrating, and that once obtained, it is much more detailed than they want or need (Turnbull & Turnbull, 1982). Developers of parent training programs must be responsive to the parents' available time, interest, and willingness to participate.

Given that the two most significant predictors of successful community placement are parental acceptance of and involvement in community-based programs (Schalock, Harper, & Genung, 1981), professionals must examine their negative assumptions about parents and begin to evaluate parent behavior within a more positive framework (Donnellan & Mirenda, 1984).

Because of the changing conditions that affect children over time, the variety of pressures and circumstances that influence parents' priorities and choices, and the fragmentation that runs rampant through this country's adult service system, all personnel training programs must incorporate a greater respect for the parents' role. At a minimum, service providers and parents must learn to work more effectively with each other (Arnold, 1985).

CONSUMER TRAINING

Social and political action since the late 1960s has resulted in the emergence of a new societal perspective that views people with disabilities as citizens who have the right to live and participate as integrated members of their communities. Browning, Thorin, and Rhoades (1984) suggest that "the progressive move to deinstitutionalize and mainstream people back into society quite naturally awakened a self-help/self-advocacy movement that continues to flourish quietly throughout the country" (p. 226).

Self-advocacy has been defined as a social movement organized and controlled by people with developmental disabilities in order to promote their efforts to achieve equality, independence, and recognition as full members of society (Rhoades, 1986). These voluntary organizations, usually with assistance from nondisabled advisors, work to ensure and protect legislated civil rights as well as the rights of consumers to participate actively in the human services delivery system. The individual consumer groups have no formalized structure on the national level; rather, they represent a grass-roots movement that consists primarily of locally based chapters.

Through the self-advocacy movement, people with developmental disabilities are beginning to use their organizations to make an impact at both individual and system levels. Better transportation, expanded vocational opportunities, and improved accessibility are among the examples of progress cited by self-advocates. Members are also assuming positions on advisory boards and policy committees in areas that affect their daily lives, and some are even becoming active in evaluating their own services.

Obstacles to Consumer Training

Consumers with developmental disabilities are often characterized as dependent and incapable of accepting the rights and responsibilities that accompany citizenship in this country. Historically, they have been isolated and denied the opportunity to engage in activities that allow them to demonstrate their competence. Self-advocates, therefore, face the challenge of overcoming long-standing negative perceptions in order to convince society that the self-advocacy movement is credible. As the movement becomes stronger and participants more visible, this obstacle may diminish (Rhoades, 1986).

Another significant problem in the self-advocacy movement is the lack of peer advisors and the resultant dependence on nondisabled advisors to provide direction. Rhoades (1986) suggests that the role of the advisor is a sensitive self-advocacy issue, in that the advisor must provide the consultation and group facilitation necessary while simultaneously respecting the nature of the group as a consumer organization. As groups evolve and progress, there is the expectation that they will rely less upon advisors and more on peer role models. Until that time, however, self-advocates are in the potentially vulnerable position of sharing power with group advisors.

Training Needs

Exercising greater control over one's life is a significant benefit that can be derived by acquiring self-advocacy skills. Indeed, many people with developmental disabilities can become articulate spokespersons on their own behalf if given sufficient training and information to do so. A major component of a self-advocacy group is the local chapter meeting. Chapter meetings are often instructional in nature and focus on learning about rights and responsibilities as consumers of services as well as citizens of the community (Browning et al., 1984). Experienced self-advocates or advisors often serve as group instructors in various content areas. Resource guides are available (Hallgren, Norsman, & Bier, 1977) that outline some of the topics to be addressed in a self-advocacy curriculum. There is still a need, however, for materials designed for use by individuals who are nonverbal and multiply handicapped.

Equally important as training consumers to advocate for themselves is the necessity to sensitize paraprofessionals, parents, professionals, and the general public to understand and respect these expressions of rights. As Dybwad (1985) noted, although the person now has a voice of his or her own, the question is, "Are we ready to listen?" Some parents and professionals may fail to take the self-advocacy movement seriously.

Furthermore, self-advocacy need not be limited to those who speak for themselves. There are many consumers who are unable to anticipate their needs even though they, like everyone else, need to have a chance to make decisions. The "kinds of decisions we get satisfaction out of are different and that should also be respected" (Boggs, 1985). Whether they communicate with their words or with their behavior (Donnellan, Mirenda, Mesaros, & Fassbender, 1984), we must learn to "listen."

CONCLUSION

This chapter has reviewed the training needs of paraprofessionals, professionals, parents, and disabled consumers. Without question, each of these groups has continuing unmet needs to acquire better skills. Additional training needs consist of finding ways to encourage and support the use of new skills after they have been acquired. These are organizational and system issues that have not yet received much attention in the developmental disabilities field (Gardner, Karan, & Cole, 1984).

It is especially critical to address these issues as we progress toward even more integrated community options for consumers with complex needs and/or challenging behaviors. In the authors' opinion, the key to full community integration for adults with developmental disabilities is a service system that can encourage and support competent participants. In particular, when it comes to those who spend the most time with consumers, namely paraprofessionals, the authors believe that the quality of their working life is inextricably linked with the quality of life of those whom they serve.

REFERENCES

Allen, D.A., & Hudd, S.S. (1987). Are we professionalizing parents? Weighing the benefits and pitfalls. *Mental Retardation, 25*(3), 133–139.

Arnold, M. (1985). Parent training and advocacy. In M.G. Fifield & B.C. Smith (Eds.), *Personal training for serving adults with developmental disabilities* (pp. 99–116). Logan: Utah State University Developmental Center for Handicapped Persons.

Bilvosky, D., & Matson, J. (1977). *Community colleges and the developmentally disabled*. Washington, DC: American Association of Community and Junior Colleges.

Boggs, E. (speaker). (1985). *Are we ready to listen?* [Video]. Produced by Research and Training Center, University of Wisconsin–Madison.

Browning, P., Thorin, E., & Rhoades, J. (1984). A national profile of self-help/self-advocacy groups of people with mental retardation. *Mental Retardation, 22,* 226–230.

Bruininks, R.H., Kudla, M.J., Wieck, C.A., & Hauber, F.A. (1980). Management problems in community residential facilities. *Mental Retardation, 18,* 125–130.

Donnellan, A.M., & Mirenda, P. (1984). Issues related to professional involvement with families of individuals with autism and other severe handicaps. *Journal of The Association for Persons with Severe Handicaps, 9*(1), 16–25.

Donnellan, A.M., Mirenda, P.L., Mesaros, R.A., & Fassbender, L.L. (1984). Analyzing the communicative functions of aberrant behavior. *Journal of The Association for Persons with Severe Handicaps, 9*(3), 201–212.

Dybwad, G. (speaker). (1985). *Are we ready to listen?* [Video]. Produced by Research and Training Center, University of Wisconsin–Madison.

Frederikson, L.W., & Johnson, R.P. (1981). Organizational behavior management. In M. Hersen, R. Eisler, & P. Meller (Eds.), *Progress in behavior modification* (pp. 67–118). New York: Academic Press.

Gardner, W.I., Karan, O.C., & Cole, C.L. (1984). Assessment of setting events influencing functional capacities of mentally retarded adults with behavior difficulties. In A.S. Halpern & M.J. Fuhrer (Eds.), *Functional assessment in rehabilitation* (pp. 171–185). Baltimore: Paul H. Brookes Publishing Co.

Gartner, A. (1979). *Career ladders and a training model for the (re)training of direct service workers in community-based programs for the developmentally disabled.*

New York: City University of New York, Center for Advanced Study in Education, New Careers Training Laboratory.

Guralnick, M.J., Richardson, H.B., & Heiser, K.E. (1982). A curriculum in handicapping conditions for pediatric residents. *Exceptional Children, 48,* 338–346.

Hallgren, B., Norsman, A., & Bier, D. (1977). *Life, liberty, and the pursuit of happiness: A self-advocacy curriculum.* Madison: Wisconsin Coalition for Advocacy and the Wisconsin Association for Retarded Citizens.

Karan, O.C. (1987, May 28). *Paraprofessional training and manpower development: Current efforts and future directions.* Paper presented at the 111th annual meeting of the American Association on Mental Deficiency, Los Angeles.

Karan, O.C., & Berger, C.L. (1986). Developing support networks for individuals who fail to achieve competitive employment. In F.R. Rusch (Ed.), *Competitive employment issues and strategies* (pp. 241–255). Baltimore: Paul H. Brookes Publishing Co.

Knowles, H., & Landesman, S. (1986). National survey of state sponsored training for residential direct-care staff. *Mental Retardation, 24,* 293–300.

Lakin, K.C., & Bruininks, R.H. (1980). *Personnel management and quality of residential services for developmentally disabled people.* Unpublished manuscript, University of Minnesota, Minneapolis.

Lattimore, J., Stephens, T.E., Favell, J.E., & Risley, T.R. (1984). Increasing direct care staff compliance to individualized physical therapy body positioning prescriptions: Prescriptive checklists. *Mental Retardation, 22,* 79–84.

Matson, J. (1984). Psychotherapy with persons who are mentally retarded. *Mental Retardation, 22,* 170–175.

McDonnell, J.J., Wilcox, B., Boles, S.M., & Bellamy, G.T. (1985). Transition issues facing youth with severe disabilities: Parents' perspective. *Journal of the Association for Persons with Severe Handicaps, 10*(1), 61–65.

Pfriem, D.C. (1979). *Inservice training: A follow-up survey.* Unpublished report, REM, Minneapolis.

Rhoades, C. (1986). Self-advocacy. In J. Wortes (Ed.), *Mental retardation and developmental disabilities: An annual review* (pp. 69–90). New York: Brunner/Mazel.

Richardson, M., West, P., & Fifield, M. (1985). Preservice and professional training. In M.G. Fifield & B.C. Smith (Eds.), *Personnel training for serving adults with developmental disabilities* (pp. 67–83). Logan: Utah State University Developmental Center for Handicapped Persons.

Schalock, R.L. (1983). *Services for developmentally disabled adults.* Austin: PRO-ED.

Schalock, R.L., Harper, R.S., & Genung, T. (1981). Community integration of mentally retarded adults: Community placement and program success. *American Journal of Mental Deficiency, 85,* 478–488.

Slater, M.A., & Bunyard, P.D. (1983). Survey of residential staff roles, responsibilities, and perception of resident needs. *Mental Retardation, 21*(2), 52–58.

Turnbull, A.P., & Turnbull, H.R. (1982). Parent involvement in the education of handicapped children: A critique. *Mental Retardation, 20,* 115–122.

Whitman, T.L., Sabak, J.W., & Reid, D.H. (1983). *Behavior modification with the severely and profoundly retarded: Research and application.* New York: Academic Press.

Ziarnik, J.P., & Bernstein, G.S. (1982). A critical examination of the effect of inservice training on staff performance. *Mental Retardation, 20,* 109–114.

Ziarnik, J.P., Rudrud, E.H., & Bernstein, G.S. (1981). Data vs. reflections: A reply to Moxley and Ebert. *Mental Retardation, 19,* 251–252.

14

Enhancing Employment Outcomes through Habilitation Planning for Social Competence

Carl F. Calkins and Hill M. Walker

It is clear from the changing economic and industrial environments, state and federal funding priorities, and changing perceptions of the role of adults with disabilities that employment is an important and continuing national priority. It is equally clear that some states and programs are demonstrating that creative reorganization of resources is both possible and necessary to increase employment options. As emphasized in other chapters in this volume, programs and technology are available to produce the outcomes necessary for successful competitive employment. The question then becomes: Why are we not applying what we know on a more comprehensive basis? Perhaps, as Thomas Gilbert (1978) points out in *Human Competence,* there are not enough human performance engineers with the tools necessary to demonstrate these outcomes. This chapter describes a habilitation planning tool that targets a critical element in enhancing employment outcomes—social competence. The habilitation planning tool discussed is the primary outcome of a national consortium of four university affiliated programs. The project's major product was a guide titled *Enhancing Employment Outcomes: A Practical Guide to the Habilitation Planning Process* (Calkins & Walker, 1988).[1] The principal topics covered in the guide are addressed here: 1) the need for a habilitation planning guide focusing on social competence, 2) a rationale and description of the conceptual model

Appreciation is expressed to Peter Griggs for his insight and editorial comments and to Norma Damon for her continuing dedication to format and production.

[1]The project was funded by the Administration on Developmental Disabilities and represents the joint efforts of university affiliated programs at the University of Missouri Institute for Human Development, the University of Oregon Center on Human Development, the Westchester Medical Center Mental Retardation Institute, and Boston's Children's Hospital.

underlying the planning guide, 3) an overview of the *Enhancing Employment Outcomes* habilitation planning package, and 4) anticipated outcomes.

NEED FOR HABILITATION PLANNING GUIDE FOCUSING ON SOCIAL COMPETENCE

The purpose of the *Enhancing Employment Outcomes Guide* (henceforth, *EEO Guide*) is to improve the ability of community-based, habilitation practitioners to facilitate successful, employment-related outcomes for people with developmental disabilities within competitive employment settings. The guide is both a natural extension and further application of the data/information compiled and developed by Calkins et al. (1985) and Walker and Calkins (1986). Results of recently reported program development efforts in the area of aging by Kultgen, Rinck, Calkins, and Intagliata (1986) clearly document that the effectiveness of individual habilitation plans (IHPs) can be improved by the development of an exemplary habilitation planning guide and by direct instruction of case managers in its use, with systematic attention given to relevant content areas including age-specific factors, interpersonal needs, and social adjustment domains of elderly persons.

The present authors believe that a planning guide of this type is a feasible and urgently needed response to the significant social competence problems that people with disabilities have experienced in adjusting to the behavioral demands/requirements of competitive employment settings (Chadsey-Rusch, 1986; Kiernan & Stark, 1986; Rusch, 1986; Salzberg, Likins, McConaughy, Lignugavis-Kraft, & Stowitschek, 1986; Walker & Calkins, 1986). These problems have prevented such persons from effectively accessing competitive employment settings and have contributed to their involuntary termination from employment. It is broadly agreed that such persons are more likely to be involuntarily terminated owing to "social" reasons than to insufficient mastery of technical job skills (Calkins et al., 1985; O'Connor, 1983). Follow-up studies of mentally retarded adults 1 year after placement indicate that only approximately 50%–60% are still employed. A minimum of 40% of such job losses are due exclusively to social reasons (Salzberg et al., 1986).

The current employment status of persons with developmental disabilities within community settings is extremely problematic. National studies and surveys consistently indicate that the percentage of persons with handicaps who are unemployed is between 50% and 75% (U.S. Commission on Civil Rights, 1983). Further, underemployment and low wages are characteristic of large numbers of persons with handicaps who are employed (Horner, Meyer, & Fredericks, 1986; Rusch, 1986). Factors influencing the employability of such persons include: the general economic climate, the attitudes of employers, the attitudes and effectiveness of employment training and placement staff, and the vocational competence of the individual.

Salzberg et al. (1986) argue that vocational competence is a product of three interacting factors: job responsibility, task-production competence, and social-vocational competence. Job responsibility refers to behavioral indicators that suggest job commitment, including punctuality, low rates of absenteeism, working continuously at job tasks, and so forth. Task-production competence is indicated by completion of work tasks that meet accuracy and efficiency standards within the work setting. Social-vocational competence refers to the adequacy of the individual's interactions with co-workers and supervisors, as well as an ability to comply with the formal and informal rules of the workplace.

Foss and his associates (Foss, Bullis, & Vilhauer, 1984; Foss & Peterson, 1981) have provided extensive empirical documentation of the social competence problems experienced by persons with handicaps in a range of employment settings. They have classified their findings into two major types of problems, including difficulties with supervisors (accepting criticism or correction, requesting assistance, accepting instructions) and difficulties with co-workers (disagreement over work tasks, lack of cooperation, conflicts over teasing and provocations). Similarly, Chadsey-Rusch (1986), in her review of valued social behaviors within competitive employment settings, concluded that employers want their workers to be able to communicate verbally their basic needs, to be compliant, to avoid disrupting the work setting, and to follow directions. Social-vocational competence problems commonly cited by investigators in this area include social interaction problems with supervisors and co-workers, not following directions, not listening to others, not understanding people and settings, failing to cooperate, not requesting information or assistance when needed, conversational problems, aberrant behaviors, sexual misconduct, and hygiene problems. Calkins et al. (1985), in their national survey of program models and exemplary model programs, sampled community-based residential, vocational, and combined program types, and found that vocational programs were significantly more socially restrictive in their behavioral expectations and in the demands made of their client populations. In addition, vocational programs invested far less attention to fostering social support forms of client adjustment (for example, facilitating friendships and the development of social support networks) than the other two program types. Vocational program types were strongly directed toward compliance, behavioral self-control, and control of disruptive or inappropriate forms of behavior.

Foss, Walker, Todis, Lyman, and Smith (1986) have recently developed a social competence model for community employment settings. This model argues that three major types or forms of social competence are required for successful adjustment to competitive employment settings, including: 1) compliance skills (control of disruptive behavior, conforming to interpersonal rules and conventions); 2) basic interaction skills (positive interactions with supervisors, co-workers, and others); and 3) relationship-building skills (developing friendships and social support networks). These forms of social competence serve different purposes for persons with developmental disabilities within competitive employment settings. For example, behavioral compliance skills are essential to remaining within these settings. Basic interaction skills determine, to a large extent, the adequacy of the person's adjustment and quality of life within the setting. Relationship-building skills permit such workers to take advantage of the numerous opportunities that employment settings provide for developing friendships and social support networks. The latter are extremely important in offsetting the effects of stress and depression and reducing loneliness and feelings of alienation (Romer & Heller, 1983). To date, comprehensive social competence training programs that incorporate these elements have not been available. The authors believe that the empirical research and knowledge base exists to develop effective solutions to the complex problems that people with developmental disabilities continue to face in adjusting to the demands of competitive employment settings. Unfortunately, current knowledge in this area is not being synthesized and made available to community-based practitioners in a manner that can be readily used to improve the social competence of such persons to levels necessary for successful adjustment in various settings. The goal of the *EEO Guide* is to do exactly that—to enhance social competence.

RATIONALE AND DESCRIPTION OF
CONCEPTUAL MODEL UNDERLYING THE *EEO GUIDE*

Figure 14.1 is a graphic representation of the conceptual model that supports the development of the habilitation planning guide.

This model makes two major assumptions that govern the development of the habilitation planning guide. These are, first, that an effective habilitation planning process will contribute significantly to an improved quality of life for workers with developmental disabilities within competitive employment settings; second, that the availability of a practical guide to habilitation planning that is geared specifically toward enhancing employment outcomes in the area of social competence will contribute significantly to more effective adjustment to competitive employment settings. The major program components of this planning guide (see Figure 14.1) involve achievement of a satisfactory person-environment fit and attention to developing adequate program-environment fit. Both of these processes are judged essential for addressing adequately the complexities involved in facilitating effective adjustment to competitive employment settings. The potential for utilization of the *EEO Guide* will need to be demonstrated effectively at two levels: 1) the training of pre- and inservice level professionals in its use, and 2) effective demonstrations of its use within field settings by habilitation planners and

Instrumentation	Expected Outcome
Habilitation planning process	→ Improved quality of life
A *User's Guide* and *Resource Manual to Habilitation Planning for Enhanced Employment-Related Outcomes*	→ Effective adjustment to competitive employment settings

EEO User's Habilitation Planning Guide

Program Components

Level I—Person-environment fit
(EEO match scale)
(EEO intervention strategies profile)

Level II—Program-environment fit
(Program capacity checklist)
↓

Implementation

Training of pre- and inservice personnel
(*Resource Manual*)

Demonstrated use at field sites

Quality assurance for social competence
and employment-related outcomes
↙   ↘

Exemplary program practices	Relevant attention to domains of social competence that enhance successful adjustment to employment settings

Figure 14.1.   Conceptual model for enhanced employment outcomes. (Based on information in Calkins et al. [1985] and Walker & Calkins [1986].)

practitioners. If these applications are successful, the guide will help to assure the quality of social-competence–related employment outcomes. The authors expect that the guide's adoption by field agencies and practitioners will ultimately facilitate exemplary program practices in the development of social competence within competitive employment settings, and will focus practitioners' attention on relevant domains of social competence that will assist people with developmental disabilities in meeting and adjusting to the behavioral demands of these settings.

The authors have approached the development of this guide from a behavioral or social ecological perspective (Kernan, Begab, & Edgerton, 1983; Romer & Heller, 1983). This appears to be the only perspective that can deal adequately with the complexities of community integration and adjustment and simultaneously take into account individual needs/characteristics and the performance requirements/demands of settings. A number of leading scholars and researchers in the developmental disabilities field have argued strongly for a recommitment to this approach and for efforts toward its effective application (Landesman & Butterfield, 1985; Rusch, 1986; Schalock, Gadwood, & Perry, 1984; Sundberg, Snowden, & Reynolds, 1978). Calkins et al. (1985) and Calkins, Walker, and Bacon-Prue (1986) developed a conceptual model describing the community adjustment of developmentally disabled people that is based upon a behavioral ecological approach of this general type. A behavioral ecological approach should be based upon four assumptions (Schalock et al., 1984). These are: 1) individuals cannot be separated from their living environments; 2) both persons and environments can be assessed; 3) the mismatch between persons and their environments can be reduced through development of behavioral skills, use of prosthetics, and/or environmental modification; and 4) intervention should focus on caregivers and settings as much as on persons with disabilities. All of these assumptions have guided the activities undertaken in the development of the *EEO Guide*.

Person-environment (P-E) fit or match is a central feature of a behavioral ecological approach and refers to the degree of congruence between an individual's skills or behavioral capabilities and the performance requirements and behavioral demands of settings and environments. P-E fit is one of the more powerful contributions of behavioral ecology to the study of social settings and is a direct measure of adjustment status. It requires that settings and individuals be assessed on the same dimensions and that intervention efforts consider altering settings as well as changing the individual. Two general types of person-environment fit are usually recognized. The first concerns the match between an individual's social skills and behavioral competence, and the demands of the settings in which he or she is expected to function. The second relates to the support systems, resources, and response opportunities within the settings that are available to respond to the person's needs. Achievement of this fit or match requires a careful assessment of the setting and of its behavioral/performance demands or critical functions that are essential to adjustment within the setting. The behavioral status and skill levels of the individual on these critical functions must also be assessed in order to achieve a satisfactory P-E fit. Research indicates that both generic and setting-specific critical functions can and should be identified in this assessment process (Calkins et al., 1985; Walker, 1984, 1986). The *EEO Guide* specifies implementation guidelines, describes techniques, identifies decision-making criteria, and contains supplemental materials and resource lists, all designed to achieve a satisfactory person-environment fit in the area of social competence in competitive employment settings for persons with disabilities. It emphasizes a practical decision-making process and is designed to bring best practice strategies and standards within the reach of community-based habilitation planners.

Person-Environment Fit Module

The P-E fit module of the *EEO Guide* is based upon ecological assessment procedures of an exemplary nature. Assessment of social/behavioral ecologies in community settings has a long tradition dating from the pioneering efforts of such investigators as Gump (1977), Moos (1979), and Moos and Insel (1974). These investigators demonstrated the feasibility of environmental assessment procedures but did not operationalize them in a manner that would allow them to be used prescriptively. Some recent advances in this methodology have moved the field dramatically toward the effective applied use of these techniques in community settings. Work reported by Schalock and Jensen (1986) describes a goodness-of-fit index (GOFI) that makes it possible to: 1) assess the actual congruence that exists between a person's behavioral capabilities on a series of either community living or vocational skills; 2) determine the performance requirements that exist within the person's living/working environment; and 3) derive a discrepancy score that can be used in selecting settings, in planning interventions, and in evaluating adjustment status.

Walker (1984, 1986) has developed and reported a similar ecological assessment and intervention model for use in the mainstreaming and social integration of pupils with handicaps in school settings. This chapter focuses on the application of Walker's assessment model to the social competence of persons with developmental disabilities within community employment settings. Furnham and Schaeffer (1984) have reviewed the literature and have reported empirical research that documents strong relationships between person-environment fit, job satisfaction, and mental health. They suggest that the strong interrelationships among these three factors make it imperative that investigators attend carefully and systematically to the development of required levels of social competence for persons with disabilities placed within competitive employment settings.

Program-Environment Fit

The guide also gives equal emphasis to the concept of program-environment fit (Calkins, Griggs, & Walker, in preparation). The present authors see this concept as vital to the continuity, maintenance, replication, and adoption of programs designed to improve the social competence of persons with disabilities (Paine, Bellamy, & Wilcox, 1984). Program-environment fit refers to the match between the features of the intervention program and the ecology of the service delivery system in which it is implemented. These variables are only rarely attended to in habilitation practice but are often the source of program failure and lack of progress by clients. Setting ecology variables relating to program-environment fit would include philosophical or social validation preferences of social agents in the setting (employers, supervisors, managers, and co-workers), normative behavioral expectations for client competence/behavioral compliance, receptivity to and value placed on best practice standards, technical assistance capabilities, support systems for facilitating the intervention program, and so forth.

Program-specific features relating to program-environment fit include philosophical or ideological compatibility issues, the intrusiveness or disruptiveness of the program to the setting, the response cost associated with program implementation, the required resources, the power or efficiency of the program in addressing the problem(s) to which it is applied, training issues, and so on. The authors believe these variables have an enormous impact upon the ultimate value of programs and interventions to consumers, directly affecting the probability of the setting's acceptance, adoption and long-term maintenance of same. An assessment procedure with appropriate decision-making criteria and recommendations is included in the *EEO Guide* for addressing the critical variables in program-environment fit. There is ample evidence (see Schalock, Chapter 10, this volume) to suggest that much of the variance in program failure outcomes within a range of residential, employment, and school settings can be attributed to insufficient attention to these program-environment variables. Achieving satisfactory levels of implementation fidelity and maintaining program-related gains over the long term are, in the authors' view, virtually impossible in the context of an inadequate program-environment fit.

OVERVIEW OF EEO HABILITATION PLANNING PACKAGE

Powerful methods are currently available to assist job coaches, employment training specialists, or other professionals concerned with successful adjustment in competitive employment settings. In order to conceptualize these methods effectively, a complete package was designed as part of the EEO project that incorporates the technical knowledge bases and simultaneously prepares the habilitation planner to address complex issues in social competence. The package allows individual components to be used singly or in combination. It also outlines a decision-making process for both the professional and the placement agency. Two primary components are contained in the package: the *EEO User's Guide* and the *EEO Resource Manual* (Calkins & Walker, 1988). It may be helpful to again review Figure 14.1, which outlines the relationship between the package and overall social competence outcomes. Each component is briefly described in the paragraphs following:

User's Guide

The *EEO User's Guide* contains three sequential sections that allow both the agency and the placement specialist or other professional to make decisions about the most effective placements for successful long- or short-term adjustment. Using this decision-making tool, the professional gathers appropriate information and pinpoints critical functions that need to be addressed relating to the employment site, the worker, or the resources available to the agency. Section I, the EEO match scale, assesses the person-environment match between the work environment, employer expectations, and the target employee. This scale is organized according to 16 critical items that either impair or enhance the process of obtaining or maintaining a job (see Chapter 10, this volume). Discrepancies are then identified in terms of a best "fit" relating to job-related social competence skills or job-specific social competence demands of the work setting. This information is important to staff as they review alternatives for achieving best matches for either the person or the employment setting.

Section II, the EEO intervention strategies profile, is a decision-making instrument that enables the practitioner to review best practices where interventions are required to assure social competence. Information gathered in the EEO match scale offers useful data necessary for selecting interventions and/or placing them in priority order. The intervention component uses a social validation approach, documented by experts, that provides guidelines to professionals and consumers in selecting intervention strategies for remediating behavioral deficits or problems identified by the EEO match scale. This component provides important information regarding three dimensions in the strategy selection process. These are: 1) criteria relating to when intervention should occur as prompted by the severity of the deficit or problem; 2) preferred intervention strategies matched to specific deficits or problems; and 3) the acceptability of available intervention strategies in terms of their intrusiveness cost, efficacy, and so forth. This component also provides information on rules to follow in the implementation of these intervention strategies.

Section III, the program capacity checklist, builds on information gathered in the preceding components. This checklist reviews the agency's ability to maintain the necessary support services for successful job placement over time. The alternate goal of this tool is to continuously review the necessary requirements in the broader system to which an agency should respond for effective placement and job maintenance.

Resource Manual

The *Resource Manual* is designed as a supplement to the *User's Guide* through its presentation of selected reading and resource materials. The *Resource Manual* contains a series of information briefs on topics such as social competence, competitive employment, person-environment fit, and selected intervention strategies. A glossary of terms is also provided to assist habilitation planners. It is anticipated that these materials will be used extensively during inservice and preservice training programs for job coaches or other professionals interested in learning about the *User's Guide*.

ANTICIPATED OUTCOMES

As the preceding sections have established, enhancing employment outcomes for people with developmental disabilities is a complex process requiring attention to domains of social competence and exemplary program practices. In order to effectively influence this process, a practical habilitation planning tool has been developed. The anticipated results of the research and development project described herein will produce three levels of effect. These include: 1) an increase in the knowledge base available to decision makers regarding employment, habilitation planning, and the adjustment of adults with developmental disabilities; 2) directed improvement in system variables that affect the habilitation process; and 3) measured effects on the quality of life of persons with developmental disabilities. At each of these levels improvement in and/or a departure from existing practices is expected.

1. An Increase in the Knowledge Base for Decision Makers While a knowledge base does exist that describes solutions to the complex adjustment problems that people with developmental disabilities face resulting from the demands of competitive employment settings, this information has not been synthesized and integrated to make it available in the everyday practice of habilitation planning. The project described here has integrated this information into the conceptual model underlying the planning guide. A systematic review of this information reveals that it assembles not only best practices but also specifies for decision makers those critical functions to which they must attend in the habilitation planning process (see Figure 14.1).

2. Directed Improvement in System Variables that Affect the Habilitation Process As previously cited, the habilitation process can be improved by the provision of direct training and resource materials designed to improve decision making (Kultgen et al., 1986). The practical guide and activities resulting from this project are designed to improve the traditional training that habilitation planners (e.g., employment training specialist, job coaches, rehabilitation counselors) receive and to focus resources through systematically designed habilitation procedures. As habilitation planners focus on the employment adjustment and social competence problems faced by people with developmental disabilities, they will have to confront some redefinition of roles. Specifically, job descriptions and responsibilities in the area of facilitating successful adjustment will necessarily shift away from more traditional facility-based responsibilities for the person's individual habilitation plan and toward identifying, specifying, and carrying out the different critical activities involved in adjustment training focused on more complete integration into the community. New competencies and roles for service providers will evolve, and organizational structures of agencies involved in planning for adjustment services may change. Interagency cooperation in service delivery should also be improved. The criteria for the selection, matching, and evaluation of competitive employment placements should be operationalized much more fully, particularly as we learn more about person-environment and program-environment fit factors and how to influence them. The desired effect on improving the service systems that support habilitation planning should be significant. While it is widely recognized that habilitation planning can be effective in meeting the overall needs of developmentally disabled persons, unless these planning procedures are clearly specified, the system of services will remain fragmented, with little or no follow-up and continuity of service provision.

3. Measured Positive Effects on the Quality of Life of Persons with Developmental Disabilities The ultimate outcomes anticipated by the application of the *EEO Guide* are clearly reflected, in another context, in the words of Landesman (1986):

> Once we define quality of life and propose measurable standards (both subjective and objective), service providers and families will be better able to pursue innovative programs to achieve these outcomes; social scientists can focus on developing strategies to measure specific, sensitive outcomes; and administrators and policymakers can adopt more reasonable and effective means for monitoring their programs on a regular basis. (p. 142)

The methods and procedures specified in this project are designed to produce standard practices that can be introduced into the habilitation planning process and will lead to socially valid quality-of-life outcomes. The extension of these practices into the habilitation planning process can result in improved quality assurance practices. The benefits of this project should be of value to policy makers, administrators, habilitation practitioners, parents, and, most important, persons with developmental disabilities themselves.

SUMMARY AND CONCLUSIONS

In conclusion, this chapter has outlined an approach to enhancing employment outcomes by applying what has been learned through research about social competence and the adjustment process in a practical, useful way. The importance of social competence as a primary mediator of job success continues to be demonstrated in the literature and as a focus of exemplary habilitation practices. The need for a habilitation planning tool that adequately addresses this potential is required if practitioners are to make the most of available knowledge and technology. The EEO project's habilitation tool is a direct response to that need. The most salient components of the tool were outlined in this chapter and described in terms of two key paradigms: 1) person-environment fit (i.e., the *EEO User's Guide* containing the match scale and intervention strategies profile); and 2) program-environment fit (i.e., program capacity checklist). In addition, the need for supplemental resources to support training and to develop an adequate knowledge base for decision making is addressed through a companion *Resource Manual*. These components constitute a complete habilitation planning package that may be utilized to produce several anticipated outcomes, including an increase in the knowledge base for decision makers, an improvement in system variables that affect the habilitation process, and measured positive effects on the quality of life of persons with developmental disabilities.

By improving the habilitation process as it relates to achieving employment outcomes, we can anticipate an improved quality of life for persons with developmental disabilities. As the *User's Guide* and *Resource Manual* are utilized by job coaches and other professionals, more effective job placement practices and improvements in job maintenance can be anticipated. In the most direct application of the *EEO Guide* and in keeping with the theme of the current volume, we may be much closer to achieving the goal identified by O'Connor (1983) in her American Association on Mental Deficiency presidential address:

> Although it is admittedly futuristic, wouldn't it be exciting if we could get to the point that one could identify community interventions that involved enlisting and/or instructing natural helpers to deliver categories of supportive behaviors that have been empirically identified as predictive of adjustment for mentally retarded persons in various types of settings? (p. 191)

REFERENCES

Calkins, C.F., Griggs, P., & Walker, H.M. (in preparation). *Program-environment fit: A conceptual model and directions for research.*

Calkins, C.F., & Walker, H.M. (Eds.). (1988). *Enhancing employment outcomes habilitation planning package: Improving the social competence of workers with developmental disabilities in integrated employment settings.* Kansas City: Enhancing Employment Outcomes Project, Institute for Human Development, University of Missouri–Kansas City.

Calkins, C.F., Walker, H.M., & Bacon-Prue, A. (1986). Learning and adjustment: Future implications. In W.E. Kiernan & J.A. Stark (Eds.), *Pathways to employment for adults with developmental disabilities* (pp. 229–240). Baltimore: Paul H. Brookes Publishing Co.

Calkins, C.F., Walker, H.M., Bacon-Prue, A., Gibson, B., Martinson, M., & Offner, R. (1985). *Learning and adjustment: Implications for a national profile of development for adults with developmental disabilities* (Technical Report No. 3). Logan: Utah State University.

Chadsey-Rusch, J. (1986). Identifying and teaching valued social behaviors in competitive employment settings. In F.R. Rusch (Ed.), *Competitive employment issues and strategies* (pp. 273–288). Baltimore: Paul H. Brookes Publishing Co.

Foss, G., Bullis, M., & Vilhauer, D. (1984). Assessment and training of job-related social competence for mentally retarded adolescents and adults. In A.S. Halpern & M.J. Fuhrer (Eds.), *Functional assessment in rehabilitation* (pp. 145–158). Baltimore: Paul H. Brookes Publishing Co.

Foss, G., & Peterson, S. (1981). An identification of social/interpersonal skills relevant to job tenure for mentally retarded adults. *Mental Retardation, 19,* 103–106.

Foss, G., Walker, H.M., Todis, B., Lyman, G., & Smith, F. (1986). A social competence model for community employment settings. In P. Ferguson (Ed.), *Issues in transition research: Economic and social outcomes* (pp. 92–123). Eugene: University of Oregon, Specialized Training Program, College of Education.

Furnham, A., & Schaeffer, R. (1984). Person-environment fit, job satisfaction, and mental health. *Journal of Occupational Psychology, 57,* 295–307.

Gilbert, T.F. (1978). *Human competence: Engineering worthy performance.* New York: McGraw-Hill.

Gump, P. (1977). Ecological psychologists: Critics or contributors to behavior analysis. In A. Rogers-Warren & S.F. Warren (Eds.), *Ecological perspectives in behavior analysis* (pp. 133–147). Baltimore: University Park Press.

Horner, R.H., Meyer, L.H., & Fredericks, H.D.B. (Eds.). (1986). *Education of learners with severe handicaps: Exemplary service strategies.* Baltimore: Paul H. Brookes Publishing Co.

Kernan, K., Begab, M., & Edgerton, R. (1983). *Environments and behavior: The adaptation of mentally retarded persons.* Baltimore: University Park Press.

Kiernan, W.E., & Stark, J.A. (Eds.). (1986). *Pathways to employment for adults with developmental disabilities.* Baltimore: Paul H. Brookes Publishing Co.

Kultgen, P., Rinck, C., Calkins, C.F., & Intagliata, J. (1986). *Final report: Expanding the life chances and social support networks of elderly developmentally disabled persons.* Kansas City: University of Missouri at Kansas City, Institute for Human Development.

Landesman, E., & Butterfield, E. (1985, June). *Normalization and deinstitutionalization of mentally retarded individuals: Controversy and facts.* Paper presented to the annual meeting of the American Association of University Affiliated Facilities, Seattle.

Landesman, S. (1986). [Guest editorial]. Quality of life and personal life satisfaction: Definition and measurement issues. *Mental Retardation, 24*(3), 141–143.

Moos, R. (1979). Improving social settings by social climate measurement and feedback. In R. Meunoz, L. Snowden, & J. Kellay (Eds.), *Social and psychological research in community settings* (pp. 81–102). San Francisco: Jossey-Bass.

Moos, R., & Insel, P. (1974). *Issues in social ecology.* Palo Alto, CA: National Press Books.

O'Connor, G. (1983). Social support of mentally retarded persons. [AAMD presidential address]. *Mental Retardation, 21*(5), 187–196.

Paine, S.C., Bellamy, G.T., & Wilcox, B. (1984). *Human services that work: From innovation to standard practice.* Baltimore: Paul H. Brookes Publishing Co.

Romer, D., & Heller, T. (1983). Social adaptation of mentally retarded adults in community settings: A social-ecological approach. *Applied Research in Mental Retardation, 4*(4), 303–314.

Rusch, F.R. (Ed.) (1986). *Competitive employment issues and strategies.* Baltimore: Paul H. Brookes Publishing Co.

Salzberg, C.L., Likins, M., McConaughy, E.K., & Lignugavis/Kraft, B. (1986). Social competence and employment of retarded persons. In N.R. Ellis & N.W. Bray (Eds.), *International review of research on mental retardation* (Vol. 14, pp. 225–257). New York: Academic Press.

Schalock, R., Gadwood, L., & Perry, P. (1984). Effects of different training environments on the acquisition of community living skills. *Applied Research in Mental Retardation, 5,* 425–438.

Schalock, R., & Jensen, M. (1986). Assessing the goodness of fit between persons and their environments. *Journal of The Association for Persons with Severe Handicaps, 11*(2), 103–109.

Sundberg, N., Snowden, L., & Reynolds, W. (1978). Toward assessment of personal competence and incompetence in life situations. *Annual Review of Psychology, 29,* 179–221.

U.S. Commission on Civil Rights. (1983). *Accommodating the spectrum of individual abilities* (Clearinghouse Publication #81). Washington, DC: Author.

Walker, H.M. (1984). The SBS Program: A systematic approach to the integration of handicapped children into less restrictive settings. *Education and Treatment of Children, 6*(4), 421–431.

Walker, H.M. (1986). The AIMS (*A*ssessment for *I*ntegration into *M*ainstream *S*ettings) assessment system: Rationale, instruments, procedures, and outcomes. *Journal of Clinical Child Psychology* [Special Issue on Social Skills in Children and Adolescents], *15*(1), 55–63.

Walker, H.M., & Calkins, C.F. (1986). The role of social competence in the community adjustment of persons with developmental disabilities: Processes and outcomes. *Journal of Remedial and Special Education, 7*(6), 46–53.

IV

OVERVIEW
Support Mechanisms
in Integrated
Employment Environments

Section III outlined recent developments and applications in natural work settings in relation to a number of technological and training strategies, including instructional technology, person-environment analysis, job accommodations, prosthetics, staff training procedures, and habilitation planning for social competence. The section emphasized the changed attitudes toward working with persons who are disabled in natural employment settings, in which the most sophisticated and current state-of-the-art strategies are used to ensure job success. But this process may take considerable time and require extensive "ongoing support." Such a need was recently recognized in the final regulations for supported employment (*Federal Register, 52*(157), August 14, 1987, pp. 30546–30552). In those regulations, supported employment means

> competitive work in an integrated work setting with ongoing support services for individuals with severe handicaps. . . . Ongoing support services mean continuous or periodic job skills training services provided at least twice weekly at the work site throughout the term of employment to enable the individual to perform the work. The term also includes other support services provided at or away from the work site, such as transportation, personal care services and counseling to family members, if skill training services are also needed by, and provided to, that individual at the work site. (p. 30551)

Section IV of this book continues the theme of integration and support in the natural setting. This section begins with Chapter 15 by L. DeStefano, which gives an overview of how best to facilitate the transition from school to adult life for youth with developmental disabilities. The issue of poor employment opportunities for graduates from special education has provided considerable impetus for the supported employment initiative referred to in earlier chapters. The chapter includes an update on the progress to date on implementing individualized transition plans, interagency collaboration, community-based life and work skills curricula, staff development strategies, and program evaluation.

Chapters 16 and 17, by F. R. Rusch, J. Trach, D. Winking, J. Tines, and J. Johnson; and P. Sale, W. Wood, J. M. Barcus, and M. S. Moon, respectively, center on the critical roles played by the job coach. Chapter 16 discusses two major issues that affect the movement of persons with disabilities into industry. One relates to job coach training, including qualifications, salary, turnover rate, and academic background. The second involves assessing the technical assistance needs of industry-based supported employment programs. The authors summarize data and survey findings, primarily from Illinois, regarding each of these issues. Chapter 17 approaches the job coach issue from a different perspective, defining the functions of a job coach in supported employment, determining the necessary competencies for each function, and then implementing a staffing model based on a number of staff utilization parameters. The major job coach functions discussed include program development, implementation, management, evaluation, and interagency collaboration.

The new supported employment initiative has significantly changed our perception and approach to employment opportunities for persons with disabilities. Chapter 18, by J. H. Noble, Jr., and R. W. Conley, reviews this new initiative, along with its prospects, potential problems, and accompanying controversy. The authors also address some of the barriers to effective implementation, including goal displacement, cost shifting, client selection, and constraints on interagency collaboration.

Two areas not typically addressed in rehabilitation literature in the disabilities field are the subjects of the section's last two chapters. The promise and potential of employee assistance programs (EAPs) are summarized by B. Googins in Chapter 19, along with a discussion of their history, nature, functions, and components. Googins concludes his chapter by addressing the issues of EAPs and disability, some of the barriers to EAP involvement with disabilities, and strategies for EAPs and disabled people. In Chapter 20, J. Stark, M. Breder, and T. L. Goldsbury discuss the important cooperative role that industry, insurance companies, and the federal government must play to move a large number of persons with disabilities into the employment sector. The chapter discusses the demographics of the injured and ill worker, the injury process and economic impact, the disability insurance and workers' compensation systems, and a potential model of care based on a trans-systems approach.

Each of the support mechanisms summarized in this section is vital to help ensure the employment success of individuals with disabilities. This (long-term) support is a new thrust in our rehabilitation efforts. Readers will find these chapters productive, informative, and very useful.

15

Facilitating the Transition from School to Adult Life for Youth with Disabilities

Lizanne DeStefano

The term *transition* refers to the process that occurs in late adolescence and early adulthood when a student moves from secondary or postsecondary education into employment (Will, 1984). In 1983, the U.S. Office of Special Education and Rehabilitative Services (OSERS) announced a national priority of aiding the transition process for students with disabilities. This interest in transition came on the heels of the discovery that special education students were not faring very well once they left the mandated services of public education.

A number of studies have analyzed data relating to students with disabilities leaving secondary education (Hasazi, Gordon, & Roe, 1985; Mithaug & Horiuchi 1983; Wehman, Kregel, & Seyforth, 1985). These studies commonly found that students face an inadequate array of employment, education, and independent living options. They frequently encounter waiting lists for adult services and community living arrangements. Instances of significant problems with funding and actual exclusion from services are common occurrences as students move from the mandated services of public education to an adult service system that is based on eligibility. A high percentage of those adults with handicaps who did gain entry into publicly supported day and vocational services experienced low wages, slow movement toward employment, and segregation from nondisabled peers (Bellamy, Rhodes, Bourbeau, & Mank, 1986; U.S. Department of Labor, 1979).

These and other data (Harris & Associates, 1986) indicate that the post–PL 94-142 emphasis upon integration of persons with disabilities into the mainstream of society and the mandate of educational services aimed at maximizing independence for everyone have little meaning if schools continue to prepare students to transition into a life of dependence and segregation. Consequently, in the Education of the Handicapped Act (EHA) Amendments of 1983 (PL 98-199), Sections 625 and 626 extended the responsibility of public education beyond the school-age population to deal specifically with transition services from school to adult life. One indication of the impact of this policy change is evidenced by an 88.3% increase (1979–1986) in the number of students of transition age receiving public school services (U.S. Department of Education). This legislation also authorized $6.6 million annually in grants and contracts intended to strengthen and coordinate education, training, and related services to assist youth in the process of transition.

The bulk of this discretionary money was used to fund over 100 model projects in transition or postsecondary education across the United States, which demonstrated newly conceived transition/postsecondary education models that could be replicated either whole or in part in future years. Subsequent reauthorization of the EHA in 1986 (PL 99-457) has continued the allocation of funds for the creation of new model demonstration projects as well as advocating for the creation of local planning teams, the development of individualized transition plans (ITPs), and state reporting on students of transition age. The remainder of this chapter combines information from research on transition and the model demonstration projects to identify several critical elements in the transition process. These elements are included in a majority of the model demonstration transition programs and either represent areas where much work has been done or where much activity is currently focused or projected. The elements are: 1) early intervention; 2) interagency collaboration; 3) systematic interdisciplinary, multiagency planning; 3) appropriate integration; 4) community-based life and work skills curricula; 5) marketing and employer relations; 6) staff development; and 7) program evaluation. The chapter concludes with a number of suggested future directions for transitional research and demonstration.

ELEMENTS IN AN EFFECTIVE TRANSITION PROGRAM

Early Intervention

If the goal of education is to prepare students to be fully participating members of the community, then educational planning and instruction should be aimed at maximizing students' integration and independence in adult society including the areas of work, residence, and leisure. Toward that end, transition planning should begin as soon as a child is identified as having special needs. Often, however, this does not happen. Most state transition plans target the ages of 14 through 16 to begin transition services, and in the OSERS-funded transition projects, the average age of the individual's first service is 20, with a range of from 6 to 60 years old (Dowling & Hartwell,

1987). As transition activities become established, it is hoped that the average age at which transition planning begins will decrease, reflecting a consideration of the needs of adult life throughout a student's public school program.

Interagency Collaboration

Making a successful transition from school to adult life requires coordination and collaboration among disabled students, their parents, the school, and the adult service delivery systems in a planned and systematic process that begins before the student leaves public school and continues until independent living and productivity are maximized. The issues that can be addressed through interagency collaboration are varied. For example, agencies may differ from schools in their terminology and eligibility criteria. There may be cases of service duplication between the school and adult service agencies, or there may be a lack of adult programming to maintain a student in his or her current employment or independent living status. Political and attitudinal barriers may exist that prohibit agencies from working together to create a smooth system of service delivery. Interagency collaboration can resolve territorial disputes and funding problems by examining each program's philosophies and values, arriving at a commonality of purpose and developing a plan for working together.

As a vehicle for interagency collaboration, staff members from schools and adult service agencies such as vocational rehabilitation and developmental disability services should meet regularly and exchange information on legislative mandates, types of services provided, eligibility criteria, and planning procedures for each agency. This community transition team should work together to assess service needs and community resources, to place targeted needs in order of priority, to identify key players to be involved in planning for the future, and to develop an information base from which to plan (Lagomarcino & Rusch, 1987).

Interagency collaboration efforts can involve other community agencies, including the state department of vocational rehabilitation, Job Training and Partnership Act (JTPA) services, guardianship and advocacy, local community colleges, vocational-technical centers, and representatives of business and industry. Through these collaborative efforts, duplicate services can be eliminated and more appropriate employment training and job placement programs can be initiated. For example, in many localities school districts have worked with vocational rehabilitation counselors assigned to that region to develop cooperative school-work agreements to provide additional employment-related services for students beyond those that the local educational agency could provide. Such arrangements also have been developed between the school and JTPA, allowing schools to provide on-the-job training in actual work environments.

Systematic Interdisciplinary, Multiagency Planning

A critical part of the transition process is the development of an ITP for each student. Federal legislation and associated regulations are not specific with regard to the timeline, format, or procedure used to develop an ITP, but some states and many localities have adopted a form and procedure that parallels the individualized education program (IEP) process (Wehman, Kregel, Barcus, & Schalock, 1986). Given the lack of specificity of federal regulations, local school districts and adult service agencies across the United States typically raise many questions regarding the development of ITPs. Some of their most common concerns are discussed here, based on an aggregate of state transition policy and observation of the practices of the model demonstration projects.

1. *Who should receive transition planning?* Ideally, every student in the public school system should receive some assistance in planning his or her postschool status. The transition initiative, however, is targeted toward those students who received special education services in secondary school or toward other groups at risk for postschool failure such as educationally disadvantaged, drop-out, and minority students.
2. *Who should initiate the planning meeting?* Public schools should take the initiating or convening role. But out of respect for their initiative, they should expect the full cooperation and participation of adult service agencies and other participants.
3. *When should the planning sessions be held?* Individual sessions should be held at least yearly, in conjunction with the existing individualized planning meetings.
4. *Who should be involved in the planning?* At the local level, the individualized planning team may vary with the type and severity of handicapping conditions, but participants may include special education teachers, vocational education teachers, rehabilitation counselors, adult service providers, parents, and the student.
5. *What should the transition plan include?* Transition planning meetings should serve as a forum in which issues related to a specific student's transition and the resulting service implications are discussed. In addition to vocational placement and employment-related goals for the student, other issues that may be appropriate include residential placement, guardianship, transportation, independent living goals, and income support. The ITP should also include annual goals and short-term objectives that reflect the skills required to function on the job and in the community. These goals should be incorporated into the IEP, and responsibilities for programming and services related to each goal should be clearly delineated among the members of the planning team.

Appropriate Integration

Another common element in effective transition programs is the effort to maximize appropriate integration. It is important for students with disabilities to be prepared to live and work in settings with nondisabled persons. Education and employment preparation in appropriate integrated settings allow students to experience and learn to meet the vocational and social demands and expectations of significant others in their work and community living environments. By *appropriate,* this author means age-peer activities, age-peer standards, integration with nondisabled persons, and the avoidance of all separate activities, facilities, and groupings. In cases of postgraduation-age students, this may involve moving postsecondary education and employment service programs from high schools to community college campuses. Provision of training, and work experience in an integrated setting, are essential aspects of all transition programs. Use of public transportation for work-related and leisure needs should be a part of students' training. In general, encouraging the use of community resources such as public libraries, YMCAs, parks, and recreational programs maximizes the individual's integration outside the work environment.

COMMUNITY-BASED LIFE AND WORK SKILLS CURRICULA

Inappropriate and inadequate preparation by secondary education programs have been cited as major causes of postschool adjustment problems among adults with disabilities (Harris & Associates, 1986). Efforts to promote the transition of students from public schools into integrated, independent adult life will be in vain unless schools offer meaningful life and work skills curriculum that are community referenced and community based (Rusch, Chadsey-Rusch, & Lagomarcino, 1987). Developing a community-referenced curriculum requires school personnel to assess the type of jobs or postsecondary education opportunities that are or will be available. These opportunities are then analyzed in terms of the specific academic, vocational, social, and work-related skills required for admission to a program or for acceptable job performance.

To maximize the generalization of skills taught in the curriculum, secondary instructional content and training should occur in community-relevant settings that have immediate value to the student. Community-based training includes mobility training conducted on buses and subways, shopping and consumer skills taught in grocery and department stores, and vocational training in actual, integrated work settings.

Recent research has shown that those students who have paying jobs in high school are more likely to be employed after high school (Hasazi et al.,

1985). In light of this evidence, effective transition includes actual work experience as part of the high school program. Enabling students to gain work experience prior to graduation serves two purposes. First, by providing students with an opportunity to work at actual jobs, the students gain a better understanding of the demands of the work environment and of the expectations of employers and co-workers. Second, the successes and failures experienced by students in real work settings provide transition program staff with a means of evaluating the curriculum content and training offered by their program on the basis of real-world standards (Lagomarcino & Rusch, 1987).

MARKETING AND EMPLOYER RELATIONS

To develop jobs effectively in which to place students, many transition projects have devoted time and effort to analyzing the labor market and creating a marketing program. The reader is referred to Chapters 5 and 6 in Section II of this book for a discussion of the application of marketing concepts.

STAFF DEVELOPMENT

The shortage of well-trained staff is a major problem encountered in the operation of transition programs (see also Chapter 13, this volume). In a survey of OSERS-funded model demonstration transition projects, hiring and training of new staff were commonly cited as major causes of delays in program start-up (DeStefano & Stake, in press). Personnel preparation efforts should include inservice opportunities for direct service personnel as well as for administrators. Staff development activities within and across agencies promote better working relationships through increased communication. Vocational educators, special education teachers, and school counselors need to become well informed about issues that will have an impact on their students' lives.

PROGRAM EVALUATION

Evaluation of transition programs should answer two questions: What happens to students after they leave public education? What happens to students as a result of the transition programs? To assess the effectiveness of school instruction and adult service employment efforts, practitioners must keep abreast of what former students are doing as adults. Evaluations should focus on both qualitative and quantitative outcomes. Transition program staff need to collect information about transition outcomes such as job type, wages earned, benefits, hours worked, job tenure, employer ratings of job performance, level of integration, access to community support services, participation in the community at large, and consumer satisfaction with the transition process. Information on quality of life, life-style satisfaction, and cost-benefit analyses are also important indicators of transition program effectiveness. Findings of evaluation studies on transition are useful for validating and "fine tuning" program activities of the program being evaluated. Other transition programs also can use these reports to guide their own program development and assess the relative efficiency of their own program.

A great deal has been accomplished in the initial years of the transition initiative. In but a short time, the priority on transition is evident in local demonstrations, personnel preparation programs, public information efforts, and parent advocacy group activities. Unfortunately, the magnitude of the transition problem is commensurate with this ambitious level of activity. The priority assigned to transition is a direct reaction to the inequity that is still present in the quality of adult life of individuals with handicaps.

Despite one's best efforts, as people with disabilities leave special education programs, many still face unenviable odds against finding suitable employment or entering services that lead to employment and independent living. Joblessness and waiting lists for services are still common, and those who do enter postschool employment services often are subjected to trivial wages and segregation from community life. For service providers, transition is also a stressful time of funding uncertainties and service discontinuities. And for those responsible for public policies, transition is a time when the effectiveness of one's collective investment in education, rehabilitation, and income maintenance services is put to the ultimate test. The final section of this chapter addresses directions that it is hoped the transition initiative will take in its next few years of implementation.

FUTURE DIRECTIONS

1. *Emphasize the importance of local transition planning.* Successful movement from school to work and independent living require different supports for different people in different circumstances. No generic strategy of staff development, interagency collaboration, service delivery, evaluation, or funding will be appropriate in all localities. For this reason, the field should resist the temptation to identify transition with any one strategy, but, instead, should identify effective strategies for particular circumstances. In this manner, progress toward the goal of employment and improved quality of life for persons with handicaps requires that communities identify major problems with service availability and quality of work in their locality and collaborate to produce solutions to their unique problems.

2. *Include all disabled people in transition planning.* Previous efforts to link school and work have emphasized collaboration among vocational rehabilitation, vocational education, and special education, and consequently

have focused on students with mild educational handicaps. Employment and independent living outcomes are equally important for all groups, and one's efforts should reflect this. If transition is to be available to all students with disabilities, state mental retardation agencies and postsecondary education agencies must become participants in the transition process.

For transition to succeed, educators, adult service providers, and the private sector must embrace the notion that all individuals have the right to learn, work, and live in the most integrated setting possible. Recent changes in adult service legislation, and jointly funded efforts by OSERS and the Rehabilitation Services Administration (RSA) should help to communicate this attitude to the field (see Chapters 3 and 4, this volume).

3. *Emphasize transition strategies without formal services.* Not all transition requires publicly funded services. In the most effective transition, a student simply graduates into a job without relying on postschool services. Formal services can help many persons find suitable employment, but many persons with handicaps may achieve this result equally well through family and friendship networks and experiences with local employers while in school. Educational programs, therefore, must not preclude the development of social networks through segregation from nondisabled peers or removal from the local community for services. The more that appropriate integration and work experience are promoted by transition programs, the more opportunities persons with handicaps will have to secure available jobs without undue dependency on social services.

4. *Evaluate and publicize what works in transition.* Although there are differences in transition across communities, there are also shared problems. Effective generalizable procedures and programs for dealing with those shared problems are critically needed so that future programs can cumulatively build on the most successful approaches. To this end, there is a need to design research studies to document the efficiency of various transition strategies.

CONCLUSION

In conclusion, 5 years after its start, the transition initiative offers both excitement and frustration to those engaged in furthering its goals. It is becoming clear that the transition period can have a significant impact on the overall quality of an individual's adult life. Instead of a transfer of responsibility of services, transition has come to be characterized in terms of independence, participation and integration, community living status, and employment. There is tremendous activity and enthusiasm among those working in and being served by transition programs. These feelings helped to provide momentum to overcome obstacles that threatened the beginning of the initiative. Additional momentum is needed, however, to maintain the vitality of the concept in the second phase of the initiative, as implementation becomes more widespread and as transition services become institutionalized as part of the special education and adult service delivery system.

REFERENCES

Bellamy, T., Rhodes, L., Bourbeau, P., & Mank, D. (1986). Mental retardation services in sheltered workshops and day activity programs: Consumer benefits and policy alternatives. In F.R. Rusch (Ed.), *Competitive employment issues and strategies* (pp. 257–271). Baltimore: Paul H. Brookes Publishing Co.

DeStefano, L., & Stake, R. (in press). *Issues in evaluating federal transition programs.* Champaign: University of Illinois, Transition Institute.

Dowling, J., & Hartwell, C. (1987). *Compendium of project profiles, 1987.* Champaign: University of Illinois, Transition Institute.

Harris & Associates. (1986). *The ICD Survey of disabled Americans: Bringing disabled Americans into the mainstream: A nationwide survey of 1,000 disabled people.* New York: Author.

Hasazi, S.B., Gordon, L.R., & Roe, C.A. (1985). Factors associated with the employment status of handicapped youth exiting high school from 1979 to 1983. *Exceptional Children, 51*(6), 455–469.

Lagomarcino, T., & Rusch, F.R. (1987). Supported employment: Transition from school to work. *Interchange, 8*(1), 1.

Mithaug, D.E., & Horiuchi, C.N. (1983). *Colorado statewide follow-up of special education students.* Denver: Colorado Department of Education.

Rusch, F.R., Chadsey-Rusch, J., & Lagomarcino, T. (1987). Preparing students for employment. In M.E. Snell (Ed.), *Systematic instruction of persons with handicaps* (pp. 471–490). Columbus, OH: Charles E. Merrill.

U.S. Department of Education. (1986). *Eighth annual report to Congress on the implementation of the Education of the Handicapped Act: To assure the free appropriate public education of all handicapped children* (Vol. 1). Office of Special Education and Rehabilitative Services, Special Education Programs. Washington, DC: U.S. Government Printing Office.

U.S. Department of Labor. (1979). *Sheltered workshop study: Workshop survey* (Vol. 1). Washington, DC: Author.

Wehman, P.H., Kregel, J., Barcus, J.M., & Schalock, R.L. (1986). Vocational transition for students with developmental disabilities. In W.E. Kiernan & J.A. Stark (Eds.), *Pathways to employment for adults with developmental disabilities* (pp. 113–127). Baltimore: Paul H. Brookes Publishing Co.

Wehman, P., Kregel, J., & Seyforth, J. (1985). Employment outlook for young adults with mental retardation. *Rehabilitation Counseling Bulletin, 29*, 90–99.

Will, M. (1984). *OSERS programming for the transition of youth with disabilities: Bridge from school to working life.* Washington, DC: U.S. Department of Education, Office of Special Education and Rehabilitative Services.

16

Job Coach and Implementation Issues in Industry
The Illinois Experience

Frank R. Rusch,
John Trach, Debbie Winking,
Jeffrey Tines, and John Johnson

Two critical issues affecting the movement of persons with disabilities into industry relate to the development of job coaches and assessing the technical assistance needs of an industry-based supported employment program. Chapter 17 describes in detail the responsibilities of a job coach. The current chapter also briefly discusses the duties of the position, but is principally devoted to examining training issues involving the job coach. In addition, the chapter describes an instrument, referred to as the Degree of Implementation (DOI) instrument, that provides a standard by which one can evaluate the implementation of supported employment and a method for assessing the technical assistance needs of individual programs. The data presented are based on supported employment programs in Illinois.

SUPPORTED EMPLOYMENT IN ILLINOIS

In Illinois, supported employment serves more than 625 handicapped individuals. These services are provided by means of three models: individual placements, enclaves, and mobile work crews. According to the data reported by 27 model programs ($N = 334$), 71% of those receiving supported employment services are employed under the enclave model. Most lower-functioning workers receive services under this model, including 94% of those with severe and profound mental retardation. Predictably, individuals working in enclaves have a lower average full-scale IQ score than individuals in either individual placement or mobile work crews, and 34% of all individuals in enclaves previously received services from developmental training programs.

The individual placement model in Illinois serves target employees with an average full-scale IQ of 61 or more. In addition, 56% of all workers in individual placement previously received services in a regular work program. Mobile work crews serve the fewest number of workers ($N = 35$). Characteristically, the majority of these workers are classified as mildly mentally retarded (63%). Their average full-scale IQ score is higher than that of workers in the enclave model, but lower than that of workers in individual placement jobs. It is also interesting that members of this group earn substantially less if they are employed on mobile work crews than if they are employed in enclaves or individual placements.

ANALYSIS OF JOB COACH INTERVENTION

The job coach has emerged as the key staff member in facilitating this new community employment option for persons traditionally employed in sheltered workshops. The job title given to these direct service providers varies across agencies, and includes: job coach, vocational training specialist, employment training specialist, and community supervisor. However, the function is the same: to enable persons with handicaps to enter into the mainstream of society through community employment.

Job Coach Duties

The position of the job coach differs from that of other direct service personnel employed by adult service agencies in the type and variety of skills performed (see also Chapter 17, in this volume). Because supported employment is community based, job coaches must function on a day-to-day basis without the array of support staff present in the traditional sheltered workshop. Job coaches are required to perform management as well as direct service functions, and to represent the agency to the businesses providing employment and the community at large. The job coach is the liaison between all the groups involved in the supported employment process, including the employer, parents, co-workers, agency personnel, and the worker.

The duties of the coach include direct training responsibilities of specific job and social skills on site, job development, worker advocacy, and agency public relations. Flexibility is an essential trait for the successful job coach. For example, on a given day, a job coach's tasks may range from teaching a worker a single component of a floor-sweeping task to meeting with a group of employers and line supervisors concerning job enlargement possibilities. The two tasks obviously require very different competencies. However, because of the level of disability of individuals targeted for service in (supported) employment programs, much of the job coach's time is spent on intervention activities.

Intervention Time

Information on the number of hours job coaches spend on intervention activities is essential for those responsible for establishing efficient and cost-effective staffing patterns across job sites. Intervention time includes time spent on specific activities that enable workers to learn their jobs and maintain employment. Intervention activities include:

Direct training—training of all specific job tasks (e.g., dishwashing, assembly filing)
Indirect training—training of all job-related skills (e.g., social behavior, travel training, time telling)
Observation—supervision without hands-on training
Follow-up—trainer activities after the worker has acquired the basic skills necessary for job retention (e.g., employer contacts, scheduled site visits for retraining)

Data analysis has been completed on 105 target employees from 16 model programs in Illinois for the major job coach activities just listed for 6 consecutive months from October, 1986 through March, 1987. Among the four activities, job coaches in enclave placements spent the most hours in direct training (average hours per month = 24.78) and the least hours in follow-up activities (average = 2.81). In individual placements, the greatest number of average hours was devoted to follow-up and observation activities (average = 3.72 and 3.71, respectively), with the least number of hours involved in direct training and indirect training (average = 3.03 and 1.58, respectively). The 8:1 ratio of direct training activities in enclave versus individual placements is understandable, since individuals involved in group placements or enclaves usually are those in need of more intensive training time owing to the severity of their disability. These results support the contention of Lagomarcino, Trach, Rusch, and McNair (in press) that generally, lower-functioning individuals who require more direct training and supervision may be most effectively served through a group placement or enclave model.

JOB COACH TRAINING ISSUES

Because the role of job coach requires competence in the business world as well as a working knowledge of the social services system and behavior principles, there is little consensus about the qualifications necessary to be successful in the position. The debate of those responsible for staffing supported employment programs concerns whether the most effective job coaches have social services or business-related backgrounds. In the first instance, the individual must learn the priorities and philosophy of the business world in order to establish and maintain relations at the worksite; and in the second, the individual must be taught the behavior change strategies utilized in social services to provide effective behavioral programming for individuals with severe disabilities.

Data from a survey of 27 supported employment programs in January, 1987 provide extensive information about job coaches employed in Illinois. The survey was conducted with supported employment program coordinators using an interview format. Information reported included the qualifications that agencies required of applicants as well as the work experience and educational background of those they hired, salary and benefits paid, turnover rate, and reasons for termination.

Qualifications

Survey results showed that programs are increasingly specifying business experience in addition to experience with persons with disabilities as a condition for employment. The following description provides a composite of qualifications specified in program job descriptions as well as of individuals actually hired as job trainers in Illinois:

Of the programs responding, 58% required a bachelor's degree, and 23% required a high school diploma.

Of the agencies responding, 52% specified 1–2 years of work experience with people with disabilities, 3% required only experience in the business sector, and 39% required both experience with disabilities and experience in business.

Of the 144 job coaches actually hired, 34% had a bachelor of science or bachelor of arts degree in a related field (special education, rehabilitation, psychology, social work), and 4% had a master of science degree.

Of those hired, 34% had only a high school diploma.

Of those hired, 58% had experience in working with individuals with developmental disabilities on a paid or voluntary basis.

Of those hired, 7% had business experience that related to the work they would be performing as job coach, 17% had unrelated business experience, and 4% had a combination of experience in business and social services.

Salary

Although almost 60% of the 31 programs surveyed required a bachelor's degree and almost 70% required some college hours, results showed that the mean salary for job coaches in Illinois programs was only $12,648 for those without experience and $13,392 for those with experience. An examination of the demographics of job trainers actually hired in the state shows that only 34% held bachelor's degrees in a related field and only 10% had degrees in unrelated fields. Job coaches received the same benefit packages as all agency employees, except for a few instances in which the job coach was working only part time.

How does this salary schedule compare with that of other direct service positions within the agency? As of January 1, 1987, 39% of the 27 agencies reported that the job coach's salary was approximately the same as that of floor supervisor or day trainer in the sheltered workshop. Twenty-nine percent stated that the job coach's salary was higher than the comparison group. Thirteen percent of the agencies responding were not facility based and therefore had no comparison group, and the remaining 19% did not respond.

Given the scope of duties and degree of autonomy inherent in the position, it is recommended that supported employment job coaches be paid on a salary schedule that is separate from that of other direct service personnel who staff programs in sheltered workshops. These findings support recommendations made in a recent Delphi study on job coach responsibilities, which stated that salary levels of supported employment job coaches should be made commensurate with traditional professional positions in rehabilitation and education (Cohen, Patton, & Melia, 1985).

Turnover Rate

Consistency of training is a crucial factor in measurable behavioral gains of individuals with severe disabilities (Snell, 1983). The high turnover rate of the job coach is an obvious threat to consistency of programming at the job site. Survey results indicated that 69 of the 144 job coaches hired were terminated (a *termination* refers to any job separation); that is, 2 individuals were hired for every available job coach position over a 12-month period. The number of job coaches terminated across individual programs ranged from 9 to 0. Forty-one of the 69 reported terminations were explained by the categories of money, promotion within the agency, and promotion outside the agency. Given that the majority of reasons for termination were related to money and promotion, and that promotion implied an increase in money or prestige or both, it appears that it was difficult to retain job coaches in the field at the January 1, 1987, salary levels.

ASSESSING TECHNICAL ASSISTANCE NEEDS

The second major issue influencing the movement of persons with disabilities into industry relates to assessing the technical assistance needs of industry-based supported employment programs. The Degree of Implementation (DOI) instrument that the authors have developed is based on the research literature related to national model demonstration development of supported employment programs (in Illinois, Oregon, Vermont, and Virginia). The intent of the DOI is to provide both a standard by which one can evaluate the implementation of the supported employment initiative and a method for assessing the technical assistance needs of individual model programs.

The DOI is used to: 1) provide structure for beginning projects to establish supported employment programs by informing them of relevant activities identified through the literature, 2) analyze the progress of supported employment projects and document the projects' efforts in relationship to a specified time frame, 3) investigate and identify possible variables that might facilitate program development, 4) analyze the proposed model in relationship to actual documented services being provided, and 5) investigate the relationship of the model to selected outcome variables (such as level of worker served, hourly wage, and tenure). The instrument lists 28 steps or indicators that are categorized according to five components of supported employment programs: 1) job survey and analysis, 2) job match, 3) job acquisition and maintenance, 4) conjunctive job services/interagency coordination, and 5) job fit. Using written documentation provided by model programs, the evaluator scores the presence or absence of each indicator by scoring a 0 (meaning No—nonexistent), a 1 (meaning Emergent—present but incomplete), or a 2 (meaning Yes—present and complete). Preestablished written criteria determine the scoring of each indicator and serve as a manual (available to readers from the senior author of this chapter) for the administration of the instrument. The overall reliability obtained from the last set of ratings was 0.89 (Range = 0.70 to 1.00).

The results of efforts at implementing the proposed model of (supported) employment in Illinois are presented in Table 16.1. Level of implementation

Table 16.1. Percentages of overall scores by quartile degree of implementation

Quartile	Percentage of projects at each level of implementation			
	March–April 1986	May–June 1986	December–February 1987	June 1987
1. 0%–25% implementation	42	30	13	14
2. 26%–50% implementation	21	33	47	46
3. 51%–75% implementation	27	18	27	21
4. 76%–100% implementation	9	18	13	19

Note: See text for further explanation.

is expressed in the table in quartiles. The first quartile (0%–25%) is the lowest level of implementation and indicates the extent (percentage of DOI activities) to which a particular project has been implemented. The fourth quartile (76%–100%) is the highest level of program implementation. Table 16.1 provides the percentages for each quartile in each round of data collection. The most current data demonstrate that 86% of the projects are in the top three quartiles of implementation and that the most growth has occurred in the second quartile, whereas the third and fourth quartiles have remained relatively constant. As of Fall, 1987, 19% of the model programs scored at least 42 out of a possible 56 total points, or implemented approximately 21 or more of the 28 supported employment activities (fourth quartile). The items implemented most frequently are those activities that survey the community (#1), target specific jobs (#3), task-analyze potential jobs (#6), identify requisite skills (#8), assess and observe vocational skills (#12 and #14), and reassess through observation the client's maintenance of vocational skills (#26). The percentage of implementation of this group of activities has remained relatively the same across most of the rounds of data collection.

Although the items cited in the previous paragraph represent the core of activities that most projects are implementing, they do not necessarily indicate all of the activities associated with successful supported employment programs. There are important activities that many projects are not implementing. For example, the identification and assessment of social skills are implemented at a significantly lower rate than items related to vocational aspects of employment. Ironically, research literature indicates that persons with disabilities lose their jobs most often because of social skills deficits (Greenspan & Shoutz, 1981). It would seem important, therefore, for projects to conduct social skills assessment and intervention activities. It is encouraging that more social skills assessments occurred in the last round than in previous rounds. It could be that the need for attention to social skills becomes evident as projects gain experience.

Although it was initially troubling that there was a lack of systematic training, data collection, and withdrawal, those projects implementing this activity (#16) increased from 37% to 53% in the last 6 months. This increase was a positive sign, but activity within the job acquisition and maintenance component will need to increase substantially to guarantee future success. The low-level implementation of job acquisition and maintenance activities may be attributed to the level of worker being served by the initiative. There is some indication that there is an inverse relationship between the level of worker functioning and scores on the job acquisition and maintenance component of the DOI. This finding has been interpreted to mean that workers with higher IQ scores do not require as much training as workers with lower scores (Trach & Rusch, 1987).

SUMMARY

In summary, this chapter has attempted to sensitize the reader to critical job coach and program implementation/technical assistance issues. The results of the DOI data collection indicate that since June, 1985, there has been a positive trend toward increasing the implementation of supported employment activities in Illinois. There has been an increase in documented training activities, and those projects in the upper two quartiles have maintained the high-quality level of services for 2 years. It is also encouraging that 18% of the programs improved their degree of implementation status, whereas 11% of the projects experienced some slippage, which seems to indicate that there continues to be some movement to improve model implementation. Overall, there were 19 activities that increased, 8 that decreased, and 1 that remained at the same level of implementation. Job survey and analysis and job match are the most widely implemented components; the remaining three components—job acquisition and maintenance, conjunctive job services/interagency coordination, and job fit—are implemented at consistently low levels. Some possible reasons for nonimplementation of DOI activities include: 1) lack of documentation, 2) inability to implement because of insufficient staff resources or lack of technology, 3) staff resistance to change, 4) low level of worker functioning, and 5) philosophical differences. The remaining chapters in this section address a number of these issues.

REFERENCES

Cohen, D.E., Patton, S.L., & Melia, R.P. (1985). Staffing supported and transitional employment programs: Issues and recommendations. *American Rehabilitation, 11*(4) 20–24.

Greenspan, S., & Shoutz, B. (1981). Why mentally retarded adults lose their jobs: Social competence as a factor in work adjustment. *Applied Research in Mental Retardation, 2,* 23–38.

Lagomarcino, T.R., Trach, J.S., Rusch, F.R., & McNair, J. (in press). *Overview of practices and emerging trends in employment services.* In R. Barrett & J.L. Matson (Eds.), *Developmental disabilities: A life span approach.* New York: Grune & Stratton.

Snell, M.E. (1983). *Systematic instruction of the moderately and severely handicapped.* Columbus, OH: Charles E. Merrill.

Trach, J.S., & Rusch, F.R. (1987). Validation of an instrument for evaluating supported employment programs: The degree of implementation. In J. S. Trach & F. R. Rusch (Eds.), *Supported employment in Illinois: Program implementation and evaluation* (Vol. 1, pp. 51–73). Champaign-Urbana: University of Illinois, Secondary Transition Intervention Effectiveness Institute.

17

The Role of the Employment Specialist

Paul Sale,
Wendy Wood, J. Michael Barcus,
and M. Sherril Moon

The decade of the 1980s has seen a major expansion of the ways in which people with disabilities gain access to vocational opportunities. Supported employment is one of the new approaches available to assist consumers with disabilities in finding and maintaining meaningful paid employment. The development of this model has been spurred by empirical demonstration of its success in increasing job numbers, wages, retention, and cost-effectiveness (see Chapter 24, this volume). The model has also been designated through legislation as a viable service delivery option (Vocational Rehabilitation Amendments of 1986).

Personnel implementing supported employment training perform differing functions and thus require different competencies than traditional rehabilitation personnel. This chapter defines these functions primarily from the perspective of the employment specialist who is implementing the individual placement model (cf. Mank, Rhodes, & Bellamy, 1986, for other placement models). The chapter also outlines critical competencies needed by personnel for these functions. The term *function* refers to groups of activities performed by an employment specialist—for example, providing program implementation. Major functions must often be subcategorized into *activities*. In supported employment, program implementation involves many activities from job placement to follow-along. The term *competencies* refers to the knowledge, skills, and abilities needed to perform a function and related activities. For example, to perform the function of program implementation, the employment specialist should be fluent in the use of systematic instruction, including task analytic assessment, reinforcement, prompting, and the eventual fading of nonnatural instructional cues.

DEFINING FUNCTIONS IN SUPPORTED EMPLOYMENT

Supported employment services for people with disabilities is an employment process that focuses on the individual. The basic activities of supported employment programs for these persons relate to program development, program implementation, program management, program evaluation, integrity, and collaboration (Danley & Mellen, 1987; Moon, Goodall, Barcus, & Brooke, 1986; Rusch, 1986; Wehman, 1981; Wood, 1988).

Efforts to develop supported employment nationally have generated a variety of new personnel roles. In 1985 the U.S. Office of Special Education and Rehabilitative Services sponsored a project to identify essential competencies for operating supported employment programs. The results of this project indicated two main roles for staff within supported employment programs: employment training specialists and managers (Harold Russell Associates, 1985). Kregel and Sale (1988) suggest that the key role in supported employment is the employment specialist, a position that has also been variously referred to as an employment training specialist (Cohen, Patton, & Melia, 1986), a job coach (Wehman & Melia, 1985), and a job coordinator (Kregel & Sale, 1988).

An employment specialist provides individualized services in all aspects of the employment process for persons with severe disabilities. This community-based professional provides services in actual work settings rather than in a training facility. The employment specialist may work out of a nonprofit placement program, traditional adult service program (agency), or a secondary education program (Wehman & Melia, 1985). Coordination and careful planning with individual workers, parents or guardians, employers, co-workers, adult service providers, rehabilitation counselors, and other human services providers are key roles for this specialist. Performing the functions of an employment specialist requires the utilization of a variety of strategies and the completion of numerous activities, summarized in Table 17.1.

Program Development

Initially, an employment specialist screens the community for potential jobs that are appropriate for persons with disabilities. The purpose of this general job market screening is to determine the types of employment available within the community. It is recommended that the job market screening be updated every 6–12 months (Moon et al., 1986).

After a general screening has been completed, an employment specialist begins contacting employers about specific job openings. The employment specialist may telephone a company to gather specific information about the job such as job duties, hours, location, wages, and benefits. If the position seems appropriate, an appointment to meet with the employer is made.

During the initial site visit, the employment specialist reviews with the employer the services the program offers. The work capabilities of individuals with severe disabilities and the level of interest in the available job are described. The role of the employment specialist in training the worker is explained, as is the fact that the employment specialist will remain available for follow-up services even after fading from the job site. Finally, the employment specialist arranges to observe someone performing the job. When observing, it is important to identify the major job duties, the sequence of these duties, critical vocational and nonvocational skills, and the time spent in each work area. Employment specialists are frequently required to use the strategies outlined in Table 17.2 during the program development phase.

Concurrently with job development, the employment specialist conducts consumer assessments to determine the strengths and training needs of several consumers in order to establish a referral pool of potential workers who may fill job openings as they become available. Employment specialists promptly acknowledge receipt of individual referrals to the program. They ensure consumer confidentiality regarding all records released to and developed by the supported employment program. Employment specialists make arrangements for personal interviews with the consumer and family to explore their ideas and address family questions and concerns. The family is counseled on benefits and disincentives to employment for their son or daughter. The employment specialist arranges time to observe the consumer directly to determine individual factors such as endurance, strength, communication, and response to supervision. The data are then summarized for all assessments. The employment specialist informs the consumer, family, and referral source of the results of the screening. This consumer assessment provides the employment specialist, consumer, family, and referral source with an overall view of the individual with regard to placement into employment.

Program Implementation

Once a job has been identified, the function of an employment specialist is to determine which candidate can be placed and trained in this particular position. This requires a review of both the job analysis information gathered during job development and the consumer assessment information. Once a consumer has been identified, an interview with the employer ensues. If the interview goes well, the employment specialist negotiates a starting work date. Then the consumer's family is notified so that arrangements can be made for the individual to start work. The employment specialist explains to the consumer and to his or her family the job benefits package, the pay rate, hours, job responsibilities, and the ramifications of employment with regard to the individual's Social Security benefits.

Next, the employment specialist provides direct, systematic instruction of job tasks and related behavioral skills to the consumer at the job site. The

Table 17.1. Employment specialist functions and activities within each supported employment component

Function	Component	Activities
Program development	Job development	Conducting community job market screening Making specific employer contacts Conducting employer interview Conducting environmental analysis Competing job analysis
	Consumer assessment	Conducting consumer interviews Observing consumer Interpreting formal records Completing task analysis Interviewing family, consumer, and others
	Program marketing	Public relations Sales/marketing Diplomacy Advocacy
Program implementation	Job placement	Conducting job compatibility analysis Facilitation, job interview
	Job-site training	Orienting the worker to the job site Orienting the worker to the community Training initial skill acquisition Stabilizing worker performance Fading from the job site
	Ongoing support	Advocacy On-site visits Communication with family, worker, and employer Counseling, career advancement Case management
Program management	Individual placement case management	Recording intervention time

(continued)

Table 17.1. *(continued)*

Function	Component	Activities
		Collecting instruction intervention data Collecting probe data Collecting product data Collecting on-/off-task data Interpreting data Problem solving Record keeping
	Caseload management	Ongoing support to workers stabilized in a job Provision of follow-along Scheduling new placements
Program evaluation	Follow-along	Collecting employer evaluation Completing progress reports Communicating with parent/guardian Conducting on-site observations Maintaining contact with employers Retraining job skills
Interagency collaboration	Coordinating services with various community human services providers	Communication with: Rehabilitation services MR/DD adult services School services Social services MH services Welfare Medical insurance Transportation Unemployment compensation Knowledge of federal and state regulations that apply to supported employment

Adapted from Buckley, Albin, and Mank (1988); Cohen, Patton, and Melia (1986); Danley and Mellen (1987); Kregel and Sale (1988); and Wood (1988).

period of on-site training can vary from several weeks to several months, depending on the skill levels of both the employment specialist and the worker and the complexity of the job duties (Moon et al., 1986). Job-site training

Table 17.2. Employment specialist job activities development strategies

Advertise your services in the community so that agencies and businesses are aware of your program.

Contact local chamber of commerce for current and future job trends.

Contact state employment commission for current and future job trends.

Become familiar with potential employer listings in the local Yellow Pages.

Read and screen classified ads.

Contact local vocational rehabilitation counselors, job placement services, civic groups, sheltered workshops, and Private Industry Council.

Talk directly with potential employers.

Telephone employers with and without advertised job openings.

Visit employers with and without advertised job openings.

Interview employers to discuss current job openings and to market the supported employment approach.

Explain the capabilities of workers to employers.

Describe and explain incentives and benefits of hiring workers with disabilities using the supported employment models.

Assess the routine of job duties required if job looks favorable.

Observe job and employees and analyze the environment.

Observe job and employees and analyze the specific job.

Source: Adapted from Moon, Goodall, Barcus, and Brooke (1986).

phases have been identified as job orientation and assessment, initial skill training and acquisition, and stabilization. Specific activities for each are summarized in Table 17.3.

Program Management

The employment specialist is responsible for assuring that placement, training, and ongoing support are effectively managed. The success of an individual worker's placement frequently hinges on the employment specialist's ability to direct all aspects of the placement. Initially, the employment specialist will want the consumer information gathered during consumer assessment, as well as the sequence of job duties, job duty analysis, and employer interview information for the position in which an individual is placed. During the initial weeks of the placement (orientation and assessment), this information, along with observations of the individual worker's performance at the job site and feedback from the employer, enables a review of the job-worker compatibility.

When initial skill training begins, it is important to have written instructional programs for all job duties. Instructional programs should include the

Table 17.3. Activities for job-site training

Orientation and assessment	Initial skill training	Stabilization
Establish rapport with supervisors and co-workers.	Develop a training schedule.	Increase production to company standards.
Orient the worker to other work environments in relation to her or his primary work area (restrooms, supply room, break areas, lunch areas, supervisor's office, emergency exits, etc.).	Task analyze job duty(ies) to be instructed. Determine the employees's initial work performance. Establish an instructional program that includes: training schedule, individualized job duty analysis, reinforcement procedures, training procedures, and data collection procedures.	Stabilize job performance under natural environmental conditions (program natural cues, consequences, and reinforcers; and expand performance across supervisors and job situations).
Orient the worker to the community (location of bus stops, getting to and from work, etc.).		Expand performance across all job duties.
Identify sequence of job duties.		Involve supervisors and/or co-workers.
Analyze specific job duties.	Implement instructional program.	Implement procedures to systematically fade trainer presence from the job site.
Assess job/worker compatibility.	Collect instructional data and analyze. Work out job modifications if needed. Systematically fade instruction. Keep family/guardian aware of worker's performance. Encourage co-worker socialization. Always model appropriate work behaviors.	

Adapted from detailed breakdown of job-site training strategies in Barcus, Brooke, Inge, Moon, and Goodall (1987).

training schedule, individualized job duty analysis, reinforcement procedures, and plans for fading instruction (Barcus, Brooke, Inge, Moon, & Goodall, 1987; Gaylord-Ross & Holvoet, 1985). Once an instructional program is implemented, it is imperative that probe data (recording of a worker's independent performance of a job duty without training instruction) and instructional data be collected (Rusch, 1986; Snell, 1987). This information enables the employment specialist to analyze the growth in the worker's performance and to make decisions regarding any changes that may need to be instituted in the instructional program.

Once a worker performs all steps of the job duty, the employment specialist must assure that the work has been performed according to the employer's standard. At this point, it is important to gather probe and instructional data regarding the worker's production performance, which will assist in the development of appropriate production training strategies. Once the worker is performing the job duty at the employer's standard without the presence of the trainer, it is helpful to continue production data collection, as well as perform checks on the worker's on- and off-task performance, and, at the same time, begin repeating this process for the next major job duty targeted for instruction. The process is repeated until all job duties are being performed under natural worksite conditions.

An accurate account of how much intervention time is spent with an individual enables the employment specialist to determine the specific areas of strength and weakness for that placement. The employment specialist should record intervention time by dividing it into specific categories such as time at the job site spent actively training a worker, time spent on the job site between periods of active intervention, and other intervention directly related to job skills training (transporting the worker, training money handling, grooming, etc.).

During the initial skills training and stabilization phases of job-site training, analysis of intervention data assists the employment specialist in determining when to begin fading support. Regular review of the intervention data can also reveal how the employment specialist's time is being spent and can help in identifying areas in which the employment specialist needs to spend more time. In addition, intervention time data can aid the employment specialist in billing various support agencies for the reimbursement of the cost of placement (Kregel, Hill, & Banks, 1987).

In addition to facilitating individual case management, the employment specialist will be responsible for managing a growing caseload of workers. Several factors will determine the intervention time an employment specialist spends with each person and the number of persons that can be served. Experience will aid the employment specialist in estimating training time for a particular placement, and intervention data can be used to decide when to become involved in placing a new worker, how to schedule follow-up visits for persons already placed, and strategies to use for covering emergency situations.

Program Evaluation

Ongoing assessment and follow-along activities begin the first day an individual is placed on a job and continue long after the employment specialist has faded from the worksite. It is essential that an employment specialist establish methods for regular, ongoing assessment of a worker's performance. Periodic employee evaluations by the employer, progress reports to the family and worker, parent/guardian questionnaires, ongoing site visits to observe the worker, telephone contacts with employers, and discussions with family members are a few of the activities for gathering follow-along information that have been found effective (Moon et al., 1986). Systematic collection of information regarding the worker's performance is critical for an employment specialist in order to minimize the chance of the employee's termination. Table 17.4 provides examples of program evaluation activities performed by employment specialists at Virginia Commonwealth University's Rehabilitation Research and Training Center in Richmond.

Interagency Collaboration

Placing and maintaining an individual with severe disabilities in employment requires the employment specialist to coordinate activities ranging from Social Security payments to living accommodations. Therefore, the employment specialist must communicate regularly with other service providers and be actively involved in assisting the worker to access other services that may be necessary to achieve and maintain successful employment. In addition, the employment specialist may need to assist the worker in accessing additional programs or support services. Such services may include: rehabilitation counselor services, personnel case attendant services, co-worker support arrangements, transportation, recreation/leisure opportunities, unemployment compensation, alternative living arrangements, access to support groups, and many others (Wood, 1988). The employment specialist takes a lead role in coordinating the support services necessary for continued successful employment and in collaborating with other service providers to address and solve problems that are impeding job stability (Hill, 1988; Wood, 1988).

COMPETENCIES NEEDED BY EMPLOYMENT SPECIALISTS

"'Competency' is a kind of motherhood and apple pie word around which everyone can rally" (National School Public Relations Association [NSPRA], 1978, p. 14). Supported employment and other rehabilitation personnel have indeed rallied around the task of delineating competencies (Danley & Mellen, 1987; Kregel & Sale, 1988; Leahy, Shapson, & Wright, 1987). There is, however, little uniformity in the definition of what a *competency* is or in methods for determining specific competencies. For the purposes of this chapter, the definition of *competency* put forth by McAshan (1979) has been adopted: "the knowledge, skills and abilities or capabilities that a person achieves, which become part of his or her being to the extent he or she can satisfactorily perform particular cognitive, affective and psycho-motor behavior" (p. 10). The collection of specific knowledge, skills, and abilities is the foundation that allows the employment specialist to engage in the myriad of activities required to execute each function.

Table 17.4. Program evaluation activities of employment specialists

Orientation and assessment	Initial skill training	Stabilization	Follow-along
Supervisor completes evaluation 2 weeks after first day of work.	Supervisor completes evaluation once a month for next 5 months.	Supervisor completes evaluation once every 3 months for next 18 months.	Continue to collect supervisor evaluations of the worker on established schedule (one every 6 months for duration of employment).
Prepare progress report based on evaluations.	Prepare progress report based on each evaluation.	Prepare progress report based on supervisor evaluation schedule.	Continue to complete progress reports.
Review progress with worker and family/guardian.	Review progress with worker and family/guardian.	Review progress with worker and family/guardian.	On-site visits at least twice a month.
Parents complete questionnaire.	Parents complete questionnaire once a month for next 5 months.	Parents complete questionnaire once every 3 months.	
Supervisor completes evaluation at 1 month.			
Prepare progress report.			
Review progress with worker and family/guardian.			
Parents complete questionnaire.			

Source: Virginia Commonwealth University/Rehabilitation Research and Training Center data management system (1987).

There are several methods through which supported employment competencies can be delineated, including: expert opinion, empirical research that identifies variables significant in achieving consumer outcomes, social validation, and specification of competencies according to organizational outcomes (Buckley, Albin, & Mank, 1988). Although attempts to define specific competencies through social validation techniques are emerging, "expert" opinion has been the major method used to date to establish competencies required by supported employment specialists. Given the relatively short time that supported employment models and resulting roles have been in existence, the paucity of outcome research and/or social validation data is not unexpected.

A number of unpublished lists of competencies associated with providing supported employment services have been developed by long-standing supported employment providers. Several competency listings that have emerged recently in the professional literature are summarized in Table 17.5. A number of comments relative to Table 17.5 are in order. First, Danley and Mellen's (1987) competencies were developed for use specifically in supported employment programs for individuals with mental illness. In contrast, Buckley et al. (1988) and Kregel and Sale (1988) have provided competencies relative to providing supported employment to a more nebulous group of consumers identified as having severe disabilities, which may include individuals with mental illness. Danley and Mellen's list has been included to illustrate the commonalities and differences in competency requirements based on the consumer group utilizing supported employment services. As the supported employment model is applied to various consumer groups, the competencies required of supported employment specialists will differ. For example, the three competency listings presented in Table 17.5 do not address mobility training competencies that may be needed as supported employment services are utilized by persons with limited vision. Likewise, competencies such as family and substance abuse counseling skills needed to serve persons with traumatic brain injury are not specified.

In addition to these specific consumer group differences, the authors of this chapter believe that a substantial commonality of competencies is required of all supported employment specialists. For example, surveying local labor opportunities is reported as a needed competency by each author in Table 17.5. Similarly, skill in data collection techniques has been identified by expert opinion as a necessary competency of an employment specialist in any supported employment program (Kregel & Sale, 1988).

The reader should also note the variety of organizational schema utilized by each of the authors cited in Table 17.5. Although all competencies were presented within the context of personnel preparation, there is little uniformity in competency grouping. This is not inherently problematic; however, it again illustrates the need to move from competency lists based on expert opinion to more socially valid and empirically documented competency delineations.

Table 17.5.   Representative supported employment specialist competencies

Danley & Mellen (1987)	Buckley, Albin, & Mank (1988)	Kregel & Sale (1988)
Attitude reflective of the supported employment initiative	*Make available* paid employment opportunities. Generate work opportunities. Maintain access to employment.	*Philosophical,* legal, and policy
Knowledge needs such as reflected in the functions listed in Table 17.1		*Program* development
Skills that include: Basic communication Job/worksite analysis Functional assessment Coaching Advocacy Teaching Behavior programming Service planning Research development Evaluating progress Job site modification Job counseling Documentation Consultation with family, employer, and other service providers	*Analyze work* and train employees. Organize jobs and tasks for performance. Maintain work performance. *Integrate* employees. Identify and access opportunities. Maintain employee integration. *Maintain* organizational capacity. Establish organizational capacity. Manage organizational capacity. *Meet* individual service coordination needs. Hire employees. Deliver employee services. Maintain employee services. Provide transition from school programs.	*Program* management *Program* evaluation *Systematic* instruction *Transition* planning

Each list presented in Table 17.5 and many other unpublished listings represent equally valid descriptions of the competencies needed to perform activities associated with the supported employment specialist's functions. Rather than adding other "expert" opinion, this chapter identifies several potential research issues that may ultimately assist in providing social validation to competency listings and in tying competencies "required" of personnel to employment outcomes for consumers with disabilities. First, one should more fully investigate the actual activities performed by employment specialists. Empirically demonstrating the frequency and topography of the activities engaged in by employment specialists is a critical first step in documenting required competencies. Leahy et al. (1987) provide one possible methodology for addressing this problem. Second, one needs to determine how each activity and its related competencies enhances actual employment outcomes for persons with disabilities. Are competencies advanced as required actually necessary if they do not enhance employment outcomes? The methodology used to answer this question requires numerous primary and secondary subjects and extensive measurement across time (Buckley et al. 1988).

STAFFING MODELS

The various functions and activities of the supported employment models have been accommodated within several different staffing designs. In one staffing arrangement, the holistic model, the employment specialist is responsible for all the various functions and activities described so far in this chapter (i.e., program development, implementation, management, evaluation, and interagency coordination). A second staffing plan, the partitioned model, divides the responsibilities between the job development and job-site training functions, with activities of the other functions evenly or unevenly distributed between the staff persons responsible for these two major functions. A third option divides the staff three ways, using the partitioned models plus a third person to carry out follow-along responsibilities after a large body of individuals has become stable in their employment situations. A fourth option uses the holistic model but again with a second staff person to provide the follow-along coverage.

The advantages and disadvantages of these various staffing models are discussed in this section. Issues related to status assignment, organizational hierarchy, recruitment, efficiency, burnout and staff turnover, pay scales, and skill development are presented as they may be affected by each model.

Holistic Employment Specialist Staffing Model

In the holistic staffing example, all of the major components with their various activities and functions are performed by each employment specialist. The specialist is given the names of persons with disabilities who are being referred for supported employment services and then implements the sequence of activities involved within each component. A simplistic description of this sequence is as follows: The employment specialist gathers relevant information through a process of consumer assessment, develops jobs through contacts with local employers, and carefully compares consumer assessment and job analysis information to determine compatibility. When compatibility is established, the employment specialist arranges for a job placement, develops and implements systematic training procedures, fades intervention according to data indications, and maintains a schedule of follow-along contact with the employee with a disability and the employer through follow-along service provision.

Advantages When one person is responsible for both functions of program development and implementation, ownership and commitment to the implementation are enhanced. The processes of developing the job, completing the consumer assessment and job analysis processes, and then making the placement decision are likely to be executed with greater care when the employment specialist knows that he or she will be providing intensive training on the job site. Jobs well matched to the consumer's abilities, interests, likes, dislikes, and so forth, can greatly lessen the difficulty of the job-site training experience, facilitate the efficiency of the entire process, and in fact make the difference between successful employment retention or termination from the employment situation.

When the employment specialist has experience as a trainer he or she gains greater competence in the area of job analysis, because the job-training activity exposes the employment specialist to many aspects of the job that are often missed by an inexperienced eye. Some of these more subtle aspects may constitute a major impediment to a disabled person's ability to be independent in the employment situation. Placement decisions may in some cases need to be reversed because of details missed during the preplacement job development and job analysis activities. Also, the intensive involvement in the job-training role with employees who exhibit challenging behaviors develops skills in consumer assessment.

With regard to efficiency, it saves time for one person to complete the preplacement (program development) activities and the postplacement training activities, because the information otherwise has to be transferred to a second staff person. There is less confusion for all concerned if there is only one person with whom to communicate regarding pre- and postemployment issues.

Other advantages to this staffing plan involve the attractiveness of the position to potential employment specialist candidates. Many applicants with the skill level necessary to be good job trainers want the diversity of the holistic employment specialist role rather than being limited to job-site training. Being able to alternate between job development and job-site training roles prevents long periods of stress, boredom, and, ultimately, burnout that can occur from continual job-site training activity.

Disadvantages It has been recommended that pay scales for persons hired to be employment specialists be commensurate with professionals in the fields of rehabilitation and education (Cohen et al., 1986). Some programs may have difficulty funding an adequate number of positions to keep up with the demand for services. It is very difficult for a program to be successful with just one full-time employment specialist.

The diversity of functions required of the holistic employment specialist role requires a highly competent and versatile person. Some applicants who may be qualified for higher paying positions might agree to accept a lower paying employment specialist position because of the position's diversity, while others may feel that the job is too demanding for the salary offered. In other words, the diversity may help or hinder recruitment of quality personnel, depending on the salary that can be offered (see Rusch, Trach, Winking, Tines, & Johnson, Chapter 16, in this volume).

Until supported employment and the position of employment specialist has enjoyed greater longevity, it is unlikely that applicants for this position will be experienced in carrying out all of the different functions of this complex role. Usually persons with skills in behavioral and systematic training procedures are not very well acquainted with the business world or the basics of job development. Persons comfortable in the business community, however, do not usually have training in systematic instruction or counseling. Therefore, after hiring staff persons, training will generally be required to develop skills in unfamiliar areas.

Another disadvantage to the holistic employment specialist staff arrangement is the time delay between each placement for each employment specialist. As the employment specialist begins to fade intervention from one job site, the specialist must refamiliarize himself or herself with consumer assessment information from his or her caseload, and start the process of job development all over again. Although this is usually an enjoyed activity change after the intensity of job-site training, it can take anywhere from 2 to 6 weeks to locate a job for someone in the referral pool.

Organizational Implications Although one full-time employment specialist can implement the individual placement model of supported employment, this same person should not be the sole staff person trained in the functions of supported employment within even a small organization. At a minimum, one part-time person is required to provide backup coverage or relief from the job-training period should a need arise. A disabled consumer employed in a 40-hour work week might require the employment specialist to be working 45 hours or more each week during the initial training period until the disabled employee begins to exhibit independence for parts of the workday. Although this situation may occur infrequently, a staff person needs to be available to provide coverage in case the employment specialist needs to take sick leave or compensatory time. Once fading begins, the second trainer can take over training while the original trainer begins job development for a second client.

Partitioned Staffing Model

The partitioned staffing model utilizes two or more employment specialists, each of whom performs a narrower scope of activities. In the most common partition model, the major activities of job development and job-site training are assigned to two different staff persons. The activities of individual consumer assessment for the purpose of compatibility analysis may be performed by the developer or the trainer or in some cases by both. The job developer may complete the job analysis activity and write the more detailed task analysis, or the trainer may write the task analysis. A period of orientation and assessment is usually required during the first week or two after the placement is made (Moon et al., 1986). In this connection, the job trainer will be modifying preliminary drafts of a task analysis during this period. Development of intervention strategies may be initiated by the job developer or the job trainer, with modifications made on the job site as indicated by the day-to-day data collected by the trainer.

Advantages With this staffing plan, it is easier to hire staff persons who are skilled in or have strengths in either of the two activities (job developing or training). Also, with a well-matched staff, there may be less downtime between each placement because the developer can be finding jobs for referrals while the trainer is occupied in job-site training. By specializing, the staff persons occupying the different positions can become highly competent in the two separate activities.

Disadvantages It may be easier to recruit individuals for the positions that split the functions, but it may not be entirely beneficial from a standpoint of effectiveness and overall program efficiency. The advantages of the holistic staffing model explain the disadvantages of splitting the position. The holistic design may require more time between placements, but that model can operate with the equivalent of just one and a half full-time staff persons. The split position may need three to four job trainers to keep the job developer busy. Alternately, an employee with one-quarter to one-half time committed to job development can provide enough jobs for one or two trainers. Ongoing job development can turn up many more jobs than can be filled by job trainers serving consumers who are truly in need of supported employment services.

A serious problem that often occurs from splitting the position is the purposeful or inadvertent assignment of lower status to the trainer position. Some programs start by offering higher salaries for the job development position. The job developer in most cases will need to dress in businesslike clothes. The image of this position is that of a professional, interacting with members of the business community. The trainer often dresses in a manner comfortable for close interaction with the disabled employee on the job site. This may mean wearing a uniform or tennis shoes, T-shirt, and jeans. The work required of job trainers may be seen by many professionals as menial and unskilled. In some cases, the job developer is placed in a supervisory role over the lower paid job trainers.

The danger here is the devaluing of the job-site training activity. To serve the individuals that supported employment is designed to serve, the skills of the training staff are the most critical. In fact, it is much easier to find jobs for individuals with severely challenging behaviors than it is to apply the training procedures to bring about successful employment retention. The training technology that is being developed is extremely refined and sophisticated and is difficult to implement. Program managers considering staffing plans need to value this training technology and offer salary levels and organizational status commensurate with its importance. The authors highly recommend that job developers and trainers receive equivalent pay and benefits.

Organizational Implications First, there is a need to hire more staff in the initial stages of a program so that work activity is somewhat evenly distributed. This could be a program start-up issue depending on the program's funding capabilities. Also, if the job developer is needed to act in a program supervisor role, it will be difficult to equalize the status among the developer and the trainers. If the developer has functioned as a trainer previously this may help, but the act of promoting staff out of training implies that it is a less valued activity.

Separate Follow-Along Case Manager

With either of the two models previously discussed, a follow-along case manager can be utilized to provide maintenance coverage for employees with disabilities who have been well stabilized in their employment situations. After a program is a couple of years old, it may be efficient to hire a follow-along person to relieve some of the routine employer and consumer contacting and the paperwork requirements from employment specialists who are actively involved with initial placement and job-site training activities. Although there is no established rule, an employment specialist with 1 employee in initial training and 12–15 employees on his or her follow-along caseload could benefit from being relieved of some follow-along duties. For some follow-along cases, a lesser skilled staff person can handle minor issues or monitor the status quo on the job site for long-employed consumers. In the event that there is a serious crisis, the former employment specialist can either guide the follow-along coach through the situation or intervene directly if necessary.

Advantages Some organizations may choose to use the follow-along position as training for a full employment specialist rank. In this role, the follow-along coach gains experience observing disabled employees in their work situations, collecting data, and communicating with the employee, employer, family, and other agency representatives. There is no documentation, however, establishing follow-along activities as less complex than other activities. Again, because efficient follow-along is crucial, the authors highly recommend equivalent rank and salary for this position.

Disadvantages As with any change of personnel in a supported employment approach, to switch the contact person after a stable relationship is developed between the employment specialist, employee, employer, family members, and agency representatives could potentially cause a problem. In most cases the current employment specialist will need to make the rounds and explain to all of the appropriate persons just listed that a new follow-along coach will be taking over. Employment specialists do change or leave their

204 / Sale, Wood, Barcus, and Moon

jobs, and replacements are periodically required even without a reassignment to a follow-along coach. So, in this respect, it is not a disadvantage to reassign, but an ultimate reality that a long-standing employee's employment specialist will change at some point.

Organizational Implications   Utilizing a follow-along case manager requires several organizational considerations. First, documentation regarding job development and job-site training must be especially thorough when delineating follow-along activities. Second, obviously this documentation must be readily available to the follow-along person and present in both subjective (narrative) and objective (hard data) terms. This is crucial to ensure maintenance of acquired employee skills to company standards. Finally, the organization must have in place a mechanism to provide intensive retraining of new or lost case manager skills. The follow-along person should not be encumbered by the potentially great amount of time required for training and still be expected to provide adequate follow-along for the remaining caseload.

SUMMARY

Supported employment is a relatively new phenomenon. The functions, activities, competencies, and staffing designs related to implementing the models discussed in this chapter are gradually being refined and reported in the professional literature. As supported employment becomes further embedded within the service delivery system, it is hoped that the functions, activities, competencies, and staffing plans presented in this chapter will receive extensive social validation. The mix of competencies needed for the best service delivery model or models has not yet been empirically demonstrated.

Social validation and other empirical demonstrations of the crucial functions, activities, and required competencies of employment specialists will foster greater acceptance of these individuals as professionals. Likewise, as social validation is provided, it is predicted that better salaries and more clearly defined credentialing of supported employment specialists will be set forth. Such measures will ultimately result in improved services to consumers with disabilities.

REFERENCES

Barcus, M., Brooke, V., Inge, K., Moon, S., & Goodall, P. (1987). *An instructional guide for training on a job site: A supported employment resource* (Monograph). Richmond: Virginia Commonwealth University, Rehabilitation Research and Training Center.
Buckley, J., Albin, J., & Mank, D. (1988). Competency-based staff training for supported employment. In G.T. Bellamy, L.E. Rhodes, D.M. Mank, & J.M. Albin

(Eds.), *Supported employment: A community implementation guide* (pp. 229–246). Baltimore: Paul H. Brookes Publishing Co.

Cohen, D.E., Patton, S.L., & Melia, R.P. (1986). Staffing supported and transitional employment programs. *American Rehabilitation, 12*(2), 20–24.

Danley, K., & Mellen, V. (1987). Training and personnel issues for supported employment programs which serve persons who are severely mentally ill. *Psychosocial Rehabilitation Journal, 11*(2), 87–102.

Gaylord-Ross, R., & Holvoet, J. (1985). *Strategies for educating students with severe handicaps.* Boston: Little, Brown.

Harold Russell Associates. (1985). *Supported and transitional employment personnel preparation study.* Boston: Harold Russell Associates.

Hill, M. (1988). Supported competitive employment: An interagency perspective. In P. Wehman & M.S. Moon (Eds.), *Vocational rehabilitation and supported employment* (pp. 31–54). Baltimore: Paul H. Brookes Publishing Co.

Kregel, J., Hill, M., & Banks, P. (1987). An analysis of employment specialist intervention time in supported competitive employment: 1979–1987. In P. Wehman, J. Kregel, M. Shafer, & M. Hill (Eds.), *Competitive employment for persons with mental retardation: From research to practice* (pp. 84–111) (Monograph). Richmond: Virginia Commonwealth University, Rehabilitation Research and Training Center.

Kregel, J., & Sale, P. (1988). Preservice personnel preparation of supported employment professionals. In P. Wehman & M.S. Moon (Eds.), *Vocational rehabilitation and supported employment* (pp. 129–144). Baltimore: Paul H. Brookes Publishing Co.

Leahy, M., Shapson, P., & Wright, G. (1987). Professional rehabilitation competency research: Project methodology. *Rehabilitation Counseling Bulletin, 31*(2), 94–106.

Mank, D.M., Rhodes, L.E., & Bellamy, G.T. (1986). Four supported employment alternatives. In W. E. Kiernan & J. A. Stark (Eds.), *Pathways to employment for adults with developmental disabilities* (pp. 129–138). Baltimore: Paul H. Brookes Publishing Co.

McAshan, H. (1979). *Competency-based education and behavioral objectives.* Englewood Cliffs, NJ: Educational Technology Publications.

Moon, S., Goodall, P., Barcus, M., & Brooke, V. (1986). *The supported work model of competitive employment for citizens with severe handicaps: A guide for job trainers* (Monograph). Richmond: Virginia Commonwealth University, Rehabilitation Research and Training Center.

National School Public Relations Association. (1978). *The competency challenge: What schools are doing.* Arlington, VA: Author.

Rusch, F.R. (Ed.). (1986). *Competitive employment issues and strategies.* Baltimore: Paul H. Brookes Publishing Co.

Snell, M. (1987). *Systematic instruction of persons with severe handicaps* (3rd ed.). Columbus, OH: Charles E. Merrill.

Wehman, P. (1981). *Competitive employment: New horizons for severely disabled individuals.* Baltimore: Paul H. Brookes Publishing Co.

Wehman, P., & Melia, R. (1985). The job coach: Function in transitional and supported employment. *American Rehabilitation, 11*(2), 4–7.

Wood, W. (1988). Supported employment for persons with physical disabilities. In P. Wehman & M. S. Moon (Eds.), *Vocational rehabilitation and supported employment* (pp. 341–363). Baltimore: Paul H. Brookes Publishing Co.

18

The New Supported Employment Program

Prospects and Potential Problems

John H. Noble, Jr.
and Ronald W. Conley

Among the major changes in the service system for persons with disabilities, described by Conley and Noble in Chapter 4, is the new program of supported employment authorized by the 1986 Amendments to the Rehabilitation Act of 1973 (*Federal Register*, May 27, 1987). The number of potential clients who may qualify for the supported employment program is enormous. There is increasing consensus that a significant number of the 4.5 million adults of working age drawing payment for Social Security Disability Insurance or Childhood Disability Benefits (SSDI/CDB) and/or Supplemental Security Income (SSI) could be employed in jobs paying more than the substantial gainful activity (SGA) earnings level of $300 per month (Conley, Noble, & Elder, 1986; Conley & Noble, 1988). In addition to Social Security beneficiaries, there are many other potential candidates. According to the National Council on the Handicapped (1986), only one person in three of working age who has a disability draws benefits from the SSDI/CDB or SSI programs.

Of course, not all these recipients are candidates for supported employment services. Some may be too near retirement age or have disabilities that are too severe for them to benefit. Others may be able to find employment without receipt of ongoing services if existing barriers to employment are removed.

The number of persons drawing support from Social Security who might become candidates for supported employment services runs into the millions, and raises a controversial policy issue. What should be the stance of the U.S.

Social Security Administration if these individuals turn down opportunities to work in supported employment at or above the SGA level of $300 per month?

The new supported employment program has potentially high costs not only because of the large number of possible clients but also because of the extended duration of the services that they may require. Nevertheless, the authors believe that the net effect of the new program will be a substantial gain to society. The increase in dollars expended on supported employment services will be offset by expected savings resulting from lesser client reliance on SSDI/CDB, SSI, Medicare, Medicaid, sheltered workshops, work activity centers, day activity care, and other social service programs. In addition, the gross national product and the taxes collected by government may be perceptibly enhanced.

OUTLOOK FOR SUPPORTED EMPLOYMENT

Notwithstanding its potential, the immediate prospect for the new supported employment program is one of constricted growth for several reasons, as follows:

1. *The amount of funds authorized for the supported employment program is insufficient to serve a large number of clients.* The current budget (1987) of slightly less than $25 million understates the total funds that will be spent on supported employment clients, since the basic vocational rehabilitation program is required to pay for its customary services to people who eventually will be placed into the supported employment program. Other state and local government as well as private, nonprofit agencies are expected to pay for continuing supported employment services after 18 months. However, because basic vocational rehabilitation program funds are also limited, one can anticipate restrictions on their use for persons who qualify for the supported employment program. Similarly, other state and local government and private, nonprofit agencies must choose among the competing uses for available resources. The extent to which these resources will be augmented through tax dollars or other means is beyond the authors' ability to predict.

2. *The ability of state vocational rehabilitation agencies to use available funds will be limited until the technical capacity to provide services to supported employment clients is greatly expanded.* Trained personnel, working relationships with other government agencies and employers, adaptation of supported employment techniques to local economic conditions, and so forth, are necessary. Judging from the experience of the deinstitutionalization movement, the process of developing the capacity for providing supported employment will take many years.

3. *Many other barriers to employment remain that society will be slow to resolve.* The following examples are illustrative:

a. The service system creates massive financial disincentives to work even at marginal levels (Conley, Noble, & Elder, 1986). The average monthly payment in 1986 to an SSDI beneficiary drawing a family benefit was $893 per month. Earnings of only $300 per month would eventually cost that beneficiary all of his or her entitlement to SSDI and Medicare benefits. SSDI beneficiaries who had not waited the requisite 2 years to qualify for Medicare entitlement would lose eligibility for the 3-year extension of Medicare benefits, which is granted to Medicare-eligible SSDI beneficiaries who lose their entitlement to SSDI benefits because of employment. Such beneficiaries would clearly hesitate to return to work until they had first remained on SSDI for 2 years, even though long delays greatly increase the difficulty of returning to work.

b. The adverse attitudes that many persons with severe disabilities have toward work will take time to change. These attitudes are caused by conditioning eligibility for income support on proof of current inability to work and the prediction of continuing incapacity; general lack of awareness among persons with disabilities and their families of the service system as a whole; the complexity and internal contradictions and inconsistencies within the service system (e.g., the different treatment of persons on SSDI/CDB as compared to SSI); and general distrust of the intentions of service system bureaucrats and providers.

Negative attitudes are not limited to clients. Under the ethical principle of "first do no harm," responsible service providers may advise many persons with severe disabilities not to accept supported employment services because they are uncertain about how clients may fare under the arcane rules governing the income support, health care, and social service programs.

CONTROVERSIES OVER SUPPORTED EMPLOYMENT

Significant skepticism continues about the value and desirability of the new supported employment program. Continuing controversy surrounds several questions:

1. *Can a significant number of persons with severe disabilities engage in substantial work in integrated employment settings?*

Many believe that persons with severe disabilities are incapable of substantial work in integrated employment settings. This belief underlies the legislative premise and operating practices of most programs that provide income support (e.g., SSDI/CDB, SSI) and health care financing (e.g., Medicare, Medicaid) to persons with disabilities. Assumptions about the incapacity to work or to carry on a major activity form the basis for identifying people with disabilities in almost all surveys, including the ongoing National Health Survey and the decennial national census. Such attitudes are also reflected in countless statements by public officials and academicians. For example, Ray Marshall, former Secretary of Labor, defined the two purposes of workshops as "preparing the less severely handicapped worker for employment in the competitive labor market, and providing long-term sheltered employment and supportive services for the more severely handicapped person who is not likely to function independently in the community" (U.S. Department of Labor, 1977, p. 10). Similarly, Greenleigh Associates (1975) asserted: "Clients in the work activities centers represent a level of functioning from which only a minimal degree of work productivity can be expected . . ." (p. 80).

The low productivity of the disabled client is too often attributed to the client's limitations rather than to the inherent economic inefficiency of work activity centers and the lack of meaningful alternative employment options. Frequently, service providers "blame the victim" rather than look to the limitations of their programs. The too-easy and pernicious *assumption* that persons with severe disabilities cannot work with greater productivity in integrated settings is accepted as *evidence* in the absense of hard findings from properly designed studies that explicitly address this contention.

Moreover, some of the more influential economic studies of disability perpetuate the belief that people with severe disabilities have very limited vocational potential. Burkhauser and Haveman (1982) concluded: "It is clear that the cost of creating jobs for the most severely disabled is high and the value of output from such jobs low" (p. 74). They appear to argue that only a few persons on SSDI or SSI could earn more than the SGA level of wages, and that for these few people, it is the level of income benefits available from the SSDI and SSI programs that determines whether or not they will seek benefits from these programs rather than go to work. These authors fail to appreciate the strength of other factors in the equation, such as the need for income security, lack of vocational support, and even the unavailability of suitable jobs. Similarly, Berkowitz (1980) concludes: "All of the evidence points to the fact that there is a group of people on disability rolls, although possibly small in number in comparison to the total number receiving benefits who are good candidates for rehabilitation" (p. 67).

The current authors disagree with the judgments of these studies as well as with the policy conclusions drawn. Burkhauser and Haveman (1982), for example, conclude: "Concentrating limited rehabilitation resources on the most severely disabled seems questionable" (p. 71). It appears, however, that this conclusion was based on the benefits and costs of sheltered workshops and not on the benefits and costs of the new technologies for supported employment in integrated settings that are being developed.

Similarly, referring to a proposal to reduce earnings by one dollar for every two dollars of earnings over the SGA level for SSDI beneficiaries (as is currently done for SSI recipients), Berkowitz (1980) argues:

A more fundamental objection is that this method of paying benefits contradicts the rationale for a DI program. At present, the program is designed to pay benefits to those who have been determined to be totally disabled. The whole concept of the program would be changed with the adoption of a variant of the retirement test, and we would be moving toward a system of payment for partial disability. (pp. 41–42)

Berkowitz's argument is valid only if it is believed that methods can be devised to restrict SSDI eligibility *exclusively* to persons unable to work at the SGA level. Some analysts apparently believe that this is both possible and desirable. Leonard (1986) argues:

While benefit schedules could be adjusted to minimize the disincentives to work, the issue of replacement rates would probably be of little importance if the screening process could be improved to keep out undeserving beneficiaries and keep in the deserving. (p. 94)

Such thinking is a vestige from the Elizabethan Poor Laws era. The authors believe the preponderance of evidence argues against the possibility or even desirability of devising eligibility conditions that would exclude from SSDI persons capable of earning above the SGA level. In an exhaustive treatise on the history and problems of determining when a person should be counted as disabled for purposes of being declared eligible for SSDI, Stone (1984) concludes that it is frequently impossible to determine when a medical condition will prevent a person from being able to work, and that attempts to do so are often harmful. The authors believe that efforts to define more restrictive eligibility conditions for SSDI would simply perpetuate present procedures, which cause large numbers of persons with severe disabilities to cease efforts to obtain substantial work.

Negative stereotypes based on these economic studies, unfortunately, weigh heavily in the decisions of government officials when formulating the types of changes to make in reforming disability programs. More important, since significant change almost invariably requires that some people relinquish cherished beliefs, and often threatens the jobs and economic security of the persons who administer existing programs, the academic treatises that reinforce and support these negative stereotypes are often eagerly grasped and used to resist programmatic changes. Because of entrenched beliefs and fears for job security, it is not surprising that some workshop directors are critical of the supported employment program. One can also anticipate that administrators of income support and health care financing programs will resist fundamental change and the associated disruption in the routine of their jobs. Some academicians, too, can be expected to resist change that conflicts with their previous published writings.

This entrenched resistance to change explains part of the reason for the slow pace of change in the service system for persons with disabilities, even when overwhelming evidence indicates that the system impedes the independence of the person with a disability. The institutional bias of the Medicaid intermediate care facilities for the mentally retarded (ICF/MR) program, for example, is inexplicable in the face of federal policy that for at least 25 years has encouraged the use of community-based residences as an alternative to institutional care.

There is a small but growing body of data indicating that the negative stereotypes of persons with severe disabilities are factually incorrect. Consider, for example, the favorable empirical evidence regarding the employability of persons with severe disabilities derived from a small number of fairly well-documented demonstrations relating to people with mental retardation and cerebral palsy (in chronological order: Wehman, 1981; Boles, Bellamy, Horner, & Mank, 1984; Poole, 1985; Rhodes, Ramsing, & Valenta, 1986; Noble & Conley, 1987). Consider also the evidence, derived primarily from several psychosocial rehabilitation programs, on the efficacy of providing supported employment to persons with mental illness who have severe difficulties in retaining employment, most notably as implemented by Fountain House in New York City, Horizon House in Philadelphia, and Thresholds in Chicago. Despite weaknesses in the data, sufficient information exists to argue that all forms of employment—supported, transitional, and sheltered—are more productive in terms of earnings and less costly to provide than adult day care.

Noble and Conley (1987) compared earnings and costs among day care programs in Virginia and Minnesota, specialized training programs (STP) in the Pacific Northwest, the Physio-Control enclave in Washington State, the job coach model of supported competitive employment in Virginia and a Wisconsin variant, and sheltered workshops and work activity centers in Virginia and Wisconsin. Taking into account weaknesses in the data, they demonstrated that earnings are clearly higher when employment is in integrated, regular job settings. Even the Wisconsin variant of supported employment, which combined elements of the Virginia Commonwealth University job coach model with volunteer work in integrated settings, produced higher average hourly wages than sheltered workshops and work activity centers. Obviously, the wages paid in each of the sheltered and supported employment alternatives exceeded the zero wage outcome of placement in adult day care, and was generally attained at lower cost.

In two of the employment models (sheltered workshops/work activity centers and STP), the average monthly cost exceeded client earnings (Noble & Conley, 1987). However, this was not construed as evidence that these programs are not meritorious, since it could reasonably be assumed that the absence of these programs would result in placement of their clients in adult day care at an even higher monthly cost with zero earnings—a point often overlooked when assessing the benefits and costs of supported work programs. Thus, adding the monthly savings in adult day care costs to the average monthly earnings of clients makes the observed benefits of all of the employment programs far greater than the costs of operating them.

One important caveat should be kept in mind when interpreting these benefit-cost comparisons. Persons with severe disabilities are extremely heterogeneous in terms of service needs and potential productivity. Programs most effective for one group may be completely ineffective for another. It follows, therefore, that any attempt to shift clients from one service model to another with a higher benefit-cost ratio will likely reduce overall benefits and increase costs.

Logic argues that if clients with less severe disabilities are placed in a program serving persons with more severe disabilities, the former should do at least as well as the latter. Since the clients served by the Physio-Control enclave and the Virginia Commonwealth University job coach model had higher earnings and lower costs compared to sheltered workshops and work activity centers, and since the clients in the sheltered workshops and work activity centers often had disabilities of equal or even less severity, Noble & Conley (1987) concluded that many clients in sheltered workshops and work activity centers should be shifted to programs that provide gainful work to persons with severe disabilities in integrated job settings.

The importance of this conclusion cannot be overemphasized. If a significant percentage of persons with severe disabilities is capable of gainful employment when suitable services are provided, then the premises under which most of the programs of the service system operate at an annual cost of billions of dollars are incorrect.

2. Should vocational rehabilitation agencies be responsible for providing supported employment services?

The supported employment program represents a major change from the traditional focus of vocational rehabilitation agencies on providing time-limited services. Actually, the new supported employment program could be said to represent a compromise in which vocational rehabilitation agencies provide postemployment services on a time-limited basis with eventual assumption of responsibility for payment of these services by other organizations.

While the timing of the new supported employment formula grant program is awkward because it catches many states in the midst of an earlier federally funded planning effort that was calculated to expand supported employment options for persons with severe disabilities on a demonstration basis, it must be said that creation of the new federal formula grant program provides a powerful stimulus for states to accelerate whatever planning and implementation activities they may have initiated.

3. Will the new supported employment program reduce the quantity of vocational services that are provided to other Americans with disabilities?

The answer to this question is self-evident. Diversion of funds away from other potential clients is inevitable because the federal-state vocational rehabilitation program has experienced constrained appropriations for a number of years and still confronts substantial unmet needs among persons who could benefit from its services. The funds to provide basic services to new supported employment clients are not coming out of the meager appropriation for the new program but out of the basic program. This, unfortunately, creates a situation in which destructive and self-defeating conflict will unavoidably arise among diverse groups of persons with disabilities and their advocates over who should have access to limited vocational rehabilitation funds.

No responsible person who supports establishment of the new program wishes to see persons with less severe disabilities deprived of needed vocational services as a consequence of its creation. Equally, no responsible person who is concerned about diversion of funds wishes to see persons who could benefit from supported employment continue to be deprived of such services.

We are confronted with a situation where there are no villains and only one solution. The amount of money allocated to vocational rehabilitation agencies should be increased to pay for both the basic vocational rehabilitation services and the supported employment services that the newly eligible clients require. Such a budget increase can be defended on the grounds that it will be partly or totally offset by the savings in other public programs as the result of increased employment among clients with severe disabilities who receive supported employment services.

4. Should vocational rehabilitation agencies serve fewer of their traditional clientele?

Occasionally, one hears vocational rehabilitation agencies criticized for "creaming," (i.e., serving those individuals with the least severe disabilities and the greatest prospects of locating employment). Allegedly, some of these individuals would have found employment without vocational rehabilitation services. The implication is that some of the funds involved should be diverted to serving persons with more severe disabilities.

The conclusion, however, does not necessarily follow from the premise. From the standpoint of an agency trying to maximize social benefits with a limited budget, "creaming" is the logical and sensible policy to follow. It becomes a problem only if "creaming" becomes so abused that the agency knowingly begins to serve persons who obviously do not need rehabilitation services. Two situations must be distinguished. One is where the agency, in order to claim credit for a job placement, provides vocational services to persons whom they *know* could obtain suitable employment in a timely manner without services. The authors do not believe that this happens often. The other situation is where vocational rehabilitation counselors provide services to clients who *might or might not* obtain employment or who *might* take much longer to obtain a job without services. If anything, this is what the authors suspect is typical in the case of most vocational rehabilitation clients.

Under the circumstances, no responsible person would wish to destroy services to persons with disabilities who otherwise would remain at substantial risk of joblessness (even though a few may find jobs without vocational rehabilitation services). Unfortunately, it is *virtually impossible* to determine who among a group of persons with disabilities would or would not find employment without services. An interesting question to pose to persons concerned with "creaming" is: How high should the probability of finding a job be before denying services to a person with a disability—75%, 50%, or 30%? The authors suspect that consensus of opinion will be hard to achieve.

BARRIERS TO EFFECTIVE IMPLEMENTATION

Whenever a new program is created, it raises consciousness and arouses the interest of existing service constituencies and providers alike. Expectations about services and outcomes (jobs in this case) are elevated.

Unfortunately, programs rarely evolve in a way that meets these high expectations. Sometimes the original expectations are too high. Sometimes program managers administer the program in ways that differ from what was expected. In addition to the constraints on program growth and controversy about the value of the new supported employment program, one can anticipate other barriers to effective implementation.

1. *Goal Displacement* Service providers could respond by relabeling their existing operations rather than by either reconfiguring their old program or creating a new program that conforms to the legislative intent of the new supported employment program. One is reminded of the effects of the federal legislation that required sheltered workshops to pay at least one-half of the minimum wage to clients. The prompt response of many workshops was to designate part of the workshop as a work activity center rather than to seek ways of enhancing productivity and earnings.

The proposed regulations for the supported employment program offer at least one loophole that could lead to goal displacement. The proposed regulations define an *integrated work setting* (*Federal Register*, 1987, Section 363.7[a]) as one in which there is a maximum of eight individuals with severe disabilities and where most co-workers are free of disabilities. This does not preclude perpetuation of de facto segregated work in sheltered workshops if sheltered workshops begin to recruit nondisabled "workfare" recipients as part of an expanded work force. Given the current popularity of "workfare" (i.e., diversion of income support payments to pay for the work activities of welfare recipients), sheltered workshops could easily pool funds from a local workfare program and the new supported employment program in contravention of the latter's intended goal of promoting integrated work for persons with severe disabilities. Such pooling of the severely disabled and workfare population would be reminiscent of the Elizabethan Poor Laws, which placed beggars, paupers, the sick and disabled, miscreants, and other devalued persons in alms and workhouses and required them to work in order to defray a portion of their upkeep.

The federal regulations governing supported employment should be amended to prevent emergence of late-20th-century "workhouses." This can be done by redefining an "integrated work setting" so that the persons free of disabilities with whom severely disabled persons are to have significant contact would be counted only if they were not service providers or employees whose earnings are wholly or substantially derived from diversion of income from support payments or other government subsidies.

2. Cost Shifting Service providers and/or the states may utilize funds from the supported employment program to pay for other services that would have been provided in any event. For example, the proposed definition of *ongoing support services* (*Federal Register*, 1987, Section 363.7 [a][3] of the proposed regulations for supported employment) encompasses transportation, personal care services, and family counseling. Other federal and state programs (e.g., the Social Security Act Title XX Social Services Block Grant, Title XIX Medicaid, and state mental retardation and developmental disabilities agencies), are also authorized to provide these services. The possibility of using supported employment program funds to supplant funds being used for these current ongoing services is obvious and a temptation whenever the need to trim state budgets arises.

3. Client Selection Providers may follow their natural tendency to identify and select candidates for the supported employment program who have the best chance of succeeding in job placement. Such "creaming" would not be difficult to accomplish. Many clients who are trained in, or employed by, sheltered workshops are capable of working in competitive jobs, and in fact many should be so placed in the normal course of events. The danger is that program managers, in order to demonstrate the "success" of their supported employment program, will begin to inappropriately select these highly employable clients who do not need long-term postemployment services and, in so doing, neglect persons with more severe disabilities who do need these services.

The solution to the client selection problem would be to require state vocational rehabilitation agencies to assess via some standardized measure the probability that persons being evaluated for participation in the new supported employment program could be successfully placed in a competitive job without postemployment services. If such a measure of employability could be developed, eligibility for the supported employment program could be limited to persons whose competitive employability index (i.e., the likelihood of successful employment without postemployment services) fell below some threshold level (e.g., 70%, 50%, or 30%). The development of such an employability index is difficult, but there are numerous instruments devised for this purpose (such as the Preliminary Diagnostic Questionnaire [PDQ]

[Moriarty, Walls, & McLaughlin, 1987] being used by New York State). While possible, the New York State vocational rehabilitation agency has set no PDQ threshold level for determining supported employment program eligibility.

4. *Constraints on Interagency Collaboration* The ultimate success of the new supported employment program hinges on the willingness of other public and private nonprofit agencies to honor their commitments to pay for ongoing support on and off the job site after the vocational rehabilitation agency has paid for up to 18 months of service. To assure this outcome, vocational rehabilitation agencies will have to reconcile the differing histories, cultures, and political constraints that influence how other public and private nonprofit agencies operate. Several types of problems are likely to arise.

a. Differing Treatment Philosophies The public and private agencies with which state rehabilitation agencies interact often operate under diverse premises about the treatment of clients. For example, the mental health system tends to view clients as sick and in need of medical treatment if they are to recover. The sick person is expected to become a "patient" and to submit to a medically prescribed course of treatment. In contrast, the vocational rehabilitation system tends to view clients as functionally impaired but capable of surmounting the impairment to achieve specific vocational objectives if assisted through counseling and retraining.

In consequence, as vocational rehabilitation and other public and private agencies attempt to coordinate their services, one can anticipate some clashes of intervention philosophies, expectations, and financial interests. The authors would, however, anticipate fewer conflicts of this nature between mental retardation/developmental disabilities agencies and vocational rehabilitation agencies because of the greater focus placed on independence and employment by mental retardation/developmental disabilities agencies.

b. Modifying the Prevailing Vocational Rehabilitation Philosophy Many agencies, including providers of vocational rehabilitation services, will need to alter their treatment philosophies in order to implement the supported employment program. Vocational rehabilitation services assume that behaviors are learned in specific developmental sequences and are transferable from one setting to another. The new supported employment philosophy, in contrast, rejects this assumption. Instead, on-the-job training through individualized applied behavior analysis and planning is stressed in recognition of the facts that most persons with severe disabilities are unable to generalize behaviors learned from one setting to another and that behaviors are best taught in settings and under circumstances where they are expected to be performed. The problem of modifying the prevailing vocational rehabilitation response to people with varying types and levels of disabilities is further complicated because it is not clear in every case which approach would best suit the needs of individual clients.

c. Resistance to Changes Some public and private agencies will resist change because their revenues and jobs are threatened. For example, the network of sheltered workshops in the United States was developed to provide sheltered employment to persons unable to benefit from the traditional vocational rehabilitation approach of first providing transitional training and then placing clients in a regular competitive job. Obviously, the supported employment program will create dramatic changes both in the types of jobs that are required in order to assist persons with severe disabilities to obtain paid employment and in the size and types of revenues that are available to sheltered workshops.

The competition for revenues will be particularly acute in states where sheltered workshops, work activity centers, and adult day care programs receive funding from a number of public agencies, including the vocational rehabilitation agency. Sheltered workshops and work activity centers can be expected to lobby for the same or a higher level of funding from the state vocational rehabilitation agency and other public agencies that are expected to finance extended services to supported employment clients. Medicaid-funded adult day care programs will continue to compete for state revenues to satisfy the federal cost-sharing formula.

d. Problems in Public Accountability Differences in methods of case documentation and public accountability may interfere with easy collaboration between vocational rehabilitation and other public and private, nonprofit agencies. These differences are nowhere more strikingly revealed than in the comparison of the vocational rehabilitation and mental health service systems. Mental health agencies largely maintain ongoing ''process'' records for cases that are seldom closed. Even if stated, process objectives are diffuse and vary as a function of manifest symptomatology and the changing life circumstances.

In contrast, the vocational rehabilitation agency record conforms to the specifications of a nationwide case closure reporting system that captures the essential steps and costs of the vocational rehabilitation process—a progression along the pathway to a unitary goal: closure into a regular job, sheltered workshop, self-managed or family business, or homemaker status. If the goal cannot be achieved, the case is closed as ''unsuccessful.''

To the extent that service agencies with differing traditions of public accountability cannot agree over how much and what kinds of reporting will be necessary for joint ventures, the expansion of supported employment services to people with severe disabilities may be delayed. To the extent that private agencies, such as those that provide mental health services, become involved as vendors of supported employment services, they may find the vocational rehabilitation case-reporting and cost-funding practices nit-picky, distasteful, and onerous. For their part, state vocational rehabilitation agencies with a long tradition of standardized reporting are unlikely to react sympathetically to the often-heard rationale that private agencies use to defend their own tradition of record keeping: ''The choice is between paper and services; you can't have more of both.'' Deeply ingrained traditions and operating practices are not easily changed.

RESOURCE ALLOCATION DECISIONS

As the new supported employment program is implemented, state vocational rehabilitation, mental retardation/developmental disabilities, mental health, and other agencies must decide how much to invest in the program. They will surely find themselves embroiled in conflicts with service constituencies and providers over decisions they make. These conflicts will often be difficult to resolve because of considerable uncertainties about the benefits and costs of the programs and about the most cost-efficient approaches for serving persons with varying types and severity of disabilities (e.g., mental retardation, cerebral palsy, severe learning disabilities, epilepsy, traumatic brain injury, chronic mental illness). The situation is ripe for conflict and for politicization of the decision-making processes, with ultimate negative impacts on the efficiency with which resources can be allocated.

As noted earlier, there is as yet only limited and scattered evidence on the benefits and costs of supported employment. More important, there have been no rigorous comparative assessments of the benefits and costs of different approaches to supported employment for individuals with the same types and severity of disabilities. Nor have there been rigorous assessments as to the extent to which the existing successful demonstrations of supported employment modalities (e.g., the mobile work crew, enclave, job coach, or transitional employment program [TEP] models) can be widely replicated in populations with varying kinds of severe disabilities (Noble & Conley, 1987). Moreover, assessments have yet to be conducted of the ways in which these successful demonstrations will need to be modified to take into account varying economic conditions in different areas of the country in order to serve persons with severe disabilities in ways comparable to those in the successful demonstration programs. What is more, it is unknown whether the initial level of success attributed to specific models of supported employment for persons with mental retardation or cerebral palsy will be maintained when organizations other than the model originator attempt to replicate the model with the same or different populations of severely disabled people.

In principle, resource allocation decisions should rest on evidence of the comparative cost-effectiveness of alternative interventions with severely disabled populations. This evidence should assist state and local governments in determining the size and composition of their supported employment networks, and the forms of supported employment to which different clients should be referred. In practice, these resource allocation decisions are based on hunches, intuition, good intentions, and hope.

To improve resource allocation decisions, the authors recommend that the federal government conduct extensive, in-depth evaluations of the supported employment programs. These efforts should not only measure the benefits and costs of separate supported employment modalities but should also determine which modalities are best suited for clients with varying types and severity of disabilities. While belief in the potential utility of supported employment for persons with disabilities other than mental retardation and cerebral palsy is sustained by internal logic, there is need to document as fully as possible the range of social benefits and costs that may result from the provision of services. In this regard, the authors reject Berkowitz's (1980) speculation that "one is tempted to make the radical suggestion that perhaps not a great deal more is needed in the way of further research. Further research may tell us more about the extent of the problem, but it is unlikely to tell us how it can be overcome. The facts are that we know a great deal now about what needs to be done" (p. 70). The current authors take an entirely different view. In the authors' opinion, the threshold of learning what can be done to promote the employment of persons with severe disabilities has only recently been reached.

Documenting benefits and costs is a complicated enterprise—one for which program administrators have little stomach until called to an accounting by legislators or executive branch budget officials. Such documentation should focus on a social benefit-cost comparison. The social costs are those additional expenditures that society did not previously bear (i.e., would not incur in the absence of the program). Sometimes these costs are entirely borne by a single public agency, sometimes they are shared by two or more public agencies, and sometimes private agencies and individuals share in these costs. Normal living expenses (e.g., food, shelter, clothing, and medical care) should not be included as part of the costs of supported employment, since they would be incurred in the presence or absence of the program.

Ideally, documentation of the social benefits of supported employment will take into account not only the increased earnings of the client but also the release of family members and possibly others from caregiving responsibilities, enabling them to accept remunerative employment, or to work longer hours, or to switch to more demanding and/or higher paying work. Also important to a full accounting of benefits are the intangible effects that work may have on the moods and feelings of the clients, their families, and others around them. While difficult to measure, these intangible benefits are nonetheless important and are often valued by the beneficiaries as much as, if not more than, the earnings that are easily measured and attributed to the supported employment programs. Social benefits must also include the reduction, often substantial, of the costs of other programs (e.g., day activity centers, work activity centers, sheltered workshops) that result from placing clients in supported employment.[1] Failure to consider savings in other program costs led Burkhauser and Haveman (1982) to conclude: "The evidence on the direct benefits of sheltered workshops suggest that such programs may well not be cost effective unless a significant value is placed on socio-psychological benefits" (p. 79). When account is taken of other program savings, a different conclusion is reached (Noble & Conley, 1987).

To assure strict comparability of data across programs, and to assure that the data can be aggregated nationally, it will be necessary for state agencies to require provider agencies to adopt a uniform accounting system capable of tracking the benefits and costs that accrue from the time specific clients enter a program until they leave. Future funding decisions to expand and/or contract given supported employment modalities for persons with varying kinds of severe disabilities could then rely on sound evidence of benefits and costs.

REFERENCES

Berkowitz, M. (1980). *Work disincentives*. Falls Church, VA: Institute for Information Studies.

Boles, S.M., Bellamy, G.T., Horner, R.H., & Mank, D.M. (1984). Specialized Training Program: The structured employment model. In S.C. Paine, G.T. Bellamy, & B. Wilcox (Eds.), *Human services that work: From innovation to standard practice* (pp. 181–205). Baltimore: Paul H. Brookes Publishing Co.

Burkhauser, R.V., & Haveman, R.H. (1982). *Disability and work—the economics of American policy*. Baltimore: Johns Hopkins University Press.

Conley, R., & Noble, J. (1988). Americans with severe disabilities: Victims of outmoded policies (pp. 924–941). In J. Goodgold (Ed.), *Handbook of rehabilitation medicine*. St. Louis: C.V. Mosby.

Conley, R., Noble, J., & Elder, J. (1986). Problems with the service system. In W.E. Kiernan & J.A. Stark (Eds.), *Pathways to employment for adults with developmental disabilities* (pp. 67–83). Baltimore: Paul H. Brookes Publishing Co.

Federal Register. (May 27, 1987). 52(101), 19817–19920.

Greenleigh Associates, Inc. (1975). *The role of the sheltered workshops in the rehabilitation of the severely handicapped* (3 vols.) (Report to the U.S. Department of Health, Education & Welfare, Rehabilitation Services Administration). New York: Author.

Leonard, J. S. (1986). Labor supply incentives and disincentives for disabled persons. In M. Berkowitz & M.A. Hill (Eds.), *Disability and the labor market* (pp. 64–94). Ithaca, NY: ILR Press.

---

[1]See Conley and Noble (1988) for a full discussion of what should and should not be included as either a *social* benefit or cost in the conduct of a benefit-cost analysis. Income support programs (e.g., SSDI or SSI) and normal medical care, even though paid for by Medicare or Medicaid, are *not* considered costs but, rather, ordinary transfer payments taken from the consumption of some members of society for the benefit of others. Only the additional expenditures that society makes as the result of providing a *special* program are appropriately considered in a comparison of benefits and costs.

Moriarty, J., Walls, R., & McLaughlin, D. (1987). The Preliminary Diagnostic Questionnaire (PDQ): Functional assessment of employability. *Rehabilitation Psychology, 32*(1), 5–15.

National Council on the Handicapped. (1986). *Toward independence.* Washington, DC: U.S. Government Printing Office.

Noble, J., & Conley, R. (1987). Accumulating evidence on the benefits and costs of supported and transitional employment for persons with severe disabilities. *Journal of The Association of Persons with Severe Handicaps, 12*(3), 163–174.

Poole, D. (1985). *Supported work services employment project* (Grant No. 90-DD-0065, final report). Richmond: Virginia Commonwealth University, School of Social Work.

Rhodes, L., Ramsing, K., & Valenta, L. (1986, November 7). *An economic evaluation of supported employment within one manufacturing company.* Paper presented at the 1985 annual TASH conference, San Francisco. Eugene: University of Oregon.

Stone, D.A. (1984). *The disabled state.* Philadelphia: Temple University Press.

U.S. Department of Labor. (1977). *Sheltered workshop study. A nationwide report on sheltered workshops and their employment of handicapped individuals* (Vol. 1 and Appendix). Washington, DC: Author.

Wehman, P. (1981). *Competitive employment: New horizons for severely disabled individuals.* Baltimore: Paul H. Brookes Publishing Co.

19

Support in Integrated Work Settings

The Role Played by Industry through Employee Assistance Programs

Bradley Googins

The relationship between adults with disabilities and the workplace is moving into a new era, largely as a result of the economic and social trends reshaping the institution of work. The boundaries between work settings and the surrounding world continue to dissolve as the mutual needs of each create increased interaction and interdependence. The spillover of home issues into the American workplace has reconceptualized and reorganized traditional worksite structures, policies, and behaviors. For the adult working population, this is most evident in its attempt to balance work and home roles and responsibilities (Googins & Burden, 1987). The influx of women, and particularly of women parents, into the workplace has to a large extent destroyed the myth that the world of work and its outside environment are two separate spheres (Kanter, 1977).

In the midst of these changes, Employee Assistance Programs (EAPs) have emerged in many corporations. EAPs are designed as a support for employees in resolving personal and family problems and as a vehicle for handling the stress in balancing work and home-life roles and responsibilities. While EAPs focused initially on substance abuse problems, their scope has broadened considerably in the last several years to include a range of problems that are encountered by employees in their home lives and brought into the workplace. This chapter discusses the Employee Assistance Program's development, nature and function, along with its potential for addressing the problems of adults with disabilities. In regard to the latter, it should be mentioned first that EAPs can greatly assist disabled employees as the disability field attempts to better the position of such individuals within business and industry. However, this potential must be tempered by several stark realities:

Most EAPs have little knowledge of the population of persons with disabilities.

The stereotyping and attitudinal barriers found within the general population are likewise found among EAPs.

There has been little interaction between EAPs and persons with disabilities or the agencies and advocates that serve them.

These realities constitute significant roadblocks for persons with disabilities. In order for these individuals to realize the potential of EAPs, there must be increased awareness and understanding of EAPs, a realization of the constraints under which they operate, and, ultimately, a strategy for enabling EAPs to work with and on behalf of employees with disabilities.

DEVELOPMENTAL PERSPECTIVE ON EAPS

In their present configuration, EAPs can be regarded as programs whose position and structure within the corporation are suited ideally to assist and support employees with disabilities and to integrate them into the workplace. This dramatic positioning of EAPs has come about after several decades of advocacy, of model building, of securing a broad range of support, and of finding means of integrating the EAP into the corporation.

In many respects, the development of EAPs has served as a catalyst in opening the doors for other human and social interventions such as wellness, stress management, and child care programs. Prior to EAPs, issues related to individual employee problems or family concerns were solely the responsibility of the individual, the family, or private and public health and welfare institutions. As indicated earlier, the introduction of EAPs highlighted dynamic linkages existing between individual and family lives and the corporation, in which a problem in one area often spilled over into the other. Corporations were shown that the savings realized through rehabilitation legitimized the breaking down of traditional boundaries between work roles and responsibilities and those of the family and the community.

It was just such a link between personal problems and the impact on productivity that promoted the early forerunners of EAPs to develop a program that has come to be termed American welfare capitalism (Brandes, 1976). During the latter part of the 19th century, the early industrialists set up a broad range of programs and services, from child care to employee counseling and even to establishing whole communities often referred to as company tours, in order to socialize employees to the industrialized workplace. Although the movement, which was pervasive from 1880 to 1920, ultimately failed owing to its paternalism and the rise of unions, it constituted an early model of management that recognized the importance of addressing employees' home lives and personal problems to ensure high rates of productivity. The prevailing message in these early developments of industrialization is important: Economic institutions take precedence over home, family, and social institutions. No organization operates outside of its perceived self-interest. The concept of a corporate humanitarianism under which many social and human services institutions have oriented their strategies toward the business community is for all practical purposes subsumed under the prevailing laws of vested interest. EAPs likewise came about not out of a sudden concern for alcoholic employees and their families; rather, it was because treatment and rehabilitation was demonstrated to be cost-effective for companies. After much education, demonstration, and dialogue, some businesses decided that it was in their interest to do something about the problem of alcoholism rather than ignore it.

As the initiating problem around which EAPs were initially focused, alcoholism is of particular interest to those attempting to develop programs for workers with disabilities, since persons burdened by either alcoholism or physical or mental disabilities are the victims of many common misconceptions and stereotypes about their capacities, motivation, and behavior. Such stereotypes have made the development of EAP programs difficult. The nature of both alcohol and disabilities tends to isolate the individual from the normal population either through moral or physical attribution or other negative perceptions.

Both the alcoholic and disabled communities have a highly committed group of supporters who are active in their cause, often because of individual or family experiences. For the alcoholism movement to translate this cause into the work world through EAPs, it was necessary for corporations to recognize a linkage between the cause and the company's self-interests. As the rehabilitation community seeks to provide effective means to integrate adults with disabilities into work organizations, it has much to learn from the EAP experience. Similar linkages will be needed for the employee with a disability to realize more than token or paternalistic actions by today's corporations.

NATURE AND FUNCTION OF EAPS

During the early 1970s, what had existed for several decades as a scattered series of occupational alcoholism programs began to develop into a coherent movement through the creation of a professional organization, the Association of Labor and Management Administrators and Consultants on Alcoholism (ALMACA), and through significant government infusion of financial resources and leadership through the newly formed National Institute on Alcohol Abuse and Alcoholism. The most recent estimate of EAPs indicated a growth from about 50 EAPs prior to 1960 to over 10,000 today (Bureau of National Affairs, 1987). This dramatic transformation was made possible through a number of core strategies and mechanisms, including (Roman & Blum, 1985):

1. EAPs were tied to job performance. Employees were not confronted with drinking problems, but they were held responsible for job performance problems. This allowed supervisors to stay within the realm of their supervisory role.
2. EAPs could properly be seen as an aid to management. Because alcohol-related behavior spilled over into productivity, EAPs became a vehicle through which managers could deal with employees whose performances had become impaired. Some have seen the EAPs as more properly called supervisory assistance programs (Phillips & Older, 1977).
3. The EAP blended job performance with a humanitarian strategy. Rather than simply appealing to the human side of enterprise, the EAP offered a model that existed on a parallel with a disciplinary approach and offered a treatment alternative that was cost-effective. All of these aspects operated to integrate the EAP within the company with little disruption in corporate policies or procedures.

A similar set of external forces also took place during the 1970s that accelerated the development and acceptance of the EAPs. The interpretation and coverage of workers' compensation was considerably broadened during this time. A number of court decisions and arbitration rulings occurring after the mid-1960s also suggested employers were increasingly liable for employees' drug and alcohol problems. These developments led many labor management consultants to advise companies to take an active role in preventing problems through the implementation of EAPs. In addition, federal legislation in the early 1970s prohibiting discrimination against persons with handicaps was construed to include drug and alcohol abusers. If employers suddenly dismissed such a person without any effort to rehabilitate him or her to a productive status, they would be vulnerable legally.

Thus, the backdrop for EAP adoption became more favorable through both external issues and the creation of a program that meshed with the policies, procedures, structures, and culture of the organization. Figure 19.1 presents a schema developed by Erfurt and Foote (1977), outlining the major EAP functions.

As shown in Figure 19.1, an EAP consists of three primary systems, including casefinding, assessment/referral/follow-up, and treatment. Each is described briefly next.

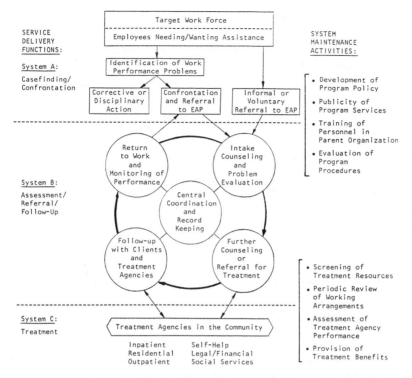

Figure 19.1. Schema of major EAP functions. (Reprinted, by permission, from Erfurt, J., & Foote, A. [1977]. *Occupational employee assistance programs for substance abuse and mental health problems*, p. 213. Ann Arbor: University of Michigan, Institute of Labor and Industrial Relations. © 1977 by Institute of Labor and Industrial Relations, The University of Michigan.)

System A: Casefinding

The identification process within the EAP Occurs either through self-referral or through referral by a supervisor because of work performance problems. In the supervisory referral, the supervisor identifies a job performance problem and confronts the employee with it. The supervisor then institutes parallel procedures: appropriate disciplinary action as spelled out in corporate policy; and referral to the EAP for assessment of any problems underlying the job performance problem.

System B: Assessment/Referral/Follow-up

Assessment/referral/follow-up constitute the core of EAP practice. Having been referred into this system, the employee is diagnosed and evaluated, is provided counseling (usually limited to assessment), is referred to community resources, is followed-up, and returns to work where the supervisor monitors job performance. This system operates much like other human service or social service agencies in providing support, assistance, and treatment through the utilization of community resources. However, the continuous interaction with the work organization, particularly in the case of supervisor referrals, requires an intimate working knowledge of the corporation's policies, procedures, communication systems, power structures, and decision making, as well as a good grasp of corporate culture.

System C: Treatment

The treatment system for most EAPs is located in the community through an extensive network of health and social services. The EAP is responsible for knowing these agencies, for achieving a good referral of the employee, and for providing a link between the employee, the company, and the treatment agency.

EAP COMPONENTS

The preceding processes are common to all EAPs but operate with numerous variations. The treatment systems also encompass a number of common components, discussed next.

1. *Written policy and procedures.* These serve to set a series of mutual expectations between the company, the employee, and the EAPs. Trice and Roman (1972, p. 180) cite three major purposes for a written policy related to alcohol and drugs, including: 1) informing employees of the consequences of using alcohol and drugs in conjunction with job performance, 2) spelling out the distribution of authority and responsibility involved in policy implementation, and 3) eliminating the possibility of ambiguity or favoritism.
2. *Provision of constructive attention to substance abuse problems.* Although EAPs have broadened to include a wide range of problems and issues, substance abuse problems are always at the core. The mechanisms for constructive confrontation and the use of impaired job performance are particularly well suited for dealing with the detail involved with substance abuse. Thus, all EAPs have to ensure that their programs are well designed to assist in the identification, documentation, confrontation, and treatment of these problems.
3. *Supervisor training.* Training of supervisors about EAPs is generally considered essential to successful EAPs. Such training helps bring about changes in knowledge and attitudes that enable the EAP to realize its objectives within the organization. Since supervisors are the gatekeepers

in work organizations, their training becomes critical in making referrals and utilizing the EAP to accomplish their managerial functions.

4. *Labor-management cooperation.* Many labor leaders have argued that unless a program has both management and labor support, labor will be suspicious and management will be tempted to misuse the power inherent in EAPs. Thus, joint cooperation and sponsorship is suggested to mitigate the traditional contentiousness between labor and management.

5. *Diffusion of program information to the workforce.* EAPs develop a variety of outreach strategies to inform employees about the EAP. This strategy couples prevention awareness with educational materials on specific health and social problems. Through brochures, presentations, and articles in company newsletters, the EAP attempts to inform, reduce stigma, and provide up-to-date information on a wide range of health problems, while helping create a culture of prevention.

6. *Linkage to treatment community.* Since EAPs are rarely complete treatment centers, referral mechanisms are necessary to link the program with the external treatment system. EAPs must be thoroughly familiar with this system to facilitate effective information and referral services to employees. Likewise, community agencies need to be educated about the dynamics and functioning of the workplace so that they can effectively treat the problemed employee.

7. *Total confidentiality.* The EAP's mission and credibility hinge on its ability to maintain confidentiality. Because of the delicate relationship between discipline and treatment, EAPs have to ensure that their program protects the individual from company intrusion into primarily personal information. If employees perceive the EAP as essentially an arm of management or not able to keep information confidential, then the EAP's future is dubious.

In summary, EAPs constitute a subsystem of the corporation that must be carefully established and monitored to meet its assistance mission. The EAP through its various components must mesh with and complement the inherently complex structures that make up organizations. The growth of EAPs speaks forcefully to their success in providing a support for employees and assistance to corporations in promoting healthy and productive environments.

EAPS AND DISABILITY

EAPs are currently relatively uninformed about the characteristics and needs of employees with disabilities. This generalization holds true for the individual corporation in which the local EAP operates and on a national level where groups like ALMACA set policy and standards and provide leadership for the EAP field. A number of factors, however, argue strongly for EAP involvement with the disabled population.

1. *Natural fit.* There is a natural philosophical fit between the needs of employed persons with disabilities and the mission of the EAP. The EAP's essential purpose is to assist employees who are experiencing personal problems that actively or potentially interfere with job performance, so that both the employee and the corporation benefit through the intervention of the EAP. Such a supportive role is critical to the employment success of a person with a disability and to his or her integration into the workplace; yet, such support is largely not available in worksites where disabled persons are employed. The importance of supports cannot be underscored. A recent study on family stress in a general working population revealed that as the movement of adults into the work force accelerates, and as the cutbacks in governmental funds for social services increase, employees are increasingly losing community and family supports and are relying on workplaces for formal and informal supports (Googins & Burden, 1987).

2. *Decreased stigma.* EAPs have waged a consistent battle to reduce the stigma of alcoholism and to locate a social service program within the work domain. Extensive public education programs and the positive experience of EAP use by large numbers of employees have served both to diminish the stigma and to gain wider acceptance of EAPs by the corporate world. Since the EAP has been able to operate with a significantly lowered rate of stigmatization, it has high potential for working productively with populations such as those with disabilities who often have to break through similar barriers.

3. *The broadening of EAPs.* EAPs have developed considerably from their early years, in which they focused exclusively on alcoholism, to today's EAP practice that reflects a diversity of both subjects and functions. If one were to examine a random selection of 10 EAPs, a wide range of activities would be found in addition to the core counseling. These activities might include a program for assisting the company with issues of day care, elder care, and retirements, as well as initiatives in health promotion, work-family stress, AIDS, and drug testing. Today's EAP caseload reflects the types of problems found in any mental health or counseling agency. This broadening provides a legitimacy and an openness in addressing the needs of employees with disabilities on both micro and macro levels.

Barriers to EAP Involvement with Disabilities

Despite the favorable climate and natural fit, a potential chasm between EAPs and disability remains. Because there is no historical linkage between EAPs and the disability field, EAPs need to adapt to serve persons with disabilities. A number of barriers currently exist that need to be recognized and for which strategies must be developed if EAPs are to address this population. Such barriers include:

1. *Lack of understanding.* Employees with disabilities rarely come to the attention of the EAP either on an individual or collective basis. Thus, such persons, not unlike the alcoholic a few years prior, constitute a hidden population. EAP staff represent a cross section of the general population, often exhibiting the stereotypical attitudes frequently associated with the presence of a disability. Because they have little contact with disabled persons, the chances of reducing or eliminating stereotypes are lessened.

2. *Multiplicity of demands.* The other side of broadening the EAP function is the pulls and tugs that EAPs are feeling from different constituencies. Where the alcoholism community once commanded sole attention, it often complains of excessive dilution and inattention by the EAP as other types of problem employees are brought under the EAP umbrella. If employees with disabilities are to receive the attention of the EAP, the EAP must find a way to juggle its resources to respond appropriately to them, while also attempting to satisfy the needs of other interest groups.

3. *Experience with disabilities.* EAPs have no models from which to develop activities and programs for working with employees with disabilities. This lack of experience, along with the previously mentioned minimal level of understanding among EAP staff, makes meaningful cooperative ventures difficult. In stark contrast to American counterparts, the European equivalent of EAPs was found, in a recent study of occupational social work in Europe, to play a very active role in working with disabled employees (Googins, Reisner, & Milton, 1986). Programs in several countries employed social workers who facilitated the disabled employee's ability to make early and appropriate decisions about return to work, and negotiated job accommodations and worksite interventions on behalf of the employee. This facilitating role has not been built into the evolution of EAPs and, to date, is not part of their culture.

Many of these barriers are reflected in a recent national survey of EAP roles in disability management, conducted by the Center for Workplace Policy of Columbia University's School of Social Work. The survey's major findings included:

1. Responsibility for employees with disabilities may be dispersed through many offices in a worksite, as well as the EAP, in areas such as medical benefits, risk management, workers' compensation, personnel matters, and health and safety.

2. In some instances the EAP plays a central role in disability management; but more typically, disability management is generally considered outside the EAP's major responsibilities. This is particularly true if *disability* is defined more as a physical condition than as an emotional or substance abuse problem.

3. Some EAPs negotiate with supervisors on behalf of returning employees for specific accommodations to a job on a case-by-case basis. However, few EAPs have regular policies that identify this as a routine goal for EAP clients, or procedures to follow in such negotiations.

4. Few EAPs view disabled workers as a target population, and therefore few EAPs have formal outreach mechanisms to identify these employees.

In summary, EAPs are well positioned to assist disabled employees in the work world and are philosophically compatible with them. Nevertheless, serious barriers exist that threaten to negate the potential for linking EAPs to the needs of this employee population. To overcome these barriers and encourage EAPs to work with and for such employees, a series of strategies must be adopted by the disability community. The next section suggests a number of such strategies.

STRATEGIES FOR LINKING EAPS WITH DISABLED EMPLOYEES

No one strategy has emerged or will suffice to link EAPs with the needs of employees with disabilities. A series of strategies must be employed in a number of areas to obtain EAP understanding and support for integrating this population into the workforce. Among these strategies are informing and educating EAPs, developing models and joint projects, and increasing advocacy on macro and micro levels.

1. *Education of EAPs* Because EAPs have evolved from a primarily alcohol-oriented mission, activities aimed at educating EAPs to the needs of disabled employees and of linking EAPs with them will probably encounter resistance similar to that experienced by the broad brush proponents. As stated earlier, EAPs have no training or education regarding disability and frequently have had little contact with this population within the work environment. Thus, a strategy to effectively inform EAPs about the needs of employees with disabilities should feature the following components:

a. *Provision of information.* EAPs can potentially be informed through the usual channels of articles, books, films, and videos. How to ensure awareness is more of a challenge, however. For example, articles in the *ALMACA Newsletter (ALMACAN)* or *EAP Digest* are more likely to be read by EAP staff than in a journal on disability. Many EAPs, too, have regular inservice training, which could provide an ideal forum for educating EAP staff about the disability field. Similarly, disabled employees with substance abuse problems often serve as a catalyst for educating the EAP on disabilities. Linking community agencies serving persons with disabilities with the EAP will go a long way to sensitize EAPs on disability issues.

b. *Conference presentations.* There are several national EAP organizations, such as ALMACA and EASNA (Employee Assistance Society of North America), that constitute another means for educating EAPs. Both have national conferences that are major meeting points for the profession. Well-positioned seminars and presentations on the issue of disability would fit naturally within most conference themes. Co-sponsoring such an initiative with one or more of the nationally recognized EAP practitioners would provide a national exposure to both the needs of persons with disabilities in the workplace and the presence of organizations focused on disabilities who are interested in working with EAPs. There are also local ALMACA chapters in most metropolitan areas whose monthly meetings attract the majority of EAP practitioners. Their format allows for presentations on subject matters related to the EAP field, such as the needs of disabled employees.

c. *Unions.* Outside of New York, there has been little union involvement with disabled persons in relation to the EAP. Often the EAP and unions work closely together for the benefit of the employee. This cooperative venture could easily be expanded to the disabled arena, but appropriate guidance will be needed. A joint effort between unions, EAPs, and the disabled community could result in an additional sector of advocacy within the work environment.

2. *Developing Models and Joint Projects* A second strategy moves from the level of information to one of demonstration. While education is essential and useful, a more visible strategy is often more effective. A number of rehabilitation facilities and other such projects already provide one model. An alternative model would be a project between the EAP and an Equal Employment Opportunity (EEO) office that might serve to mainstream the disabled population in a manner not available in an isolated sheltered workshop. In large corporations, EEO offices often have staff concerned primarily with employees with disabilities. In conjunction with the EAP, a pilot project could be conducted to assist both populations. For example, EAPs routinely conduct supervisory training sessions for managers on how to deal with employees who are experiencing problems at work. Through a joint effort, the EEO and EAP could develop a parallel series for managers who have employees with disabilities, thus broadening the EAP concept while staying under its cloak. Similarly, the EAP could sensitize the general supervisory population by utilizing examples of such employees in their training programs.

Another effective EAP model was the Human Resource Counselor's Council (HRCC). This comprised representatives from all of the areas within a corporation that dealt with the human resource aspect of employees including: medical, EAP, EEO, training, legal, personnel, and community relations. The council was charged to examine all of the human resource issues that cut across the corporation. For example, the HRCC addressed the area of stress and recommended introducing a carefully monitored pilot project of stress management training. Similarly, it also examined the problem of working parents and provided feedback about policy and programs for child care. Such a mechanism could easily be utilized to educate the range of human resource personnel within a corporation who would have significant interaction among employees with disabilities. In addition, the mechanism would be a critical group to initiate action planning to address the needs of these employees.

3. *Micro and Macro Advocacy* A final strategy for linking EAPs with the disabled community rests on an advocacy base. Attempts should be made to reconcile the EAPs' weak position in this area, as reflected in the lack of awareness or understanding, in stereotyping, and in sparse programmatic initiatives for persons with disabilities by advocating for greater supports and resources for and attention to them. This advocacy needs to occur on both micro and macro levels.

a. *Micro level.* Within the corporation, advocates need to get the corporate EAP informed and active on behalf of persons with disabilities. A concerted effort will be required to coordinate the EAP within the corporation, the EAP field, and employees with disabilities. The mobilization of these constituencies is critical to pushing the disability issue to the top of the EAP agenda. It will most likely require a combination of instructional material, publicizing of case examples, and political pressure.

b. *Macro level.* Advocacy within the wider EAP field is equally important, as new initiatives and priorities often trickle down to the local chapters and programs from the national level. The influence of the national ALMACA board and of EAP publications in the EAP field cannot be overlooked. Any effective advocacy strategy must incorporate a macro-level set of activities. This will obviously require that a different cast of individuals and activities be identified, coordinated, and set into action. National organizations for persons with disabilities will be in the best position to introduce this strategy.

SUMMARY

In summary, just as EAPs have emerged as a potent vehicle for assisting troubled employees in American corporations, they also offer unique opportunities for employees with disabilities to obtain support and assistance in maintaining their job status and in addressing problems related to their home and work functioning. Because EAPs have served to legitimize corporate involvement with individual employee problems, they have the potential to assist persons with disabilities in reducing stigma attached to them and in integrating them into the general employee population. From a strategic perspective, there could be no more propitious time for persons with disabilities to achieve a meaningful place within American corporations. The economic projections of serious labor shortages toward the year 2000 create a window of opportunity in which these employees will be in high demand. The disabled community can capitalize on this opportunity by using the already existing mechanisms of EAPs to help provide the necessary supports within the work environment, while at the same time endeavoring to break down the barriers facing employees with disabilities in the world of work. To be successful, an alliance between employees with disabilities and EAPs must overcome a mutual ignorance of each other and a perceived lack of common interests. The challenge remains for the disabled community, their advocates, and EAPs to create a true partnership that will move persons with disabilities from the fringe of the American workplace to a position alongside all employees and employers, resulting in productive and healthy work environments.

REFERENCES

Brandes, S. (1976). *American welfare capitalism,* Chicago: University of Chicago Press.
Bureau of National Affairs. (1987). *Employee assistance programs.* Washington, DC: Author.
Erfurt, J., & Foote, A. (1977). *Occupational employee assistance programs for substance abuse and mental health problems.* Ann Arbor: University of Michigan, Michigan Institute of Labor and Industrial Relations.
Googins, B., & Burden, D. (1987). Vulnerability of working parents: Balancing work and home roles. *Social Work, 32*(4), 295–300.
Googins, B., Reisner, E., & Milton, J. (1986, Spring). Industrial social work in Europe. *EAP Quarterly,* 1–24.
Kanter, R. (1977). *Work and family in the United States: A critical review.* New York: Sage Publications.
Phillips, D., & Older, H. (1977). A model for counseling troubled supervisors. *Alcohol, Health, and Research World, 2*(1), 24–30.
Roman, P., & Blum, T. (1985). Core technology. *ALMACAN, 15*(3), 8019.
Trice, H., & Roman, P. (1972). *Spirits and demons at work.* Ithaca, NY: Cornell University Press.

20

Injured and Ill Workers
Interface between Industry, Insurance, and Government

Jack A. Stark,
Marcia Bredar, and Tammi L. Goldsbury

$\mathbf{W}$e are entering an unprecedented era that will provide tremendous opportunities for disabled workers. Due to a shortage of workers via the "birth dearth" era which began in 1988, individuals with disabilities due to injury or illness have approximately a 10-year period in which to enter the labor force. Often, however, disabled workers face insurmountable barriers that preclude their participation in gainful employment particularly at a time when they are needed.

This chapter addresses the critical cooperative role that industry, insurance systems, and the federal government must play to move large numbers of disabled individuals into the employment sector. The chapter focuses on those individuals who have been previously employed but, due to injury or illness, need to be reemployed via the rehabilitation process. The six sections in the chapter focus on the following topics: basic demographic issues of disabled workers, with a description of how industry, insurance systems, and the federal government are involved in job training programs for disabled individuals; the injury process and its economic impact; the disability insurance system; the workers' compensation system; a new model of care involving each of these systems and addressing the role of the family and the health care system in assuring success for the disabled worker; and future directions.

DEMOGRAPHICS OF THE INJURED AND ILL WORKER

A record 126 million people, or 69% of the nation's working-age population, held jobs during the 1986 year, according to the U.S. Bureau of Labor Statistics. This represents a 2.3 million increase over 1985, with 2 million of these being full-time, permanent jobs. This increase has resulted in 1 million fewer part-time jobs during the last 4 years (Bureau of the Census, 1987).

237

In 1986, approximately 29 million women held full-time jobs, representing roughly half of all employed females and 30% of the entire female population age 16 and over. In contrast, only 21% of all working women and 21% of the female population age 16 and over held full-time jobs in 1970. Although our economy is creating more than 20 million jobs every 10 years, we are witnessing a decline in the number of middle-class workers. This phenomenon is due mainly to the diminution in high-wage, union jobs, which is causing a bipolarization resulting in only high- and low-wage jobs. In the last 5 years approximately three-fifths of all new jobs were those of the low-wage category, paying less than $7,000. Most of the new jobs were created in the services sector (i.e., health care, financial services, food, lodging, recreational, and social areas). Employment in the area of manufacturing has not declined appreciably in absolute terms over the last 2 decades. However, manufacturing employment, as a share of the total employment, fell from 26% in 1973 to 20% by 1985. Despite this percentage drop, the absolute number was maintained owing to an increase in productivity gain.

The U.S. Department of Labor Task Force on Economic Adjustment has indicated that $1 billion have been spent in federal training programs to assist the 1 million displaced workers during the last 5 years. The traditional job training process does not seem to be able to meet the needs of this particularly hard-to-place population, who usually do not have readily transferable skills. During the last 25 years, the federal government has spent over $100 billion on job training programs. Not all of these programs have been successful, however. It appears that some of these program failures are due to economic disincentives such as a dropping off in federal program support, which conflicts with the goals of industry.

The 1980 U.S. Census showed that 12.3 million persons in the work force reported that a disability interfered with their ability to work, and 51% of these believed that their disability prevented them from working altogether (Bowe, 1981) (see Figure 20.1).

Only one disabled male in every three and only one disabled woman in five has a full-time job. These statistics indicate that 58.2% of all disabled men and 76.5% of all disabled women are totally out of the labor force. This compares with the nondisabled working-age population percentages of almost 9 out of every 10 men and 6.4 out of every 10 women participating in the labor force (*Source Book of Health Insurance Data*, 1988). These statistics indicate that disabled persons are currently underutilized (see Figure 20.2).

Although disabled people are underutilized, employers may be reluctant to turn to them to fulfill their staffing needs, because of negative myths and stereotypes that persist about them. Many of these myths concern anticipated increases in insurance costs, increases in absences, and increases in the job turnover rate, to mention only a few.

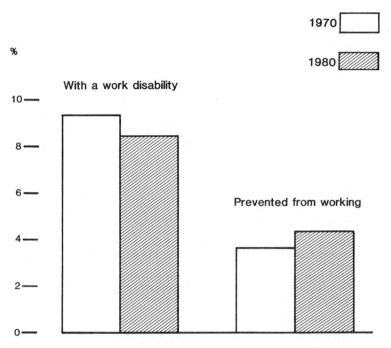

Figure 20.1. Percentage of noninstitutionalized Americans, ages 16–64, who have a work disability and who are prevented from working, 1970, 1980. Adapted from U.S. Bureau of the Census (Bowe, 1981).

THE INJURY PROCESS AND ECONOMIC IMPACT

In 1985, there were 9 million disabling injuries, at a cost to the United States of approximately $107.3 billion. This indicates that an injury occurred every 4 seconds at a cost of $12 million per hour. These costs represent wage loss, medical expense, insurance administration cost, property damage in motor vehicle accidents, fire loss, and other indirect losses from work accidents. Of the 2 million on-the-job injuries, 70,000 were permanent impairments. Of the 3.1 million home accidents, 80,000 were permanent impairments (National Underwriter Association, 1987).

In 1983, 4.7 million work-related injuries resulted in 36.4 million lost workdays. Short-term, nonoccupational illnesses resulted in $45.6 billion of total income loss. During this same year, $6.4 billion was paid in workers' compensation benefits (National Council on Compensation Insurance, 1984).

The most frequent single cause of lost work time and on-the-job fatalities is highway accidents. Highway accidents cost the work industry $70 billion a

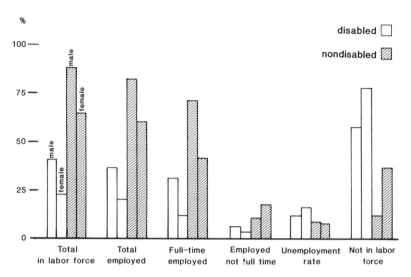

Figure 20.2. Percentage of labor force and employment status of male and female noninstitutionalized disabled and nondisabled populations, ages 16–64, as of March, 1981 (Bowe, 1981).

year in lost productivity, insurance, property loss, legal expenses, and medical care (Washington Business Group on Health, 1987). In addition, chronic pain (back, headaches, arthritis, etc.) affects some 196 million individuals (duplicate count) at an annual cost of $67 billion dollars.

A startling statistic is revealed in Table 20.1, which shows that a 25-year-old has a 34% chance of becoming disabled for 6 months before reaching age 65. A 30-year-old has a 33% chance, and a 40-year-old has a 32% chance. These statistics show how important it is for both the employer and

Table 20.1. Chance likelihood of disability before age 65

| | Term of possible disability | | | |
If you are now	6 months (%)	1 year (%)	2 years (%)	5 years (%)
25 years old	34	27	22	15
30 years old	33	26	22	15
35 years old	33	26	21	15
40 years old	32	25	21	15
45 years old	30	24	20	14
50 years old	28	23	19	14

Source: National Underwriter Association (1987).

Note: Only 23 million persons in the United States have any long-term disability insurance.

employee to develop strategies and support mechanisms to assist each other in adjusting to disabilities, whether they be permanent or temporary.

THE DISABILITY INSURANCE SYSTEM

Whenever a productive employee becomes disabled, the employer, employee's family, and medical providers are all involved to some extent in adjusting to and dealing with the disability. Figure 20.3 illustrates the process a productive employee goes through when he or she becomes disabled. With short-term disability with no lasting residuals, the process may be as simple as assisting the disabled person to utilize the company's sick leave program and filling out insurance claim forms. This process is illustrated on the left side of Figure 20.3. However, if the disability is long term and/or involves permanent residuals, the process may be as involved as working with medical providers in determining if job accommodations are available, developing trial work agreements, or attempting to revise job requirements to accommodate the disability. This process also entails assisting the employee with utilizing the sick leave program and completing insurance claim forms. The process frequently includes dealing with the workers' compensation carrier if a work-related injury or illness is present. This process is illustrated on the right side of Figure 20.3.

Whether the disability is long or short term, almost all employers have the same goal—that of returning the employee to his or her status as a productive employee. In attaining this goal, open-mindedness and motivation are the keys, especially when the disability is long term and/or involves permanent residuals. The employer must be open-minded to the fact that the

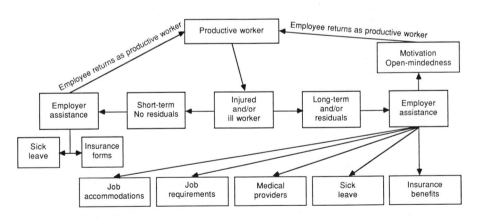

Figure 20.3. The disability process for injured or ill productive workers.

employee may be able to return to work even if he or she is not fully re-
covered, provided some accommodations are made and/or the job requirements are revised to accommodate the disability. The employee and his or her
family must also be receptive to this possibility. According to the National
Underwriter Company (1987), only 23 million Americans have any long-term
disability insurance. Figures from 1984 indicate that 87 million persons have
some form of disability insurance, while only 2 million have both long- and
short-term disability insurance (*Source Book of Health Insurance Data*,
1986). Considering the fact that the 1980 U.S. Census showed that 144.7
million Americans are of working age, the preceding statistics show that most
Americans are not protected against the loss of income resulting from a
disability (Bureau of the Census, 1987).

Disability insurance differs from major medical or major hospital insurance in that it is designed to help replace the loss of income that results
directly from a covered disabling condition. Frequently the benefits provided
are a specified amount for each month the disability continues. More recently,
policies coordinate their monthly benefits with payments from Social Security; consequently, the initial monthly benefit may later be reduced by an
award from Social Security. It should be noted that most disability policies
limit the maximum monthly benefit to two-thirds of the insured's salary. This
limit is imposed to give the insured an incentive to return to work.

Often in attempting to understand the insurance disability system, one is
confused by the fact that similar terminology is used in varying forms not only
for disability insurance but for the Social Security system and the workers'
compensation system. It is imperative that one understand the terms as used in
each system, and also be aware of the ramifications of each. Throughout this
chapter the term *disability* is used frequently. A basic working definition of
disability with which most professionals in the field would agree is "a condition that results in a physical and/or mental impairment" (Bowe, 1981, p.
12). Unfortunately, neither insurance policies nor the Social Security or workers' compensation systems utilize this term in exactly the same way. Rather,
these systems speak in terms of *total disability, partial disability, permanent
disability, temporary disability, permanent partial disability, temporary partial disability, permanent total disability, temporary total disability*, and *percentage of body disabled*, to mention a few. The next several paragraphs
define each of these terms.

Total disability, which can be permanent or temporary, frequently con-
notes a state of helplessness or of absolute mental and/or physical incapacity.
This connotation is not a requirement under most insurance policies, nor
under the Social Security or workers' compensation systems. Under Social
Security, usually two requirements are necessary to meet the definition of
total disability. First, there must be a physical and/or mental impairment that

is expected to be of a long or indefinite duration (at least 12 months) or result in death. Second, the impairment must result in an inability to engage in any substantial or material gainful activity.

The workers' compensation requirements for total disability are similar to those of Social Security, yet are different enough to warrant further elaboration. First, there must be a physical and/or mental impairment that may or may not be incapacitating. Second, there must be a causal relationship between the impairment and the accident or occupational disease. Finally, there must be a diminished earning power or capacity (wage loss) due to the impairment, which relates to the availability of work in one's trade (or of work of a similar nature) in the community.

Disability insurance policies usually discuss the terms *total* and *partial* disability in the definitions section of the policy. It should be noted that some policies make a distinction between *occupational disability* and *nonoccupational disability*. The occupational disability clause insures one against disability from one's current occupation. It does not require disability from *any* occupation. A nonoccupational disability clause usually requires the insured to be disabled from *any* occupation for which he or she is suited by reason of education, training, or experience in order to receive benefits. Sometimes disability policies will provide occupational disability benefits for 1 year, and then provide those benefits beyond the 1-year period only if the insured is disabled from *any* occupation for which he or she is suited by reason of education, training, or experience.

Partial disability is generally defined as the impaired ability to perform in one's usual or customary occupation. Under workers' compensation, that work must be of the same type of work and character that was performed on the date of injury or illness. It should also be noted that *partial disability* usually means that the employee has the ability to engage in some other gainful employment for which he or she is suited by reason of education, training, or experience.

Permanent disability means the impairment of a physical and/or mental function that is expected to be continuous and of indefinite duration. Furthermore, one's actual and presumed ability to engage in gainful activity is reduced or absent. *Temporary disability* anticipates either a complete recovery or healing to the extent that one's actual or presumed ability to engage in gainful activity is no longer reduced by an impairment of a physical and/or mental function.

Finally, the term *percentage of body disabled* is frequently presented to medical providers. This term is usually involved in workers' compensation cases where responses in terms of total or partial disability are inappropriate. Terms such as *total* or *partial, permanent* or *temporary* merely modify the percentage of body disabled. The provider is asked to indicate what percentage of the body is disabled so that this percentage can be quantified under the applicable workers' compensation statutes into monetary terms.

With the preceding as background, the workers' compensation system is briefly discussed next, followed by the presentation of a new model of care.

THE WORKERS' COMPENSATION SYSTEM

Workers' compensation is a means of replacing income lost owing to disability. Eligibility for workers' compensation benefits extends to almost all workers disabled in the course of their employment. The cost to U.S. businesses is more than $32 billion each year in disability payments, workers' compensation, lost productivity, and poor morale (Turkington, 1987).

The average age of workers at the time of disability is 40, with approximately 99% of all claims being short-term disabilities. As shown in Table 20.2, 95% of the claims made involve lost work time of 1 year or less (National Council on Compensation Insurance, 1984).

Another 4% of claims are for lost work time of between 1 and 5 years. For workers' compensation, nominal benefit levels are set by statute and are determined using earnings-based formulas. Because workers' compensation comprises a collection of state systems, there are differences in benefit structures across states. The norm for most states is to provide benefits equal to two-thirds of the worker's average weekly wage at the time of disability, subject to some minimum and maximum weekly benefits. Several elements that would normally affect a nondisabled person's wages should also be taken into consideration when figuring long-term compensation, such as age of the worker, inflation, and wage growth net of inflation. These elements are described next.

It is often difficult to determine if the benefits provided are adequate for the individual, because the judgments of adequacy and of equity are often subjective. The trick with compensation is determining what a worker would have earned in the absence of disability. Thus, basic guidelines and data are available that do not involve such value judgments. For example, compensation is normally based on the worker's earnings at age of disability. A prob-

Table 20.2. Distribution of workers' compensation cases, by duration of disability

Duration	Cases (%)
1 year or less	95.2
1–2 years	2.4
2–3 years	0.9
3–4 years	0.4
4–5 years	0.3
Over 5 years	0.8

Source: National Council on Compensation Insurance (1984).

lem with this, however, is that a worker's earnings typically increase as his or her experience and productivity increases. The workers' compensation, as shown in Figure 20.4, usually does not increase accordingly.

Figure 20.4 illustrates annual replacement rate of lost income, which is the annual replacement rate at which lost earnings are replaced by benefits for each year of disability. It shows how much spendable income a disabled worker would receive at any point during disability, relative to what would have been received had there been no disability.

To help deal with inflation, some jurisdictions utilize a cost of living or supplemental benefit adjustment for workers' compensation benefits for long-term disabilities. Again, long-term disabilities are those that last more than 1 year. In most states, benefits are paid to the worker for the duration of the disability. However, as of 1986, 15 states place some type of limit on benefits that can be paid for a single disability, which is usually defined in weeks. Two states (Kansas and Massachusetts) have set a limit on the dollar amount that can be paid.

It should also be noted that employer-paid fringe benefits are not considered in figuring the worker's lost earnings. And, for those who are classified as having a long-term disability, other forms of reimbursement, such as Medicare coverage, do not start until 29 months after the onset of disability, which leaves a gap in coverage.

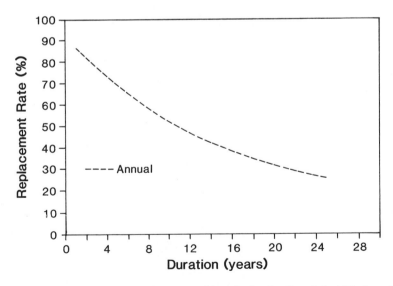

Figure 20.4. Annual income replacement of benefits by duration of disability for a 40-year-old unmarried male worker, earning $20,000 annually at injury, who suffers a total disability and who would have worked continuously until age 65 but for the disability. From Workers' Compensation Research Institute (1986).

A NEW MODEL OF CARE: A TRANS-SYSTEMS APPROACH

What happens to an individual who becomes disabled owing to injury or illness and is no longer able to perform the same job duties? The answer to this question varies dramatically from company to company and community to community. Essentially, there is no agreed-upon system of coordinating care, and often litigation may be brought against a company as a way of ensuring that an individual receives proper care. It is indeed difficult to coordinate all of the components necessary to provide for successful reentry into the job market. For example, a person may be involved with the medical care system, with the insurance claims agent, the company for which the employee works, rehabilitation agencies, the U.S. Social Security Administration, and the workers' compensation system, not to mention all the health care personnel from whom the individual must receive services.

Rehabilitation models that currently exist for an injured or ill worker are shown in Figure 20.5. Generally, when a disability case involving a smaller

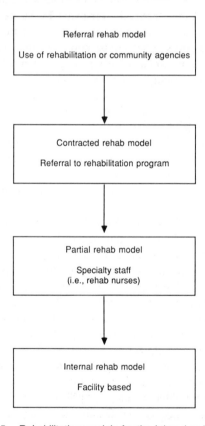

Figure 20.5. Rehabilitation models for the injured or ill worker.

company or corporation occurs, the injured or ill worker is referred to local rehabilitation agencies for assistance with their particular case. Usually, an individual works with the family physician or a specialist, who may then refer the client to a rehabilitation agency consisting of various rehabilitation staff working via a team approach to aid the person in returning to work. In some cases, larger companies will have their own rehabilitation program, with in-house nursing staff who can help coordinate the case by working with other governmental rehabilitation agencies or rehabilitation programs. However, if the company is large enough, it may have its own rehabilitation facility for employees. This is generally rare, since such company rehabilitation agency facilities often have to be centrally located, and the costs of travel and traumas the injured worker experiences from being separated from his or her family can often preclude the feasibility of such an approach.

Most employers are acutely aware of the extensive costs of retraining and replacing an individual, not to mention the expenses due to lost work time, medical care, and costs mentioned in the previous sections. Some companies have tried to control this approach somewhat by hiring their own internal rehabilitation staff or contracting with outside rehabilitation agencies and their staffs. It is these authors' contention, however, that a new rehabilitation model is needed that would involve an integrated rehabilitation approach, which, through a consortium concept, would coordinate various systems in a holistic approach to the total needs of the injured or ill worker. Figure 20.6 demonstrates this proposed rehabilitation model, which would integrate six components, as described next.

1. *Industry.* Industries are the purchasers of these services, and therefore they can be much more sophisticated and concerned about coordination of services because of escalating costs. The authors foresee more and more agencies combining their services in a joint effort to better utilize resources and funds.

2. *Insurance care.* The insurance industry is currently undergoing a reorganization and reevaluation of payment of health care, and specifically of rehabilitation services, in addition to reevaluating the overall management of claims. Insurance companies enjoyed a very profitable period from 1976 to 1983, in which much of their premium incomes were reinvested during double-digit inflation. However, from 1983 to 1987, insurance industries suffered major financial losses due to increasing competition and underwriting losses. For example, for every dollar collected in premiums in 1986, the insurance industry paid $1.59 for malpractice insurance, $1.44 for business liability, and $0.22 for workers' compensation. Currently, the timing is advantageous for the insurance industry to look at alternatives in the delivery of care to injured and ill policy holders (Capousis, 1987).

3. *Health care industry.* The health care industry is a $350+ billion business, which has witnessed a three-fold increase above the consumer price

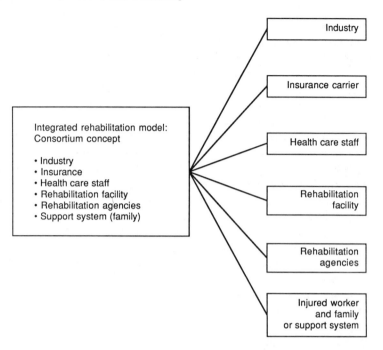

Figure 20.6. Proposed rehabilitation model.

index for health care costs during the last 10 years and a seven-fold increase in hospital costs. In addition, insurance premiums have increased some 20% a year during the last 2 years, including an increase of 72% in the cost of general disability insurance and a 43% increase in the cost of medical malpractice insurance. The health care system is experiencing unprecedented problems, particularly among hospitals. Hospital occupancy was 75% in 1980, 60% in 1985, and is expected to be 50% by 1990. As hospital admissions have dropped and Medicare has slowed down, hospitals are eager to look at alternative delivery of services and may be eager to play a significant role along with multispecialty groups to become more involved in the rehabilitation process. Certainly, physicians in private practice are also in need of expanding their traditional set of services, since only 53% tend to be working at full capacity. Patient visits to doctors' offices have decreased some 20% in the last 8 years, and the doctor-patient ratio has seen a greater increase, with a surplus of physicians who are witnessing the growth of new models in medicine such as health maintenance organizations, preferred provider organizations, and individual provider organizations (Gest, 1983).

4. *Rehabilitation facility.* A more comprehensive rehabilitation facility is needed that is able to work with industry and insurance carriers, health care staff, various federal agencies, and with the individual and the family to

provide an orderly return to competitive employment. Since the federal government has significantly decreased its role in this process, this will most likely need to be done on a private basis, which can be an extremely costly process to initiate and maintain. However, the model that the authors envision here would consist of groups of professionals working independently who would come together in perhaps one facility or network of facilities in the community and would work as a team to coordinate and treat each rehabilitation case. This team would consist of medical and nursing staff, along with physical and occupational therapy, psychology, and vocational rehabilitation staff, working together to form a plan of action utilizing all the resources in the community. This approach would ensure continuity of care without people falling through the various cracks in the system. Smaller communities may need to utilize regional programs or consortium networks.

5. *Vocational rehabilitation.* The vocational rehabilitation (VR) system can also play a role, particularly in evaluation and training efforts for disabled or injured individuals. Federal and state expenditures for vocational rehabilitation now amount to almost $2 billion, with close to a million applicants processed for eligibility, and 60% of these accepted for some type of services. Annually, some 250,000 people are successfully placed into gainful employment—approximately a 63% success rate (Kiernan & Stark, 1986).

6. *Family or support system.* Injured or ill workers will need a great deal of support to enable them to navigate through the maze of people and services in the course of their rehabilitation process. Frequently, psychological care and assistance will be needed. In particular, the individuals who receive adequate support seem to develop a better *raison d'être,* as they may become depressed in attempting to return to their previous level of functioning and by their need to be retrained to be reintegrated into the employment system. The support system is an area that has not been granted sufficient attention, and is where the rehabilitation facility or network of professionals can provide a significant service to increase the chances of successful integration.

FUTURE DIRECTIONS

As the baby boomers begin to reach early retirement in the 1990s, employers will be increasingly forced to turn to the disabled population to fill their staffing needs. There will be an increasing need to fill jobs in the service-related industries, often at lower paying wages. Certainly these jobs can be filled by injured or ill workers, who can be extremely productive (Kiernan & Stark, 1986).

Sociological systems research has indicated that in order for a new social system to be successful and to "grab hold," the timing must be right. As indicated at the beginning of this chapter, we now have before us a decade of opportunity in which to make major gains for the disabled population, particularly in the employment area. If human services personnel can unite and develop management systems, such as have been proposed here, the unemployment rate for disabled Americans may be permanently reduced. At the same time, we may see disabled individuals fully integrated into the community, living satisfied and productive lives.

REFERENCES

Bowe, F. (1981). *Disabled adults in America. A statistical report drawn from Census Bureau Data.* Washington, DC: Health Insurance Association of America.

Bureau of the Census.(1987). *Statistical abstract of the United States 107th edition.* Washington, DC: U.S. Department of Commerce.

Capousis, H. (1987, January 16). Payouts outpay premiums. *U.S.A. Today,* pp. 1-B.

Gest, T. (1983, December 19). For doctors, too, it's a surplus. *U.S. News and World Report,* pp. 1-B.

Kiernan, W.E., & Stark, J.A. (1986). *Pathways to employment for adults with developmental disabilities.* Baltimore: Paul H. Brookes Publishing Co.

National Council on Compensation Insurance. (1984). *Annual report, 1984.* Washington, DC: National Council on Compensation Insurance.

National Underwriter Company. (1987).*The 1987 national report.* Washington, DC: National Underwriter Association.

Source book of health insurance data. (1986). Washington, DC: Health Insurance Association of America.

Source book of health insurance data. (1988). Washington, DC: Health Insurance Association of America.

Turkington, C. (1987, August). Help for the worried well. *Psychology Today,* 44–48.

Washington Business Group on Health. (1987). *Annual report.* Washington, DC: Washington Business Group on Health Institute.

Workers' Compensation Research Institute. (1986). *Annual report.* Washington, DC: Author.

V

OVERVIEW
Accountability Issues

In Chapter 4, R. Conley and J. Noble emphasize the tremendous number of people with disabilities who currently receive some type of habilitation services. In Chapter 18, they bemoaned the fact that little data are available to evaluate the efficiency and effectiveness of these services—hence, the increasing need being recognized by many to demonstrate program accountability. But that process is easier said than done. For one thing, accountability is based on measurability and reportability, factors frequently lacking in today's human services systems. Second, accountability is perceived as risky to many program administrators who face unstable funding patterns and a vocal, heterogeneous constituency that frequently requests different types of accountability. Third, many programs have few resources to devote to program evaluation and to the necessary data-gathering and analysis equipment and procedures.

Although this is not a book about program evaluation, Section V contains valuable suggestions regarding accountability and program evaluation strategies. The editors encourage readers to look carefully at the individual chapter reference sections for additional helpful resources. The accountability issues discussed in this section include:

Factors that predict success in employment
Designing decision support systems
Different perspectives or costs
A benefit-cost model for evaluation of employment outcomes
Contradictions and inconsistencies in the service system

The section begins with Chapter 21, by W. E. Kiernan and S. Rowland, who address the key factors emerging from business and industry research that have been found to influence the success or failure of the individual in the workplace. The authors first explore the relationship between industry's expectations and the needs of the individual and the importance of making the two congruent. Next, they examine positive and negative factors influencing an individual's employment status. The authors report that the reasons for hiring, promoting, or terminating a worker are often both production and personality based, and that frequently one's dependability and interpersonal skills are as vital to job success as are technical and production skills.

The next chapter, by S. M. Boles, B. A. Wald, and Y. Xiaoyan, discusses the evaluation and use of a decision support system developed by the authors to collect, monitor, analyze, and disseminate outcome data from vocational programs that provided services to individuals with severe disabilities in Washington State. After describing the system and the data generated, the authors propose that a decision support system is useful in collecting, analyzing, and monitoring the outcomes generated by publicly supported vocational/employment programs.

Chapter 23 is appropriately titled *Perspectives on Costs*. "What does it cost?" is a frequently asked question concerning generic employment with supports, and C. V. D. Thornton, S. M. Dunstan, and J. Matton provide a timely discussion of the financial side. Using the example of transitional employment, the authors discuss cost analytical perspectives that involve the program administrator, participants, employers, the taxpayer, and society. P. Wehman and M. L. Hill expand this discussion in Chapter 24 and outline an approach to (and results from) a benefit-cost analysis of a supported employment program in Richmond, VA. The material presented in both of these chapters is beneficial to anyone confronting one or more "accountability issues."

The section concludes with a detailed discussion by R. W. Conley and J. H. Noble, Jr., of some of the contradictions and inconsistencies in the service system for adults with disabilities. Many of these concerns relate to aspects in the system that foster dependence, work disincentives, barriers to job enhancement, lack of coordination, and inconsistent rules and regulations. Of special interest to the reader is the authors' discussion of "prospects for change."

Accountability is a term that will continue in the forefront of disability concerns. This section does not give answers to all the accountability issues one might face, but readers are provided significant suggestions and guidelines to aid the solution-finding process.

21

Factors Contributing to Success and Failure in the Work Environment
An Industry Perspective

William E. Kiernan and Sean Rowland

As noted in several chapters in this book, employment plays a critical role in establishing the worker's identity as well as in providing a mechanism for achieving a level of economic self-sufficiency. Acknowledgment of this central role has triggered much of the research into the significance of the relationship between the worker and the industry-employer. The business literature is replete with studies examining issues such as critical factors in hiring, characteristics leading to promotion, variables contributing to job satisfaction, and reasons for job termination (Hendrickson, 1987; Herring, 1986; Melohn, 1987). However, in examining the role that employment plays for persons with disabilities the focus of the literature is more restrictive. Much of the research into employment of persons with disabilities has concentrated not on issues of job selection, job satisfaction, or job growth but on reasons for job termination or failure (Foss & Peterson, 1981; Greenspan & Shoultz, 1981; Hanley-Maxwell, Rusch, Chadsey-Rusch, & Renzaglia, 1986).

This chapter examines the key factors emerging from business and industry research that have been found to contribute to the hiring, maintenance/promotion, or termination of the individual in the workplace. Knowledge of what is expected from industry in these three key areas will allow employment and training organizations to respond more effectively to the needs of the marketplace. This knowledge should allow those organizations to modify training, employment, and support services based not upon the perception of what industry expects but upon the actual factors industry utilizes in hiring, promoting, or terminating its workers.

A MODEL FOR THE RELATIONSHIP
BETWEEN THE INDIVIDUAL AND THE INDUSTRY

In analyzing the key factors contributing to successful employment, it is helpful to examine the conceptual model of social behavior developed by Jacob Getzels and Egon Guba (1957). This model looks at the interrelationship of the individual's needs and the expectations of the industry-employer. To understand the issues related to obtaining, maintaining, and terminating employment, one must look at employment more broadly than as a job or variety of jobs. A job is not an isolated event; it is part of a larger social system. A social system looks not just at the products or services delivered in the workplace but also at the personal goals, interpersonal relationships, and specific needs of the worker as these relate to the goals and expectations of the industry.

Relationships within the Model

As stated, Getzels and Guba's (1957) social system model (see Figure 21.1) presents a framework for examining the relationship of the individual to the industry and depicts the specific elements that constitute this complex relationship. The two key components are, naturally, the individual and the industry. For the industry, a series of roles must be assumed if the goals of the industry are to be met. It is industry's expectation that the worker will adhere to these roles. These roles and the associated expectations define what the individual should and should not do so long as he or she is employed in that position by that company.

To understand the social behavior exhibited in the workplace, it is not enough to know industry's expectations; the nature of the needs of the individuals employed by the industry must also be known. The model (see Figure 21.1) presents the essential element of the individual as personality. For their purposes, Getzels and Guba (1957) define *personality* as the representation of the needs and wants of the individual, with the behavior of the individual reflecting the process utilized to satisfy those needs and wants. Thus, the model presents the individual as a reflection of his or her personality, which in turn reflects the specific needs of the individual.

The success of the relationship between the individual and the industry depends upon the congruence of the role and expectations of the industry and the personality and needs of the individual. When the two are compatible, a

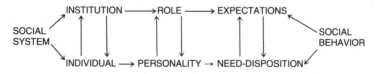

Figure 21.1. Social system model. (Adapted from Getzels and Guba [1957].)

level of satisfaction is achieved on the part of both the individual and the industry. However, when there is divergence or lack of compatibility, there is conflict on the part of the individual, the industry, or both and, correspondingly, a degree of dissatisfaction is present. Getzels and Guba (1957) refer to this as *conflict.*

Conflict Situations

From this theoretical model it is easy to see where the opportunities for conflict arise: from role-personality conflict, role conflict, and/or personality conflict. These possible conflict situations warrant further explanation here.

The role-personality conflict reflects a situation in which industry's expectations clash with those of the individual. This may happen, for example, when the individual is independent and nontraditional in his or her beliefs and the industry expects strict compliance with the rules and regulations of the company. In this situation if the individual asserts his or her independence or nonconforming behaviors, his or her personality needs will be met, yet industry's expectations will not. However, if this individual decides to follow the rules and regulations to the letter, the company's expectations will be satisfied but not the needs of the individual. Specific examples of role-expectation conflict can also reflect such basic issues as personal appearance related to dress codes (e.g., sneakers versus business shoes, open shirt versus tie, jeans versus suit) or length/style of hair.

In cases where there is role-expectation conflict, the resolution is often a compromise of the needs of the individual and the expectations of the industry. When there is no compromise, the end result frequently is termination by the employer or, at best, extreme lack of job satisfaction on the part of the employee. In the latter case, ultimately this level of job dissatisfaction will need to be resolved through either termination of the working relationship by one or both parties or by some level of compromise and thus reduction in the level of conflict.

The second conflict situation, role conflict, occurs when the individual is required to conform simultaneously to many expectations that are mutually exclusive or inconsistent. In this case adjustment to one set of expectations makes it impossible to adjust to another set. This type of conflict frequently reflects industry disorganization or lack of clarity in expectations rather than a deficit in the individual worker. Situations when there is a change in the mission of the industry may lead to role conflict. Shifts in market demand, philosophy, funding resources, and so forth can create a situation where the roles of the workers must be altered. In this case there is often a lack of clarity of mission or inconsistent communication of roles and role expectations.

Role conflict can also occur when the workplace undergoes a change in the supervisory structure. For instance, a new manager may want to alter the way things are done both from a task and an interrelationship perspective. In addition, independence and initiative, valued qualities under the previous manager, may not be as acceptable now. This type of change will not necessarily lead to role-expectation conflict, in that the industry's basic expectations remain the same. However, for the individual, some of the more qualitative aspects of the job may be changed, which may affect the satisfaction of his or her needs. A similar situation may emerge for the worker employed in a small family business that is taken over by a larger company, with the result that the "personal touches" and "family atmosphere" are no longer present. Again the issue is not one of change in expectation but change in the work environment such that the individual's basic needs are no longer met. In any of these situations, as in role-expectation conflict, there must be a resolution, frequently in the form of a compromise in which both the individual and the industry reconsider the situation and modify their stands. In role conflict, modifications may be more appropriate for the industry, although there will clearly need to be some change in how the individual satisfies his or her ongoing needs as well.

The third type of conflict situation, personality conflict, occurs when the individual's needs and disposition conflict with industry's expectations. For instance, the individual may misinterpret what the company expects of him or her, either because of a misunderstanding of the company's basic mission or because the employee assumes he or she will be able to change the industry's expectations. An employee concerned primarily with quality and not quantity, and who is working in an industry where numbers or units of production are key, may experience personality conflict. For example, in the human services field, frequently the clinical staff will be expected to see or provide services to a certain number of clients. To accomplish this goal, the quality of the services delivered, in the opinion of that professional, will not be of the standard required to meet the needs of the client. The conflict between optimal, adequate, and inadequate levels of service delivery is one that occurs daily in human services agencies.

In some instances, company expectations no longer are able to successfully respond to new needs that have emerged for the individual and thus there is personality conflict. An example of this would occur in an individual who, in his or her early years of employment, is more interested in level of economic return than in job security. In later years, however, when security may be the need, the job's role and expectations may not be able to fulfill this concern. A salesperson who works solely on commission over the years may experience this change in need. In the areas of education and human services, sources of support are important; thus tenure and hard-money positions, as opposed to time-limited grant support or soft money, may be more important for the professional as his or her career progresses. In these situations often the individual experiences a declining level of job satisfaction as the change in personal needs progresses and there is no change in role expectations. Frequently the resolution is one of job change, with the individual seeking out a new role that is more compatible with his or her new needs.

Each of the preceding conflict situations leads to stress and lack of congruence between the individual's needs and the expectations of the industry. Resolution of these conflicts is central if an increased level of satisfaction is to be experienced by both the individual and the industry.

Through an examination of the application of this social system model, one can begin to understand the significance of the relationships of industry expectations to the needs of the individual and why it is important to ensure that the two are in agreement. Clearly, a delicate balance between the employer and the employee must be maintained. The current emphasis upon matching individual abilities and interests to job requirements and work environments is critical for all workers. This concept is referred to elsewhere in this book as the person-environment match or the goodness-of-fit of the worker's abilities and interests to the demands and attributes of the job.

The matching of the individual's abilities to industry's needs creates acceptable social behaviors and thus a good fit of the person to the position and vice versa. When this matching is not done at the time of hiring, or for that matter over the entire period of employment, potential for conflict emerges. The needs of the individual and the expectations of the industry are not static but dynamic, changing over time. Looking at the match of the needs to the expectations can give both a measure of satisfaction for the individual and the industry and establish criteria that can be used both to advance individuals in the workplace and to change the working relationship when necessary. The following section examines the key factors reported by business and industry that lead to hiring, maintaining/promoting, and terminating employees.

CHARACTERISTICS FOR HIRING

Many different jobs are available in a wide range of industrial settings. These jobs carry with them a variety of tasks and responsibilities. However, in reviewing the various sources in the business literature, it appears that there are a number of consistent variables that industry considers when recruiting staff to fill positions (see Table 21.1). Personality traits such as maturity, self-confidence, compatibility, cooperation, flexibility, thoughtfulness, dependability, and agreeableness with others are the most frequent factors noted by industry in the hiring of new employees (Hendrickson, 1987). These personality traits will often be the key determining factors once the company has verified that the applicant possesses the qualifications to perform the required job tasks (Dumaine, 1978; Herring, 1986; Melohn, 1987).

Factors such as previous experiences on similar jobs, the presence of related skills, and specific training in the job area also play a role in the job

Table 21.1. Factors contributing to hiring

1. Personality traits: Maturity, self-confidence, compatibility, cooperation, composure, flexibility, adjustment, responsibility, thoughtfulness, sense of humor, caring, friendliness, dependability, creativity, attitude, agreeability

2. Experience (related work experience): Similar industry experience, training

3. Qualifications for job: Age, good reference, physical and mental ability to perform the job, sufficient health, reliable transportation, reliable communication, good attendance/punctuality, technical skills, appearance, and intelligence as needed for the job

4. Work history (past performance in the following areas): Attendance, compatibility, ability to get along with other people, ability to follow instructions, quality and quantity of work

5. Motivation: Drive/aggressiveness, initiative in conversation, alertness, aspirations, pride in work, commitment to employer, enthusiasm toward company and job, being hard-working

6. Education: Educational and technical background

7. Other: Potential, scholastic ability, extracurricular intelligence, and capacity to learn

selection process. These variables reflect industry's attempt to identify whether the capabilities of the applicant are compatible with the job duties. Once the applicant's personality is felt to be compatible with the work environment and the skills of the individual are deemed present to perform the required tasks, other qualifications such as good references, health status, reliable transportation, technical skills, and appearance enter into the decision-making process.

Previous work history can play a role in determining the appropriateness of the applicant; however, this is viewed more from the perspective of worker traits and behaviors than from the actual duties performed. Specific traits such as the ability to relate to both co-workers and supervisors are of high interest to the prospective employers. In looking at past work histories, the quality of work done is frequently examined. However, factors such as cooperation and dependability are verified with a former employer as often as is the quantity of the work produced or the actual tasks performed.

Factors such as pride in work, motivation, commitment, and enthusiasm toward the company are important to the employer. At the time of the interview the worker can demonstrate his or her level of motivation and investment in working for the company and often compensate for lack of previous or related work experiences. To reiterate, the capabilities of the worker to perform the required tasks is important. However, the major factors in the determination to hire an individual applicant reflect traits such as dependability, punctuality, and capacity to relate to others. Development of these traits in a worker is as essential, and in many cases more essential, as is the development of the specific job skills.

As pointed out by Getzels and Guba (1957), one must look not only at the expectations of the industry but at the needs of the individual as well. For the individual, Bewayo (1986) noted that the needs of the first-time or new worker differ from those of the older worker (see Table 21.2). The new worker looks for opportunities to advance, to have some security in the position, and to be challenged by the job. For the employee looking at subsequent employment opportunities, pay is the most significant factor, with the use of a wide range of skills and the opportunity to assume responsibility on the job also being important. Opportunities for advancement are less significant as the worker develops more job experience. Although the needs do vary depending upon whether the applicant is a new entrant into the labor market or a veteran worker, challenging work, opportunities to assume responsibility, rate of pay, and range of benefits offered are all important for the worker in the job selection process.

In examining the variety of traits that an employer looks for in hiring an employee, it is clear that personality traits and individual characteristics play more of a role than specific skills or past experiences in determining the goodness-of-fit between the employee and the job responsibilities. For the employee, challenge, responsibility, and reimbursement are all important factors whether the worker is beginning an employment career or is well established in a career. This is consistent with the discussion of the social system model presented earlier, where needs and expectations must be compatible for an effective and efficient match to occur between the individual

Table 21.2. What employees are looking for

In the first job

Advancement opportunities
Benefits
Use of varied skills
Pay
Challenge
Security
Work atmosphere

In subsequent jobs

Pay
Use of varied skills
Responsibility
Benefits
Advancement opportunities
Security
Work atmosphere

duties and the abilities of the worker. Both the capacity to perform the tasks and the compatibility of the role expectations of the company to the needs and disposition of the individual are critical.

FACTORS LEADING TO PROMOTION

As important as is matching the individual to the job is the capacity for the individual to maintain job satisfaction and for the industry to feel that the individual is producing at a level that meets its expectations for that specific job.

Given that the average worker will have 10 or more jobs during a work history and that fewer than 1% of the population stay in their first job for more than 10 years, the world of employment has become extremely mobile (see Chapter 1 of this volume). It is thus critical that industry examine not just the traits to be sought in hiring a new worker but also those traits that are considered desirable for enhancing industry's capacity to maintain and promote workers who have achieved company expectations.

In reviewing the general area of promotion and career opportunities, a number of specific factors emerge (see Table 21.3). These factors, although somewhat consistent for jobs in general, do vary depending upon the type of employment setting, service, or production. Table 21.3 presents the list of factors that industry found significant in the evaluation and promotion of its workers (Bureau of National Affairs, 1988). For both service and production employees, it is essential that the quality and quantity of work performed meet industry standards. Beyond that, however, a number of specific traits including initiative, cooperation, ability to get along with others and dependability must be present. The rank order of these specific traits is somewhat different for the service and production industries.

For the service employee, initiative, cooperation, and ability to get along with others are chief factors leading to promotion. These jobs often require face-to-face interaction with the customer or a co-worker. The ability to relate is key in meeting industry's expectations—that is satisfying the needs of the customer.

Production workers will have less occasion to relate directly to the customers; thus, cooperation and ability to get along with others, although important, are less critical than the factors of dependability, attendance, and job knowledge. For these employees, meeting the deadline is more important than meeting and interacting with the customer. However, interpersonal relations and ability to relate to others, co-workers, and/or customers are key elements leading to job promotion within most industry environments.

These data contain specific implications for employment and training

Table 21.3. Factors contributing to promotion in rank order

Service and production employees have the following needs:

Service employees

 Appropriate quality of work
 Appropriate quantity of work
 Initiative
 Cooperation/ability to get along with others
 Dependability
 Job knowledge
 Attendance
 Need for supervision

Production employees

 Appropriate quality of work
 Appropriate quantity of work
 Dependability
 Attendance
 Job knowledge
 Initiative
 Cooperation/ability to get along with others
 Need for supervision

programs. Such programs should focus upon the development of skills that are critical to enhancing the worker's value to the company, in addition to the development of traits that will assure that the individual will be able to obtain employment. The traits that industry regards as essential to promotion and advancement include not just quantity and quality of work done but cooperation, dependability, and initiative.

FACTORS LEADING TO TERMINATION

The previous two sections examined the traits that contribute to obtaining a job as well as to job advancement. This section discusses some of the factors that lead to termination (see Table 21.4). It is important for the reader to distinguish between termination initiated by the employer and employer-motivated job leaving. A number of workers leave jobs for reasons that can be viewed as positive. Such reasons could include, among others, job advancement, chance for increased responsibility, higher wages or benefits, and career growth. The following paragraphs discuss reasons for negative termination, or those terminations that do not enhance the individual's career growth, independence, or economic status.

Table 21.4. Factors contributing to termination

1. Unacceptable work performance issues: incompetence, unacceptable skill level (i.e., quality/quantity), inexperience, physical/psychological "disqualifications," inability to learn the job, failure to improve, lack of knowlege of job

2. Unacceptable work behavior issues: unreliable/undependable, ineffective human relations (inability to get along with people, interpersonal differences between employer and employee, discourteous, not helpful, uncooperative), lack of initiative and ingenuity, poor judgment, ineffective communication skills, absenteeism

3. Positive misconduct: rule violation—theft, dishonesty, insubordination, intoxication/drug use on the job, carelessness, "trouble breeding"

4. Other: appearance, personality traits, defects of character

As with job promotion, a central variable in job termination is the quantity and quality of production by the individual worker. If the employee is unable either to deliver the amount of output expected or his or her work does not meet company standards, initially additional training and support may be provided. If poor production persists, the employee will have to be either reassigned or terminated. Other nonproduction-related issues such as misconduct, appearance, specific personality traits, and an inability to get along with others can also lead to job termination.

Unacceptable work behaviors such as lack of dependability or inconsistency in relationships with others will create a situation where role and expectation conflict will develop. Industry is looking for dependability so that it can meet the established goals and objectives. If a worker cannot be depended upon for whatever reason, his or her utility to meeting company expectations is minimal. Unacceptable work behaviors can also indicate a lack of personal needs fulfillment for the worker. In this instance, since the job is not meeting the individual's needs, the worker's level of satisfaction and degree of motivation is diminished. This diminution of both satisfaction and motivation is reflected in reduced productivity and/or poor quality in workmanship.

Society rule violations such as stealing and substance abuse can also lead to job termination. In situations such as these there may be an immediate termination or at least the initiation of a progressive disciplinary procedure. The magnitude of the response is generally a reflection of the nature of the issue in comparison to the rules and regulations of the company.

Less significant factors such as appearance and interpersonal traits that are incompatible with other persons in the work area can also lead to termination. Clearly the previously mentioned factors are more substantial issues in job termination. Except for gross societal rule violations, in most instances the factors previously noted lead to initial intervention efforts by the employer prior to termination. If no resolution is possible, then the employment relationship will be ended. As with the factors that are critical in hiring and promoting the worker, personality issues or concerns are most frequently the reasons for initiating a progressive disciplinary procedure or terminating the employee.

CONCLUSIONS

A review of the industry research shows that in many instances attributes such as dependability, ability to get along with others, and cooperation are as valuable as the technical or production skills one brings to the job. The reasons for hiring, promoting, and terminating workers are often both production and personality based.

This finding would imply that employment and training programs need to look at the development of both skill levels and personality traits if persons with disabilities are to obtain and maintain employment. Programs will need to encourage the development of traits such as dependability, initiative, and cooperation if disabled people are to be adequately prepared to assume a productive role in industry. The use of on-site training and support, which aid in both the development of the productivity and social capacity of the worker with a disability, will be essential as these employment and training programs respond to industry's expectations for its workers now and in the future.

REFERENCES

Bureau of National Affairs. (1988, May 26). *BNA policy and practice series for the personnel executive: Personnel management.* (No. 681, pp. 207; 11–207:130 and 207:951–207:1022). Washington, DC: Author.

Foss, G., & Peterson, S.L. (1981). Social-interpersonal skills relevant to job tenure for mentally retarded adults. *Mental Retardation, 19,* 371–375.

Getzels, J.W., & Guba, E.G. (1957). Social behavior and the administrative process. *School Review, 65,* 423–441.

Greenspan, S., & Shoultz, B. (1981). What mentally retarded adults lose jobs: Social competence as a factor in work adjustment. *Applied Research in Mental Retardation, 2,* 23–38.

Hendrickson, J. (1987). Hiring the right stuff. *Personnel Administration, 32,* 70–75.

Hanley-Maxwell, C., Rusch, F., Chadsey-Rusch, J., & Renzaglia, A. (1986). Reported factors contributing to job termination of individuals with severe disabilities. *Journal of The Association of the Severely Handicapped, 11*(1), 45–52.

Herring, J.J. (1986). Establishing an employee recruitment system. *Personnel, 63,* 47–54.

Melohn, T. (1987). Screening for the best employees. *Inc., 9,* 104–110.

22

Designing Decision Support Systems

Shawn M. Boles,
Bruce A. Wald, and Yan Xiaoyan

 This chapter describes the evolution of a decision support system (DSS) that was developed to collect, monitor, analyze, and disseminate outcome data from vocational programs providing services to people with severe disabilities in Washington State (Boles, 1985). The chapter reviews the history of the system's development and implementation and describes the user groups and the construction of the dataset resulting from the system's use. A dataset is a collection of systematically obtained and archived data relating to a generic topic area; in this case, vocational outcome data from persons with disabilities in Washington State. Next, the data generated by the system are presented in relation to key employment indicators. Finally, those results are examined in terms of the usefulness of such a DSS. This discussion is particularly timely in light of recent state and federal employment initiatives that have shifted funding priorities that pay for work support in segregated settings to paying for providing work support in integrated settings (*Federal Register,* 1984; Office of Special Education and Rehabilitative Services, 1984). Additionally, changes in the Social Security Act have removed work disincentives from individuals receiving Supplementary Security Income (Social Security Disability Benefits Reform Act of 1984, 1984). The authors argue that a DSS such as that described here would be useful in collecting, analyzing, and monitoring the outcomes generated by the infusion of federal money into state system changeover.

HISTORY OF THE DECISION SUPPORT SYSTEM

The statewide data system developed in Washington State was facilitated by three factors, including changes in vocational service models, advances in information processing technology, and a commitment to consumer outcomes.

Changes in Vocational Service Models

At a public cost of nearly a third of a billion dollars annually, state developmental disabilities agencies are administering some 2,000 adult day programs for over 100,000 developmentally disabled citizens in the United States (Bellamy, Sheehan, Horner, & Boles, 1980). The programs administered by those agencies have traditionally been viewed as the first step in a continuum of services that would eventually lead service recipients (consumers) to vocational rehabilitation and employment in the private sector. In this traditional view, meaningful work opportunities and work-related services have been reserved for advanced programs, while adult day programs have been intended to enhance development of personal and social skills to enable individuals to enter and benefit from work preparation services at a later time.

The result of traditional practices has been the exclusion of many people with developmental disabilities from both work and work-related services as reflected in the following findings: 1) studies in two large states revealed that progression through vocational services was limited to 5% of the day program participants being served in a given year (California Department of Finance, 1979; New Jersey Bureau of Adult Training Services, 1981); 2) progression through the continuum of services has been virtually impossible within the working life span of the typical day program participant (Bellamy, Rhodes, Bourbeau, & Mank, 1986); and 3) meaningful work opportunities commensurate with consumer skills have not been available across the service continuum (U.S. Department of Labor, 1979).

Federal, state, and local responses to the failure of traditional vocational service practices have focused on the development of alternative service strategies such as those described in Chapters 23 and 24 in this text. Despite their diversity, these program alternatives share a common commitment to assessing their impact in terms of direct benefits to consumers. Rather than simply expecting employment opportunities at the end of a lifelong continuum of services, these alternative service models emphasize current work opportunities and the direct benefits received by working individuals.

Effective management of adult day programs by responsible state agencies requires coordination of several decisions about the service providers responsible for funding, contracting, regulation, and monitoring. In addition, as alternative programs succeed in improving economic conditions for disabled service consumers, there is a need for regular information on wages and program costs, and for processes to link these data to program evaluation and funding decisions at all levels of the service system.

Advances in Information Processing Technology

The second factor leading to the development of the DSS was the explosive growth over the past decade in the availability of inexpensive and powerful information processing tools (Boles & Wheeler, 1981). The application of these tools in social services management has been limited by the lack of software that reflects the actual management decisions made by administrators of such programs in ensuring service quality. Recent developments in the design of microcomputer-based decision support systems that link hardware, software, people, and management practices have provided a means of overcoming this problem. These developments provide a framework for designing and implementing systems that embody the concept of feedback loops to represent the process by which outcomes are planned for, performance is measured, and decisions are directed to reduce the discrepancy between actual and desired levels of performance.

Unique Consumer Needs

Each consumer has unique system needs. In reference to Washington State, the features desired in a decision support system included:

The system would provide frequent and reliable information on consumer benefits that reflected the vocational focus of services. The information would be organized and presented in the context of a feedback loop.

The system would summarize this information in a form and schedule that would enable use by the many decision makers with program management responsibility. This includes managers of provider agencies, county program managers, state agency staff, state legislative bodies, and external advocacy groups.

For each of the users, information on consumer benefits would be accompanied by supporting materials that would facilitate use in decision making. For example, county decision makers, responsible for selecting and contracting with providers, would be assisted by clear procedures for linking consumer outcome data to performance-based contracts.

Information on consumer outcomes would be linked systematically to cost data, which would enable state-level administrators to evaluate the public costs of achieving desired consumer benefits and to determine future allocation of scarce resources.

The unit of reporting would be service programs/vendors, and input data would come from standardized forms used by the state for program reimbursement purposes.

USER GROUPS

Four user groups were identified as beneficiaries of the DSS, including the researcher, consumer, purchaser, and provider. The researcher group can be found in both university settings and evaluation units of state governments. The consumer group consists of people with disabilities, their individual advocates, and advocacy groups representing them. The purchaser groups consist of those governmental bodies that provide the funding for the services provided. The provider group consists of the organizations that provide the services.

SYSTEM DESCRIPTION

A decision support system is an organization of hardware, software, and operating procedures that provide accurate, timely, and relevant information to groups of decision makers. In social services systems, this information is combined with additional documentation to form a basis for decisions regarding the organization of resources to produce valued outcomes for a specific group of citizens across a variety of service settings. The structure of a particular DSS is determined both by the settings where the outcomes are to occur and by the decision roles involved in achieving the outcomes.

Each of these user groups requires a DSS to provide planning, performing, measuring, and reporting functions associated with feedback on those outcomes that are affected by the group's decisions. In addition, a DSS must minimize the response cost entailed in recording and reporting outcome data, as well as ensure that adequate communication links exist among the user groups. The requirements of relevant feedback, minimum response cost, and adequate communication links formed a set of constraints that controlled the development of the system. In essence, the system addressed these constraints in a particular service system (Washington State Supported Work Services for Severely Handicapped Adults), using a combination of applied system analysis (Gilbert, 1978) and microcomputer technology (Boles & Wheeler, 1981). Figure 22.1 is a diagram of the system that was developed using this approach.

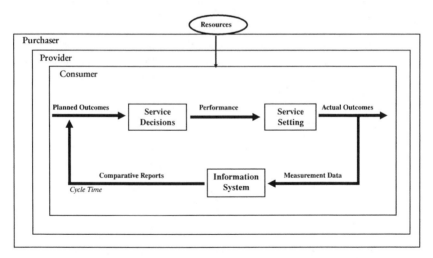

Figure 22.1. Diagram of decision support system. For all figures in this chapter, see the text for further explanation.

This figure shows resources available to consumers, providers, and purchasers being used to support the performance of activities necessary to achieve planned outcomes valued by the users. In the loop, performance is changed as a result of decisions made by these groups. These decisions, in turn, are based on comparison reports that indicate discrepancies between actual outcomes achieved in service settings and outcomes targeted by users. These reports are generated by a microcomputer information system that is used to manage the collection, aggregation, scheduling, and communication activities required for each user group.

Initial work in Washington State identified the components required in an effective management system for vocational programs. Public investment efficiency, consumer benefit, and economic feasibility from the perspective of service providers served as a set of indicators for the management and analysis of investments in services. Public investment efficiency (cost-effectiveness—CE) is measured by the public dollars that must be invested to generate one dollar of wages for a consumer with a disability. Consumer benefit (CB) is measured by the monthly wages paid to these consumers. Program economics feasibility (self-sufficiency—SS) is measured by the proportion of program revenues that derives from commercial operations.

Different reports, as described in the next section, were generated depending on the user group to which they were addressed. For each report, the three indicators (SS, CE, CB) allowed quick analysis of the economic feasibility, public investment efficiency, and consumer benefit generated by each program by region and for the state as a whole.

1. *Self-sufficiency (SS)* Self-sufficiency is the measure of how fiscally sound a program would be without government payments. The measure is derived by dividing gross commercial revenue by the sum of gross commercial revenue and government funding. The measure approaches a value of 1.0 as the relative contribution of company-generated revenue grows. Clearly, this measure is useful only when describing a facility-based or small business organization. In the time frame reported in the "Results" section, facility-based programs formed the predominant model used to employ individuals with severe disabilities.

2. *Cost-effectiveness (CE)* CE measures the success of a program in paying wages to workers with disabilities as a percentage of government funding paid to a program for providing services. The measure is calculated by dividing total worker wages by total county payment. The minimum acceptable value is one dollar in wages paid for each dollar received in fees for services, or 1.0. This is clearly a measure that is applicable to a vocational program regardless of whether it carries out activities that add value to a product or if the sole purpose is to provide placement services.

3. *Consumer Benefit (CB)* CB is an exploitation measure. It is calculated by dividing the wages paid to workers by the total commercial revenue.

Worker exploitation is avoided only if this value falls in the 0.25 to 0.50 range. Exploitation of the state occurs if the value is greater than 1.0, since at that point taxpayers' dollars are used to subsidize worker wages.

Data collection timelines were arranged to ensure that data were verifiable and that additions or corrections could occur. A second data distribution 5 months after the end of the month in which the data were collected gave programs the opportunity to correct any faulty entries. Allowing these corrections increased data collection accuracy. In addition to permitting programs to self-correct data entries, funders were also given the opportunity to determine whether programs were complying with data provision to the state-level funders. Each outcome data report included a "control" report, which showed missing values or values that were not calculable. The latter could have occurred either because values were missing (and needed to be made available before the second data compilation) or because the type of service did not generate those data (e.g., a placement company that did not generate commercial revenue).

RESULTS

Raw data have been collected monthly since July, 1983. The results described here are based on five 6-month periods (beginning with the period July 1, 1983, to December 31, 1983, and ending with the period July 1, 1985, to December 31, 1985). There are 499 6-month blocks of data represented in the 30 months reported. Each 6-month block represents the data for one program for that time period. The number of programs reporting data in any 6-month block ranged from 95 to 104, with 159 different programs reporting over the 30-month period. Recall that the unit of reporting was the service programs/vendors in the state.

The major worker outcome data presented are related to: 1) worker wages, 2) self-sufficiency, 3) cost-effectiveness, and 4) consumer benefit. The data are presented summed across all 6-month blocks by Region and broken out by Regions across 6-month blocks. The number of programs remained relatively constant (range 95–104) over the five periods from which data are presented. There was a considerable turnover in programs over the 30-month duration. The number of programs increased slightly in Regions 3, 4, and 6 and decreased slightly in Regions 1, 2, and 5 over the 30 months.

Worker Wages

Figure 22.2 shows that wages generally increased across data collection periods for all regions, except Region 1. The assumption that small programs would result in higher worker wages was not borne out by the data; wages were low regardless of program size.

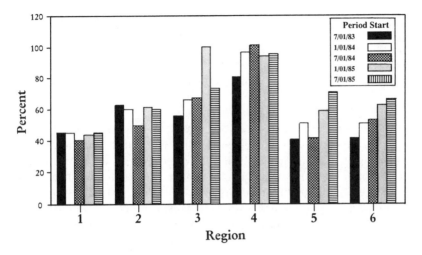

Figure 22.2. Average monthly worker wage, by region and period.

Self-sufficiency

Figure 22.3 shows that average regional SS never got above 0.50, indicating that the average program always got more than half of its income from governmental sources. There were programs at both ends of the continuum— those that generated no commercial revenue and those that had values greater than 0.90 on this measure. There were never more than 5 programs in any 6-

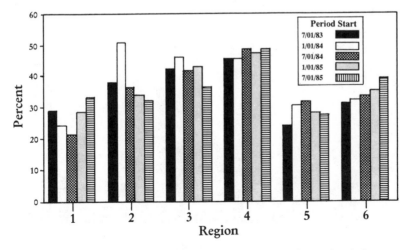

Figure 22.3. Average regional self-sufficiency, by region and period.

month block at or above 0.90 (range 2–5), and the number of programs generating no commercial income ranged from 17 to 21 across blocks. Over the 30-month period, 19% of the programs generated no commercial income, while slightly over 3% generated 90% or more of their income from commercial sources. This outcome variable also had no relationship to program size.

Cost-effectiveness

Average CE for a region never exceeded 0.53, as shown in Figure 22.4. This value was reached only in Region 4 and was about 0.35 or lower in the remaining regions. This means that the average program was never returning one dollar in wages to workers for each dollar received in government funds. Unfortunately, of the 499 6-month blocks of reports, only 17 (3%) reported returning one dollar or more in wages to workers for each government dollar received. Again, there was little or no relationship between program size and this variable.

Consumer Benefit

Average consumer benefit for the six periods by region is shown in Figure 22.5. The profile of these data is somewhat different from that of the other outcome measures. Remember, however, that acceptable values for this measure fall between 0.25 and 0.50. Values below this range demonstrate employee exploitation, values between 0.50 and 1.0 demonstrate poor business acumen, and values 1.0 or above show exploitation of the state. No regional average falls below 0.30 and none is above 1.0. Regions 2 and 6 did rise higher than 0.50, suggesting some problems with business operations with at least some of the programs in those regions.

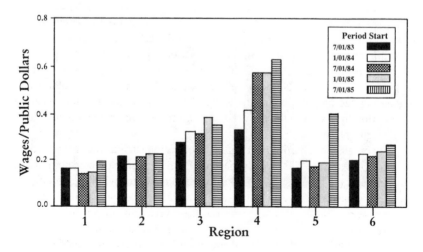

Figure 22.4. Average cost-effectiveness, by region and period.

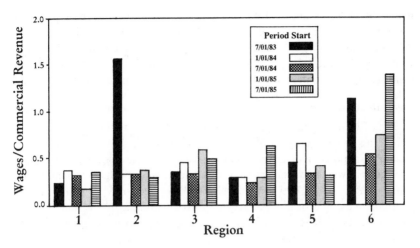

Figure 22.5. Average consumer benefit, by region and period.

DISCUSSION

These data demonstrate that a statewide DSS designed to monitor vocational outcomes generated by providing services to individuals with disabilities is possible in a large state bureaucracy. Although data had never before been available systematically on a statewide basis, the system described in this chapter made the data available in a timely manner and should have made it possible for county and regional managers to make decisions based on the indicators (SS, CE, CB) identified as important in evaluating employment services. Data were unfortunately not collected on the frequency with which government monitors used exemplary performers to provide consultation or information on methods that would allow less exemplary performers to increase their expertise. Nor are data available that indicate the actions of monitors based on poor indicators. Regardless of the uses made of the data, it is clear that they were publicly available in a timely manner and available to all user groups.

In conclusion, all consumers need information such as that generated by the DSS, to examine the effectiveness of the recent employment initiatives. Only through the use of such public information systems will it be possible to openly evaluate the effects of public policy and the use of public funds. It may be the case that future data will bear out the convictions of practitioners that individuals with severe disabilities can earn significant wages in integrated settings. It is hoped that the DSS discussed in this chapter will facilitate that process.

REFERENCES

Bellamy, G.T., Rhodes, L.E., Bourbeau, P.E., & Mank, D.M. (1986). Mental retardation services in sheltered workshops and day activities programs: Consumer benefits and policy alternatives. In F. Rusch (Ed.), *Competitive employment issues and strategies* (pp. 257–271). Baltimore: Paul H. Brookes Publishing Co.

Bellamy, G.T., Sheehan, M.R., Horner, R.H., & Boles, S.M. (1980). Community programs for severely handicapped adults: An analysis of vocational opportunities. *Journal of the Association for the Severely Handicapped, 5,* 307–324.

Boles, S.M. (1980). *STP information system summary.* Unpublished working paper, University of Oregon, Specialized Training Program, Eugene.

Boles, S.M. (1985). *Final report: A decision support system for managing work programs serving developmentally disabled adults.* (HDS Contract No. 90DDD0041/01, University of Oregon/Washington State DDD). Eugene: University of Oregon, College of Education, Specialized Training Program.

Boles, S.M., & Wheeler, R.W. (1981). Microcomputers in social service systems. In *Proceedings of the Johns Hopkins University's first national search for applications of computing to aid the handicapped* (IEEE # TH0092-7) (pp. 86–101). Baltimore: Johns Hopkins University Press.

California Department of Finance. (1979). *A review of sheltered workshops and related programs (Phase II): To Assembly Concurrent Resolution No. 206. Volume II, final report.* Sacramento: State of California.

Federal Register. (September 25, 1984). Developmental Disabilities Act of 1984. Report 98-1074.

Gilbert, T.F. (1978). *Human competence: Engineering worthy performance.* New York: McGraw-Hill.

New Jersey Bureau of Adult Training Services. (1981, June). *Movement of adult activities clients to vocational programs.* Paper presented at the New Jersey Bureau of Adult Training Services Regional Supervisors' Meeting, Trenton.

Office of Special Education and Rehabilitative Services. (1984). *Supported employment for adults with severe disabilities: An OSERS initiative.* Unpublished manuscript.

Social Security Disability Benefits Reform Act of 1984. (1984). *Report from the Committee on Ways and Means, March 14, 1984.* Washington, DC: U. S. House of Representatives.

U.S. Department of Labor. (1979, March). *Study of handicapped clients in sheltered workshops* (Vol. 2). Washington, DC: Author.

23

Perspectives on Costs

Craig V.D. Thornton, Shari Miller Dunstan, and Janine Matton

Cost information is essential to the development and implementation of public policy. It provides a measure of the resources required to operate a program and a benchmark for assessing the magnitude of any program-induced impacts. Legislators and administrators are understandably reluctant to undertake programs or policies in which the cost implications are not well understood. Thus, one of the first questions asked of any proposed initiative is: What does it cost?

The importance of cost information is well illustrated by the growing interest in the costs of transitional employment. This program is a means of assisting persons with disabilities to obtain, learn, and hold jobs in the competitive labor market. When this approach was proposed 15 years ago as a means of fostering the economic and social independence of people with disabilities, the primary question was: Will it work? As transitional employment techniques have been used and refined in the ensuing years, there has been growing interest in implementing this type of intervention on a larger scale. This has led, not surprisingly, to intensified concern over the costs of transitional employment as policy makers seek to fit this program into the current service system.

This chapter endeavors to meet the need for greater cost information about transitional employment by reviewing the operations costs observed in *The Transitional Employment Training Demonstration* (TETD) (Thornton, Dunstan, & Schore, in press). In this demonstration, the U.S. Social Security Administration funded eight transitional employment projects in 13 cities from June, 1985 to June, 1987. These programs served persons who were receiving Supplemental Security Income (SSI) payments, who were between the ages of 18 and 40 years, and who had a diagnosis of mental retardation that was sufficiently severe to meet the disability criteria for the SSI program. The demonstration was undertaken, in part, to determine the costs of the intervention and its effectiveness in promoting the financial self-sufficiency of the SSI recipients.

The financial estimates derived from the experiences of these eight demonstration projects offer a sound basis for estimating the costs of this intervention in general. The projects were conducted in diverse economic and geographic environments, ranging from predominantly rural counties to very large cities. The projects also took different approaches to selecting the persons they served and to providing transitional employment services. Thus, their experiences, when taken as a whole, suggest the range of likely costs for transitional employment programs. In addition, the authors' review of the literature indicates that the costs incurred by these demonstration projects are generally similar to those reported by other projects.

WHAT IS TRANSITIONAL EMPLOYMENT?

The concept of transitional employment is still evolving as more is learned about effective training strategies. The key element of this method, well expressed in the term *transitional employment,* is time-limited training in a real work–employment setting. The technique is a vehicle for providing training to facilitate the transition to regular employment. In addition, the technique stresses training on regular jobs, rather than preplacement or work-readiness training. Consequently, transitional employment places persons on regular jobs more quickly than many traditional programs.

Transitional employment can be thought of as proceeding in five stages. The first is the recruitment and assessment of appropriate persons. Second, persons are matched with and placed on competitive jobs. Third, program staff train the persons on their jobs and provide them with assistance in adapting to those jobs (this assistance includes help with travel arrangements, co-worker relations, and housing and other nonvocational skills and needs). Fourth, the training and assistance are gradually faded in order to promote independence on the job. Finally, the program works to see that the person will be able to obtain any future services necessary to retain his or her job. In some cases, the program provides these long-term job retention services directly, and in other cases, it arranges for other agencies to provide the services.

The intention of transitional employment is to provide a bridge to employment rather than ongoing support. The actual duration of transitional employment services varies, but the goals of the program are always to fade out services and to promote independent employment. In the TETD, the services were limited to 1 year, although long-term job retention services were anticipated to continue beyond that point (such services had to be funded by a source other than the demonstration).

The amount of ongoing services required depends on the individual needs of the client. Persons with more debilitating forms of mental retardation or other handicapping conditions may require more support than others. To date, there is little clear information available regarding the specific types, duration, intensity, and costs of the job retention services to be provided.

COST PERSPECTIVES AND ANALYTICAL FOCUS

The answer to the question "What does it cost?" depends on the perspectives of the person asking the question. Different groups of persons will be affected differently by transitional employment and so will perceive different costs. Specifically, program administrators, participants, employers, taxpayers, and society as a whole will all view the costs of operating a transitional employment program in varying ways.

Thornton (1985) and Schalock and Thornton (1988) discuss these various perspectives and their interrelationships. This chapter considers only the perspective of the program administrator. In particular, the discussion focuses on the resources needed to operate a transitional employment program: the wages and fringe benefits paid to project staff, the materials and supplies used by the program, transportation, facilities, and the costs of general program administration.

An administrator may not actually make cash expenditures for all of the resources used to provide the transitional employment services. Some resources may be obtained at a reduced charge or free of charge from other programs, individuals, and organizations. However, administrators need to consider the value of these items regardless of the expenditures made for them. By focusing on the costs of all resources used, administrators can gain a better understanding of the intervention, independent of the means by which the program is financially supported. Such a focus is also useful to others who plan to replicate the program, since they may not have the same access to donated resources and will have to purchase those resources.

This chapter's focus on costs as seen by program administrators provides a useful but incomplete picture of transitional employment. Here one sees only the bad news—the costs that must be incurred to provide the transitional employment services. A complete analysis would see these expenditures as investments in the futures of the participants and thus would need to assess the returns, or benefits, generated by this investment. These benefits potentially include net savings to the government if the transitional employment services substitute for alternative services; increased earnings, self-esteem, and community integration for the participants; savings to income-support programs such as Supplemental Security Income; and benefits to employers in the form of an increase in the available labor pool. There may also be additional costs if program participants increase their use of some programs that complement the transitional employment program or if the participants take jobs that otherwise would have been held by other workers.

Thus, while the material presented here is only one part of such a comprehensive evaluation, it is, nevertheless, a key component. Efforts to implement transitional employment programs will need cost information to prepare budgets and assess the alternative approaches to service delivery. The broader benefit-cost picture is provided by Kerachsky, Thornton, Bloomenthal, Maynard, and Stephens (1985), who present a comprehensive analysis of benefits and costs for the transitional employment programs fielded in the Structured Training and Employment Transitional Services (STETS) demonstration; and by Noble and Conley (1987), who provide an overview of several benefit-cost studies for transitional employment programs.

DATA SOURCES

Information on costs was obtained from expenditure reports that were submitted by the eight demonstration projects. These organizations prepared monthly cost reports that listed all project-related expenditures, including those funded by the Social Security Administration, as well as those funded by other sources (all of the projects were required to obtain at least 25% of their funding from sources other than the Social Security Administration). While these cost reports were unaudited, project directors did certify that they were accurate. In addition, the authors confirmed much of the information and collected additional cost information from discussions with project managers and financial staff. Thornton, Dunstan, and Schore (in press) describe the data collection process.

This chapter's analysis excludes three specific types of costs. The first is the costs for wages paid to participants. For the most part, these wages were paid by private employers, but some of the projects provided wages for participants during the early stages of their training. Those costs have been ignored here so that the analysis can focus on operations costs—that is, those costs incurred to provide the services. Programs that plan to offer wage subsidies or participant stipends will need to add those costs to the figures presented here.

The second group of costs excluded are the initial start-up costs incurred before the projects enrolled any participants. These costs grew to be substantial as the projects sought to hire and train their staff and implement their outreach activities. The average expenditure was approximately $50,000 per project. While such costs will be incurred by all new programs and technically should be amortized over the life of the program, they are excluded in this analysis. In the long term, these initial start-up costs will be relatively unimportant.

Finally, the costs incurred by the Social Security Administration to monitor and fund the demonstration projects are excluded. Ongoing projects will require some degree of monitoring by the funding agencies, and these costs should be considered in the analysis. However, the fact that the projects were fielded as part of a demonstration made it difficult to isolate the costs of "normal" monitoring from the costs of the demonstration evaluation. As a result, the authors have omitted these costs and concentrated on the project-level operations costs. Agencies that plan to field transitional employment programs will need to consider the central administrative costs necessary for effective program monitoring.

COSTS OF TRANSITIONAL EMPLOYMENT SERVICES

For the most part, this analysis focuses on average operating costs *per client enrolled* in a transitional employment program; that is, the total costs incurred by the program to recruit, screen, place, and train participants during a given period divided by the number of persons enrolled in that period.

The number of clients enrolled is only one of several bases that could be used to calculate average costs. The authors selected this basis since it is relevant from an administrative perspective when deciding whether to enroll a client in a transitional employment program. This figure indicates, on average, the costs an administrator should expect to incur for each client enrolled. Other cost averages that are used to assess program costs and performance include the average costs per placement or the average costs of stabilizing an individual in competitive employment. These average cost figures will be higher than comparable average costs per client, since not every client enrolled will progress through the program to be placed in or stabilized on a job. Some enrolled clients, for example, may only receive assessment services but will not go on to be placed or trained.

However, since screening is imperfect, it is often quite difficult to determine the likelihood of a person's achieving competitive employment. Thus, in practice, some transitional employment clients will not move into competitive employment (Kiernan & Stark, 1986, discuss the alternative outcomes). Nevertheless, resources will be spent on providing these individuals with services, and these are as much a part of program costs as are the costs of successful placements. Using the average operational cost per client enrolled in calculating total program operational expenses is then a reasonable practice, in that it accounts for the costs spent on those unsuccessful clients that will inevitably represent some portion of the participants enrolled.

The average cost across the eight demonstration projects ranged from $3,800 to $14,000 per client enrolled. Costs also varied within each project, from relatively low costs, which were incurred for those clients who dropped out or were terminated early in their year of eligibility, to costs in excess of $25,000, which were incurred for some particularly difficult and time-consuming cases.

The level of cost reflects decisions about myriad aspects of program operations. The aspects reflect particular characteristics of the clients served, the program models adopted, client-to-staff ratios, staff salaries, the duration and intensity of services provided, the extent of support services, and the settings in which the programs were fielded.

Because the authors observed only eight projects and there are hundreds of factors that can cause cost to vary, it is impossible to determine the specific effect each of these factors has on cost. However, conclusions can be drawn about some of these key factors on the basis of the authors' observations of the projects during the 2 years of the demonstration.

An obvious factor explaining costs in the demonstration is the fact that the demonstration schedule implied that the projects never had a chance to operate in a "steady-state" mode where they resembled an ongoing program. Instead, the demonstration timetable required projects to build up their enrollment and begin providing services quickly during the first year. But then during the second year the projects had to stop enrollment and complete all the necessary services for the remaining clients. This meant that for most of the time they were not at their optimum scale and that they had to juggle their staff in response to the changing client intake requirements.

To estimate what the average cost would have been had the projects been able to operate more like ongoing programs, the authors sought to identify the direct labor costs of the interventions and then add to those costs the various indirect costs that would be incurred in an ongoing program. The direct labor costs are the wages and fringe benefits paid to staff for the time they devoted to working directly with or on behalf of clients. These costs were estimated on the basis of records maintained by project staff and from information on staff wage rates. For the most part, these direct labor costs can be expected to be representative of the direct labor costs that would be incurred by an ongoing program.

Two types of indirect costs were added to these direct labor costs. The first indirect cost captured wages and fringe benefits for the time that the service staff spent not working directly with specific clients. This time included general job development, staff training and development, general outreach and recruitment, interagency coordination, and, in some cases, downtime for job coaches between clients. The second indirect cost captured general program administration, as well as other direct costs of program services, such as travel, occupancy, and telephone.

Both types of indirect costs appear to be higher in the demonstration than they would have been in an ongoing program. To estimate the magnitude of these costs for each ongoing program, the authors used their value during 1986. This year, in the middle of the demonstration, was the period when the demonstration projects most closely resembled an ongoing program, although indirect costs might still be higher than their long-term levels for this period.

When these two types of indirect costs were added to the estimates of direct labor cost, the resulting estimates indicated that average costs in an ongoing program similar to the demonstration would be approximately 25%

less, overall, than those actually observed during the demonstration. The variation in costs was also reduced. Estimated ongoing costs ranged from $2,800 to $8,100 per person enrolled, with the average cost for the eight projects being $5,600 per person enrolled.

The figure of $5,600 per person enrolled represents the authors' best single estimate of the costs of operating a transitional employment program like those in the demonstration. It is based on observations from the eight projects and reflects the experiences of serving 375 SSI recipients with mental retardation. Of course, since average costs for the projects ranged $2,500 above and below that $5,600 average, it is clear that there is room for substantial variation around this single estimate.

When interpreting these costs, it is essential to note that they reflect estimated costs for services provided within each participant's year of demonstration eligibility. These costs indicate the resources needed to recruit, assess, place, train, and stabilize SSI recipients with mental retardation in competitive jobs. Many of the clients continued to receive services after leaving the demonstration. These postprogram services were funded by nondemonstration sources and were generally intended to help participants retain the jobs they obtained while in the demonstration. However, the use of these longer term services implies that the total resources needed to place and maintain a person in competitive employment will exceed the costs observed in the demonstration.

As noted earlier, data on the costs of job retention and follow-up services for transitional employment programs, as well as the extent of the need for these services, are not well documented to date. However, it is necessary to estimate these costs so that they can be included in a comprehensive cost assessment of transitional employment. These costs can be estimated on the basis of the average salaries paid to job coaches and the average number of persons that could be served by a single coach.

In the eight demonstration projects, job coach salaries averaged approximately $13,500 per year. The costs of fringe benefits and of program management need to be added to this salary to estimate the total cost of a job coach position. Using the data collected during the demonstration, it appears that these costs are approximately equal to the job coach's direct salary, making the total cost of the position approximately $27,000 per year.

To estimate the average job retention cost per client, the authors divided the cost of the job coach position by an estimate of the number of clients a job coach could reasonably serve in a year. The TETD did not cover long-term job retention services, so this information had to be obtained from other sources. Wehman and Hill (see Chapter 24, this volume) report that at the program at Virginia Commonwealth University the average job coach serves 13 clients. Jim Moss (personal communication, December 15, 1986) reports that the client-to-staff ratio at the transitional employment project at the University of Washington is 20 to 1. Other transitional employment programs have proposed ratios ranging from 5 : 1 to 35 : 1. Consequently, according to these estimates, the cost of follow-up services per client can range from $771 per year for the program serving the most clients per staff member to $5,400 per year for the program serving the fewest number of clients per staff member. Using the ratio of 13 : 1 as a middle value, the authors computed that the average annual cost of job retention services would be just over $2,100 per client. Not all clients who are enrolled will receive job retention services, however, and so the average cost per person enrolled will be less than $2,100.

Having estimated the average operating cost per client, administrators still need to project the total cost of the program. Given that the demonstration projects generally operated on a scale that would have enabled them to enroll and serve 30 persons a year, the authors' average cost estimate suggests that it would cost approximately $170,000 a year to run an average-size transitional employment program on an ongoing basis, if it was providing only the initial placement and training services. Judging from the actual costs incurred in the demonstration from start-up and for running the programs, it could cost an additional $100,000 over the first year of operation to establish the program.

The long-term job retention services, to the extent that they are necessary, would have to be budgeted separately and would depend on the number of persons who progressed through the program and were successfully placed and stabilized on competitive jobs.

Total project costs, including both initial and job retention costs, will depend on the mix of people being served. For example, in the first year the cost of serving 30 persons would be approximately $170,000 (ignoring any start-up costs). In the second year the costs would include those of providing initial services to another 30 persons, in addition to the costs of job retention services for the persons successfully placed by the program in the previous year. As pointed out by Wehman and Hill (Chapter 24, this volume), as time passes, the proportion of clients receiving job retention services grows relative to the proportion of those receiving initial services. Thus, job retention costs get proportionately larger with each year.

WHY DO COSTS VARY?

So far this chapter has accounted for only one of the many factors that influence costs—the demonstration schedule. The authors' observations of the eight projects over 2 years, plus information from the earlier-mentioned STETS demonstration (Kerachsky et al., 1985) suggest the roles played by many other factors. While the specific magnitudes of these roles cannot be identified from these observations, several considerations emerge.

First, the various decisions administrators make about program operations interact. As a result, it is difficult to make simple statements about factors that would raise or lower costs. Consider, for example, staff-to-client ratio. As seen in the discussion of job retention services, increasing this ratio will raise costs if all other factors remain unchanged. However, other factors often vary, so that projects with relatively more staff members per client may not have higher costs.

In the TETD, some projects were able to operate with relatively more staff per client and still have relatively low costs by keeping the fraction of time staff spent working directly with clients high and by keeping program administration costs low. In other words, differences in the indirect costs could compensate for differences in direct costs. Another compensating factor was staff wages. One project was able to hire undergraduate students who worked at low wages and on an on-call basis (that is, the students were paid only for the hours when they were working with clients, with no allowance for normal downtime). This enabled the project to provide participants with a relatively high amount of direct staff intervention, yet still keep overall average costs low.

Another project incurred relatively high average costs, yet provided relatively little direct staff time per participant. This situation arose because of difficulties in recruiting SSI recipients for that project. These difficulties prompted the project to spend substantial staff resources on outreach and recruiting, which raised indirect costs. When the project was unable to enroll as many persons as it planned, it was left with relatively more staff and administrative capability per person enrolled than planned. This also increased the average indirect costs at that project and contributed to the higher overall average cost.

Of course, low cost need not always reflect low staff-to-client ratios, low staff wages, or low indirect cost rates. The fraction of persons who are enrolled and then actually placed in jobs and provided training is also a key factor. Overall, the demonstration projects were able to place almost 68% of the SSI recipients with mental retardation who were enrolled. In contrast, the project with the lowest average cost in the demonstration placed 40% of its clients in jobs. While this project was quite successful with the clients who were placed, it spent relatively little resources on the persons who were not placed. When costs are averaged across all persons enrolled, regardless of whether they were placed in jobs, the resulting average costs were quite low.

Participant characteristics are a major influence in determining program costs. The individuals in TETD all had a diagnosis of mental retardation. They came to the program with specific needs and placed specific demands on the project. Other groups might require a different intensity and duration of services. Other things being equal, the less intensive the services and the shorter the length of participation, the lower will be the average cost per client. It should be noted, however, that the severity of the disability was not a good predictor of the intensity of services required in the demonstration.

Rather, service intensity depended on several factors, including motivation and previous work experience (Thornton et al., in press, chapt. 6).

Different screening practices will also influence costs. To the extent that program administrators can accurately predict which clients are likely to be placed in the program at a low cost, and enroll only these clients, costs will fall. As programs try to open their doors to a wider range of clients, many of whom will require more extensive services, average program costs per client would then likely rise unless offsetting changes in program efficiency, indirect costs, or staff wages could be achieved.

Another source of differing costs is variations in compensation paid to staff. The wages and fringe-benefits for nonadministrative staff in the TETD accounted for half of all project costs. Thus, differences in compensation rates greatly influence overall costs. For example, the wages paid to job coaches in the demonstration ranged from a low of about $4 per hour with no fringe benefits to an annual salary of almost $24,000 plus a full fringe-benefits package. Not surprisingly, the projects at the extremes of the compensation range were also at the extremes of the range of estimated ongoing average costs.

CONCLUSION

Data from the Transitional Employment Training Demonstration suggest that it would cost from $2,800 to $8,100 per person enrolled to provide the initial placement and training services in a transitional employment program. The exact size of the costs will depend on a variety of decisions about program structure and operation. These decisions interact in complex ways to influence costs and program performance. In general, all else being equal, it appears that the low average costs are associated with low staff-to-client ratios, staff wages, indirect cost rates, and placement rates. Costs will also be influenced by the needs of the persons enrolled and by the programmatic and economic environments in which a program operates. Of course, these factors are likely to affect program performance as well as costs.

In interpreting this range of costs, it is important to note that demonstration projects were encouraged to enroll a wide range of SSI recipients with mental retardation, even if they were not entirely sure about the persons' chances of success. The authors' discussions with project managers indicate that program placement rates could have been higher and average costs lower if the projects had been able to evaluate program applicants more intensively to screen out inappropriate applicants.

These costs represent a substantial investment, and need to be compared to the benefits they produce. While little long-term data are available about the impacts of transitional employment, it does appear that these programs have the potential to produce net benefits to participants, to the government, and to society as a whole (see Hill, Hill, Wehman, & Banks, 1985; Kerachsky et al., 1985; Noble & Conley, 1987). A key factor will be the extent to which transitional employment represents an alternative to other services (and therefore has the potential to generate net savings to the government) or represents an extension of services to previously unserved or underserved populations (in which case, it will increase government expenditures but will also increase the employment and community integration of persons with disabilities). Another factor will be the extent to which persons need long-term job retention services in order to hold their jobs.

It is clear that transitional employment represents a substantial investment. What is needed is more information about the long-term impacts and job retention costs so that a comprehensive assessment can be made of this approach to increasing the employment, earnings, self-sufficiency, and community integration of persons with handicaps.

REFERENCES

Hill, M., Hill, J.W., Wehman, P., & Banks, D. (1985). An analysis of monetary and nonmonetary outcomes associated with competitive employment of mentally retarded persons. In P. Wehman & J.W. Hill (Eds.), *Competitive employment for persons with mental retardation: From research to practice*. Richmond: Virginia Commonwealth University Rehabilitation Research and Training Center.

Kerachsky, S., Thornton, C., Bloomenthal, A., Maynard, R., & Stephens, S. (1985). *Impacts of transitional employment on mentally retarded young adults: Results of the STETS demonstration*. Princeton, NJ: Mathematica Policy Research.

Kiernan, W.E., & Stark, J.A. (1986). Comprehensive design for the future. In W.E. Kiernan & J.A. Stark (Eds.), *Pathways to employment for adults with developmental disabilities* (pp. 103–112). Baltimore: Paul H. Brookes Publishing Co.

Noble, J.H., & Conley, R.W. (1987). Accumulating evidence on the benefits and costs of supported and transitional employment for persons with severe disabilities. *Journal of the Association for Persons with Severe Handicaps, 12*(3), 163–174.

Schalock, R.L., & Thornton, C. (1988). *Program evaluation: A field guide for program administrators*. New York: Plenum.

Thornton, C. (1985). Benefit-cost analysis of social programs: Deinstitutionalization and education programs. In R.H. Bruininks & K. C. Lakin (Eds.), *Living and learning in the least restrictive environment* (pp. 225–244). Baltimore: Paul H. Brookes Publishing Co.

Thornton, C., Dunstan, S.M., & Schore, J. (in press). *The transitional employment training demonstration: Analysis of program operations and in-program impacts*. Princeton, NJ: Mathematica Policy Research.

24

Competitive Employment for Persons with Mental Retardation
A Benefit-Cost Analysis of Outcomes

Paul Wehman and Mark L. Hill

A significant number of states appear to be moving toward adopting supported employment programs for people with severe disabilities. While these programs have not been without controversy, the combination of strong federal initiatives in this area plus high unemployment and underemployment of persons with significant disabilities has resulted in serious evaluation of how current rehabilitative and adult day services are being provided. Although there are a variety of different forms of supported employment, one that has received major attention is the supported work model of competitive employment (Wehman & Kregel, 1985). With this model, two important outcomes of supported employment, decent pay and community integration, result. Furthermore, it has been demonstrated that this approach can occur on an attractive cost-benefit basis (Hill & Wehman, 1983). This chapter focuses on the benefits and costs associated with the competitive employment of persons with developmental disabilities.

Hill and Wehman (1983) previously addressed the benefits and costs associated with supported competitive employment through an analysis of employment data over a 4-year period. In that analysis, the public's cumulative savings were estimated at over $620,000, while expenditures during the 4 years were estimated at $530,000, leaving a direct benefit to the taxpayer of about $90,000. Most participants (59%) were labeled moderately mentally retarded and had collectively earned over $500,000. This chapter provides an extension of these 1983 results by reporting cumulative data from September, 1978 to June, 1986. First, cumulative benefit and cost data are presented with respect to a population of 214 individuals served through the demonstration programs operated by the Rehabilitation Research and Training Center (RRTC) at the Virginia Commonwealth University, Richmond. Second, information is presented that illustrates the specific impact of competitive employment on persons labeled moderately and severely mentally retarded.

STUDY PARTICIPANTS

Table 24.1 presents demographic and employment outcome data from the 214 consumers participating in supported competitive employment from 1978 to 1986. The majority (51%) of the 214 consumers were described as moderately mentally retarded. These consumers were most frequently employed in entry-level, nonskilled positions such as food service or housekeeping. Approximately 70% of all consumers placed into supported competitive employment remained employed for at least 6 months; the average length of time that consumers remained employed during the study period was 21 months. The consumer's average duration of employment, with respect to the number of months a program has operated, is an important reference point for interpreting the benefit-cost analysis. The longer a program has been operating, the greater is the expectation for increased consumer job duration.

It should be emphasized that all consumers participated in individual placements; no group-supported employment options such as enclaves or work crews were developed. Furthermore, all consumers earned the federal minimum hourly wage or above. The project did not place any individuals in jobs where they would earn less than the federal minimum wage.

Table 24.1. Key consumer demographic and employment outcomes, 1978–1986 (*N* = 214)

Gender	
Male: 66.2%	
Female: 33.8%	
Average age: 30	
Average IQ: 51	
Previously diagnosed functioning level:	
Severe: 6%	
Moderate: 51%	
Mild: 33%	
Not retarded: 10%	
Annual salary for year before referral:	$229.00
Average hours worked per week:	28 hours
Average monthly wage after placement:	$406.51

ANALYTIC PROCEDURES

The general analytic procedures used in this report were adapted from an accounting model presented elsewhere (Hill et al., 1987; Thornton, 1984). This model provides a description of the actual monetary outcomes resulting from the supported employment program. Data were generated from the Rehabilitation Research and Training Center's Management Information System (MIS), which contains permanent consumer information supplied by individual employment specialists. These data were then analyzed in terms of their effect on consumer outcomes and governmental expenditures.

Several specific steps were taken to maximize the reliability of the data reported. The collection of data regarding the monetary outcomes of specific consumers was the responsibility of the individual employment specialists assigned to the consumers. These employment specialists were required to participate in inservice training in the center's MIS, and to follow specific procedures for data collection outlined in the MIS operations manual. All data submitted were reviewed twice for completeness and accuracy, first by the director of employment services, who forwarded the data for analysis, and second by the center's statistician, who verified the data both before and after data entry. While the data included in this chapter encompass an 8-year period and represent the efforts of over 20 employment specialists, the authors believe that the data verification procedures in effect during the course of the project resulted in a data base of acceptable reliability.

The effects of fluctuating economic factors (inflation and discounting) were examined, owing to the longitudinal nature of the data. All dollar figures across the 94-month period were converted to constant dollars expressed in 1986 (quarter 1) figures. To complete the conversion, the gross national product implicit price deflator was applied to actual dollar amounts expended. *Discounting* refers to the manner in which dollars change in value over time (Conley, 1973). In this analysis, discounting was applied to both benefits and costs. All reported data were analyzed using a 5% discount rate; however, sensitivity tests using discount rates of 3% and 10% were also employed to examine the effects of lower and higher rates on the data. As is seen later in the chapter, varying the discount rate did not change the overall effect of the benefit-cost analysis to any degree.

BENEFITS AND COSTS

Several variables from the RRTC data base were used to complete the cumulative and individualized benefit-cost analyses. These variables included: months worked, intervention time, ratio of service quotient (RSQ), Supplemental Security Income (SSI) saved, estimated alternative program cost, estimated total taxes paid per consumer, total public savings per consumer, Targeted Jobs Tax Credit to employer (TJTC), project expenditures per consumer, consequence to the taxpayer, and consumer cumulative wages. These variables are described in the paragraphs following.

1. *Months worked*. The number of months worked represents an accumulation of all jobs held by 11 consumers over the 8 years of the project. When information regarding the number of months employed is provided for specific consumers (as is seen in Table 24.2), information is also provided regarding the number of months between the individual's first placement and the end of the analysis period (June, 1986). This allows for a comparison of the amount of time the consumer could have potentially remained in employment.

2. *Staff intervention hours*. The amount of time that direct service staff spent with each consumer was monitored over the 94 months of operation. Various procedures for tracking intervention time have been used over the 8-year period. These variations entailed adding categories to the recording sheets to allow greater discrimination among the types of service being provided. Specific logs of trainer time with individual consumers began in June, 1979. Approximately 9 months of intervention time previous to this date was reconstructed by interviewing each trainer and by reviewing the consumer's information file. Since there were very few intervention hours provided during this period in relation to all intervention time during the course of the 8-year project, any error in measurement due to reconstruction would be negligible.

3. *Ratio of service quotient (RSQ)*. The overall amount of time spent by all trainers represents the total direct service effort. The hours invested in each consumer are a portion of the 100% effort. To provide an individual analysis of the effects of competitive supported employment, a fraction of the overall effort is computed for each participant. This computation indicates each individual's staff effort requirement relative to total staff hours expended by all direct service staff. The ratio of service quotient represents the total number of hours spent with a specific client divided by the number of hours spent with all participants. The RSQ is reported as a decimal rounded to the thousandths level.

4. *Supplemental Security Income (SSI)*. The SSI payments were derived by computing actual SSI reductions to each consumer's earned income over the period of employment. Pay raises, periodic SSI inflation rate adjustments, and consumers' living arrangements all affect the SSI payment on a month-to-month basis and have been included in each consumer's SSI computation. The figures presented in Table 24.3 represent the amount of SSI lost by all consumers due to increased income from supported employment. SSI is the only income maintenance program included in the present analysis. Recipients of Social Security Disability Insurance (SSDI) represented less than 2% of the project participants.

Table 24.2. Cross section of moderately and severely mentally retarded consumers: Demographics

Code name	Work status	Disability level	Probable program alternative	Age	Number of jobs held	Months worked	Number of months since first placement	Intervention time (hours:minutes)	Ratio of service quotient (RSQ)
Ted	Working	Moderate	Day program	63	1	85.7	88.5	617:58	0.01722
Bill	Working	Moderate	Sheltered workshop	33	3	82.5	87.2	567:44	0.01582
Len	Terminated	Moderate	Sheltered workshop	30	2	61.1	91.8	411:40	0.01147
Clyde	Working	Moderate	Sheltered workshop	27	1	26.6	29.4	65:10	0.00182
Donald	Working	Moderate	School/sheltered workshop	26	2	36.1	52.0	360:57	0.01006
Jason	Working	Moderate	Sheltered workshop	51	1	19.4	22.1	56:45	0.00158
Charlotte	Working	Moderate	Sheltered workshop	25	1	12.2	14.9	22:30	0.00063
Ralph	Working	Moderate	Sheltered workshop	19	1	12.2	15.0	108:35	0.00303
Dottie	Terminated	Moderate	Sheltered workshop	28	1	1.5	60.4	6:20	0.00018
Arnold	Working	Severe	Public school	21	1	2.6	5.4	111:00	0.00309
Horace	Terminated	Moderate	Day program	22	1	0.3	4.4	37:10	0.00104
Andy	Resigned	Severe	School/day program	24	3	8.1	40.5	222:04	0.00619
Cheryl	Terminated	Moderate	Sheltered workshop	33	1	5.2	68.3	36:35	0.00102
Sara	Terminated	Moderate	Sheltered workshop	33	1	1.8	85.5	45:00	0.00125
Harry	Resigned	Moderate	Public school	30	3	3.4	43.4	127:22	0.00355
Rudy	Laid off	Moderate	Day program	67	2	32.4	86.4	508:05	0.01416
Frank	Working	Severe	Public school	19	2	13.6	20.2	485:02	0.01352
Wanda	Resigned	Moderate	Sheltered workshop	38	4	21.4	59.6	389:50	0.01086

Table 24.3. Financial ramifications of competitive employment (1978–1986)

	Individual labeled moderately or severely mentally retarded ($N = 117$)	Individual labeled mildly mentally retarded or not retarded ($N = 97$)	Total population ($N = 214$)
Months worked	2,873	1,649	4,522
Intervention time	23,934	11,954	35,888
Ratio of service quotient	0.692963	0.307037	1.000000
Reduction in Supplemental Security Insurance payments	$306,765.83	$145,797.67	$452,554.50
Estimated alternative program costs savings	$1,055,194.83	$748,409.33	$1,803,604.16
Estimated total taxes paid	$351,689.76	$235,855.72	$587,545.48
Total public savings	$1,713,641.42	$1,130,062.72	$2,843,704.14
Targeted Jobs Tax Credits	$192,730.44	$103,569.38	$296,299.82
Total project expenditures	$1,212,117.88	$575,594.70	$1,787,712.58
Consequences to taxpayers	$525,071.88	$531,919.68	$1,056,991.56
Total wages earned	$1,503,779.72	$1,050,765.86	$2,554,545.58

5. *Estimated alternative program cost.* Decreased service expenditures, which represent the decrease in costs to governmental service agencies as consumers, are transferred from alternative programs (i.e., sheltered workshops, day activity centers, or public schools) into supported employment. The "estimated alternative program costs savings" figure presented in Table 24.3 represents the savings across all consumers, and is based on their most recent or probable alternative program attended and the number of months they remained employed.

Noble (1985) provided cost estimates for sheltered workshops ($3,744) and day activity programs ($5,916) in Virginia for 1985. Estimates of sheltered workshop and day activity center costs for the remainder of the analysis period were calculated by applying the effects of inflation to the figures provided by Noble (1985). The figures estimating yearly cost of sheltered workshops and day activity centers during the analysis period were divided by 12 to compute a monthly program cost, and then all dollar values were converted to 1986 (quarter 1) dollars.

Actual individual student costs for public education in Virginia were provided by the National Education Association (NEA) for the entire length of the analysis period. While no figures are available on the state or federal level for the costs of special education, special education costs have been estimated at two to three times the cost of public education (Kakalik, Ferry, Thomas, & Carney, 1981).

The figures provided by the NEA were multiplied by two (the more conservative estimate) to obtain individual student costs for special education in Virginia. These annual projections of the cost of special education for individual students were divided by 10 to compute a monthly cost estimate based on an academic year. These monthly estimates were subsequently multiplied by the number of months each school-age consumer (i.e., consumers less than 22 years of age) remained competitively employed.

6. *Taxes paid.* The figure for taxes paid is an estimate of taxes (income, payroll, sales, and excise) paid by consumers placed into supported competitive employment, and is calculated at 23% of each consumer's gross income, a figure reported by Pechman & Okner (1974) as an effective tax rate for low-wage earners. The resulting individual figures are an estimate of taxes paid by each consumer, based upon individual gross earnings. These taxes are paid by the consumer and are realized in savings to the taxpayer.

7. *Total public savings.* The entry for "total public savings" in Table 24.3 is computed by combining the three previously discussed taxpayer benefits: savings in SSI payments, costs for the projected traditional alternative programs, and consumer taxes paid.

8. *Employer Targeted Jobs Tax Credit (TJTC).* Employer tax credits represent an amount of money deducted from the employer's tax debt for hiring an individual with disabilities. TJTC essentially provides a rebate to the employer for the first 2 years of employment. As of December, 1986, the TJTC program allows a rebate in the first year only. The figures presented in Table 24.3 represent the amount of credit rebated to the employer for hiring the individuals in the sample.

9. *Total project expenditures.* Project expenditures comprise direct service, administrative, and clerical staff salaries and fringe benefits, as well as all appropriate nonpersonnel costs including travel, supplies, space leasing, telephone, duplication, and so forth. Program expenditures are first computed on a yearly basis and totaled across all project years to obtain a cumulative project cost. To provide an individualized program expenditure analysis, as well as the subsample comparisons contained in Table 24.3, each consumer's RSQ is multiplied by the funds expended within each of the years in which the consumer received services. Each individual program year, which is considered separately, is adjusted differently for inflation, discounting, and total staff intervention hours. For consumers who received services in more than 1 year, each year's expenditure was summed to determine the total cost reported in Table 24.3. Likewise, the RSQ for each consumer in Table 24.2 is a cumulative figure over the 94 months, rather than an individual year of participation.

10. *Consequence to taxpayer: benefit vs. cost.* The net consequence to the tax-paying public for each consumer is computed by subtracting the costs from his or her employment.

11. *Consumer earnings.* Earnings or gross income are listed for each participant. However, consumer *net* income may be substantially less. All the participants benefited financially when net income was computed ([gross wages + fringe benefits] ÷ [SSI reductions + taxes paid + foregone access to sheltered workshop earnings]). A detailed analysis of consumer net income concerning the entire population is discussed in Hill et al. (1987).

PROGRAM ANALYSIS RESULTS

Cumulative program data regarding the financial outcomes of 8 years of program operation are contained in Table 24.3. A cumulative total of 35,888 staff intervention hours were spent with all participants ($N = 214$), and 23,934 hours were devoted to consumers labeled moderately and severely retarded ($N = 117$). Consumers who have participated in this supported competitive employment program have worked a cumulative total of over 4,500 months, with mean months employed being just over 21. The mean number of intervention hours spent on this population is 168. For the moderate and severe subpopulation, the cumulative months employed totaled 2,873, and the mean months employed totaled 24.6. The mean number of intervention hours needed to attain this level of employment was 205. Program expenditures totaled over $1.7 million was spent for all program expenditures throughout the 8-year period.

In Table 24.3, it can be seen that $452,554 ($306,765 for the subsample of persons labeled moderately and severely mentally retarded) has been saved so far in SSI payments. The cost of the estimated alternative service programs for these workers, had they not been working, would have been $1.8 million (nearly $1.1 million for those with moderate and severe retardation). When the total state and federal taxes of $587,545 paid by workers are added to the estimated alternative program cost plus SSI savings, total public savings of over $2.8 million (over $1.7 million for those with moderate and severe retardation) result. When the program expenditures of $1.79 million are subtracted from the $2.8 million of total public savings, a final positive financial consequence accrues to the public of nearly $1.1 million ($525,071 for those with moderate and severe retardation).

The total worker cumulative earnings of the 214 participants totaled almost $2.6 million, and for the group with moderate and severe retardation $1.5 million. This amount, when divided by the total of program expenditures of $1,787,713 ($1,212,118 for those with moderate and severe retardation), yields a ratio of about 1:1.43. Stated another way, for every $1.00 of public tax dollars spent on this program, consumers earned $1.43 ($1.24 for persons labeled moderately and severely retarded).

Tables 24.2 and 24.4 include descriptive characteristics on 18 representative consumers (with coded fictitious names) from the study who were labeled moderately or severely mentally retarded. The format of these tables allows the reader to see a cross section of the study population.

An additional analysis was conducted to examine the effect of time on the benefits accruing to taxpayers from operation of the program. The results of the analysis are continued in Table 24.5, in which a taxpayer benefit-cost index is computed and presented for each year of the project. The taxpayer benefit-cost index represents the relationship between the factors that result in financial savings to the taxpayer (taxes paid by the consumers, reduced SSI payments, and reduced alternative program costs) and the factors that represent financial expenditures on the part of the taxpayer (TJTC monies and project operating expenditures). Stated another way, the taxpayer benefit-cost index represents the amount of money returned to the taxpayer for each dollar invested in the program.

From the data contained in Table 24.5, it is apparent that the program over time results in a substantial return on each dollar invested. However, the data also clearly indicate the costs involved in starting a program such as this one. In the first 2 years of the program (1979 and 1980), the taxpayer benefit-cost index was less than $1.00. That is, the program cost more than was returned to the taxpayer through savings in SSI, alternative programs, and taxes paid by the consumer. It was not until the third year of operation that the program actually began to result in financial savings. Since then, savings have continued to increase over time.

DISCUSSION OF IMPLICATIONS

The results presented in this chapter lend credence to the assertion that supported competitive employment programs yield powerful financial benefits for people with moderate and severe mental retardation, as well as for the taxpayer. It can be anticipated that the amount of increased expendable income available to these individuals is likely to increase their opportunities for community integration. Furthermore, the savings to society generated by supported employment are quite important in a time when every education and human services dollar must be scrutinized closely.

Despite the positive results, one should also be aware of cautions and limitations regarding interpreting a study such as this. First, the primary population consisted of people labeled as moderately mentally retarded. Therefore, the benefit and cost conclusions of this study apply only to this population. Second, this analysis only reflects one supported employment

Table 24.4. Financial ramifications of competitive employment: Cross section of moderately and severely retarded consumers

Code name	Reduced SSI	Est. alt. program cost	Est. total taxes paid	Public savings	TJTC	Project expenditures	Consequence to taxpayer	Cumulative wages
Ted	$23,266.62	$51,560.44	$15,517.78	$90,398.84	$ 0.00	$30,542.78	$59,856.06	$67,703.38
Bill	17,391.81	31,150.88	17,473.53	66,016.22	0.00	40,633.09	25,383.13	75,971.88
Len	11,095.71	24,508.29	11,615.21	47,219.20	0.00	28,404.58	18,814.62	50,500.90
Clyde	1,530.37	8,974.34	1,970.34	12,475.05	0.00	2,014.81	10,460.25	8,566.71
Donald	3,193.94	13,941.30	3,086.09	20,221.33	3,420.79	13,488.18	6,733.14	13,417.77
Jason	810.18	6,416.40	1,398.77	8,625.35	2,466.17	3,786.38	4,838.97	6,081.59
Charlotte	0.00	3,971.74	628.04	4,599.78	1,347.80	1,838.37	2,761.41	2,730.60
Ralph	0.00	3,994.04	918.30	4,912.34	1,978.72	4,341.26	571.08	3,992.61
Dottie	0.00	585.71	98.04	683.75	0.00	380.52	303.23	426.25
Arnold	0.00	2,062.48	199.80	2,262.28	0.00	2,313.06	–50.78	868.70
Horace	0.00	183.90	37.26	221.16	0.00	772.92	–551.77	161.99
Andy	0.00	4,570.46	652.00	5,222.46	121.45	5,916.54	–694.09	2,834.76
Cheryl	0.00	2,142.54	969.14	3,101.68	2,106.83	4,869.52	–1,767.84	4,213.65
Sara	0.00	795.92	217.26	1,013.18	0.00	3,197.51	–2,184.33	944.63
Harry	0.00	1,922.97	591.44	2,514.41	804.47	5,045.82	–2,531.41	2,571.50
Rudy	6,853.43	21,145.76	6,646.53	34,645.72	4,918.16	37,556.30	–2,910.58	28,897.95
Frank	168.00	7,802.60	636.97	8,608.45	1,384.71	12,033.27	–3,424.82	2,769.42
Wanda	1,242.51	7,760.81	2,702.10	11,705.41	3,472.74	18,557.39	–6,851.98	11,748.26

SSI = Supplemental Security Income.
TJTC = Targeted Jobs Tax Credit.

Table 24.5. The effects of time on the benefits accruing to taxpayers (individual program year data)

Fiscal year (July–June)	Clients served	Taxes paid	SSI reduction	Alternative program cost	TJTC cost	Project expenses	Taxpayer B/C index
1979	16[a]	$ 10,408.05	$ .00	$ 33,577.83	$ .00	$230,391.44	$ .19
1980	41	53,467.82	7,482.61	145,427.75	21,679.48	239,013.15	.79
1981	59	73,630.05	45,070.01	202,578.40	36,485.10	209,708.13	1.30
1982	72	76,313.55	55,886.98	244,729.97	35,867.29	194,170.31	1.64
1983	86	88,807.27	72,557.24	280,348.55	58,134.90	182,651.91	1.83
1984	99	104,215.21	100,769.52	339,340.36	43,906.89	174,572.25	2.49
1985	104	96,027.24	113,409.23	344,414.96	49,149.16	137,384.07	2.97
1986[b]	112	88,408.47	107,628.31	332,338.04	52,873.14	127,270.75	2.93

SSI = Supplemental Security Income.

TJTC = Targeted Jobs Tax Credit.

B/C = benefit-cost.

[a]This is the number of persons receiving any intervention time during the individual years; in years after 1979 there are duplicate counts (persons receiving intervention in more than 1 year).

[b]Data for 1986 are incomplete; 10 of 12 months are reported here.

model (supported competitive employment). Again, to generalize these findings across different vocational models would be spurious. Third, and perhaps most significantly, the program efforts were based at a university and involved potential subject selection biases, plus indirect support services. For example, consumers were accepted into the program both on the basis of their need and also on the specific research and demonstration goals of the program.

In conclusion, results of this study showed a substantial savings to society from utilization of this model, along with significant financial benefits to workers with moderate and severe disabilities. It is equally important to note the documented expansion of benefits over time. These figures do not reflect theoretical projections but, rather, direct placement data. This information will, it is hoped, provide encouragement and direction for managers and other policy makers who make fiscal decisions related to supported competitive employment.

REFERENCES

Conley, R.W. (1973). *The economics of mental retardation.* Baltimore: Johns Hopkins University Press.

Hill, M., Banks, P.D., Hendrick, R., Wehman, P., Hill, J., & Shafer, M. (1987). Benefit-cost analysis of supported competitive employment for persons with mental retardation. *Research in Developmental Disabilities,2*(1), 63–81.

Hill, M., & Wehman, P. (1983). Cost benefit analysis of placing moderately and severely handicapped individuals into competitive employment. *Journal of The Association of the Severely Handicapped, 8,* 30–32.

Kakalik, J.S., Ferry, S.W., Thomas, M.A., & Carney, M.F. (1981). *The cost of special education* (Prepared for the Department of Education). Santa Monica: RAMP.

Noble, J. (1985, July). *The benefits and costs of supported employment and impediments to its expansion.* Presentation to the Policy Seminar on Supported Employment, Virginia Institute for the Developmentally Disabled, Richmond.

Pechman, J., & Okner, B. (1974). *Who bears the tax burden?* Washington, DC: Brookings Institute.

Thornton, C. (1984). Benefit-cost analysis of social programs: Deinstitutionalization and education programs. In R.H. Bruininks & K.C. Lakin (Eds.), *Living and learning in the least restrictive environment* (pp. 225–244). Baltimore: Paul H. Brookes Publishing Co.

Wehman, P., & Kregel, J. (1985). A supported work approach to competitive employment of individuals with moderate and severe handicaps. In P. Wehman & J.W. Hill (Eds.), *Competitive employment for persons with mental retardation: From research to practice.* Richmond: Virginia Commonwealth University, Rehabilitation Research and Training Center.

Contradictions and Inconsistencies in the Service System for Adults with Disabilities

*Ronald W. Conley
and John H. Noble, Jr.*

Chapter 4 of this book outlined a number of changes that have occurred in the human services system, which directly affect the economic and human service environments within which adults with disabilities live and work. The major changes discussed included a service system that has: 1) become large, complex, and poorly understood; 2) shifted its reliance on funding to the federal level; and 3) experienced rapid and dramatic changes over the last 40 years in its goals for people with disabilities. This chapter describes contradictions and inconsistencies that exist in the system, in the hope that readers will better understand the inefficiency and ineffectiveness that often characterize the way the system provides services to clients. The chapter begins by specifying several goals that should energize the system and then moves into a discussion of inconsistencies and contradictions that hamper the achievement of these goals. Finally, prospects for change are presented.

GOALS

To evaluate the efficiency of the service system and to identify inconsistencies and contradictions in it, one must first agree on a set of fundamental goals.

This chapter was written by the authors in their private capacity. No support or official endorsement by the U.S. Department of Health and Human Services is intended or should be inferred.

This is the most critical step in developing a national policy on disability. Although the U.S. Congress has not yet legislated a complete set of goals, one can nonetheless identify goals that should be included in such a national goal structure. These goals may then be used to assess the existing system.

The Developmental Disabilities (DD) Act of 1987 (PL 100-146) articulated the overall intent of a national goal structure as follows:

> [to] assure that persons with developmental disabilities receive the care, treatment, and other services necessary to enable them to achieve their maximum potential through increased independence, productivity, and integration into the community, . . .

and

> [to] establish and operate a system which coordinates, monitors, plans, and evaluates services which ensure the protection of the legal and human rights of persons with developmental disabilities.

Two other guiding principles underlying the developmental disabilities legislation are "normalization," which requires that people with disabilities be assisted to live lives as near normal as possible, and "independence," which requires that persons with disabilities be assisted to depend as little as possible upon public programs.

Table 25.1 summarizes eight specific goals that are needed to achieve the overall goals set forth in the Developmental Disabilities Act. They are equally applicable to all programs serving Americans with disabilities.

INCONSISTENCIES AND CONTRADICTIONS

Inconsistencies and contradictions inherent in the service system often impede attainment of the specific goals summarized in Table 25.1. The following discussion groups these inconsistencies and contradictions according to those specific goals that, in the authors' view, are most adversely affected.

Goal 1: Employment

The service system adversely affects the likelihood of employment for persons with disabilities in a number of ways.

Fostering of Dependency The service system fosters the development of adverse work attitudes and dependency. These attitudes are largely a consequence of the eligibility conditions for income support and health care financing programs (e.g., the Social Security Disability Insurance/Childhood Disability Beneficiary [SSDI/CDB], Supplemental Security Income [SSI], Medicare, and Medicaid programs). In order to establish eligibility for SSI or SSDI/CDB, persons with disabilities must show that they cannot engage in substantial employment. At present, this means they must establish that they cannot earn over the substantial gainful activity (SGA) level of $300 per month, the equivalent of about one-half of the federal minimum wage. If they

Table 25.1. Specific objectives that need to be attained to achieve the overall goals set forth in the 1984 Developmental Disabilities Act

1. *Employment.* Whenever possible, employment should be in integrated work settings and involve jobs that are suitable to persons with disabilities, given their functional capacities and skills.

2. *Community-based services.* It is believed that most people with disabilities can be served in the community and do not need to be placed in institutions. The guiding principle is the "least restrictive" setting. It is preferable to keep persons with severe disabilities with their natural families as children, although this may not always be the preferred form of residential arrangement for adults.

3. *Family stability.* Children with disabilities should be assisted to remain with families. Families should be encouraged to be supportive of family members throughout their lifetimes.

4. *Avoidance of poverty.* Persons with disabilities should receive income that is above poverty level and should be allowed to accumulate and maintain assets.

5. *Savings.* Persons should be encouraged to save, not only in order to accumulate assets, but also to promote economic growth and to make a stronger economy.

6. *Equity.* The service system should not discriminate among different categories of persons with disabilities.

7. *Coordinations.* The programs in the service system should reinforce and complement each other.

8. *Efficiency and dynamism.* The system should achieve social goals at the least cost. Cost should be measured over the entire system, rather than limited to any one program. The system should also continually strive toward always seeking more cost-efficient and effective ways of achieving social goals. The assumption should not be made that an existing package of services, even if state of the art, is the most efficient or effective possible.

have not worked since the onset of the disability, and they have one of a long list of physical or mental conditions that are contained in Social Security regulations, or if they have conditions that are equivalently disabling, then they are regarded as presumptively unable to earn at the SGA level and automatically become entitled to benefits. At present, persons who have one of the listed conditions are usually regarded as presumptively eligible for benefits even if they have prior earnings. This has not always been the practice. In the cases of persons who do not qualify on the basis of one of the listed conditions, a decision on capacity to earn at the SGA level must be based on the medical evidence, with some account taken of education, age, previous occupation, and work experience. If they have previously worked at the SGA level, and there has been no worsening of the disability, then in principle they should not be considered eligible for income support.

The process of establishing eligibility for these programs may last 2 months to a year, and is often marked with appeals and litigation. Almost ineveitably, the net effect is destructive to the applicant's morale and reduces his or her willingness to return to work.

Although both the SSDI/CDB and the SSI programs have been modified in various ways to encourage recipients to return to work, the need to prove inability to work in order to receive benefits stands in striking contradiction to the purpose of these modifications.

Work Disincentives Because of the ways that the amounts of income support and health care benefits are calculated in the service system, there are often few net benefits and sometimes a major financial loss if beneficiaries return to work. Many beneficiaries who return to work will, of necessity, return to jobs that are low paying; that offer no fringe benefits, particularly health insurance; and that provide no other assurance of permanence. Small companies, in particular, often do not provide health insurance, or have provisions in their coverage to exclude persons with preexisting conditions. Although persons who return to work must consider loss of all benefits from all programs, this chapter, for convenience, briefly considers each major program in turn.

SSDI/CDB The Social Security Disability Insurance/Childhood Disability Benefits program gives beneficiaries who return to work a 9-month trial period. At the conclusion of the trial work period, the beneficiaries are reevaluated, and if found capable of earning more than the SGA level of $300 per month, then they will be terminated from the program. Note that it is work capacity, not actual earnings, that is relevant. Since the average benefit for individuals in the SSDI program is approaching $500 per month (and sometimes exceeds $1,500 per month), and since the beneficiary must consider the loss of the other benefits, such as attendant care (which may be provided by state or local governments) and eventually Medicare, the disincentive to work is potentially very large.

SSI Prior to 1981, the Supplemental Security Income program used the same test as that used in the SSDI/CDB program to determine whether recipients should be terminated from the program. However, the Social Security Act was amended in 1980 to allow, on a demonstration basis, beneficiaries to earn far more than the SGA level before being terminated from the program. Initiated in 1981, this demonstration program, generally known as the Section 1619(a) program, was greatly improved and made a permanent part of the SSI program beginning July 1, 1987. The basic features of the program (as of July 1, 1987) are as follows:

There is no longer a trial work period.

Recipients who return to work are allowed to make up to $65 with no effect on their SSI benefits.

Participants may disregard another $20 in income from any source.

Additional earnings cause benefits to be reduced by $1 for each $2 of earnings.

Income from sources other than earnings causes benefits to be reduced dollar for dollar.

In 1988, the monthly SSI benefit for an individual was $354 and for a couple, $532. Consequently, an individual recipient with no SSDI/CDB benefits, and no source of income other than earnings, could earn up to $793, and a couple could earn up to $1,149 per month before all income support benefits were terminated. Since Medicaid benefits will usually be continued, SSI recipients who return to work will almost always be better off financially than if they had remained dependent upon SSI alone. Of course, persons who return to work and have earnings sufficiently high to cause them to lose entitlement to benefits under both the Section 1619(a) and Section 1619(b) programs (see description following under "Medicaid") may end up worse off if they subsequently (after 12 months) lose their job.

The Section 1619(a) program clearly creates a major program contradiction, in that applicants for SSI must first prove that they are unable to earn over $300 per month, and then are allowed/encouraged to earn two to three times that amount before losing entitlement to all SSI payments.

Medicare SSDI/CDB beneficiaries become eligible for Medicare after receiving SSDI/CDB benefits for 2 years. If they then return to work, they continue to be eligible for Medicare benefits for 3 years after the termination of the trial work period. Although this provision is designed to reduce the fear of loss of benefits, some persons, particularly those who incur large ongoing medical expenses, may be deterred from work because of concern about the loss of medical benefits after Medicare coverage is terminated.

Medicaid Most SSI recipients are entitled to Medicaid. Prior to 1981, SSI recipients who lost their entitlement to SSI usually also lost their entitlement to Medicaid. However, a special demonstration program, Section 1619(b) of the Social Security Act, was initiated in 1981 to allow SSI recipients who returned to work to continue receiving Medicaid coverage after losing entitlement for SSI benefits under certain conditions. Those conditions were: that the disability continued, that the lack of Medicaid coverage would constitute an impediment to work, and that earnings were inadequate to allow these persons to obtain benefits equivalent to those that they had prior to returning to work. On July 1, 1987, a greatly improved version of the Section 1619(b) demonstration program was made a permanent part of the Social Security Act.

Under this program, SSI recipients who return to work and do not receive equivalent comprehensive coverage from their employer are eligible to continue receiving Medicaid protection so long as they meet the conditions just stipulated. In practice, SSI recipients who return to work are eligible to continue to receive Medicaid benefits so long as their earnings fall below a threshold level, which is calculated separately for each state. This threshold is calculated by adding together the federal break-even amount for an individual, plus twice the value of any SSI supplement paid by the state, plus the average expenditure by Medicaid on recipients with disabilities in the state, plus the value of any publicly funded personal or attendant care that would be lost if the individual was not eligible for SSI. The threshold exceeds $20,000 per year in a number of states—a sum that far exceeds the federal break-even amount for the SSI program. Even persons whose earnings exceed the threshold level may continue to be eligible for continued Medicaid benefits if their expected medical expenses are above the average Medicaid expenditure. In these cases, the threshold level is increased by the amount that their expected medical expenses exceed the Medicaid average.

Residents of Medicaid-Certified Facilities   The penalty for working is particularly strong for persons who live in Medicaid-certified facilities such as nursing homes or intermediate care facilities for persons with mental retardation (ICFs/MR). In these cases, residents are entitled to keep a personal needs allowance that must be at least $25 per month but that may, at the discretion of the state, be higher. Any amount over the personal needs allowance must be paid to the facility to reduce the costs charged to Medicaid. Although no one would dispute that persons who work should use part of their earnings to assist in paying for public services that they receive, it would seem reasonable to allow persons living in these facilities to retain some portion of what they earn, if for no other reason than to encourage work effort.

Income Security   The secure benefits provided by the service system create a major disincentive for program recipients to return to jobs, particularly if the jobs themselves are low paying and insecure (see Bluestone, Chapter 2, in this volume). Several features of public programs may reduce part of the fear of loss of income security, broadly defined to include income support payments, health benefits, attendant care, and so forth. Beneficiaries of the SSDI/CDB program who return to work have 36 months after the trial work period in which they are automatically reentitled to benefits if the work effort fails (i.e., if earnings fall below the SGA level). Recipients of SSI who return to work at earnings above the break-even amount are automatically reentitled to SSI payments if they lose their job, so long as they are eligible for the Section 1619(b) program. Even if they lose their entitlement for the Section 1619(b) program, they are automatically reentitled to benefits for a year after their eligibility ends. Reducing the difficulty of reestablishing eligibility was a major improvement that the Congress made in the Section 1619(a) and (b) programs in 1987.

These program features, designed to reduce the fear of loss of income security, may not seem adequate to beneficiaries who anticipate long-term, and perhaps lifetime medical problems, or whose work history has been characterized by intermittent work. The fear of losing a job need not always be due to the limitations imposed by the disability. Many jobs are terminated because of business failure, technical change, and cyclical variation. However, when job loss does occur, persons with severe disabilities may have difficulty locating other suitable employment. At the same time, they may find it almost impossible to requalify for public benefits which requires that they demonstrate that they cannot earn above the SGA level, because they have a substantial history of earning above this level.

Unfortunately, the major public income support and health care financing programs take an "all or nothing" approach and do not make adequate provision for the reality of intermittent employment that represents the long-term prospects for many beneficiaries who return to work.

Barriers to Job Enhancement   The service system sometimes creates barriers to accepting employment with earnings above a threshold level. This is a major problem in the Section 1619(b) program, which extends Medicaid protection to former SSI recipients whose earnings fall below a threshold level. If the recipients' earnings rise about this level, they are expected to purchase their own medical insurance protection. Unfortunately, this view is unrealistic. Many people with severe disabilities are either uninsurable or insurable only at extremely high rates. Even employer-based group policies may exclude them. Consequently, there are persons on the SSI program who in order to maintain medical coverage have had to reduce their hours of work, turn down promotions, and otherwise make decisions that are neither in the private or public interest.

Insufficient Long-Term Vocational Programs   The service system often fails to provide appropriate vocational services. This is partly because there are only limited federal and state funds to provide long-term vocational service such as supported work to persons with severe disabilities. Another problem is that the federal ICF/MR program will fund day care and nonvocational services, but not vocational services. Therefore, many states place most residents of ICFs/MR in adult day care rather than employment, and make no effort to provide services that could lead to employment.

There is a minor exception in the Medicaid program. The Omnibus Budget Reconciliation Act of 1985 (PL 99-272) permitted payment for pre-vocational and supported employment services to persons leaving institutional care under a waiver from the special Home and Community-Based Services Waiver program (HCBSW). Unfortunately, the extent to which vocational services can be provided is ambiguous, and most persons with disabilities are not entitled to receive services under this program.

Goal 2: Least Restrictive Care

The service system causes large numbers of persons with severe disabilities to be placed in residential care that is more restrictive than actually required. The

ICF/MR program has frequently been criticized for having a strong institutional bias. In large part, the institutional bias derives from the underlying condition of program eligibility. In order to qualify for ICF/MR care, persons with mental retardation have to require 24-hour-a-day care. Since there is no objective measure of what constitutes this level of need, states have wide latitude in making placement decisions. But even more important is the strong financial incentive that states have to place persons with mental retardation in ICFs/MR. The program has open-ended federal funding, and there is little federal support for care in non–ICFs/MR.

The Medicaid Home and Community-Based Services Waiver (HCBSW) program, passed in 1981, was an effort to reduce the institutional bias of the Medicaid program, not only for persons with disabilities but also for all nursing home residents. The HCBSW program permits states to claim federal financial participation (FFP) from the Medicaid program for services provided in the community when these services make it possible either to deinstitutionalize a person in a Medicaid-certified facility or to avoid institutionalizing a person in the first place. These services include some that are not normally eligible for Medicaid support. Other Medicaid requirements, such as the requirement that an optional service be statewide, can also be waived. The use of the HCBSW program has been restricted, partly because persons are eligible only if the states can show that they would otherwise be institutionalized. The states must show not only that the resident has a severe handicap but also that he or she actually could have been placed in an institution. The complicated administrative provisions for approval of waivers, as well as the threat that they would be cut off at some later time, have made states wary about their use. Nevertheless, waiver programs in 32 states were serving approximately 30,000 persons with developmental disabilities in September, 1985. Several contradictions are inherent in these Medicaid programs, including:

1. To the extent that residents who could be placed in less restrictive care are instead placed in ICFs/MR, then these placements are probably of questionable legality.
2. The requirement that residents need 24-hour-a-day oversight in order to be eligible for care in an ICF/MR contradicts the purpose of creating small (under 16 clients) community-based ICFs/MR. The fundamental purpose of community-based care is to permit persons with severe disabilities to be integrated into community activities to the fullest extent possible. One measure of success should be the extent to which residents do not need constant care.
3. If services under a home and community-based services waiver enable a person to avoid institutional care, this could be taken to demonstrate that the individual did not need institutional care to begin with, making one

wonder if there is a basic contradiction in the waivers program, since eligibility first requires that a person *need* institutional care, and then the provision of services indicated that they do not need this level of care.

4. As things now stand, institutionalized persons have a better shot at community-based services than those whose families struggled to keep them at home.

The moral of these contradictions is that we would be better off if we stopped trying to categorize people as needing or not needing institutional care. Instead, we should be developing a system that will provide an array of services from which the most appropriate services can be selected for clients.

Goal 3: *Family Stability*

The service system often decreases family stability. For example, needed services, such as respite care for families, funds for housing modifications, and home health services are often not available. Families must sometimes place a child with a serious illness or a disability in a hospital or institution in order to allow the child to become eligible for Medicaid. Otherwise, the family's income and assets would be deemed as available to the child, despite the fact that the income and assets may be grossly inadequate to pay for the care that is needed. However, in some cases, Medicaid waivers make it possible to provide Medicaid benefits while a child continues to live at home.

By now, it should be evident that repeated creation of special waiver programs to correct the unacceptable results of the application of Medicaid's standards and rules to individual cases is a sign of the fundamental flaws in the program's logic. In time, Congress will undoubtedly abandon patchwork solutions in favor of fundamental reform of the whole program.

Goal 4: *Poverty*

The service system often requires people who acquire a disability to deplete their lifetime savings in order to become eligible for services. For example, in order to receive SSI or Medicaid benefits in 1988, recipients must meet an asset test that permits them to own a home, personal possessions, a car (with some limitations), burial plot, and no more than $1,900 in other countable assets (if an individual) and $2,850 (if a couple). In addition, even persons who are eligible for SSDI benefits must wait for 6 months after the onset of their disability, during which time they must subsist on their own resources. For some people, this results in a major spend-down of savings and correspondingly increased feelings of insecurity about giving up SSDI benefits for a job. And finally, SSDI beneficiaries must wait 24 months before becoming eligible for Medicare. Some, but not all, may have medical coverage that they obtained prior to the onset of their disability. Others, however, will be forced to dig deeply into their savings because they lack medical insurance. Of course, once they spend most of their savings, they can become eligible for Medicaid. This may explain why many more people with disabilities are receiving Medicaid than are receiving SSI.

Goal 5: *Savings*

Few people on SSI have any incentive to save, since the most identifiable reward is a $1 reduction in their SSI benefits for each dollar of interest income from their savings. Even for those persons receiving only extended Medicaid benefits under the Section 1619(b) program (and thus not subject to the offset), there would be little incentive to save, since the reward would be termination of Medicaid eligibility once the assets exceeded the permissible amount. These stringent limitations on assets will become increasingly onerous and socially counterproductive over time. It is likely to become a particularly irksome problem to persons receiving payments under the Medicaid Section 1619(b) program. The number of persons eligible for the Section 1619(b) program should increase over time. Even though some of these persons will have earnings in excess of $20,000 per year, their inability to acquire private insurance will force continued reliance on Medicaid, a resource that would be lost if they saved any significant sum. Some of these recipients would certainly save part of their earnings if they were given the incentive to do so.

Goal 6: *Equity*

There are many situations in which persons with similar earning limitations due to disability are treated differently in terms of eligibility for federal funds. Several of these are discussed briefly next. First, persons with disabilities who become eligible for SSI and Medicaid may continue to receive payments from both programs if they subsequently go to work, while others with similar disabilities who either continue to work after the onset of disability or accept vocational rehabilitation services and return to work will never become entitled to receive SSI benefits. This is because anyone earning over $300 per month will automatically be disqualified from becoming eligible for SSI. However, once a person becomes eligible for SSI and Medicaid, earnings will generally have to significantly exceed this amount before all benefits end. Therefore, it is advantageous for high school students with severe disabilities to establish eligibility for SSI before accepting work. Unfortunately, this frequently interferes with plans to make a swift transition from high school to work.

    Second, persons receiving SSI are clearly treated differently from persons receiving SSDI, even though the disabilities that qualified the individuals for these programs are identical. SSDI/CDB recipients can earn up to $300 without any penalty and may receive any amount of income from other sources. SSI recipients, in contrast, have their benefits reduced dollar for dollar if they receive unearned income, and have their benefits reduced by $1 for every $2 of earnings after the initial income disregards. In all cases, however, where earnings of more than $300 per month are involved, people are better off under SSI than under SSDI/CDB, because substantially higher earnings are permitted before cut-off of all SSI and/or Medicaid benefits.

Some people receive benefits from both programs. The SSI program often supplements a SSDI/CDB payment in order to bring the combined benefit up to the level of the SSI benefit. Changes made in the Section 1619(a) and (b) programs in 1987 appear to have eliminated most of the problems initially caused by receiving payments from both programs. In fact, it can be advantageous to receive benefits from both programs. Concurrent payees who return to work at less than SGA level will continue to receive the full SSDI/CDB benefit. Thus, a person with a $300 monthly SSDI benefit and a $40 monthly SSI benefit who returns to work on a job paying $250 monthly will end up with $550 monthly ($300 from SSDI and $250 from earnings). In contrast, a recipient who receives SSI only and returns to work at a wage of $250 monthly would net only 507.50 monthly ($257.50 from SSI and $250 from earnings). What happens if the SSDI/CDB recipient receives a pay raise, say to $350, and loses entitlement to SSDI benefits after a trial work period? Since the recipient would have retained eligibility for the Section 1619(b) program (extended Medicaid benefits), then he or she would still be eligible for the Section 1619(b) program and would begin receiving an SSI payment so long as earnings were below the break-even point ($221.50 in 1988). There would be a "notch" effect at the point at which the earnings of concurrent beneficiaries exceeded the SGA level, which might create a disincentive to exceed this level, however. Moreover, loss of SSDI/CDB eligibility eventually leads to loss of Medicare and reliance on Medicaid. The latter shift increases state costs, since Medicare is 100% federally funded, while Medicaid is not. For that reason, the states may discourage dual SSDI/CDB and SSI beneficiaries from taking insecure jobs.

Third, persons with blindness are given preferential treatment. In particular, their SGA level is over twice as high as for other persons with disabilities and is indexed to inflation. In addition, high earnings will not cause them to be terminated from the SSI or Medicaid programs. Payments from these programs will resume if their earnings subsequently decline.

Fourth, some people argue that the SSDI program is, in effect, an early retirement program for workers with disabilities. This, however, is not the congressional intent for the program, and it is doubtful if people with disabilities who are able to work should be allowed to retire early.

Fifth, if entitlement to the Section 1619(a) and 1619(b) programs is lost, perhaps due to an inheritance that causes the recipient to be disqualified because of excess assets, and if the loss of entitlement extends over a 12-month period, then the person will be able to requalify only if he or she can establish inability to earn over $300 monthly. If there was a significant work history under the Section 1619(a) and/or 1619(b) programs with earnings over the SGA level, establishing inability to earn may be difficult to do, unless the disability worsens.

Sixth, SSDI beneficiaries who return to work may find that their Social Security benefits are reduced if they subsequently apply for benefits. This is because: 1) they must pay Social Security taxes on their earnings (which will generally be lower than before the onset of the disability), and 2) benefits are based on their average covered earnings.

And seventh, impairment-related work expenses are deducted from earnings before the $1 for $2 reduction in benefits begins in SSI, and are subtracted from earnings in determining whether a person can work at a SGA level for purposes of deciding both initial and continuing eligibility for SSDI/CDB benefits. However, impairment-related earnings are not deducted from earnings in establishing whether a person can work at an SGA level when determining eligibility for SSI, creating an inconsistency in the way eligibility is determined for SSI as compared to SSDI/CDB.

Goal 7: *Efficiency and Dynamism*

The operations of the service system are dominated by the rules and regulations governing public programs. The lack of efficiency and dynamism in public programs has been frequently noted. There are at least two important reasons for this tendency toward stagnation in the service system for persons with disabilities. Perhaps the greatest impediment to efficiency and dynamism in the service system is the paucity of sufficient and appropriate data to show what has been accomplished, which programs have been most successful, and which programs are most effective for which types of clients. Without such data, efficient management is virtually impossible.

A second reason results from permitting the organizations that maintain programs, and that have a vested interest in their continuation, to evaluate themselves to determine if they should continue in operation. For example, the responsibility for determining whether ICFs/MR meet federal standards is, for the most part, left up to state agencies. Federal "look-behind" audits of the ICF/MR program regularly show gross violations of federal standards. Similarly, state agencies are responsible for assuring that community-based residences that are subject to the Keys Amendment standards (Section 1616[e] of the Social Security Act) actually comply with them. It should be no surprise that state agencies infrequently report out-of-compliance facilities to the federal government. Not one violation of Keys Amendment standards has been reported!

Goal 8: *Coordination*

Lack of coordination among government programs for persons with disabilities has long been lamented. Among the reasons for this lack of coordination:

The service system lacks clear-cut and realistic goals.

The service system is far from achieving a unified individualized service plan for clients.

The service system generally lacks unified intake procedures where potential clients are assessed and placed in the programs that would provide them with the greatest benefits.

Few people understand the availability and the conditions of eligibility of all the programs in the service system.

Even when enacting programs, Congress often fails to consider the supportive interactions among programs that are needed if the intent of Congress is to be met.

WORKERS' COMPENSATION: A PARALLEL SYSTEM

The foregoing discussion has been primarily focused on a service system dominated by federal programs. Workers' compensation is a parallel system that provides the same support and services to persons whose disabilities result from work-related injuries or illnesses. (See Chapter 20, by Stark, Breder, & Goldsbury, in this volume). Unfortunately, the workers' compensation system also imposes obstacles that prevent the attainment of the goals of the service system.

The number of people served by the workers' compensation system is large. Each year, almost 6 million people receive a workers' compensation award because of an industrial accident, disease, or cumulative trauma such as the cumulative effect of noise on hearing or of lifting objects on the back (Worrall & Butler, 1986). In most cases, the conditions are not serious, and workers' compensation pays for medical treatment only. However, over 1 million workers receive indemnity benefits for wage loss or as compensation for the injury or disease. Of these persons receiving indemnity benefits, about 325,000, a little less than one-third, suffer permanent disability in the sense that there is a permanent functional loss. The remaining persons receiving indemnity benefits are temporarily disabled.

These workers' compensation claims understate the full extent of temporarily or permanently disabling conditions caused by workplace exposure, since an unknown but potentially large number of persons develop occupational disease or injuries resulting from cumulative trauma for which workers' compensation benefits may not be claimed. Barth and Hunt (1980) have summarized evidence indicating widespread existence of occupational disease (see also Conley & Noble, 1979).

Workers' compensation is a state-mandated program that requires employers to provide benefits to workers who suffer a job-related injury or illness. In general, employers must pay all medical expenses; pay indemnity benefits, which are sometimes based on an assumed wage loss and sometimes based on the degree of disability; and provide rehabilitation services if indicated and desired by workers. Employers may cover their workers' compensation obligations in several ways. In most states, they may either self-insure or purchase coverage from either a state fund or a private carrier, and in a few states, the options are limited to self-insurance or coverage by the state fund. Firms that are self-insured are usually large firms that can meet state financial requirements and can predict with reasonable accuracy the number and costs of workers' compensation claims that they will incur.

Workers' compensation originated as a no-fault system in which workers with a job-related injury or illness would receive limited but assured benefits. The trade-off for accepting limited benefits was that workers would be entitled to these benefits regardless of how the injury was caused. If workers' compensation had worked as envisioned, one would expect little litigation, prompt and adequate benefits, and no disincentive to return to work. Although the workers' compensation program has probably met these expectations reasonably well in the case of temporary claims, it has fallen far short of the goals in the case of permanent disability cases, largely because of the problem of determining the extent of disability. About one-third of the permanent disability cases in workers' compensation are settled by use of a schedule that establishes a predetermined indemnity benefit for a specific type of injury. In these cases, the workers' compensation system often does work as intended. However, in about two-thirds of the permanent disability cases, the injury cannot be related to a schedule. It is these "nonscheduled" cases that create many of the problems in workers' compensation.

In nonscheduled cases, the claimant has an incentive to maximize the extent of the disability in order to maximize the size of his or her indemnity award, and the employer/carrier obviously has the opposite incentive. Given this fundamental conflict, it should come as no surprise that the workers' compensation system is characterized by extensive litigation over permanent disability cases. It has been estimated that two-thirds of the permanent disability cases involve a controversy between the employee and the carrier/employer, and that about three-fifths of these cases are litigated over the amount of the award (Conley & Noble, 1979). Resolution of these litigated cases may be prolonged, during which time the employee has an incentive to display the maximum level of disability and inability to work and often has little interest in work or rehabilitation services. Although most states require that workers' compensation provide rehabilitation services and that workers' compensation claimants accept these services, the enforcement of this requirement is weak. Even if workers are compelled to accept vocational rehabilitation services, they can accept them in such a way as to render them largely ineffectual (Worral & Butler, 1986).

About one-half of permanent disability cases in workers' compensation are settled by a formal compromise agreement (Conley & Noble, 1979). In principle, these formal compromise agreements should occur only if a fundamental disagreement exists between an employer/carrier and a claimant about eligibility for benefits or their amount. In practice, there is another incentive for carrier/employers to seek such settlements. In most cases, these agreements have the effect of ending any future liability on the part of the carrier or the employer for the workers' compensation claim. Limiting liability in this way makes such settlements particularly attractive to employers/carriers and may lead carriers to prolong litigation in order to induce claimants to accept this type of settlement. Obviously, such an agreement would also eliminate any subsequent financial incentive on the part of the employer to provide rehabilitation services to the claimant.

Such prolonged litigation is obviously detrimental to the claimant's motivation to return to work. Given these workers' compensation procedures, it is not surprising that a large percentage of claimants with permanent partial disability fail to return to work. In one study, it was estimated that one-fifth of men with permanent partial disability ratings of 10% or higher were not working 4–7 years after their injuries because of the effects of their injury and/or the problems generated by the system for obtaining compensation (Conley & Noble, 1979).

This approach to disability has been appropriately termed the "disabling system." In effect, most employers "wrote off" disabled employees, paying compensation claims and other benefits as a cost of doing business. For example, Wickersham (1983) stated that before the 3M company adopted a disability management system, the company paid "benefits to anyone who presented proof of a disabling condition" (p. 28).

It should be pointed out that there are many progressive employers and workers' compensation carriers who are developing excellent return-to-work programs for workers with industrial injuries or occupational diseases. Many firms are also adopting procedures to reduce the occurrence of work-related injuries and diseases. Nonetheless, numerous improvements are needed in the system before it can be fully supportive of the goals of the service system for persons with disabilities.

PROSPECTS FOR CHANGE

Although this chapter has been strongly critical of the existing service system, a solution exists for every problem identified here. In fact, some of these solutions are in the process of being adopted. In the last 2 years, for example, Congress has created and greatly improved the Section 1619(a) and (b) programs in the SSI and Medicaid programs in order to significantly reduce work disincentives. In addition, there are limited circumstances under which vocational services can be funded by Medicaid. As another example, educational services are in the process of being extended to handicapped children almost from the day of birth (PL 99-457). Finally, funds for supported work are now a permanent part of the federal rehabilitation legislation.

These and other legislative changes are part of a process in which existing programs are being gradually modified to conform to and support current treatment philosophies. These programmatic changes have enormous philosophical implications for the service system. In particular, the focus on providing income support and financing for health care only to persons unable to work is eroding. Because of the enormous size of these programs, change in their philosophical focus is critical to the modernization of the rest of the service system. Although prediction is always risky, the authors believe that in the not-too-distant future, there will be the equivalent of the 1619(a) and (b) programs enacted for SSDI/CDB program beneficiaries, not only because of the desire of Congress to encourage work among persons with disabilities but also because of the glaring inconsistency in the way persons on SSDI/CDB who return to work are treated as compared to those on SSI. In addition, the Medicaid ICF/MR program and the component of the Home and Community-Based Services Waiver program that pays for the services to persons with mental retardation/developmental disabilities will probably be combined and modified so that the funds can be expended much more flexibly. There is widespread agreement on the need for such a change. The major impediment is uncertainty about the budget implications of such a change.

In the future, the authors anticipate a rethinking of the eligibility conditions for all disability-related income support and health care financing programs. There is a need to coordinate conditions of initial program eligibility so that they are consistent with the conditions for remaining eligible. Unified, individualized plans that include federally operated programs will emerge as an outgrowth of the deep concern of Congress over program coordination. The authors anticipate that fewer restrictions will be placed on the amount of assets that may be owned by persons applying for SSI and Medicaid, and less severe penalties will be assessed for income produced by savings. With increasing numbers of persons becoming eligible for the SSDI/CDB program, it may even be possible to eliminate these restrictions on assets and to merge the SSDI/CDB and the SSI programs and the Medicare and Medicaid programs. The arguments in favor of such mergers are greatly strengthened when it is noted that almost two in every five persons receiving SSI payments for reason of a disability are also receiving SSDI/CDB benefits and presumably are eligible for both Medicare and Medicaid coverage in most instances.

Undoubtedly, many other changes can be suggested as serious efforts are made to change the service system so that it supports a well-articulated set of social goals. As with the development of any successful product, the system to provide services to persons with severe disabilities should be subject to continuous evaluation and modification for years to come. It must be realized that all changes will probably fall short of the ideal. We must also recognize that programmatic change itself often creates new problems that must be remedied.

If there is a moral from this, it is that we need to institute a much more effective information system and much more intensive and effective evaluation procedures than have existed to date. Failure to conduct rigorous evaluations of the effectiveness of the service system is truly penny wise and pound foolish.

REFERENCES

Barth, P., & Hunt, H. (1980). *Workers' compensation and work-related illnesses and diseases.* Cambridge, MA: MIT Press.

Conley, R., & Noble, J. (1979). *Workers' compensation reform: Challenge for the 80's.* In R. Conley (Ed.), *Research reports of the interdepartmental workers' compensation task force* (Vol. 1, p. 164). Washington, DC: U.S. Government Printing Office.

Wickersham, J. (1983, December). Disability management key to cost savings at 3M. *Business and Health, 1*(2), 26–30.

Worrall, J., & Butler, R. (1986). Some lessons of workers' compensation. In M. Berkowitz & A.M. Hill (Eds.), *Disability and the labor market. An overview* (pp. 95–123). Ithaca: New York State School of Industrial and Labor Relations, Cornell University, ILR Press.

VI

OVERVIEW
Quality of Life Issues

Quality of life (QOL) has recently become an important issue in human services, and may well replace deinstitutionalization, normalization, and community adjustment as *the* issue of the 1990s. There are a number of reasons for this interest, including concern about the quality of life of community-placed persons with disabilities, proof that social environments have considerable impact on an individual's way of life, the fact that complex human services programs require complex outcome measures, the reemergence of the holistic health perspective, and a growing conviction that all people deserve to find satisfaction and quality of life in a rapidly changing world.

The QOL issue has also moved into the workplace, with accompanying concerns about the equity, safety, enrichment, and growth-producing aspects of people's jobs. The concerns are the same for all employees, with or without disabilities. As the future of economics, industry, and disability is contemplated, it is essential that quality of life issues be examined and debated by policy makers, administrators, professionals, advocates, parents, and people with disabilities. This final section looks at this most important issue of the 1990s from a variety of perspectives, including integration in the workplace, quality of life and quality of work life (QOWL), and quality of residential/community life.

In Chapter 26, D.M. Mank and J. Buckley review strategies for integrated employment. Based on their extensive work in Oregon and elsewhere, the authors summarize the components of integration, including how to measure integration and strategies for promoting integration. The next chapter, by D.A. Goode, delves into quality of life and quality of work life. Goode summarizes the history of QOWL and then conceptualizes and operationalizes both QOL and QOWL. He also suggests that the rehabilitation field must begin to adopt the newer forms of human management aimed at increasing the QOWL of persons with disabilities and must also address the structural inequalities that mitigate against QOWL.

The final chapter in this section, by S.A. Borthwick-Duffy, focuses on the important QOL dimension of the person's living environment. The author reviews the origins of quality of life models and outlines the dimensions of the residential environment, including affective, cognitive, physical, and normalization components. Although related to a person's residential environment, these components may well also reflect one's work environment, thus underscoring the importance of including a section on quality of life in a book on economics, industry, and disability.

26

Strategies for Integrated Employment

David M. Mank and Jay Buckley

Least restrictive environment . . . mainstreaming . . . normalization . . . criterion of ultimate functioning . . . social role valorization. Over the past 15 years, these concepts have been used to enhance the degree to which individuals with disabilities live, learn, and work in regular and ordinary ways with persons who do not have disabilities. These terms have guided ideology, advocacy, law, policy, and service development aimed at integrating persons with disabilities into the mainstream of society.

The supported employment initiative represents a recent effort toward integration for people with severe disabilities; the focus is on employment in regular work settings. Supported employment is defined by law (Developmental Disabilities Act and Bill of Rights of 1984 [PL 98-527]; Rehabilitation Act Amendments [1987, PL 99-506]) by three specific outcomes: 1) paid work with 2) ongoing support in 3) integrated community job settings. Many advocates, consumers, policy makers, and practitioners share the belief that integration is the initiative's most important quality feature.

Recent initiatives and congressional action have encouraged advocates, providers, and policy makers to develop a variety of approaches to enable Americans with disabilities to work in integrated settings. The U.S. Office of Special Education and Rehabilitative Services (OSERS) announced the national supported employment initiative in 1984 (Will, 1984). At present, 27 states have demonstration grants to change the nature of employment services for individuals who traditionally would have been served in segregated facilities. The Rehabilitation Act of 1986 (PL 99-506) now makes funding for supported employment available in all 50 states.

The emphasis on integration in employment presents three issues that must be addressed if the initiative is to succeed: 1) definitions of *integration* that are operational and functional, 2) valid and reliable measurement techniques that capture information across multiple dimensions, 3) strategies for promoting integration in employment settings. This chapter discusses these three critical integration issues.

DEFINING INTEGRATION

Integration can be described in its simplest and most elegant form as a degree of community presence and participation for persons with disabilities that is no different than that enjoyed by persons without a disability label (Galloway & O'Brien, 1981; Nisbet & Callahan, 1987). In relation to employment, integration can be further described as adherence to regular and ordinary patterns of minute-to-minute and day-to-day working life. Description of social constructs, such as those of integration, may be intuitively accurate; yet, they are often insufficient to serve as functional definitions (Chadsey-Rusch, 1986; Kelly, 1982). Greater detail and specificity are needed to: 1) understand all dimensions of integration, 2) decide when a specific level of work-life integration is acceptable, and 3) guide the process of measuring integration.

Components of Integration

Developing an operational definition of integration is essential to identifying its components. The following constitute four levels of integration:

1. *Physical integration.* In reference to employment, integration requires proximity to co-workers without disabilities. It may involve required interactions (i.e., contact that is necessary for performance of the task) and incidental interactions (i.e., contact that is unpredictable).
2. *Social integration.* Social integration involves elective personal interactions that occur during work or free time.
3. *Relationships.* Relationships depend on social interactions that are ongoing and usually involve reciprocal participation in activities.
4. *Social networks.* Social networks involve repeated contact with a number of people who identify the relationships that exist within the group as "socially important." Such interactions are characterized by reciprocity among members and occur in a variety of settings (Horner, Newton, LeBaron, Stoner, & Ferguson, 1987).

Integration is both an outcome and a process. Advocates view supported employment as a way to enable individuals with severe disabilities to develop relationships and participate in social networks, as well as to gain personal advice, emotional support, material aid and service, companionship, and access to new people (Gottlieb, 1981; Horner et al., 1987). Yet the process of forming relationships and social networks begins with physical and social integration. A comprehensive definition should deal with all of these components.

Response Analysis and Ecological Factors

Viewing integration as a process requires attention to two factors. First, it must be kept in mind that most individuals with disabilities have had limited access to settings that provide opportunities for physical integration, social integration, relationships, and social networks. For individuals to become integrated, information must be available on the behavior needed for successful and regular participation.

Second, integration does not occur in a vacuum, nor is there a generic setting where the same behaviors are required in all instances. Therefore, identifying the behavior required for successful integration depends on ecological factors of specific cultures and worksites and the natural range of response variation that occurs among the individuals who participate in these environments. A functional definition of integration should be robust enough to help identify the manner in which physical integration, social integration, relationships, and social networks occur in specific jobs.

Identification and analysis of behaviors combine to define the manner in which each level of integration takes place within specific workplaces. This enables support staff to identify behaviors for instruction, assess threshold levels of integration in order to set criteria for success, and then use this information to "match" individuals to environments that will enhance quality of life. The difficulty of defining integration makes it clear that the definition depends in part on measurement strategies.

MEASURING INTEGRATION

As stated previously, components of integration include physical integration, social integration, relationships, and social networks. Further, these components can only be defined in the context of the specific work environments in which they occur. Clearly, the measurement of integration must involve attention to a number of complex variables related to both outcomes and specific environments.

A recent national seminar was convened to discuss critical elements in supported employment evaluation (Berkeley Planning Associates, 1986), but no consensus on a method for measuring integration was achieved. Seminar participants noted that adequate measurement systems for integration have not been developed. The report from this seminar states:

> The integration of individuals with severe disabilities into the work place is a key element in the supported employment effort. . . . measuring integration is not yet well-developed or well defined in the field. Thus, few concrete examples exist of measures of the performance of supported employment programs in furthering community integration objectives. (Berkeley Planning Associates, 1986, pp. 18–20)

The absence of agreed-upon methods for measuring integration gives cause for a number of concerns. First, the effect of the supported employment initiative on changing levels of integration for individuals with severe disabilities is difficult to specify. Second, the progress of an individual in increasing his or her integration cannot be tracked. Third, the degree to which a specific job enhances the quality of life of the individual involved cannot be articulated. Finally, the integration achieved in various types of jobs or in differing approaches to supported employment is subject more to conjecture than to empirical evidence.

Existing Measures

Measurement systems that have been utilized to assess integration can be grouped into three categories: capacity, progress, and life-style measures (Bellamy, Newton, Lebaron, & Horner, 1986). Such broad classifications may miss fine distinctions among instruments and techniques; however, comparison at this level is useful in reviewing important differences in the application of integration measures.

Capacity Measures A number of measurement systems address the extent to which specific environments allow integration (Budde, 1976; King, Raynes, & Tizard, 1971; Moots & Otto, 1972; Schalock & Jensen, 1986). Federal definitions and guidelines for supported employment regarding group size (eight or less in a setting) fall into this category. Such measures can provide threshold requirements of minimum acceptability.

Capacity measures and standards tend, however, to represent minimum requirements rather than actual accomplishments. That is, they can describe necessary conditions for integration without addressing whether integration actually occurs. Moreover, capacity measures tend to reflect a programmatic or organizational orientation without accounting for individual and natural variations, needs, or opportunities.

Progress Measures This category of measures assesses the quality of service in terms of its success in increasing an individual's skills, adaptive behavior, or community adjustment (Nihara, Forster, Shelhaas, & Leland, 1974). In this context, progress refers to individual behavior changes achieved in the pursuit of integration (Bellamy et al., 1986).

These measures provide a starting point in assessing the process of integration, and as such, extend the information provided by capacity measures. However, problems exist in using progress measures alone to assess the outcome of integration. An individual may make progress and develop new skills as measured on these scales, yet fail to reach acceptable levels of integration in his or her work setting. Many skills targeted in some skill sequences may have little to do with the behaviors needed for building relationships and social networks in specific work environments.

Life-style Measures   A third category of measurement system seeks to examine the lives of the individuals in the environments in which they function, rather than simply assessing the nature of the environment, the administrative structure of the program, or the number of new skills learned over time (Bellamy et al., 1986; Edgerton, 1975; Emerson, 1985; Horner et al., 1987; O'Brien, 1987). These measures provide information about the accomplishment of valued changes in the pattern of day-to-day living and working in the context of relationships and social networks. Life-style measures can provide much-needed information about personal satisfaction and quality of life. It is important to note that life-style measures depend on assurance that capacity standards are in place and that instruction and support occur on job sites.

Measurement Techniques and Dimensions of Integration

Overall, life-style measures may offer the greatest promise for tracking integration; however, such measurement relies on a number of techniques for gathering the information required to develop a comprehensive analysis of an individual's integration within a specific work environment. It thus becomes critical to identify these techniques and the dimensions of integration to which they might be applied.

Measurement Techniques   Table 26.1 presents definitions of nine techniques that might be applied to gather information about integration of individuals within work environments. These techniques are borrowed from a number of disciplines. No single technique listed in Table 26.1 would be adequate to provide all of the information needed to assess integration, yet each has value in answering specific questions regarding the complex dimensions involved in integration.

Dimensions of Integration   Use of the techniques listed in Table 26.1 depends on the need for specific information. While most or all of these techniques are needed for a comprehensive analysis of integration, there are specific dimensions of integration information to which individual techniques can be applied. Figure 26.1 presents a list of elements of integration-related information and the measurement techniques that may be appropriate for each. The dimensions presented in Figure 26.1 include information on the environment, co-worker roles, specific integration-related skills, and participation in integration opportunities by the individual with disabilities. It is doubtful that any single provider, program monitor, advocate, or government official will need, or have the opportunity, to apply all of these measure. But, as already mentioned, the application of specific techniques will help assess specific dimensions of integration.

The measurement and analysis of data collected on each of these dimensions can help develop a more functional definition of integration. The data help assure that standards for progress and outcomes rely on more than de-

Table 26.1. Measurement techniques for integration

Technique	Definition
1. Frequency counts	The observation and documentation of the occurrence of events recorded in terms of number of discrete behaviors, percentage of total behaviors, or rate within specific time frames (Agran, 1986).
2. Duration recording	The observation and documentation of the onset and completion of discrete behavior or interaction (Alberto & Troutman, 1982).
3. Checklist recording	The observation and documentation of the occurrence of discrete or continuous behavior(s) during a specified time period, or of discrete behaviors at a specified time (Agran, 1986).
4. Topographical analysis	The identification and analysis of the topography of each response involved in specific social interactions.
5. Social validity	The process of determining the acceptability and/or importance of specific behaviors as determined by experts or other knowledgeable persons (Kazdin, 1982; Wolf, 1978).
6. Likert scales	A set of attitude items considered to be of equal scale to which respondents record degrees of agreement or disagreement (Kerlinger, 1973).
7. Structured interviews	The process of eliciting choices between alternative answers to performed questions on specific topics or situations (Lofland & Lofland, 1984) within a specific interview protocol (Ferguson, Ferguson, & Jones, 1987).
8. Open-ended interviews	The use of questions that allow or require the respondent to answer with more than one- or two-word answers, using terms not supplied in the body of the questions (P.M. Ferguson, personal communication, October 10, 1987).
9. Participant observations	A process in which an investigator establishes and sustains a relatively long-term relationship involving "looking and listening" in the natural setting for the purpose of understanding human associations (Lofland & Lofland, 1984).

Desired integration information	Frequency count	Duration recording	Checklists	Likert Scale	Social validity	Topographical analysis	Structured interview	Open-ended interview	Participant observation
1. Identification of integration activities that occur in the workplace	*		*			*	*	*	
2. Analysis of activities									
a. Topography of interactions	*	*	*			*			*
b. Identification of responses (skills) utilized by participants			*			*			
3. Weight of specific activities (social value to participants)	*			*	*		*	*	*
4. Percentage of total potential interactions in which co-workers participate	*		*			*			*
5. Number of integration activities in which workers with disabilities participate							*		
a. With co-worker at worksite									
b. With general public during work									
c. With general public before and after work and during breaks									
d. With co-workers before and after work and during breaks									

Figure 26.1. Potential measurement techniques for dimensions of integration.

(continued)

Figure 26.1 (continued)

Desired integration information	Frequency count	Duration recording	Checklists	Likert Scale	Social validity	Topographical analysis	Structured interview	Open-ended interview	Participant observation

6. Duration of integration activities in which workers with disabilities participate
  a. With co-worker at worksite
  b. With general public during work
  c. With general public before and after work and during breaks
  d. With co-workers before and after work and during breaks
		*	*			*	*	*	*

7. Topography of integration activities in which workers with disabilities participate
  a. With co-worker at worksite
  b. With general public during work
  c. With general public before and after work and during breaks
  d. With co-workers before and after work and during breaks
			*			*	*	*	*

8. Demonstrated reciprocity in interactions
   a. With co-worker at worksite
   b. With general public during work
   c. With general public before and after work and during breaks
   d. With co-workers before and after work and during breaks

9. Number of weighted activities in which individual participates

10. Percentage of potential interactions in which individual participates

11. Identification of program planning goals and objectives

12. Evaluation of effect of training aimed at measuring/enhancing integration activities
   a. According to training specifications
   b. According to degree to which training affects items 5–10

327

scriptions or opinions. However, an important piece in the integration puzzle involves specifying strategies for assisting individuals with severe disabilities to develop relationships and social networks.

STRATEGIES FOR PROMOTING INTEGRATION

Service providers have the primary responsibility for promoting integration in the employment of persons with disabilities. Nisbet and Callahan (1987) provide a set of critical elements for achieving integration, including elements related to the development of individualized job placements, coordination of services, and technology. The nature and scope of these elements make it clear that it is insufficient to place an individual in a job and then hope that integration will result. Rather, it is important that service providers attend to a broad band of strategies around the working life of persons with disabilities. Emerging strategies for improving integration can be organized into three general categories: ecological analysis, environmental modification, and systematic instruction and support. Figure 26.2 presents a way in which these strategies can be applied to physical integration, social integration, relationships, and social networks.

Ecological Analysis

Attention to ecological factors associated with specific worksites is critical for promoting integration. There are at least five strategies that service providers can use to assure that the environments in which they place workers with disabilities provide the opportunity for full integration.

1. *Job development.* Service providers must plan for integration when they select businesses for marketing efforts. Job sites and types of work that allow little opportunity for integration must be avoided. Providers must be sure that the jobs developed for persons with disabilities enhance the quality of life. Job developers must be certain that the work environments have the potential for integration. Specifically, this involves ensuring that individuals work in proximity to co-workers and/or the public, that social interactions are observed among individuals in the worksite before the person to be supported begins employment, and that the individual with disabilities will have opportunities for variety and choice in social interactions.

2. *Job analysis.* A complete job analysis provides an opportunity to document details of work tasks, hour-to-hour activities, day-to-day variations, and the social interactions that take place in employment settings. A job analysis should result in a list of the individuals with whom interactions can occur and the nature and the frequency of possible interactions. A job analysis provides the opportunity to assess the potential for integration and to prepare for integration training and support. A comprehensive job

Figure 26.2. Integration components and support strategies.

Integration components	Ecological analysis					Environmental modification			Systematic instruction and support		
	Job development	Job analysis	Functional analysis	Task analysis	Trainer specialization	Negotiation with employer	Environmental adaptation	Co-worker orientation	Job match	Planning with worker/advocate	Support and instruction
Physical integration											
Contact related to proximity (i.e., required and/or incidental interactions related to work functions)	*	*	*	*		*	*	*	*	*	*
Social integration											
Elective personal or social intratask or free-time contact	*	*	*	*	*	*	*	*	*	*	*
Relationships											
Ongoing reciprocal social integration related to specific activities		*	*	*	*			*		*	*
Social networks											
Repeated social contact with a stable group in a variety of settings			*	*				*		*	*

329

analysis should enable analysts to develop a sense of the quality of the environment related to integration and make decisions about the appropriateness of the job for an individual with disabilities.

3. *Functional analysis.* One aspect of ecological analysis is the identification of the manner in which social integration, relationships, and social networks take place within a specific worksite. Different parts of the country, different industries, and specific businesses show variation in culture and therefore in the behaviors that constitute social competence and acceptance. By analyzing environments, service providers can identify specific skills needed for successful integration.

4. *Task analysis.* Once the skills involved in integration within the specific work environment are identified, preparation for instruction and support can begin. The instruction provided must be based on the stimuli, responses, and criteria that determine social integration, relationships, and social networks. The task analyses that are developed to teach individuals to converse with others, to use the lunch room, and so forth, should lead to the development of competence within the specific culture.

5. *Trainer socialization.* One important key in the integration of an individual with disabilities is the skill of the trainer in adapting to the culture of the workplace. The trainer must learn the rules and the roles that define relationships and social networks within the workplace. More important, the trainer must give evidence of respecting the culture and of fitting into the patterns of social behavior. In so doing, the trainer will be better able to impart information about the company culture to the individuals with disabilities.

Environmental Modification

A second group of strategies for promoting integration consists of ways in which providers can transform an environment that has limited promise for integration opportunities into one in which there is every reason to expect successful development of relationships and social networks. Trainer socialization (discussed earlier) is one strategy that falls into this category, since the trainer uses his or her skills to influence the environment to enhance the possibilities for integration. There are additional discrete steps providers can take to alter conditions in job sites, including the following:

1. *Negotiating with employer.* Providers may discover during job development or analysis that there are barriers related to integration in a job that may, in other respects, seem appropriate. It is possible that providers can negotiate to have barriers such as work locations, break times, or scheduled hours changed to promote integration. Under ideal circumstances, the conditions to be negotiated are identified before the worker with disabilities begins employment. However, conditions in jobs change, and

adjustments in employment conditions may be needed at any time during the worker's tenure on the job.

2. *Environmental adaption.* Once an employer agrees to some adjustment of job conditions to increase opportunities for integration, the provider must assume the responsibility for making sure that the change takes place and that the change has the desired effect. Changes in work circumstances may involve alterations in the location or physical proximity of the individual's work station (e.g., screens that block access to co-workers may be removed). By assuming as much responsibility as possible in this process, providers can help to ensure that increased integration results and that the alterations made are acceptable to co-workers.

3. *Co-worker orientation.* One means of enhancing the potential for integration is to ensure that co-workers understand the nature of supported employment. Trainers should emphasize that the employment aspirations of the person with disabilities are not different from other workers and that the individual's intention is to fit into the social patterns and work flow. Trainers must be certain that the manner in which orientation takes place is as similar as possible to the way in which other new workers orient themselves to the workplace. Special meetings with co-workers as a group to discuss disabilities in general or the particular individual's specific needs may create undue attention and diminish the possibility for smooth integration.

Individual Support and Instruction

Providers can use a number of individual support strategies to help individuals with disabilities succeed in employment. A detailed discussion of these strategies is beyond the scope of this chapter. There are, however, three individually oriented activities that can have a profound influence on integration.

1. *Job match.* To date, most procedures for job matching focus primarily on job and task performance issues. One reason for this is the fact that more strategies exist for addressing job performance requirements than for understanding and promoting integration. A second reason is that most people with disabilities have little or no experience in employment in integrated settings. As efforts in job development are increasingly aimed at matching individuals and jobs in integrated settings, consideration of individual variation must come into play. Just as it is inappropriate to assume that persons with disabilities need or desire little interaction in the worksite, it is also inappropriate to assume that every individual with disabilities should work in a job where continuous interaction during job performance is required. While projections about the kind and degree of social interaction may be difficult to determine, it is clear that individual preference must be addressed before jobs are arranged.

2. *Planning with individuals and their advocates.* Changes in integration can be considered successful only to the degree that they are valued by the individual. The only way to assure that the activities taken by support personnel to promote integration are not wasted is to plan carefully with the individuals with disabilities and their families or advocates. Most individuals, even those with limited work histories, have some preferences about types of jobs. Individuals also have preferences about social interactions and about their own particular need and desire for relationships and social networks. The participation of the individual and of his or her family or advocates can profoundly influence actions taken to enhance integration.

3. *Systematic instruction.* A number of instructional methods exist that can be applied to make sure that disabled individuals are prepared to take advantage of integration opportunities. These include general case programming (Horner, Sprague, & Wilcox, 1982), self-management training (Gifford, Rusch, Martin, & White, 1984; Mank & Horner, 1987), social behavior training (Chadsey-Rusch, 1986; Gaylord-Ross, 1980), mobility training (York & Rainforth, 1987), and communication training (Falvey, 1986; Mirenda, 1985).

Most training and support efforts are concerned with the performance of work skills. There is, however, ample reason for applying these instruction methods to the skills involved in integration activities. Lack of social skills is a commonly cited reason for job loss (Chadsey-Rusch, 1986). Job success relates to the performance of both work and social skills.

SUMMARY AND UNANSWERED QUESTIONS

Supported employment represents a national effort to integrate individuals with disabilities into the fabric of American working life. In every part of the country, programs are being developed that will allow individuals with disabilities to leave segregated settings and work alongside other members of their communities. Integration is identified in federal law and guidelines as one of the critical outcomes of supported employment. Yet, since the individuals involved historically have been denied access to integrated environments, integration is also a process that involves careful planning, analysis, and support.

Despite the fact that integration is an essential component of supported employment, adequate definitions and measurement systems of this complex construct are elusive. Definitions of integration commonly describe more than define it, and measurement systems typically measure only a single aspect of this multidimensional concept.

This chapter has suggested that integration can be viewed in terms of four components: physical integration, social integration, relationships, and social networks. Each of these components builds on the other, and the purpose of giving individuals with disabilities access to community employment is to help them develop relationships and social networks.

The difficulty in defining integration is related to problems surrounding its measurement. A number of measurement techniques can be applied to specific work environments to provide information about the nature of integration within that worksite, the skills involved in full integration, and the participation of the individual with disabilities.

Arriving at a functional definition of integration by matching related constructs with measurement techniques does little to foster integration; specific and operational strategies that help promote integration are also needed. These include a number of strategies for ecological analysis, environmental modification, and systematic instruction and support.

The degree to which we are able to clarify definitions, measurement techniques, and strategies for integration will increase one's ability to address a number of critical issues, including:

1. How one determines appropriate levels of integration in the context of individual and ecological variation
2. The degree to which the provision of job-site training and support by third-party service providers interferes with integration
3. The effect of social skills training on the development of relationships and social networks
4. How support related to the behaviors needed for developing relationships and social networks affects job retention

By successfully addressing these issues, one can help to ensure that integration is recognized as a valued outcome of supported employment and that the process involved in increasing each person's ability to build relationships and social networks is well planned and effective. Failure to deal with these critical issues may result in a situation in which one approaches integration with a ''place and hope'' strategy, leaving both the success of the individuals with disabilities and the supported employment initiative in doubt.

REFERENCES

Agran, M. (1986). Observational reporting of work behavior. In F.R. Rusch (Ed.), *Competitive employment issues and strategies* (pp. 141–152). Baltimore: Paul H. Brookes Publishing Co.

Alberto, P.A., & Troutman, A.C. (1982). *Applied behavior analysis for teachers.* Columbus, OH: Charles E. Merrill.

Bellamy, G.T., Newton, J.S., Lebaron, N., & Horner, R.H. (1986). *Toward lifestyle accountability in residential services for persons with mental retardation.* Unpublished manuscript, University of Oregon, Specialized Training Program, Center on Human Development, Eugene.

Berkeley Planning Associates. (1986). *Development of performance measures for supported employment programs. Tasks 4 and 5: Availability of existing measures and need for additional measures to address program objectives* (Contract No. 300-85-0138). Washington, DC: U.S. Department of Education.

Budde, J.F. (1976). *Analyzing and measuring deinstitutionalization across residential environments with Alternative Living Environments Rating and Tracking system (ALERT).* Lawrence: University of Kansas, Affiliated Facility Publications.

Chadsey-Rusch, J. (1986). Identifying and teaching valued social behaviors. In F.R. Rusch (Ed.), *Competitive employment issues and strategies* (pp. 273–287). Baltimore: Paul H. Brookes Publishing Co.

Developmental Disabilities Act and Bill of Rights of 1984. (1984). [PL 98-527].

Edgerton, R.B. (1975). Issues relating to the quality of life among mentally retarded persons. In M.J. Begab & S.A. Richardson (Eds.), *The mentally retarded and society: A social science perspective* (pp. 127–140). Baltimore: University Park Press.

Emerson, E.B. (1985). Evaluating the impact of deinstitutionalization on the lives of mentally retarded people. *American Journal of Mental Deficiency, 90,* 277–288.

Falvey, M.A. (1986). *Community based curriculum: Instructional strategies for students with severe handicaps.* Baltimore: Paul H. Brookes Publishing Co.

Ferguson, P.M., Ferguson, D.L., & Jones, D. (1987). Generations of hope: Parental perspectives on the transitions of their severely retarded children from school to adult life. In P.M. Ferguson (Ed.), *Transition planning and adult service: Perspectives on policy and practice* (pp. 81–123). Eugene: University of Oregon, Specialized Training Program, Center on Human Development.

Galloway, C., & O'Brien, J. (1981). *Mapping vocational services accomplishments.* Decatur, GA: Responsive Systems Associates.

Gaylord-Ross, R. (1980). A decision model for the treatment of aberrant behavior in applied settings. In W. Sailor, B. Wilcox, & L. Brown (Eds.), *Methods of instruction for severely handicapped students* (pp. 135–158). Baltimore: Paul H. Brookes Publishing Co.

Gifford, J.L., Rusch, F.R., Martin, J.E., & White, D.M. (1984). Autonomy and adaptability: A proposed technology for maintaining work behavior. In N. Ellis & N. Bray (Eds.), *International review of research in mental retardation* (Vol. 12, pp. 285–314). New York: Academic Press.

Gottlieb, B.H. (1981). *Social networks and social support.* Beverly Hills: Sage Publications.

Horner, R.H., Newton, J.S., Lebaron, N.M., Stoner, S.K., & Ferguson, P.M. (1987). *Community Network Project: Research on strategies for supporting social networks* (Grant #G0087300223). Washington, DC: U.S. Department of Education.

Horner, R.H., Sprague, J., & Wilcox, B. (1982). General case programming for community activities. In B. Wilcox & G.T. Bellamy (Eds.), *Design of high school programs for severely handicapped students* (pp. 61–98). Baltimore: Paul H. Brookes Publishing Co.

Kazdin, A.E. (1982). *Single case research designs.* New York: Oxford University Press.

Kelly, J.A. (1982). *Social skills training: A practical guide to intervention.* New York: Springer-Verlag.

Kerlinger, F.N. (1973). *Foundation of behavioral research.* New York: Holt, Rinehart and Winston.

King, R.D., Raynes, N.V., & Tizard, J. (1971). *Patterns of residential care: Socialization studies in institutions for handicapped children.* Boston: Routledge & Kegan Paul.

Lofland, J., & Lofland, L.H. (1984). *Analyzing social settings: A guide to qualitative observation and analysis* (2nd ed.). Belmont, CA: Wadsworth.

Mank, D.M., & Horner, R.H. (1987). Self-recruited feedback: A cost-effective procedure for maintaining behavior. *Research in Developmental Disabilities, 8*(1), 91–112.

Mirenda, P. (1985). Designing pictorial communication systems for physically able-bodied students with severe handicaps. *Augmentative and Alternative Communication, 1,* 58–64.

Moots, R., & Otto, J. (1972). The community-oriented programs environment scales: A methodology for the facilitation and evaluation of social change. *Community Mental Health Journal, 8*(1), 28–37.

Nihara, K., Foster, R., Shelhaas, M., & Leland, H. (1974). *AAMD Adaptive Behavior Scale.* Washington, DC: American Association on Mental Deficiency.

Nisbet, J., & Callahan, M. (1987). Achieving success in integrated workplaces: Critical elements in assisting persons with severe disabilities. In S.J. Taylor, D. Biklen, & J. Knoll (Eds.), *Community integration for people with severe disabilities* (pp. 184–201). New York: Teachers College Press.

O'Brien, J. (1987). A guide to life-style planning: Using *The Activities Catalog* to integrate services and natural support systems. In B. Wilcox & G.T. Bellamy, *A comprehensive guide to The Activities Catalog: An alternative curriculum for youth and adults with severe disabilities* (pp. 175–189). Baltimore: Paul H. Brookes Publishing Co.

Public Law 98-527. *Developmental Disabilities Act and Bill of Rights of 1984* (1984). 42 U. S. C. Sec. 6000.

Public Law 99-506. *Rehabilitation Act Amendments,* 1987. 29 U. S. C. Sec. 706.

Schalock, R.L., & Jensen, C.M. (1986). Assessing the goodness-of-fit between persons and their environments. *Journal of The Association for Persons with Severe Handicaps, 11*(2), 103–109.

Will, M. (1984). *OSERS programming for the transition of youth with disabilities: Bridges from school to working life* (Position paper). Washington DC: Department of Education. Office of Special Education and Rehabilitative Services.

Wolf, M.M. (1978). Social validity: The case for subjective measurement of how applied behavior analysis is finding its heart. *Journal of Applied Behavior Analysis, 11*(2), 203–214.

York, J., & Rainforth, B. (1987). Developing instructional adaptations. In F.P. Orelove & D. Sobsey, *Educating children with multiple disabilities: A transdisciplinary approach* (pp. 183–217). Baltimore: Paul H. Brookes Publishing Co.

27

Quality of Life and Quality of Work Life

David A. Goode

An era of concern for quality of life (QOL) is upon us in the field of human services for people with disabilities. As with many other major changes in this area, the beginning steps are small and can be traced to historical antecedents that did not foresee their current relevance for persons with disabilities. For a variety of reasons, to be discussed in this chapter, quality of life has increasingly become a focus of human services recipients, researchers, providers, and regulators. This chapter looks at the relationship between QOL and quality of work life (QOWL) and at issues related to their conceptualization and measurement.

QUALITY OF LIFE

There are indications that QOL may soon replace normalization, community adjustment, and deinstitutionalization as a guiding principle in the design, delivery, and evaluation of services for persons with disabilities and their families (Schalock, 1987; Schalock, Keith, Hoffman, & Karan, in press). Reasons for this include: a growing general social awareness of quality in work, home, and interpersonal life as evidenced in many "pop" publications; increased concern about quality of life in community placement for persons with disabilities; dissatisfaction with current approaches to monitoring and evaluation service outcomes and quality of service (Bradley, 1984); the re-emergence of a holistic perspective in services (Baker & Intagliata, 1982); recognition of the complex interaction between personal and environmental variables in determining satisfaction with life and quality of life (Edgerton, 1975); growing acceptance of the view that consumer satisfaction measures are legitimate indicators of quality of life (Heal & Chadsey-Rusch, 1985); recognition of the need for standardized categories of meaningful client-referenced evaluation data (Schalock, 1987); and acceptance of quality of life as a concept guiding clinical decision making and social policy formation.

For these and other reasons, persons are increasingly talking about quality of life, although there is still no general agreement about the meaning of the concept, about how to operationalize it, or about how to measure it. Schalock (1987) is correct in noting that quality of life research in services for disabled individuals is in its infancy, despite the 50-year history of research related to the concept beginning with the work of Thorndike (1939). Schalock (1987) nevertheless observes that one can make certain tentative conclusions about the concept of QOL in services for people with disabilities. In his review of current QOL models (Borthwick-Duffy, 1986; Halpern, 1986; Keith, Schalock, & Hoffman, 1986), Schalock (1987) cites the following common dimensions:

A concern with community involvement (recreation, clubs, events, and activities)
A concern for personal relationships (family, friends, neighbors, others)
A focus upon the living environment (degree of control, services available, safety and normalization of setting)
An emerging focus on the working environment (degree of productivity and financial productivity, enhancement of status, integration with normal workers)

In addition to recognition of these common QOL dimensions, Schalock et al. (in press) note that there are three ways in which QOL has thus far been operationalized: 1) by social indicators, which are objective indicators related to health, standard of living, education, safety, housing, leisure, and so on; 2) by two varieties of psychological indicators, including measures of psychological well-being and measures of personal satisfaction and happiness; and 3) by social-ecological measures directed at assessing the "goodness of fit" between the characteristics of an environment and an individual.

Other indicators associated with quality of life relate to staff income, stability, training, career development, the existence of quality circles and other forms of participative management technique, and staff control over conditions of labor.

QUALITY OF WORK LIFE

The quality of work life is a relatively new concept. It was popularized by Irving Bluestone, head of General Motors' (GM) Department of the United Auto Workers in the late 1960s and early 1970s. In explicitly formulating a concern for the rights of workers to make decisions affecting the conduct and conditions of labor, Bluestone coined the term *quality of work life* and persuaded GM to expand its Organizational Development Program, an expansion of Alfred Sloan's Employee Research Section, to include QOWL issues. Bluestone also convinced GM to sponsor the first national joint labor/management committee on quality of work life (Kanter, 1983). What distinguished Sloan and Bluestone's efforts was the recognition that positive employee attitude and relationships as well as participation in governance were crucial to the overall success of the production process.

As with quality of life, there was some historical precedent for this recognition. In the 19th century in this country, there were utopian experiments in governance and profit-sharing arrangements that one would today recognize as QOWL oriented. Similarly, the Hawthorne studies in the 1930s provide an example of the long-standing interest in the psychology, attitudes, and behavior of workers and their relationship to production. But Bluestone's accomplishment was different from that of the psychologists. He was the first figure in American corporate history to convince management that workers participating in decisions affecting their own work conditions and lives would significantly enhance the production process. He was the first to institutionalize in a relatively permanent way in our society the proactive approach to enhancing the QOWL for employees in the private sector.

The essence of Bluestone's approach was to improve participation by employees in problem solving and decision making in matters related to the condition of their working lives. In attempting to achieve this, resolving conflicting relationships was a primary focus. This was accomplished through changing management's attitudes to be more tolerant, caring, and concerned; through changing management's behavior to be less punitive; through stressing good interpersonal relationships; and through fostering a general concern for the clean appearance and good organization of the plant. Under Bluestone's influence, plants were created that gave the appearance of efficiency in combination with healthy employer-employee relationships (Kanter, 1983). Part of the solution was also employee participation groups, which addressed matters related to QOWL and were jointly run by management and labor.

It is important to understand that Bluestone, and the current corporate structures concerned with promoting QOWL, did not advocate his approach primarily on the basis of humanitarianism, but rather on the basis of increased worker productivity. Programs such as these require commitment from management and are expensive to run. Thus, as in most business arrangements, they are rationalized on the basis of profit. In the case of plants in which Bluestone-style management was instituted, benefits included higher product quality, lower absenteeism, lower employee sabotage, fewer grievances (from 2,000 per year to 30 per year in 2 years in one plant), and good publicity (Kanter, 1983). Today, most corporations devote considerable time and money to these democratic structures and also to worker incentive programs. They do so largely for the same reasons that motivated GM in 1970.

Concomitant with these changes in the private sector, one also sees increased attempts at operationalizing QOWL by the academic community. For example, Walton (1973) has attempted to define and operationalize

QOWL. The factors he suggests include: adequate and fair compensation, safe and healthy working conditions, opportunity to use and develop behavioral capabilities, opportunities for continued growth or security, constitutionalism in the work organization (privacy, free speech, equity and due process), normal work schedules, and a variety of jobs. The understanding that these factors are associated with high QOWL has been part of the consciousness of the private sector for many years.

CONCEPTUALIZATION OF QOWL FOR PEOPLE WITH DISABILITIES

The concept of QOWL has not yet entered the disabilities field, as it has the private sector. There have been experiments using progressive management techniques (Tjosvold & Tjosvold, 1983) that recognize that the QOWL of workers directly affects the quality of life of clients (Karan & Berger-Knight, 1986; Powers & Goode, 1986; Tjosvold & Tjosvold, 1983), as well as recognition of the general need for proactive, participatory management in the disabilities field (MacEachron, Zober, & Fein, 1985).

Perhaps the most general formulation of the significance of QOWL to the human services field is found in Powers and Goode's (1986) statement of the Quality Principle: "This principle postulates that the quality of life of a person with disabilities will vary directly and significantly with the quality of life of those 'significant others' surrounding him or her" (p. 10). This Quality Principle asserts that quality of work life is best conceptualized in terms of a social system approach, stressing positive or desirable relationships between the elements (persons) of each life setting. The relationships between these elements compose a Quality Set or Q-Set, and may be expressed axiomatically through statements such as: "The QOWL of a person with disabilities will vary directly and significantly with the QOWL of his or her coworkers." This proposition is similar to that of Walton (1973).

This axiom points to an important implication of QOWL for the disability field today and one that could have far-reaching effects on current approaches for enhancing the QOWL of people with disabilities. The implication is that the disability field must begin to adopt the newer forms of management style that are aimed at increasing QOWL; that is, the field must address the structural inequities (such as low rates of pay and poor job advancement) mitigating against higher QOWL. This will require a change in management style and technology that will necessitate a total commitment from labor and management (Kanter, 1983).

TECHNOLOGIES FOR CHANGE

One can well ask how such a total change is going to come about in employment for persons with disabilities and in the services provided them. In this regard, two current developments are laying the groundwork for this change: the recognition of the importance of client participation in job-related decisions, and the development of methods to measure and assess QOWL.

Participation in Decision Making

Commitment to progressive management has always meant a commitment to greater decision making for the worker in matters related to his or her work life. Because of the increased power that is afforded to workers, corporations are offering educational programs related to their QOWL efforts. In the disabilities field today, there is a movement toward empowering persons with disabilities to make decisions that affect their own work and residential lives. Figure 27.1 presents the author's adaptation of the Pathways model of vocational decision making (Kiernan & Stark, 1986). It is important to note the central role of decision making in vocational services for this population. The model displays a circular process that can begin with a decision point, lead to specific training and/or employment experience, stabilize, or lead back to another decision point and further vocational training or experience. Again, however, it is the emphasis upon client choice that characterizes the current approach to vocational services.

Along with an awareness of QOWL is the increasing responsibility of people with disabilities to make work-related decisions themselves. The model in Figure 27.1 recognizes that there may be some persons who do not, or cannot, relate to a vocation, and for whom a broader sense of the terms *vocation* and *production* are appropriate (Edgerton, 1975; Stark, Kiernan,

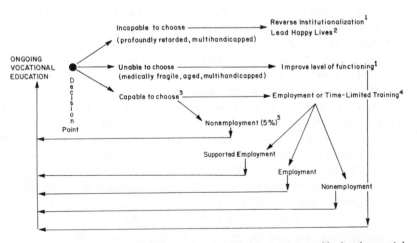

Figure 27.1. Individual employment decision making for persons with developmental disabilities. (Adapted from Kiernan & Stark, 1986). Sources: 1. Stark, Kiernan, Goldsbury, and McGee (1986); 2. Edgerton and Goode, personal communication (1979); 3. Kiernan and Stark (1986); 4. Whitehead and Marrone (1986).

Goldsbury, & McGee, 1986). There are also those who require help in making vocational decisions, or who have a particular condition that requires special training or highly technical environmental interventions. Then there are those who are fully capable of choosing from among vocational options. As Figure 27.1 indicates, these persons choose regularly between nonemployment and available training employment options. The figure also shows the importance of training and education in a philosophy of vocational services that stresses the importance of client choice.

Thus, if one adopts a QOWL focus, it may mean developing a technology to help those who need assistance to achieve this outcome behavior. Making decisions is something that needs to be taught and practiced; and there are many persons with disabilities who lack both experiences. We have a system that has historically constructed ways to minimize the client's participation in these choices and that has perpetuated a negative view of workers with disabilities that does not enhance their image as decision makers. Both these things will have to change if one is to enhance the QOWL for individuals with disabilities.

A similar change in "empowerment" must also occur for nondisabled workers who are employed within the service system in vocational, residential, and other settings. The perspicuously poor staff recruitment, development, and retention in residential services has a direct if not determinative bearing upon the QOL of persons who live in residential settings. As suggested by Powers and Goode (1986) and Karan and Berger-Knight (1986), quality of work life for persons providing service in work or residential settings is a primary determinant of the QOWL or QOL of persons with disabilities who participate in these settings. Tjosvold and Tjosvold (1983) demonstrated that progressive changes in management of a community residence resulted in clients participating more fully in decision making in the residence, and that other positive behavioral changes followed this intervention. The absence of participating forms of management all too often has the opposite effect—clients and staff make few decisions about how they spend their time together. If one wants one's clients to enjoy a high quality of work and residential life, one will also have to learn how to provide QOWL to those workers who work and live with them. This will increasingly involve availing oneself of technical resources from those in the private sector who have dealt with QOWL issues for over 20 years.

There is thus a two-edged implication to the current concern for QOWL with respect to decision making. First, disabled clients must participate in vocational decision making to the greatest degree possible; that is, decisions regarding vocational training and decision making in the workplace. At the same time, one must apply the same logic to those who work within the disabilities system. To tackle the QOWL problems that consumers face without similarly addressing these same issues for workers in vocational and residential systems would be a one-sided intervention with a minimal probability of success.

Operationalization of QOWL

The operationalization and measurement of QOWL is the second vehicle for producing positive change in the work lives of persons with disabilities. As described earlier in this chapter, there have been some attempts to conceptually clarify QOWL in the developmental disabilities field; but because there has been no shared construct of QOWL, there have been few examinations of how one might construct QOWL measures. The development of operational definitions and measures involves a complex and long-term relationship between theory, empirical research, and political definition. Attempts are already being made to lay a framework for the development of QOWL measures in the disabilities field. While it will take time, numerous scientifically defensible attempts will undoubtedly surface to measure QOWL.

Table 27.1 displays some of the kinds of indicators that have been proposed with respect to QOWL for persons with disabilities. The figure presents a benefits spectrum for employment (columns labeled on the top) and locates QOWL as one of these benefits. The left-hand column names the classes of indicators that have been proposed by the authors cited. As noted by Schalock (1987), three general classes of indicators have been employed: objective, subjective, and social-ecological. Given the current state of the literature, Table 27.1 suggests that a consensual conceptualization of QOWL that is measured through objective, subjective, and social-ecological measures is where we are headed, and where we will arrive in the not too distant future.

This figure is not presented to raise issues about the adequacy of the specific indicators listed. Its purpose is to point out that the conceptual ground for QOWL measures in the developmental disabilities field is alive and fertile. As one reads the items in the QOWL column in Table 27.1, it is interesting to note that the column summarizes most of the major issues in the field of employment services for persons with disabilities. The fact that QOWL and QOL are concepts that seem to collect these kinds of critical issues makes them powerful social policy issues. This fact may also underscore the potential clinical utility of these concepts, although this has yet to be demonstrated.

Only technical and resource problems stand in the way of the development of a psycho-social-ecological QOWL index.[1] There are both promises

---

[1]This is precisely the kind of notion that lies behind the Quality of Life Initiative sponsored by the U.S. Administration on Developmental Disabilities. In this initiative, the framework for QOL guidelines and indicators is being developed by scholars, advocates, consumers, regulators, and other members of the community of persons concerned with disabilities. In addition to the creation of indicators, it is hoped that this initiative will develop a general agenda around QOL and QOWL issues in training, social policy, research, evaluation, individual assessment, program planning, advocacy, and related areas.

Table 27.1. Relationship of quality of life (QOL) to employee benefits (partially completed)

	BENEFITS OF EMPLOYMENT*								
	Nonmonetary indicators				Monetary indicators				
Type of QOL indicator	Quality of community life	Quality of work life	Skill acquisition and maintenance	Program progression	Earnings	Taxes	Reduced alternate program expenses	Fringe benefit coverage	Reduced care subsidy payments
I. Objective social indicators	1. Mobility[a] 2. Appearance and physical condition[a] 3. Activity level and variety[c] 4. Independence, community involvement and acceptance[c] 5. Social and recreational involvement[a,c] 6. Increased decision making at home[c] 7. Living arrangements[a]	1. Decreased training and supervision[a] 2. Increased company of other persons with developmental disabilities[a] 3. Integrated work, lunch, and break areas[a] 4. Marketable skills learned[a] 5. Same work schedules as other employees[a] 6. Absence of negative stereotypes[a] 7. Variety of jobs[a] 8. Accessibility to promotions[a]	1. Increased self-help skills[c] 2. Increased skills with activities of daily life[c] 3. Communication skills 4. Decision-making skills[c] 5. Decreased negative behavior (behavioral self-control)[c] 6. Increased mobility skills 7. Adaptive behavior and generalization of learning						

	9. Increased decision making re: job 10. Increased productivity[f]		
II. Social-psychological and satisfaction indicators	1. Life-style satisfaction[b] 2. Psychological well-being and absence of stress[c] 3. Increased intimacy 4. Sexual satisfaction 5. Satisfaction with friends 6. Satisfaction with recreation	1. Job satisfaction[f] 2. Pride in workplace and job[f] 3. Satisfaction with relationships at work 4. Career satisfaction[f] 5. Satisfaction with participating in a "team process" on job[f]	1. Enhanced self-, body image 2. Enhanced social image 3. Enhanced sexual self-image
III. Person/environment fit and social-ecological (sociological) indicators	1. Increased GOFI for home environment[d,j] 2. Participatory, egalitarian role in social ecology of residence[e,f,h,j]	1. Increased GOFI for vocational environment[d,j] 2. Participatory role in decisions re: quality of work life and productivity[e,f,h,j]	1. Person specific, environment specific interventions[g,j]

Sources/references:
[a]Schalock and Hill (1986)
[b]Heal and Chadsey-Rusch (1985)
[c]Calkins, Walker, Bacon-Prue, Gibson, Intagliata, and Martinson (1986)
[d]Schalock, Keith, Hoffman, and Karan (in press)
[e]Powers and Goode (1986, n.p.)
[f]Bluestone, as cited in Kanter (1983)
[g]Romer and Heller (1983)
[h]Tjosvold and Tjosvold (1983)
[i]Karan and Berger-Knight (1986)
[j]Schalock and Jensen (1986)

and dangers inherent in such an index. The promises are significant. If constructed, the index could be seen as a way to approach measurement of service impact, which the field, while agreeing upon the importance of such measurement, has been unable to do. Impact data are now a high priority because demonstrated effectiveness of services provides politicians with the information they need to protect service programs from budgetary cuts. The development of such an assessment methodology would also seem to ground the development of assessments that are more relevant to the client's perspective and to the perspective of other significant actors in the client's life. Some of the standards that are used in quality assurance today seem to address matters that are, from the point of view of client and staff, secondary to other, more important matters. A QOWL index could begin to address the problem of relevance of program development and evaluation standards.

Powers and Goode (1986) suggested that the development of QOL indexes be linked with the development of cost-efficient proactive models of QOL (or QOWL) enhancement. Given this kind of approach, the development of any QOWL index should be linked with the development of capacity-expanding, resource-providing systems of quality enhancement mechanisms. As described by Bradley (1984), current monitoring and quality assurance mechanisms often do little more than determine compliance, or of more significance to the provider, appropriate punishment for being out of compliance. Both Bradley (1984) and Bercovici (1982) note that almost all the current quality assurance codes are administered in ways punitive to system enhancing. Often, they do nothing to address the concerns of the provider or the client. By their very nature, QOL and QOWL measures are not (or at least do not have to be) part of this kind of punitive process.

The risks of constructing QOWL monitoring methodologies are also significant. One cannot control the uses of even positive and valid social inventions. Some of what was done in the name of normalization or behavior modification might be good examples. This is a significant political and ethical dimension for professionals who are involved in QOWL research. One could easily envision an inappropriate clinical prescriptive use of QOWL standards ("Ninety-five percent of persons with Down syndrome love competitive employment, so you should listen to us and go into competitive employment") or the restriction of clients from what they consider to be desirable forms of employment because they do not score well on a QOWL setting scale. It is not difficult to imagine other inappropriate uses of measures of QOL or QOWL. This ethical/moral dimension to the scientific development of such measures will have to become a critical, ongoing component to them; if they are not managed in as self-aware and meticulous a fashion as the development of the measures themselves, the potential benefit of operationalizing QOWL will be seriously questioned.

There are also other dangers to constructing QOWL indices. We are probably already overregulated and think of reducing the regulation of services as a primary way to improve the quality of service and of our work lives. Thus, the construction of any new set of standards will have to take the expense burden of regulation into account. Finally, the ultimate danger to indices and standards is that they are often fixed and fail to change with the quick pace of history characteristic of the 20th century. Whatever standards and measurements of QOL and QOWL that we produce within the developmental disabilities field will need to incorporate the capacity for change, if such standards are to keep pace with society.

SUMMARY

In summary, it has been suggested that QOL and QOWL are two new but important concepts in the developmental disabilities field. A brief review of the conceptual and research development of QOL and QOWL was presented, along with a discussion of their relevance to developmental disabilities. With respect to QOWL, two major movements were described and analyzed. One was the recognition of client choice in vocational and employment matters, and the other was the movement toward constructing QOWL measures and indicators. It was suggested that an awareness of QOL and QOWL issues for consumers entails a corresponding awareness of those issues for workers in the disabilities service system, and that the QOL and QOWL for many consumers cannot be divorced from QOWL for these workers.

The developmental disabilities field has a dual interest in both QOL and QOWL. We all care about QOL as private citizens with legitimate concerns about the quality of our own lives. We struggle with how we are to understand what QOL is and how to best achieve it. But as professionals and advocates with concerns about the QOL of persons with disabilities, we also have a professional or career interest in this topic. The same is true for QOWL. Depending on social and economic factors that far exceed the scope of the disabilities field per se, one of the great challenges that human services professionals may face in the future will be to solve contradictions arising between self-interest in pursuing QOL and QOWL and professional interest in providing opportunities for persons with disabilities to achieve these same ends.

REFERENCES

Baker, F., & Intagliata, I. (1982). Quality of life in the evaluation of community support systems. *Evaluation and Program Planning, 5,* 69–79.
Bercovici, S. (1982). *Barriers to normalization.* Baltimore: University Park Press.

Borthwick-Duffy, S. (1986). *Quality of life of mentally retarded people.* Unpublished doctoral dissertation, University of California, Riverside, School of Education.

Bradley, V. (1984). *Assessing and enhancing the quality of services: A guide for the human services field.* Boston: Human Services Research Institute.

Edgerton, R.B. (1975). Issues relating to quality of life among mentally retarded individuals. In M.J. Begab & S.A. Richardson (Eds.), *The mentally retarded and society: A social service perspective* (pp. 127–140). Baltimore: University Park Press.

Halpern, A. (1986, May). *The dimensions of community adjustment.* Paper presented at the Annual Meeting of the American Association on Mental Deficiency, Denver.

Heal, L., & Chadsey-Rusch, J. (1985). The Lifestyle Satisfaction Scale (LSS): Assessing individuals' satisfaction with residence, community setting, and associated services. *Applied Research in Mental Retardation, 6,* 475–490.

Karan, O., & Berger-Knight, K. (1986). Training demands of the future. In W.E. Kiernan & J.A. Stark (Eds.), *Pathways to employment for adults with developmental disabilities* (pp. 253–271). Baltimore: Paul H. Brookes Publishing Co.

Keith, K.D., Schalock, R.L., & Hoffman, K. (1986). *Quality of life: Measurement and programmatic implications.* Lincoln, NE: Region V Mental Retardation Services.

Kiernan, W.E., & Stark, J.A. (1986). Comprehensive design for the future. In W.E. Kiernan & J.A. Stark (Eds.), *Pathways to employment for adults with developmental disabilities* (pp. 103–112). Baltimore: Paul H. Brookes Publishing Co.

MacEachron, A., Zober, M., & Fein, J. (1985). Institutional reform, adaptive functioning of the mentally retarded, and staff quality of work life. *American Journal of Mental Deficiency, 89*(4), 379–388.

Powers, J., & Goode, D. (1986). *Partnerships for people.* Unpublished paper, Albert Einstein College of Medicine, Bronx, NY.

Romer, D., & Heller, T. (1983). Social adaptation of mentally retarded adults in community settings: A social-ecological approach. *Applied Research in Mental Retardation, 4,* 303–314.

Schalock, R. (1986, May 28). *Current approaches to assessing a person's quality of life.* Paper presented at 110th Meeting of the American Association on Mental Deficiency, Denver.

Schalock, R. (1987). *The concept of quality of life in community-based mental retardation programs: A position paper.* Hastings, NE: Hastings College, Department of Psychology.

Schalock, R.L., & Hill, M.L. (1986). Evaluating employment services. In W.E. Kiernan & J.A. Stark (Eds.), *Pathways to employment for adults with developmental disabilities* (pp.285–302). Baltimore: Paul H. Brookes Publishing Co.

Schalock, R.L., & Jensen, C.M. (1986). Assessing the goodness of fit between persons and environments. *Journal of The Association for Persons with Severe Handicaps, 11*(2), 103–109.

Schalock. R., Keith, K., Hoffman, K., & Karan, O.C. (in press). Quality of life: Its measurement and use. *Mental Retardation.*

Stark, J., Kiernan, W., Goldsbury, T., & Mcgee, J. (1986). Not entering employment: A system dilemma. In W.E. Kiernan & J.A. Stark (Eds.) *Pathways to employment for adults with developmental disabilities* (pp. 199–206). Baltimore: Paul H. Brookes Publishing Co.

Thorndike, E.L. (1939). *Your city.* New York: Harcourt Brace.

Tjosvold, D., & Tjosvold, M.M. (1983). Social psychological analysis of residences for mentally retarded persons. *American Journal of Mental Deficiency, 88*(1), 28–40.

Walton, R.E. (1973, Fall). Quality of work life: What is it? *Sloan Management Review, 15*(1), 11–21.

Whitehead, C. W., & Marrone, J. (1986). Time-limited evaluation and training. In W. E. Kiernan & J. A. Stark (Eds.), *Pathways to employment for adults with developmental disabilities* (pp. 163–176). Baltimore: Paul H. Brookes Publishing Co.

28

Quality of Life
The Residential Environment

Sharon A. Borthwick-Duffy

As indicated in the previous chapter, quality of life has been identified as the issue in the field of mental retardation that will lead to improved services and outcomes in the late 1980s and 1990s, just as deinstitutionalization, normalization, and community adjustment have done in the past 2 decades (Schalock, 1986). Beyond the need to evaluate programs, Schalock cites America's current concern for the general welfare and well-being of its citizenry as a justification for evaluating a person's quality of life. Landesman (1986) referred to quality of life as a new "buzz-word" in mental retardation, an outcome that is sorely in need of a formal, measurable definition. In her proposal that the American Association on Mental Deficiency help develop guidelines to measure this concept, Landesman noted that lacking a definitional structure of desired outcomes and estimated relationships of client outcomes to one another, the overall evaluation of the effects of policies has been less than systematic, and has had to occur outside a conceptual framework.

The phrase *quality of life* has been used throughout the literature with regard to the home, work, and community life of persons with mental retardation in our service systems. Unfortunately, it is difficult to draw conclusions and summarize these reports because the quality of life construct has not been clearly defined and because studies frequently focus on very limited aspects of this broad concept. Moreover, a number of other terms have also been used to describe the positive outcomes that are related to residential placement, including *adjustment, adaptation,* and *success.* Yet, regardless of the general term used, the specific operational criteria employed in research studies are used interchangeably, suggesting that these concepts may not be distinguishable in the literature. For example, friendships have been said to reflect an

The preparation of this chapter was supported in part by NICHD Grants HD-14688 and HD-04612 to the University of California, Los Angeles; and NICHD Grant HD-22953 to the University of California, Riverside.

individual's adjustment (Seltzer, 1981), adaptation (Bell, Schoenrock, & Bensberg, 1981), and quality of life (Schalock, 1986). The literature contains reports of some well-executed studies that have examined a wide range of outcome variables, each important in the context of an individual's quality of life, yet bearing ambiguous relationships with other studies that have had related but different objectives.

The diversity of quality of life criteria and outcome measures has been described as almost researcher specific (Craig & McCarver, 1984; Seltzer, Sherwood, Seltzer, & Sherwood, 1981). In a discussion of community adjustment, Lakin, Bruininks, and Sigford (1981) stated that the wide range of operational definitions does not always lead to problems in interpreting results of single studies, but does make it difficult to compare and summarize research findings. In some ways this relatively undeveloped research field is faced with a dilemma. While it would be more straightforward to standardize measures of life quality and develop a universal definition, this would oversimplify what is an extremely complex phenomenon (Craig & McCarver, 1984; Eagle, 1967; McCarver & Craig, 1974). In fact, Lakin et al. (1981) have suggested that community adjustment is a matter of degree and personal preference, and is not easily quantified. They state that:

> the notion of adjustment as it has been operationalized in previous studies implies a standard or norm by which the adjustment of mentally retarded persons can be determined—that is by which one can separate those who are "adjusted" from those who are not. Such a standard can be most easily criticized in that even among nonmentally handicapped persons adjustment is at best ill-defined and represents no particular pattern of behavior. (Lakin et al., 1981, p. 383)

Quality of life is a subjective concept, the definition of which has been dependent on the perspectives and biases of the persons or groups doing the evaluation. An illustration of this point emerged from a study conducted by Intagliata, Willer, and Wicks (1981), who found that social workers and nurses assigned very different ranks of importance to various aspects of the lives of individuals with mental retardation in their care. For example, social workers ranked "encouraging independence" last, while nurses ranked it as most important in client care. In contrast, social workers placed a higher value on stability and organization of the home, and on knowledge of client needs. Similarly, Bartnik and Winkler (1981) found that employers, training staff, and parents had discrepant opinions regarding the importance of various criteria for evaluating the community adjustment of adults with mental retardation. These results clearly indicate that criterion measures can be a reflection of the investigator's view of residential care, and of the purpose it should serve, whether it be custodial, habilitative, or otherwise (Butterfield, 1985; Intagliata et al., 1981). Even though quality is often precisely defined in individual research studies, these findings support the notion that quality of life is a subjective concept, and that its interpretation may be "in the eye of the beholder."

ORIGINS OF QUALITY OF LIFE MODELS

Although life quality issues per se are relatively new to the field of mental retardation, quality of life models are common in community psychology and have been studied for several decades. With the exception of studies that have assigned overall goodness scores to cities, the concern of most model builders has been to select clusters of dimensions that are useful for understanding and evaluating community life, rather than to identify a single underlying dimension of quality (Zautra, 1983). Not surprisingly, a number of models have emerged from different perspectives on the meaning of quality of life. A recent review of some of these models suggested that four dimensions of life quality were commonly described, including residential environment, interpersonal relationships, community involvement, and stability (Borthwick-Duffy, 1986). It was also found that the dimensions of life quality that are important in the study of nonretarded populations overlap with those found in the literature on mental retardation.

Two quality of life models (Halpern, 1986; Schalock & Keith, 1984) have been proposed in the literature on mental retardation, both evolving from efforts to evaluate the rehabilitation and community adjustment of adults with mental retardation in semi-independent and independent living situations. As expected, the elements of Halpern's and of Schalock and Keith's models are basically similar. Moreover, these quality of life models for higher functioning adults with mental retardation closely resemble the community psychology models, although increased emphasis is given to utilization of community resources and leisure activities. For relatively high-functioning persons with mental retardation, the desired outcome of their residential placements is to conduct normal life activity to the greatest extent possible, and the potential exists for this to occur. Although achievements and activities may occur less frequently among such persons, quality of life for persons with mild retardation is likely to be explained with rather straightforward generalizations from normal community psychology—that is, employment, income, residential neighborhood, leisure activities, education, civic activities and citizenship, marriage, and so forth.

In the absence of existing theoretical constructs, the work of Schalock and his associates (Keith, Schalock, & Hoffman, 1986; Schalock, 1986; Schalock & Harper, 1978; Schalock, Harper & Carver, 1981; Schalock & Keith, 1984) began at the level of the conceptual model. The "Quality of Life Questionnaire" (Keith et al., 1986) was derived from this work and has proven to be an extremely useful instrument in the evaluation of programs and of individual outcomes.

Halpern (1986) has empirically tested the relationships among the hypothesized components of the four dimensions in his "Community Adjustment Model." Subsequent examination of the correlations among the four factors found the external dimensions, occupation, social support, and residential environment, to be uncorrelated; the internal dimension, satisfaction, was strongly correlated with social support and moderately with residential environment.

In light of Halpern's (1986) results, a word on the subject of client satisfaction is in order. The consideration of the preferences and perceptions of the person with mental retardation whose quality of life is being evaluated is a recurring theme in recent articles (Emerson, 1985; Landesman-Dwyer, 1985; Sigelman et al., 1981; Wyngaarden, 1981). Client satisfaction has been identified as: 1) a dimension of quality of life (Bruininks, 1986; Halpern, 1986), 2) a concept distinguishable from quality of life (Landesman, 1986), and 3) an approach to assessing quality of life (Schalock, 1986). Satisfaction, like quality of life, is multidimensional. People can be satisfied with their homes, *or* with their social activities *or* their interpersonal relationships, but not necessarily all three at the same time. Thus, measures of personal satisfaction might give an additional perspective or impression of each of the four aspects of life quality already discussed, rather than representing a separate dimension. This may provide at least a partial explanation for the significant correlations of Halpern's satisfaction dimension with his "external factors" as well as the lack of correlation among the external factors. The measured satisfaction variables were sufficiently intercorrelated to support the existence of a satisfaction factor. However, it is still possible that personal satisfaction may have been correlated with the external dimensions because it was another method of evaluation.

QUALITY OF LIFE FOR
ALL LEVELS OF RETARDATION AND FOR ALL AGES

As previously noted, the community psychology field has contributed considerably to the development of quality of life models that are appropriate for nonretarded individuals. Although the operational definitions differ somewhat across models, the same four dimensions (residential environment, interpersonal relationships, community involvement, and stability) seem adequate to describe the major aspects of the quality of life models. Operational definitions of measured variables in studies of groups of persons with mild retardation can also be explained in terms of the four dimensions just mentioned.

The application of quality of life models to groups of people with more severe degrees of retardation has not yet been tested, although the need for such a study has been acknowledged (Halpern, 1986; Keith et al., 1986). It is reasonable to assume that the same dimensions of life quality are meaningful for all levels of intelligence, but that the relevance of *specific operational* criteria used to define the dimensions might differ according to an individual's skills and ability levels.

With regard to age, some of the same arguments apply to the consideration of children and adolescents with mental retardation whose quality of life should not be judged on the basis of occupation, income, civic involvement, or other outcomes that are indicators of adult adjustment. The same broad categories of life quality might be appropriate for all clients, regardless of age; however, the specific criteria for evaluating these dimensions are expected to be different for children and adults.

The remainder of this chapter focuses on an important quality of life dimension, the residential living environment. In conjunction with work or other day activity programs, the residence is where persons with mental retardation spend the majority of their time. For everyone, and for people with severe levels of retardation in particular, many characteristics of the residential environment are reflective of their quality of life. The conceptual residential environment dimension of the quality of life model that is proposed is intended to be meaningful across all ages and levels of retardation.

QUALITY OF LIFE: THE RESIDENTIAL ENVIRONMENT

Studies of residential living alternatives for persons with mental retardation typically seek to answer variations of the question: How does the environment influence behavior? (Butterfield, 1985). However, even though a major focus of research efforts has been on the role of the environment as a "means to an end," it is generally agreed that at any one time, an individual's quality of life is at least partly defined by the characteristics of his or her residential environment (Emerson, 1985; Landesman-Dwyer, 1985; Willer & Intagliata, 1984). It has been argued that placement in the least restrictive environment is justifiable on humanitarian grounds, regardless of its effect on client behavior. According to Seltzer et al. (1981), an individual may not adapt to his or her environment in terms of behavioral change, yet "the quality of that person's life may still be improved, given the improved qualities of the environment, such as increased cleanliness, personalization and stimulation" (p. 85).

In recent decades, official policies and legislation have committed our service systems to the concept of placement in the least restrictive environment (Bachrach, 1985; Flynn, 1980; Maloney & Ward, 1979). Moreover, perceptions of environmental quality are now judged on the basis of adherence to the principle of normalization. Although empirical studies have not overwhelmingly concluded that "smaller is better" or that "normalized environments promote greater development" (Landesman-Dwyer, 1983; Landesman-Dwyer & Sackett, 1978), the commitment to these values does not appear to be in jeopardy. To the extent that normalization or other sociophysical aspects of the home enhance an individual's quality of life, regardless of their effect on other outcomes, environmental quality can be perceived of as a quality of life goal in itself (Aanes & Haagenson, 1978; McCord, 1980; Seltzer et al., 1981).

Dimensions of the Residential Environment

Volumes have been written about the issues and research related to the residential living environments of mentally retarded people, and are reviewed elsewhere (e.g., Bruininks & Lakin, 1985; Haywood & Newbrough, 1981; Kernan, Begab, & Edgerton, 1983). The purpose of this section is to discuss the rationale for the structure of the proposed residential environment quality of life model.

The assessment of residential environments is relatively undeveloped compared to work that has been done on the measurement of the characteristics of the individuals who live in them (Elardo & Bradley, 1981; Landesman-Dwyer, 1985). Until recently, category labels of facility types were used as crude environmental distinctions in the majority of studies, even though the heterogeneity within these broad classifications has been well documented (Bjaanes & Butler, 1974; Landesman-Dwyer, 1985; Rotegard, Bruininks, Holman, & Lakin, 1985). In a thought-provoking discussion of this issue Landesman-Dwyer (1985) highlighted the problems associated with using broad classification types. She recommended that more refined environmental descriptors include both qualitative and subjective impressions from multiple sources and perspectives. She further emphasized that values should not be attached to particular aspects of the residential environment, because individual differences among clients will dictate which characteristics of the environment are most relevant to enhancing a person's quality of life.

The multidimensionality of environments as well as the interrelationships among environmental dimensions should be considered in a quality of life model. The possibility that the environment can be conceptualized at different levels should also be examined. Residential environments are generally viewed as being very complex. Novak and Berkeley (1984) discussed the "innumerable, and potentially infinite components" that have emerged from attempts to describe and evaluate residential living environments. At the same time, environments are usually perceived of as a whole, rather than as a collection of separate attributes that affect those who are exposed to them (Ittleson, 1978; Landesman-Dwyer, 1985). Some studies have found dimensions of environmental care to be uncorrelated in large institutions (Raynes, Pratt, & Roses, 1979) and in smaller community residences (Pratt, Luszcz, & Brown, 1980), supporting the notion of a multidimensional environment. However, further investigation is necessary to determine whether this is indeed the case, or whether a single higher level construct can describe the environment as a whole (Ittleson, 1978).

Residential Environment Model

The proposed factor structure for the residential environment dimension of the quality of life model is drawn primarily from Bradley (1986), Crawford, Aiello, and Thompson (1979), and Jacobson and Schwartz (1983). Three comparable dimensions are described by these researchers. Bradley described three salient attributes of the environment, including socioemotional/affective, cognitive, and physical factors that contribute to an individual's quality of life. Crawford et al. summarized three similar domains, including the social environmental climate, treatment programs and skill training, and the physical environment. Nihira, Mink, and Meyers (1984) studied the child-rearing attitudes and adjustment of families with mentally retarded children and identified similar dimensions of the environment. Finally, Jacobson and Schwartz cited the social environment (client-caregiver interactions and attitudes toward client), habilitation and structured activities, and physical setting components. In addition, Jacobson and Schwartz discussed the importance of a fourth area, "homelikeness," which is an application of the normalization principle to residential environments. Integrating the frameworks just described, four general dimensions of the environment constitute the residential environment quality of life model: 1) affective environment, 2) cognitive environment, 3) physical environment, and 4) environmental normalization. They are diagrammed in Figure 28.1.

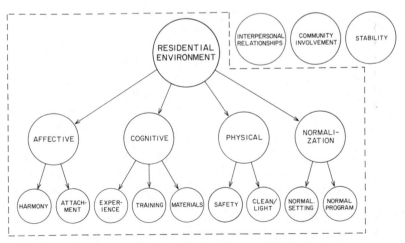

Figure 28.1. Residential environment quality of life model.

1. *Affective Component* The affective qualities of a home environment are important to the quality of life of any human being, but particularly to those individuals whose early attachments may have been less than ideal or even severed within the first years of their lives by out-of-home placement. Moreover, for individuals with mental retardation who have been placed outside their natural homes, there is an instability built into the placement, referred to by Evans (1983) as a "conditional belongingness."

Residential placements can offer a family-oriented environment, with opportunities for interaction with other persons with mental retardation in the home, with nonretarded children of the caregivers, and with primary caregivers and other staff, although these qualities are not always present (Evans, 1983). A home that reflects positive and accepting attitudes toward its residents and persons with mental retardation in general enhances the quality of life experienced by all who live in the home (Bjaanes & Butler, 1974; Jacobson & Schwartz, 1983). Characteristics of the affective home environment have been described as responsiveness, warmth, nurturance, discipline styles, and the overall positiveness of the socioemotional climate (Bradley, 1986). These qualities were summarized in the quality of life model (see Figure 28.1) as harmony in the home and attachment to the individual with mental retardation.

2. *Cognitive Component* The importance placed on the cognitive or training aspects of the home environment in the proposed model (see Figure 28.1) represents a departure from the quality of life models that have been developed for individuals who are higher functioning. Whereas employment, occupation, schooling, or workshop behavior and attendance are all training related, they actually reflect a degree of independence and stability; an entirely separate issue is the degree and quality of cognitive stimulation that occurs at home. Berkson and Landesman-Dwyer (1977) discussed the role of the caregiver as a trainer, as well as the fact that characteristics of behavior appear to be related to the environments in which individuals spend most of their time, that is, the home. Cognitive aspects of the home environment involve such characteristics as the variety of stimulation, cognitive/affective investment of caregivers, intellectuality in the home, encouragement of achievement, and so on (Bradley, 1986). The subcomponents of the cognitive environment were conceptualized (see Figure 28.1) as including cognitively stimulating experience, skill training, and cognitively stimulating materials.

3. *Physical Component* Physical aspects of the residential setting have been shown to be related to quality of life by influencing motivation, activity levels, affective behavior, and stress (Rotegard et al., 1985). The physical qualities of a home environment have also been found to reflect a resident's well-being and general life-style (Willer & Intagliata, 1984).

Frequently cited concerns regarding physical features include cleanliness, attractiveness, noise level, and lighting of the home (Bradley, 1986;

Willer & Intagliata, 1984), in addition to safety aspects of the house and outdoor yard area (Halpern, 1986). Most other physical attributes mentioned in the literature reflect the environment's adherence to the principle of normalization. Thus, in the proposed quality of life model (see Figure 28.1), the latter elements are incorporated into the normalization component, rather than the physical component. The subelements of the physical environment are concern for client safety, and that the home is clean and light.

4. *Normalization Component* The philosophy of normalization has been identified as providing the basis for the modification of several aspects of the service delivery system in mental retardation. According to Wolfensberger (1980), normalization does not necessarily mean doing what everyone else does; neither is it intended to make persons with mental retardation normal. Rather, normalization should make the life conditions of such people as close to normal as possible, by realistically assessing and respecting the degrees and complications of their handicaps (Nirje, 1980). Bjaanes and Butler (1974) distinguished between environmental normalization and client normalization, indicating that the normalization of the residential setting and program are catalysts to the development of client skills and abilities that allow people with mental retardation to engage in normalized activities.

CONCLUSIONS

The proposed dimensional structure of the residential environment quality of life model, presented in Figure 28.1, contains elements on three levels and a number of hypothesized relationships among the elements. Each feature of the environment is expected to have at least some relevance for all people with mental retardation, regardless of age or level of retardation. The importance attributed to these components will depend on characteristics of the individual, such as age, skills and abilities, functioning level, personality, health status and physical disabilities, contact with natural families, and so forth. For some clients, or perhaps the same clients at different life stages, different aspects of life quality might be emphasized.

The preceding discussion has implications regarding the match between an individual and his or her residential environment. In the past, a "success" or "failure" to remain in community settings was thought to be related to the characteristics of the individual; if a person was moved back to the institution, it was attributed to deficiencies of the person rather than to an inappropriate placement or lack of fit with the environment. In contrast, current thinking focuses on the ability of professionals and service providers to select the residential placement that will best suit the needs and abilities of the individual. Thus, a failure is more frequently interpreted as a mismatch of person and setting, rather than as a reflection of the placeability of the client.

Keith et al. (1986) examined the relationship between client "need status" and quality of life in two studies, and found that higher levels of need were associated with lower quality of life scores. These data suggest that the corresondence between client needs and abilities and environmental demands is an important predictor of life quality. Crawford et al. (1979) concluded from a review of the literature that a systematic study of environments and their differential impacts on the lives of mentally retarded people would eventually lead to an "optimal match" of person and environment. Landesman-Dwyer (1985) also noted that the characteristics of the environment are not necessarily perceived similarly by different people and that environmental evaluations should be distinguished from straightforward descriptions of environmental characteristics.

The concepts of quality of life and person-environment match are relatively new to the field of mental retardation. Not surprisingly, current theory has advanced beyond our current capacity to make accurate judgments along these lines. In order to bridge the gap between theory and practice, we must develop methods of assessing quality of life and of recognizing the optimal match between persons with mental retardation and the environments in which they live and work.

REFERENCES

Aanes, D., & Haagenson, L. (1978). Normalization: Attention to a conceptual disaster. *Mental Retardation, 16,* 55–56.

Bachrach, L.L. (1985). Deinstitutionalization: The meaning of the least restrictive environment. In R.H. Bruininks & K.C. Lakin (Eds.), *Living and learning in the least restrictive environment* (pp. 23–36). Baltimore: Paul H. Brookes Publishing Co.

Bartnik, E., & Winkler, R.C. (1981). Discrepant judgments of community adjustment of mentally retarded adults: The contribution of personal responsibility. *American Journal of Mental Deficiency, 86,* 260–266.

Bell, N.J., Schoenrock, C.J., & Bensberg, G.J. (1981). Change over time in the community: Findings of a longitudinal study. In R.H. Bruininks, C.E. Meyers, B.B. Sigford, & K.C. Lakin (Eds.), *Deinstitutionalization and community adjustment of mentally retarded people* (pp. 195–206). Washington, DC: American Association on Mental Deficiency.

Berkson, G., & Landesman-Dwyer, S. (1977). Behavioral research on severe and profound mental retardation (1955–1974). *American Journal of Mental Deficiency, 81,* 428–454.

Bjaanes, A.T., & Butler, E.W. (1974). Environmental variation in community care facilities for mentally retarded persons. *American Journal of Mental Deficiency, 78,* 429–439.

Borthwick-Duffy. (1986). *Quality of life of mentally retarded people: Development of a model.* Unpublished doctoral dissertation, University of California, Riverside.

Bradley, R. (1986). *The importance of home environment on the education of children.* Lecture given to University of California education graduate students, Riverside.

Bruininks, R. (1986, May). *The implications of deinstitutionalization for community adjustment*. Paper presented at the Annual Meeting of the American Association on Mental Deficiency, Denver.

Bruininks, R.H., & Lakin, K.C. (Eds.). (1985). *Living and learning in the least restrictive environment*. Baltimore: Paul H. Brookes Publishing Co.

Butterfield, E.C. (1985). The consequences of bias in studies of living arrangements for the mentally retarded adult. In D. Bricker & J. Filler (Eds.), *Severe mental retardation: From theory to practice* (pp. 245–263). Lancaster, PA: Lancaster Press.

Craig, E.M., & McCarver, R.B. (1984). Community placement and adjustment of deinstitutionalized clients: Issues and findings. In N.R. Ellis & N.W. Bray (Eds.), *International review of research in mental retardation* (Vol. 12, pp. 95–122). Orlando, FL: Academic Press.

Crawford, J.L., Aiello, J.R., & Thompson, P.E. (1979). Deinstitutionalization and community placement: Clinical and environmental factors. *Mental Retardation, 17*, 59–63.

Eagle, E. (1967). Prognosis and outcome and community placement of institutionalized retardates. *American Journal of Mental Deficiency, 72*, 232–243.

Elardo, R., & Bradley, R.H. (1981). The Home Observation for Measurement of the Environment (HOME) Scale: A review of research. *Developmental Review, 90*, 277–288.

Emerson, E.B. (1985). Evaluating the impact of deinstitutionalization on the lives of mentally retarded people. *American Journal of Mental Deficiency, 90*, 277–288.

Evans, D.P. (1983). *The lives of mentally retarded people*. Boulder, CO: Westview Press.

Flynn, R.J. (1980). Normalization, PASS, and service quality assessment. In R.J. Flynn & K.E. Nitsch (Eds.), *Normalization, social integration, and community services* (pp. 323–359). Baltimore: University Park Press.

Halpern, A. (1986, May). *The dimensions of community adjustment*. Paper presented at the Annual Meeting of the American Association on Mental Deficiency, Denver.

Haywood, H.C., & Newbrough, J.R. (Eds.). (1981). *Living environments for developmentally retarded persons*. Baltimore: University Park Press.

Intagliata, J., Willer, B., & Wicks, N. (1981). Factors related to the quality of community adjustment in family care homes. In R.H. Bruininks, C.E. Meyers, B.B. Sigford, & K.C. Lakin (Eds.), *Deinstitutionalization and community adjustment of mentally retarded people* (pp. 217–230). Washington, DC: American Association on Mental Deficiency.

Ittleson, W.H. (1978). Environmental perception and urban experience. *Environment and Behavior, 10*, 193–213.

Jacobson, J.W., & Schwartz, A.A. (1983). Personal and services characteristics affecting group home placement success: A prospective analysis. *Mental Retardation, 21*, 1–17.

Keith, K.D., Schalock, R.L., & Hoffman, K. (1986). *Quality of life: Measurement and programmatic implications*. Nebraska City: Region V Mental Retardation Services.

Kernan, K.T., Begab, M.J., & Edgerton, R.B. (Eds.). (1983). *Environments and behavior: The adaptation of mentally retarded persons*. Baltimore: University Park Press.

Lakin, K.C., Bruininks, R.H., & Sigford, B.B. (1981). Early perspectives on the community adjustment of mentally retarded people. In R.H. Bruininks, C.E. Meyers, B.B. Sigford, & K.C. Lakin (Eds.), *Deinstitutionalization and community adjustment of mentally retarded people* (pp. 28–50). Washington, DC: American Association on Mental Deficiency.

Landesman, S. (1986). Quality of life and personal life satisfaction: Definition and measurement issues. *Mental Retardation, 24,* 141–145.

Landesman-Dwyer, S. (1983). Residential environments and the social behavior of handicapped individuals. In M. Lewis (Ed.), *Beyond the dyad* (pp. 299–322). New York: Plenum.

Landesman-Dwyer, S. (1985). Describing and evaluating residential environments. In R.H. Bruininks & K.C. Lakin (Eds.), *Living and learning in the least restrictive environment* (pp. 185–196). Baltimore: Paul H. Brookes Publishing Co.

Landesman-Dwyer, S., & Sackett, G.P. (1978). Behavioral changes in nonambulatory, profoundly retarded individuals. In C.E. Meyers (Ed.), *Quality of life in severely and profoundly mentally retarded people: Research foundations for improvement* (pp. 55–144). Washington, DC: American Association on Mental Deficiency.

Maloney, M.P., & Ward, M.P. (1979). *Mental retardation and modern society.* New York: Oxford University Press.

McCarver, R.B., & Craig, E.M. (1974). Placement of the retarded in the community: Prognosis and outcome. In N.R. Ellis (Ed.), *International review of research in mental retardation* (Vol. 7, pp. 145–207). New York: Academic Press.

McCord, W.T. (1980). Community residences: The staffing. In J. Wortis (Ed.), *Mental retardation and developmental disabilities* (Vol. 12, pp. 111–128). New York: Brunner/Mazel.

Nihira, K., Mink, R., & Meyers, C.E. (1984). Salient dimensions of home environment relevant to child development. In N.R. Ellis & N.W. Bray (Eds.), *International review of research in mental retardation* (Vol. 12, pp. 149–175). Orlando, FL: Academic Press.

Nirje, B. (1980). The normalization principle. In R.J. Flynn & K.E. Nitsch (Eds.), *Normalization, social integration, and community services* (pp. 31–49). Baltimore: University Park Press.

Novak, A.A., & Berkeley, T.R. (1984). A systems theory approach to deinstitutionalization policies and research. In N.R. Ellis & N.W. Bray (Eds.), *International review of research in mental retardation* (Vol. 12, pp. 245–283). Orlando, FL: Academic Press.

Pratt, M.W., Luszcz, M.A., & Brown, M.E. (1980). Measuring dimensions of the quality of care in small community residences. *American Journal of Mental Deficiency, 85,* 188–194.

Raynes, N., Pratt, M., & Roses, S. (1979). *Organizational structure and the care of the mentally retarded.* London: Croom-Helm.

Rotegard, L.L., Bruininks, R.H., Holman, J.G., & Lakin, K.C. (1985). Environmental aspects of deinstitutionalization. In R.H. Bruininks & K.C. Lakin (Eds.), *Living and learning in the least restrictive environment* (pp. 155–184). Baltimore: Paul H. Brookes Publishing Co.

Schalock, R.L. (1986, May). *Current approaches to quality of life assessment.* Paper presented at the Annual Meeting of the American Association on Mental Deficiency, Denver.

Schalock, R.L.. & Harper, R.S. (1978). Placement from community-based mental retardation programs: How well do clients do? *American Journal of Mental Deficiency, 83,* 240–247.

Schalock, R.L., Harper, R.S., & Carver, G. (1981). Independent living placement: Five years later. *American Journal of Mental Deficiency, 2,* 170–177.

Schalock, R.L., & Keith, K.D. (1984). *DD client and staff variables influencing outcome of service delivery: Present and future models.* Lincoln: Nebraska Department of Health/Division of Developmental Disabilities.

Seltzer, G.B. (1981). Community residential adjustment: The relationship among environment, performance, and satisfaction. *American Journal of Mental Deficiency, 85,* 624–630.

Seltzer, M.M., Sherwood, C.C., Seltzer, G.B., & Sherwood, S. (1981). Community adaptation and the impact of deinstitutionalization. In R.H. Bruininks, C.E. Meyers, B.B. Sigford, & K.C. Lakin (Eds.), *Deinstitutionalization and community adjustment of mentally retarded people* (pp. 114–129). Washington, DC: American Association on Mental Deficiency.

Sigelman, C. K., Schoenrock, C. J., Winer, J. L., Spanhel, C. L., Hromas, S. G., Martin, P. W., Budd, E. C., & Bensberg, G. J. (1981). Issues in interviewing mentally retarded persons: An empirical study. In R. H. Bruininks, C. E. Meyers, B. B. Sigford, & K. C. Lakin (Eds.), *Deinstitutionalization and community adjustment of mentally retarded people* (pp. 114–129). Washington, DC: American Association on Mental Deficiency.

Willer, B., & Intagliata, J. (1984). *Promises and realities for mentally retarded persons: Life in the community.* Baltimore: University Park Press.

Wolfensberger, W. (1980). A brief overview of the principle of normalization. In R.J. Flynn & K.E. Nitsch (Eds.), *Normalization, social integration, and community services* (pp. 7–30). Baltimore: University Park Press.

Wyngaarden, M. (1981). Interviewing mentally retarded persons: Issues and strategies. In R.H. Bruininks, C.E. Meyers, B.B. Sigford, & K.C. Lakin (Eds.), *Deinstitutionalization and community adjustment of mentally retarded people* (pp. 351–359). Washington, DC: American Association on Mental Deficiency.

Zautra, A. (1983). The measurement of quality in community life: Introduction to the special issue. *Journal of Community Psychology, 11,* 83–87.

29

Epilogue

Economics, Industry, and Disability in the Future

William E. Kiernan, Raymond Sanchez, and Robert L. Schalock

Changes in the labor supply, current economic factors, and advances in employment training technologies for adults with disabilities, as discussed in preceding sections of this book, clearly underscore the need for an aggressive marketing approach in order for disabled persons to be recognized as a viable labor resource in the nation's economy. The demands of the marketplace, changing employment patterns, and the reduction in available workers has created an opportunity to increase employment opportunities for persons with disabilities and thereby enhance their economic self-sufficiency. This book concludes with a look at three critical issues for the future: 1) evolutions within the marketplace and the corresonding development of a marketing plan and a public relations employment solicitation effort by the U.S. Administration on Developmental Disabilities (ADD), 2) current placement patterns as reflected in the results of a national survey on employment of adults with developmental disabilities, and 3) the outlook for the quality of life for adults with disabilities.

EVOLUTIONS IN THE MARKETPLACE

Employment plays a central role in providing a means for both achieving a level of economic self-sufficiency and establishing one's identity (Wright, 1980). Changes in population trends and the economic environments and demands of the marketplace in the past 10 years have provided opportunities for persons with disabilities to enter employment (Kiernan, McGaughey, & Schalock, 1986). Such changes are consistent with the changes in the perception of the role of adults with disabilities. Emphasis upon increased independence and productivity, the provision of a wider range of choices, and a higher degree of community integration have emerged as the guiding principles in programs for persons with disabilities (Kiernan & Stark, 1986; Rusch, 1986).

Over the past 20 years in the United States, the move from a manufacturing to a service economy has caused a significant shift in the types of job opportunities (U.S. Department of Labor, 1984). Changes in the population distribution have occurred as well. The continued decrease in the number of younger workers (age 15–24) available for employment, and the increase in the number of individuals over age 65 (Bogue, 1985) have led to greatly expanded needs in the information and service industries, with considerable demand placed upon the dwindling labor resources. Furthermore, movement patterns reflecting the increase in population for the South and West and the decline in population for areas such as the Northeast imply that shifting population patterns will exert additional region-specific pressures on the labor market (U.S. Department of Labor, 1984).

Job seekers have become more mobile, and job permanence has become less significant for the new entrant into the labor market. Fewer than 1% of the population remain on their first job for more than 10 years. In addition, during the average employment history, an individual will work for 10 or more employers (Hall, 1982). Thus, the focus is on job mobility and job change, rather than on job permanence.

Continued reduction in the unemployment rates has further complicated the supply and demand balance between the expanding industries and the declining labor resource supply. Relatively low unemployment rates nationally and locally imply that competition for the available jobs is and will remain, for the foreseeable future, keen. High unemployment rates for people with disabilities also indicate that this previously untapped labor resource will be a potentially viable source for responding to the demands of the marketplace in the future (International Center for the Disabled, 1987).

People with disabilities, however, continue to be perceived by many as unable to enter the labor market. Major efforts to establish supported and transitional employment programs are helping to dispel the belief that disabled persons are not able to perform in an integrated and competitive work setting (Kiernan & Stark, 1986; Rusch, 1986). Nevertheless, as noted in a recent Harris poll, of the 1,000 persons surveyed who had disabilities, more than 67% were unemployed (International Center for the Disabled, 1986). Of that, two-thirds stated that if given the opportunity, they would engage in employment. These factors clearly indicate the need to establish a marketing strategy to bridge the information gap between industry and human services. The section following expands on the marketing section (Section II) of this book by reviewing a specific national marketing strategy implemented by the Administration on Developmental Disabilities Employment Initiative. This effort was developed to respond to the lack of information reaching industry regarding the employment capacities of adults with developmental disabilities. The public relations approach of the pledge system utilized by ADD was a strategy both for providing information/awareness and for inspiring a commitment to action.

MARKETING PLAN

As the U.S. economy shifted from manufacturing to information and services, a number of occupations emerged as high-demand areas (U.S. Department of Labor, 1984). As shown in Table 29.1, these occupations included labor-intensive service activities such as those in food services, hotels, restaurants, and health care. As a strategy to enhance employment opportunities for adults with developmental disabilities, the Administration on Developmental Disabilities initiated a major marketing campaign directed at a specific market segment—those industries experiencing high rates of turnover. This campaign utilized a pledge system where the target industries were asked to take a proactive role in creating employment opportunities for adults with disabilities by pledging jobs for these individuals. The goal was to create an awareness of the productive capacity of adults with disabilities in specific service areas and to document some of the high-demand areas in various industries.

Table 29.1. Occupations with largest growth rates. Employment projections for 1995

Occupation	Change in total employment (in thousands)	Percentage of total job growth	Percentage of change
Building custodians	779	3.0	27.5
Cashiers	744	2.9	47.4
Secretaries	719	2.8	29.5
General clerical office workers	696	2.7	29.6
Salesclerks	685	2.7	23.5
Nursing aides	423	1.7	34.8
Guards and doorkeepers	300	1.2	47.3
Food preparation and service workers (fast food)	297	1.2	36.7
Helpers—trades	190	.7	31.2
Stock clerks—stockroom and warehouse	156	.6	18.8
Delivery and route workers	153	.6	19.2

Note: Includes only detailed occupations with 1982 employment of 25,000 or more, with data for 1995 based on U.S. Department of Labor moderate trend projections (U.S. Department of Labor, 1984).

A cornerstone of this marketing campaign was the utilization of a pledge card system that would allow industries to designate a certain number of jobs that would be available for persons with disabilities. Figure 29.1 summarizes the 43,000 pledges received in calendar year 1984 and the 59,382 pledges made during calendar year 1985.

The success of this strategy in the first 2 years led to an enhanced effort during the third year. A broader market segment was identified, again using the pledge system. As seen in Figure 29.2, approximately 105,000 job pledges were received in 1986 from a wide variety of industries. This diversification reflects an increased awareness by industry of the abilities of adults with disabilities as well as an increased demand within the marketplace for employees. It is anticipated that this demand will continue to be high, due to the reduced number of available workers as compared to previous years and the increased demand in service-related occupations.

EMPLOYMENT OUTCOMES

As a component of ADD's employment initiative, two national surveys were conducted to document employment of people with disabilities over a 2-year period. Included in the survey sample were agencies, organizations, and facilities providing vocational services to adults with developmental disabilities.

A total of 1,629 agencies were identified and surveyed in the first year (October 1, 1983 to September 30, 1984), with 3,652 agencies surveyed the

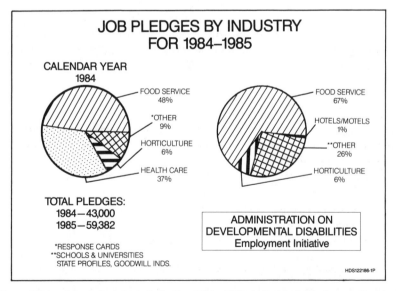

Figure 29.1. Job pledges by industry for 1984–1985, U.S. Administration on Developmental Disabilities Employment Initiative.

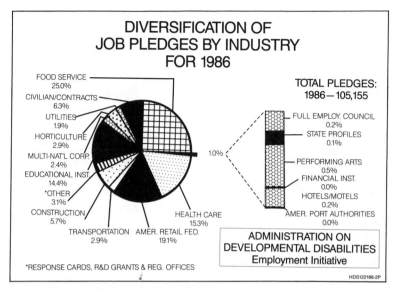

Figure 29.2. Diversification of job pledges by industry for 1986, U.S. Administration on Developmental Disabilities Employment Initiative.

second (October 1, 1984 to September 30, 1985). The surveys collected information regarding the total number of persons placed by those agencies into various occupational clusters, as well as specific earnings for those individuals. From the results of the first survey it was projected that more than 25,000 persons with developmental disabilities would have been placed had all agencies, facilities, and/or organizations responded. Actual data based on the placement of 7,075 adults with developmental disabilities showed that many of these individuals entered food service industries and janitorial types of occupations. Specific details and results from this survey can be found in Kiernan and Ciborowski (1985).

Based on the data received from the second national survey (Kiernan et al., 1986), it could be estimated that more than 62,400 persons with developmental disabilities would have been placed into competitive, supported, or transitional employment had all 2,506 eligible facilities responded. Of the actual 22,513 persons placed, the types of occupational clusters were varied, as shown in Table 29.2. Although there continued to be a heavy focus upon accessing food and janitorial services, a broad range of occupational clusters were accessed by those placed during the second survey period. This may reflect both an increased awareness by industry of the abilities of the worker with developmental disabilities and/or an increased effort among those who provide assistance in placement to access a wider variety of jobs.

A number of specific benefits have accrued to individuals with disabilities as well as to society through the expanded employment opportunities realized during the two survey periods. It is estimated that the gross earnings

Table 29.2. Placements by two-digit occupational categories[a]

Category label[b]	Absolute frequency	Relative frequency[c]
Food and beverage preparation and	2,792	22.7
service	2,088	17.0
Building service	965	7.8
Fabrication and assembly	616	5.0
Lodging and related service	444	3.6
Miscellaneous clerical	426	3.5
Packaging and handling	308	2.5
Plant farming	242	2.0
Production and stock clerk	236	1.9
Stenography, typing, filing	199	1.6
Miscellaneous personal service	169	1.4
Construction	127	1.0
Apparel service	114	1.0
Transportation	665	5.4
Other		

[a]General and detailed surveys combined.

[b]As presented in the *Dictionary of Occupational Titles* (U.S. Department of Labor, 1977).

[c]Only those job categories comprising 1% or more were included.

for those individuals placed during the two survey periods exceeded $400 million, while the savings to society in terms of reductions in transfer payments and in alternative program costs, as well as in contributions through the tax system, likewise exceed $400 million during the 2-year period.

What may be more important, however, are the advances that have been made in changing employer attitudes regarding the productivity of adults with disabilities. Jobs provide an environment in which these adults can increase their level of economic self-sufficiency. Through their earnings, they are more able to contribute to the economic well-being of society, as well as to develop a life-style that is more compatible with the mainstream.

This and various other marketing efforts have created a heightened awareness among a wide variety of industries about the abilities of this previously untapped labor resource. Over the 2-year period, there has been an increase in the number of disabled adults entering employment, in addition to the types of occupations being accessed. Employment of adults with disabilities has returns not only for the individual and industry but for society as well.

RECOMMENDATIONS FOR FUTURE EXPANSION

The potential of the marketing, placement, and support strategies described throughout this book is significant. The increased awareness of the needs of industry and of the importance of matching the individual's abilities to the demands of the job and the work environment will facilitate increased accessing of employment opportunities by adults with disabilities. Human services professionals must do their utmost to take advantage of this opportunity and to document change, not just in light of earnings and economic yield to society but in the enhanced quality of life for individuals who are placed into employment. A number of specific recommendations can be made in the areas of marketing, placement, documentation, and policy planning.

1. *Marketing* There is a continuing need to create an awareness among industry and human services providers of the abilities of disabled adults. A major marketing campaign should be designed to:

Increase the awareness of employment opportunities for adults with disabilities to parents, human services providers, educators, industry, and the disabled consumers themselves. Information sharing and demonstration of innovative programs of corporate and human services partnerships must be much more widespread.

Increase the awareness of the individual with disabilities and the employer that job change can be a positive step in the development of an employment history. Job change and job mobility will assure continued growth within an employment setting for adults with disabilities and create an opportunity for increased economic self-sufficiency in the future.

Increase opportunities for adults with disabilities to be active participants in selecting training activities and jobs. Individual choice and the acceptance of the responsibilities associated with that choice are important elements in fostering greater independence and responsibility for one's own future.

Increase the awareness of educators that employment in integrated work environments is a viable goal for special needs students and that specific job-related or functional curricula ought to be employed in the school setting to facilitate the transition from school to work.

Increase the variety of employment opportunities in high-growth areas by placing and training adults with disabilities in a wider range of service and manufacturing areas than has occurred in the past.

Increase the integration of the employee with disabilities both in the production and social environments of the work setting.

Reduce the utilization of a fragmented or piecemeal approach to human services delivery. The integration of the vocational, residential, and social needs of disabled persons will lead to a planning process that looks at the whole person in a coordinated fashion.

2. *Placement* In addition to a continued emphasis upon increased awareness, there must be an expanded effort to place persons with disabilities in careers that provide opportunities for mobility as well as variety. Specific recommendations in the area of placement include:

Continue to emphasize the marketing concept that adults with disabilities can be productive and valuable workers in those jobs where there is a good person-environment match.

Expand employment opportunities for employees with disabilities who are ready for more than entry-level positions.

Design support models such as employee assistance programs, job coaches employed by industry, and the use of industries as the employer of record for supported employment programs.

Work with industry to integrate the employee with disabilities into the social and recreational environments of the workplace.

Develop strategies to allow for supported employment programs to access fringe benefits available through the host industry.

Expand the job opportunities for adults with more severe disabilities.

Develop retirement opportunities for employees with disabilities that will allow for independence socially, economically, and emotionally in later years.

Expand efforts to access vocational education and work-study programs for special needs students with severe disabilities.

3. *Documentation* An essential component in developing good marketing/placement efforts is the documentation of the changes that occur as a result of employment for the individual, industry, and society. A number of specific documentation efforts should be developed, including:

Develop a national data collection procedure for transitional, supported, and competitive employment data that would uniformly document changes in the placement trends and benefits realized through the employment of adults with disabilities.

Develop a data collection procedure that would document changes in the quality of work life due to employment in integrated work settings for adults with disabilities.

Develop state and local evaluation systems that will provide longitudinal data on the employment, placement, training practices, outcomes, and effectiveness of the employment of adults with disabilities.

4. *Policy Planning* Beyond the efforts to increase awareness and employment opportunities, there is a need to establish forward-looking policies in the federal, state, local, and private sectors that will support the increased emphasis on employment of adults with disabilities. A number of specific issues need to be considered, including:

Conduct an in-depth analysis of the changing population trends and their impact at the national, regional, and local levels on the labor force in relationship to future industry demands.

Review the changing role of the workplace for all workers and the strategies that can be employed to integrate the employee with disabilities into the social and cultural climate of the workplace.

Examine the expanding service environment and the need to more effectively access the face-to-face service jobs by adults with disabilities and to foster attitude changes in the work environment.

Develop strategies that look at the needs of the whole person and the role of the workplace in responding to the needs of the worker with disabilities beyond the issues of production.

Review the impact of trends in the economy such as unemployment rates, national debt, interest rates, housing shortages, and transportation concerns upon the employment of adults with disabilities in the years to come.

Develop fiscal, health, social, and emotional incentives for the adult with disabilities, his or her parents, industry, and society that will support the movement from a dependent status to an independent status.

QUALITY OF LIFE ISSUES

Our efforts in promoting and interfacing economics, industry, and disability will be evaluated largely on the basis of whether the quality of the work and community lives of persons with disabilities is improved. Thus, it is appropriate to end this book with a discussion of the challenge posed by the preceding statement.

As others in this book have suggested, there is no doubt that quality of life (QOL) will be *the* human services issue of the 1990s, even though the field has yet to reach a concensus on how best to define and measure it. Our task, then, is not only to examine the QOL of the whole person, looking at the interaction of employment, residential, and recreational activities, but also to examine what constitutes the quality of work life for all persons, not just for those with disabilities.

From an economic and industry perspective, the future for persons with disabilities will be both promising and challenging. As the chapters in the book have described, opportunities for employment are being created for persons with disabilities, and technologies are being used to ensure their job success and personal growth. Our mission over the next 2 decades will be to maximize these opportunities and technologies to ensure these persons' continued independence, productivity, and community integration.

REFERENCES

Bogue, D.J. (1985). *The population of the United States: Historical trends and future projections.* New York: Free Press.

Hall, R. (1982). The importance of life time jobs in the U.S. economy. *American Economic Review, 72*(4), 716–724.

Harris, L. (1987). *Inside America.* New York: Vintage.

International Center for the Disabled. (1986). *The ICD survey of disabled Americans: Bringing disabled Americans into the mainstream* (Survey #854009). New York: Author.

International Center for the Disabled. (1987). *Employing disabled Americans.* New York: Author.

Kiernan, W.E., & Ciborowski, J. (1985). *Employment survey for adults with developmental disabilities.* Washington, DC: National Association of Rehabilitation Facilities.

Kiernan, W.E., McGaughey, M.J., & Schalock, R.L. (1986). *Employment survey for adults with developmental disabilities.* Boston: Children's Hospital, Developmental Evaluation Clinic.

Kiernan, W.E., & Stark, J.A. (1986). *Pathways to employment for adults with developmental disabilities.* Baltimore: Paul H. Brookes Publishing Co.

Rusch, F.R. (Ed.). (1986). *Competitive employment issues and strategies.* Baltimore: Paul H. Brookes Publishing Co.

U.S. Department of Labor. (1977). *Dictionary of occupational titles.* Washington, DC: Author.

U.S. Department of Labor. (1984). *Employment projections for 1995* (Bulletin 2197). Washington, DC: Author, Bureau of Labor Statistics.

Wright, G. (1980). *Total rehabilitation.* Boston: Little, Brown.

INDEX